RETHINKING WORK

This book is an innovative consideration of a changing and contested domain in society. New essays from scholars at the University of Sydney are structured around the themes of time, space and discourse to highlight the value-laden and constructed nature of these categories as they apply to the organisation of our working lives. Time is employed to establish order, construct identity and illuminate the subjective experiences of individuals at work. Imagined and material space permeates all aspects of working life and broadens our understanding of how employers and employees mobilise power in different places. Discourse offers crucial insights into the contested processes of work policies and identity formulation, as well as presenting methodological tools for analysing the metaphors and practices that govern work. Contributors draw from their expertise in strategic management, organisational theory, labour and business history, law, economics, industrial relations, human resource management, geography, and discourse and narrative analysis. Their stimulating chapters in *Rethinking Work* reflect that the study of work must itself be capable of adaptation to the profound changes reshaping this most powerful expression of human relationships and experience.

Mark Hearn has published on the historical and contemporary analysis of work and trade unions. **Grant Michelson** teaches and researches in the areas of business ethics, organisational behaviour and change, and industrial relations, and his work has appeared in many national and international journals.

RETHINKING WORK

Time, Space and Discourse

Edited by Mark Hearn and Grant Michelson

CAMBRIDGE UNIVERSITY PRESS

CAMBRIDGE UNIVERSITY PRESS
Cambridge, New York, Melbourne, Madrid, Cape Town, Singapore, São Paulo

Cambridge University Press
477 Williamstown Road, Port Melbourne, VIC 3207, Australia

www.cambridge.edu.au
Information on this title: www.cambridge.org/9780521617598

© Cambridge University Press 2006

First published 2006

Printed in Australia by Ligare Pty Ltd

A catalogue record for this publication is available from the British Library

National Library of Australia Cataloguing in Publication data
Rethinking work, time, space and discourse.
Bibliography.
Includes index.
ISBN 978 0521 61759 8.

ISBN 0 521 61759 6.

1. Work.   2. Labor.   3. Quality of work life.
I. Hearn, Mark, 1959-.   II. Michelson, Grant.

306.36

ISBN-13 978-0-521-61759-8 paperback
ISBN-10 0-521-61759-6 paperback

CONTENTS

TABLES AND FIGURE

CONTRIBUTORS

Susan Ainsworth teaches management and HRM and her research interests include identity, discourse analysis, gender, age and public policy. Susan's work has appeared in *Critical Discourse Studies*, *Organization Studies*, *Management Communication Quarterly*, *Gender, Work and Organization*, and in the *Sage Handbook of Organizational Discourse* (2004).

Marian Baird specialises in the areas of women and work, industrial relations and HRM. She applies her research to the improvement of workplace standards and works closely with policy-makers to achieve these goals. Previous research has been undertaken on greenfield sites and high-commitment work systems. Marian is an associate editor of the *International Journal of Management Reviews*.

Rae Cooper has written extensively on contemporary and historical union renewal and organising strategies. This work has been published in journals including *Labour History*, *Relations Industrielles* and the *Journal of Industrial Relations*. Rae is currently researching employer agency and union recognition in the Australian workplace.

Leanne Cutcher lectures in strategic management and HRM. Her research interests include identity, gender and customer service work. She has published her work in *Management Communication Quarterly*, *Labour and Industry* and the *Journal of Industrial Relations*.

Bradon Ellem has published historical studies of unions, local industrial relations and the Cold War. Bradon's research now examines how unionism can be understood by combining insights from the disciplines of geography, industrial relations and history. His work also examines aspects of government industrial relations policy and changes in regulation.

David Grant's primary area of research is organisational discourse, particularly in relation to organisational change. He is a co-director of the

International Centre for Research on Organisational Discourse Strategy and Change at the University of Sydney. He is also Visiting Senior Research Fellow at the Management Centre, King's College, London.

Dimitria Groutsis has a background in political economy and conducts research in the areas of gender and ethnicity, labour market policy and international labour mobility. Her work in these areas has been presented at a number of international conferences and other outlets.

Richard Hall is especially interested in the relations between political institutions, work practices and socio-economic outcomes. Richard has undertaken a number of major research projects concerning the politics of flexibility, the organisation of work, trade union strategy, telework and telecommuting, labour hire and agency work, and critical approaches to HRM. He is currently researching enterprise resource planning systems.

Mark Hearn has published on the historical and contemporary analysis of work and trade unions. He recently completed a Sesquicentenary post-doctoral fellowship in Work and Organisational Studies on 'Labour and National Identity: Work, Authority and the Australian Settlement, 1901–1920', with a methodological focus in narrative theory. He is co-editor of the online workplace relations magazine *workSite* and an associate editor of *Labour History*.

Suzanne Jamieson is a legal specialist whose main research areas include women and work, equity and equal pay in the workplace, and international comparisons in occupational health and safety law. She is active in the broader community and sits on a number of government bodies. Her research has appeared in a number of journals and books.

Jim Kitay's research interests focus on service industries. He has coordinated two international projects on the changing nature of HRM and industrial relations in retail banking. He has also been involved in a major project on the activities, careers and influence of management consultants. Jim is co-editor of *Changing Employment Relations in Australia* and *From Tellers to Sellers: Changing Employment Relations in Banks*.

Harry Knowles teaches leadership and organisational behaviour and researches in the area of business and labour history. He has published articles on trade union history and biography. Harry has a particular interest in the study of leadership in trade unions and business organisations and is currently undertaking a biographical and historical study of leadership in Burns Philp in the postwar period.

Russell Lansbury's research focuses on international and comparative aspects of employment relations. In recent years he has undertaken studies of multinational enterprises such as ABB and Hyundai. He has published on the impact of globalisation on the automobile industry. Russell is editor of the *Journal of Industrial Relations* and is an editorial board member of several international journals.

Susan McGrath-Champ specialises in labour geography and HRM with a particular interest in regional and global aspects of work processes. Susan is currently using the insights of geography to research enterprise bargaining and the employment aspects of Australian construction firms in Asia. She has published in these and other areas.

Grant Michelson teaches and researches in the areas of business ethics, organisational behaviour and change, and industrial relations, and his work has been published in many national and international journals. Grant is currently exploring contemporary discourses in business ethics as well as the role of new actors in industrial relations with an emphasis on workplace chaplains.

Tim Morris is at the Saïd Business School, University of Oxford, UK. He has researched on numerous issues in the area of industrial relations, including union mergers and the finances of British trade unions. He has also published widely on the management of professional organisations, including studies of promotion systems and change processes, and on employee commitment.

Greg Patmore is director of the Business and Labour History Group, School of Business, University of Sydney and editor of *Labour History*. Interests include Rochdale consumer cooperatives and nonunion forms of labour organisation. With other colleagues at Sydney, he is working on a history of Citigroup's operations in Australia.

John Shields has a special interest in performance and reward management and in the role of organisational justice and psychological contracts in the employment relationship. His current research focuses on executive remuneration, corporate governance and firm performance in Australian listed companies. John also has a longstanding interest in labour history and is an associate editor of the journal *Labour History*.

Diane van den Broek teaches HRM and her research interests lie in this area as well as in call centres and service industries. Diane focuses mainly on such issues as the labour process, monitoring and surveillance, teamwork, emotional and aesthetic labour, and customer relations. Her work has been published extensively in such outlets as *Economic and Industrial Democracy* and *New Technology, Work and Employment*.

Nick Wailes has a number of research interests including the impact of globalisation on employment relations and the relationship between capital market structure and firm strategy. His articles have appeared in leading international journals including *Industrial Relations*, *British Journal of Industrial Relations* and the *International Journal of Human Resource Management*.

Mark Westcott's main research interests relate to employment regulation, labour management strategies, bargaining structures, and occupational health and safety. He is presently exploring these issues in the Australian oil refinery and brewing industries.

The contact details of all contributors, except Tim Morris (chapter 16), are:
Work and Organisational Studies
School of Business
Faculty of Economics and Business
University of Sydney
Sydney, NSW 2006
[initial.surname@econ.usyd.edu.au] e.g. m.hearn@econ.usyd.edu.au

Professor Tim Morris
Saïd Business School
University of Oxford
Park End Street
Oxford, OX1 1HP
United Kingdom
tim.morris@sbs.ox.ac.uk

EDITORIAL STATEMENT

All chapters in *Rethinking Work* were peer-reviewed by an international expert in the field. The reviewers reflect the broad range of disciplinary perspectives that contribute to our understanding of work – geography, history, industrial relations, law, economics management, political science, and sociology. The editors would like to acknowledge, on behalf of all contributors, the valuable assistance of the following reviewers:

Chris Carter	University of St Andrews, UK
Andrew Cumbers	University of Glasgow, UK
Robert Fagan	Macquarie University
Steve Frenkel	University of New South Wales
Bill Harley	University of Melbourne
Andrew Herod	University of Georgia, USA
Cliff Oswick	University of Leicester, UK
Rosemary Owens	University of Adelaide
George Strauss	University of California, Berkeley, USA
Shelton Stromquist	University of Iowa, USA
Peter Waring	University of Newcastle
Tony Watson	University of Nottingham, UK
Michael Webber	University of Melbourne
Gillian Whitehouse	University of Queensland

In addition, the editors would like to thank Sid Gray, School of Business, University of Sydney for financial support as well as the production and editorial team at Cambridge University Press for their assistance.

Finally, we owe a special debt to the following: Margaret, Elizabeth, Chris and Tom (Mark Hearn) and Lisa (Grant Michelson) and thank them for their love and support.

ABBREVIATIONS

ABA	Australian Bankers Association
ABS	Australian Bureau of Statistics
ACD	automated call distribution
ACIRRT	Australian Centre for Industrial Relations Research and Training
ACTU	Australian Council of Trade Unions
AFR	*Australian Financial Review*
AGPS	Australian Government Publishing Service
AHRI	Australian Human Resources Institute
AIRAANZ	Association of Industrial Relations Academics of Australia and New Zealand
AIRC	Australian Industrial Relations Commission
AJPM	*Australian Journal of Productivity and Management*
ALP	Australian Labor Party
AMMA	Australian Mines and Metals Association
AMWU	Australian Manufacturing Workers Union
ANZ	Australian and New Zealand Banking Corporation
ATM	automatic teller machine
AWA	Australian Workplace Agreement
CAR	Commonwealth Arbitration Reports
CBA	Commonwealth Bank of Australia
CPD	*Commonwealth Parliamentary Debates*
CPSU	Community and Public Sector Union
CSO	customer service officer
CSR	customer service representative (Chapter 5)
CSR	corporate social responsibility (Chapters 11 and 12)
DIMIA	Department of Immigration and Multicultural and Indigenous Affairs
DST	daylight saving time
DWR/OEA	Department of Workplace Relations and the Office of the Employment Advocate

EA	Enterprise Australia
EFPA	Economics, Finance and Public Administration
EFTPOS	electronic funds transfer at point of sale
EGOS	European Group for Organizational Studies
FSU	Finance Sector Union
GDP	gross domestic product
HR(M)	Human Resource (Management)
HREOC	Human Rights and Equal Opportunity Commission
ICRODSC	International Centre for Research on Organisational Discourse, Strategy and Change
ILO	International Labour Organisation
IWW	Industrial Workers of the World
KPI	key performance indicator
LSIA	Longitudinal Survey of Immigrants to Australia
MMC	Monopolies and Mergers Commission
MTM	Methods-Time-Management
OECD	Organization for Economic Cooperation and Development
PMTS	Predetermined Motion Time Systems
PMU	Pilbara Mineworkers Union
PSA	Public Service Association (NSW)
SMH	*Sydney Morning Herald*
SOE	state-owned enterprise
TVE	town and village enterprise
WEA	Workers Educational Association
WOS	(Department of) Work and Organisational Studies

CHAPTER ONE

GOING TO A NEW PLACE
Rethinking Work in the 21st Century

Mark Hearn and Grant Michelson

In her contribution on international work and management, labour geographer Susan McGrath-Champ describes the experience of an expatriate manager setting up a plant in China as 'going to a new place': an abrupt and challenging shift in experience that is at once cultural and spatial, driven by the forces reshaping international capital and work organisation. *Rethinking Work* argues that work researchers must also explore new territory – engaging with challenging analytical categories to explain the rapidly evolving and multi-dimensional realm of 21st-century work.

The multidisciplinary nature of Work and Organisational Studies (WOS) at the University of Sydney has stimulated an innovative analysis of work, industrial relations, human resource management, organisations and management. *Rethinking Work* is a product of this diverse and collaborative research environment. Drawing on expertise in strategic management, discourse and narrative analysis, organisational theory, labour and business history, labour geography and the study of unions, gender and human resource management, the contributors reject a narrowly conceived approach to the study of work and employment relations. Work and workplace issues must be sensitive to the historical and contemporary context of management decision-making and organisational behaviour if they are adequately to explain and understand the internal and external forces that drive action and choice.

Rethinking Work reflects recent changes within the areas of industrial relations, human resource management and organisation studies.

1

Many of the contributors formerly worked in the Department of Industrial Relations, established by pioneering industrial relations academic Kingsley Laffer in 1953. The University of Sydney was the first Australian tertiary education institution to establish a dedicated industrial relations discipline, which developed and grew in staff numbers over the ensuing decades. The sweeping restructuring of the world of work since the 1980s – the shift to labour market deregulation and a more intensive focus on human resource issues and organisational analysis – rendered its traditional nomenclature too narrowly focused. In 2000 the department was renamed 'Work and Organisational Studies' and was located within a newly formed School of Business. Since this time WOS has experienced considerable growth in staff numbers. This transformation represents a broader and more innovative approach to studying the world of work. In particular, members of WOS seek to showcase to practitioners, students and scholars in other institutions the important principles that are now required in understanding more comprehensively all issues pertaining to work. In doing so, we argue that this book helps to identify and establish a uniquely 'Sydney School' approach to studying work and the employment relationship.

The structure of the chapter is as follows. First, we outline the major changes in work and the organisation of work over the last 15 or so years. Many of these developments are not exclusive to Australia but also reflect changes experienced in other industrialised economies. This backdrop is presented to argue why we need to construct and use more analytically robust and sophisticated tools to understand and explain the changes. In the second section, the three themes of time, space and discourse are introduced. While not all are 'new' in the study of work matters, what is new is that these themes are brought together for the first time in one place to illuminate issues in the fields of industrial relations, human resource management and work organisation. We are mindful that a comprehensive understanding of the numerous and important work changes requires more than merely presenting or privileging one theme over another. Rather, and this is the purpose of the third section, the concepts of time, space and discourse are presented in an integrated fashion. Thus although the different chapters have been classified according to one of the three organising themes or devices, in practice there is considerable overlap and there is a need to draw on two or more themes simultaneously.

CHANGING WORK: NEO-LIBERALISM AND
THE ANALYSIS OF WORK

In recent years, work and working life in Australia have undergone significant social and economic change (or 'fragmentation') in terms of industry restructuring, the shift from a rather centralised system towards a more decentralised system, the growth of non-standard (part-time and casual) forms of employment, a rise in individualism, longer and more intense hours of work, more limited prospects for skill development and training, and an increasing wage gap between the top and bottom ends of the labour market, to name but a few of these changes (ACIRRT 1999; Deery & Mitchell 1999; Callus & Lansbury 2002; Watson et al. 2003). Accompanying such changes, many of which have reflected developments evident in other countries, have been debates about the future role for the traditional workplace actors and institutions – trade unions, employer associations and industrial tribunals (for example Peetz 1998; Sheldon & Thornthwaite 1999; Dabscheck 2001) – and about how individuals might balance better their work and non-work lives (Pocock 2003).

Furthermore, changes in the world of work are increasingly being viewed through a different lens that reveals a preoccupation with the neo-liberal notions of flexibility, innovation, productivity and competitiveness. Such themes have arguably overtaken the traditional industrial relations concerns of equity, workplace justice and the regulation of conflict among public policy-makers and managers alike (Hearn & Lansbury 2005). In Australia, as elsewhere, there has been a reshaping of national policy priorities towards encouraging greater competitiveness and efficiency through such mechanisms as works councils and partnership programs (Gollan et al. 2002; Gollan & Patmore 2003).

Such changes have precipitated uneven consequences among different industries and for the field of employment relations in Australia more generally (Kitay & Lansbury 1997; Lansbury & Michelson 2003, 2005). In the broader international context, they have spurred an interest among researchers to expand the focus of enquiry to global trends in work and employment such as the rise of the service sector, the shift to an information or knowledge society, and developing better theoretical explanations of the observed phenomena (for example Warhurst & Thompson 1998; Giles 2000; Kaufman 2004). For other scholars, the changes in work and the organisation of work have further blurred and eroded disciplinary boundaries and it is argued that there is a greater need for industrial relations to engage with cognate social science areas such as law, history, economics, sociology and psychology (Ackers & Wilkinson 2003). Many earlier studies on work and how it is regulated have drawn on such disciplinary areas to present a range of insights (see, for example, Williams 1992; Ewing 1996; Richardson 1999; Hearn & Patmore 2001).

The present book similarly draws on the variety of disciplinary traditions to be found in the study of work. But unlike other publications which preserve and reinforce the bounded nature of these disciplines (for example Ackers & Wilkinson 2003), *Rethinking Work* synthesises the concepts of time, space and discourse to provide a fresh and innovative perspective on the study of work and employment relations.

Structuring *Rethinking Work* around the themes of time, space and discourse allows us to think in new ways about the organisation, management and regulation of work. It is true enough that these themes have been woven into past scholarship, and this book builds on these traditions, arguing that time, space and discourse have become increasingly powerful tools for unlocking the complexities of the world of work. While the content is largely based on developments in Australia, we contend that much of the empirical material speaks to, and will inform, the experiences of other countries. Contemporary debates, processes and events in Australia such as those surrounding the organisation and regulation of work, workplace change, employee institutions, workplace groups (migrants and older workers) and the articulation of normative ethical values at work, for instance, are also highly relevant in other parts of the world, as the concluding chapter by Tim Morris attests.

Briefly, we define our working principles and outline some of the issues that arise from analysing work through these three categories.

NEW WAYS OF THINKING ABOUT WORK

Time

Although it has been the case that history, and labour history in particular, has been a core disciplinary strand in the study of work and employment relations, it has always had to fight for that place. This seems to remain the case. Time receives too little attention among contemporary scholars in spite of recent attempts by some to argue for a place for temporality in social settings (for example Bluedorn 2002; Epstein & Kalleberg 2004). Instead the focus is on an uninterrogated present and an imagined future disconnected from their links to the past. So much attention is paid to the rapidity of social change that the past seems indeed to be as remote as a totally different country – and yet arguments about rapid change are, ironically, pre-eminently arguments about time, history and the future. We can learn from the past in order to understand the present and anticipate the future.

Time is one of the major structuring devices for human activity, and there is considerable evidence of temporal order in industrialised societies (Adam 1990, 1995). As Greg Patmore argues in Chapter 2, our deployment of time in a contemporary understanding of work must be rethought in a number of ways – in the blurred divisions of time between paid and unpaid work and leisure, and how time is not simply bestowed by nature or clock/calendar time but is organised by human agency, and is 'socially constructed'. In other words, time is embedded in a range of social interactions, structures and practices. The social construction of time can be neatly illustrated by different experiences of time ('time is dragging' or 'time passes quickly') and different orientations across national cultures suggesting that all times are not the same (see Bluedorn 2002).

Time is frequently considered as a resource in the context of work and work organisation and, as such, contains an assumption of efficiency. This idea is captured and demonstrated for example, by the themes of 'time management' and 'just-in-time' and by the statement 'gossip wastes time'. There is a desire by organisations to allocate time, part of which involves the need to impose discipline based on clock-time in order to maximise productive activity (Thompson 1967). This includes turning up to work 'on time'. However, this construction is not without its difficulties and we acknowledge the existence of a number of time-related 'problems' including the time of work (long work hours), the timing of work (the arrangement of working time), work–life balance, work stresses ('running out of time'), nostalgia (a desire to 'live in the past'), and the politics of time. On this last point, it is important to recognise that time has an essentially 'political' dimension in terms of whose time is valued in our work organisations and how this is established. Contesting the amount of work and employee control of work timing is also inherently a political struggle. Of course, this is not to deny the importance of linear time in different social contexts (Rehn 2002). But it does help to illustrate that time is more complex than is often assumed and contains both 'objective' and socially constructed features.

In addition to the politicised element of time, we also see the value of employing time in further illuminating some more familiar concepts in the work and industrial relations literature, such as gender. How is time constructed by women when they are more likely to experience absences from the labour market to have children? To what extent do men and women have shared or different understandings of time with respect to their careers? Among professional workers in one study, the perception that working long hours could be a vehicle for career progression was endorsed more frequently by men than by women; for women, time spent at work reflected a sense of professional conscientiousness. For both men and women in this study, however, work time was an expression of professional and personal identity, suggesting that working long hours may not be always be in conflict with work–life balance (Sturges 2004). Questions such as these do not negate the importance of gender in explaining work-related outcomes, but they do raise the possibility that other dimensions can enhance our understanding of the more commonly employed analytical categories. A time perspective can indeed help us explain many developments in work and employment relations. Accordingly, we privilege time as one of the three organising themes or devices in this book.

Space

Arguments in and about the world of work 'take place', we habitually say, in particular settings such as factories and offices. But we quickly move on from this evocative phrase without thinking much more about these spaces. How are spaces in and around work constructed and how do they interact with work, organisations and regulation? Echoing the view of others that space should have a more central position in analysis (for example Ellem & Shields 1999: 537), space is therefore the second of our major structuring devices to understand work, the organisation of work and employment relations.

While space is sometimes treated as synonymous with place in the literature, it is not limited to this interpretation. Space is not a 'given' where it is to be treated merely as a static environmental factor in research studies; rather, different societies organise, structure and reproduce space in different ways (Herod et al. 2003). Such spaces are often taken for granted and can communicate important symbolic and power elements in social contexts. Taking but one familiar example, the allocation of 'office space' (how much and where) can send messages to others about the relative status of individuals in work organisations (Baldry 1999). In addition, this can structure social action as well as act as a source of conflict. How space is partitioned, therefore, can provide insights into how we partition work, the world of work and employment relations. One such term that has recently helped to shape research in the field is 'globalisation'.

The rise of globalisation – a term as little defined as it is commonly deployed – makes very clear that the remaking of, and rethinking about, work is a spatial process. It is not simply an objective term but a process with multiple layers of social meaning. Changes 'take place' in different ways across both time and space and we need to understand how spatial specificity is configured or set up at the workplace, at local, regional and national scales within the global restructuring of economic and social life. Debates about the future of work need to acknowledge a number of these factors (Morris 2004).

It is also important to understand the links between these different spatial scales as well as how individuals and organisations might both 'manage' as well as resist changes in space. An illustration of this might be how many business organisations in Australia, in response to various global and national pressures, are relocating their operations partly or wholly offshore, establishing new 'greenfield' sites in other parts of the country with different employment conditions from older, more established sites, or offering some workers the option of family-friendly employment practices via working from home. However, these initiatives have not always proceeded smoothly as different groups at work have sought to reconstitute and challenge the space in which work 'takes place'. For some employees, this might involve establishing greater solidarity with others across different spaces such as through international labour networks or links with the wider community. In other words, spaces can be subjectively made and remade and are not simply the geographic context or setting in which work occurs. The remaking of space reveals the struggles or contests over how managers and employees pursue their interests at work, in turn reflecting the typically uneven patterns of how capital and labour are organised (Ellem & Shields 1999; Herod et al. 2003).

In addition to the more common localised spaces of the factory or office and, increasingly, the home, there is also evidence now of more work being carried out in a 'third place' such as the train, car and plane, suggesting that there is a mosaic of contrasting work spaces (Felstead et al. 2005: 428). New technologies such as mobile phones and laptop computers have begun to usher in a change in the places where work can be carried out. This has arguably helped to foster a new language and space associated with the 'virtual organisation' and 'networked organisation'. Work and employment relations appear to be undergoing something of a transformation in their location. Again, such shifts are symptomatic of wider changes in the landscapes and mobilities of capital and labour. An understanding of the spatial dimension is therefore critical to generating more rigorous and nuanced explanations of the changes in work, including how different actor groups shape the practice, experience and regulation of work.

Discourse

As they struggle to survive and expand within the context of globalising market forces, work and employment relations present us with a bewildering diversity of managerial strategies, policies and practices. In Part III we suggest that one way to make sense of progressively uncertain, inconsistent and fluctuating employee, managerial and organisational behaviour is for commentators to examine the ways in which discourses pertaining to work are produced, disseminated and consumed.

'Discourse' refers to the practices of talking and writing, the visual representations and the cultural artefacts that bring a range of social phenomena (objects) into being through a variety of texts (Grant et al. 2004). Texts can take many forms such as written documents, verbal reports and statements, terminology, symbols and signs. Discourse analysis involves the systematic study of these texts. A discourse does not start out in possession of meaning. Instead, and in line with their socially constructive effects, meaning is created, renegotiated and changed via interactions between different groups. This allows for a range of alternative meanings to be produced. In order to explain why particular discourses emerge or how meaning is established, as well as accounting for their effects, the historical contexts in which discourse arises must also be understood (Fairclough 1995). That is, when individuals use language they employ a variety of terms that have been provided by the past.

Discourse analysis is particularly useful in work settings, for instance to show how employees and managers construct meaning and their own reality (maybe to justify an action or to attribute blame). Discourse can be mobilised by different actor groups as a strategic resource, and this shapes and constructs outcomes in their favour (Hardy et al. 2000). These constructive processes help to further reveal and illuminate underlying power relations in social structures as dominant meanings associated with a particular discourse emerge by way of contestation (Grant & Hardy 2003). The dominant meaning occurs as alternative discourses are marginalised or subverted. However, this outcome is by no means secured as there is an ongoing struggle among competing discourses. In the current work and industrial landscape in Australia, these different discourses (for example those surrounding 'fairness' and 'more jobs') and how they are articulated represent the interests of different groups such as federal and State governments, employers, trade unions, industrial courts, legal practitioners, churches, welfare agencies and so on.

This point might be further shown in the shift from 'personnel management' to 'human resource management' (HRM). This change in terminology from around the mid-1980s was arguably an attempt to make people issues more central or strategic to business decision-making, and while HRM has certainly become the favoured nomenclature, the adoption of HRM in practice in Australia has been slow (Michelson & Kramar 2003). In part this is due to senior organisational managers being unwilling to cede strategic authority to human resource (HR) managers. Other language has recently begun to emerge which refers to the idea of 'human capital'. This latest development (which might or might not take hold in business circles) highlights the fluid and contested nature of discourse in work and other social contexts. We believe that asking apparently simple questions of discourses helps to lay bare the intricate dynamics of work. Accordingly, chapters in this section of the book ask questions such as who uses the particular discourse under scrutiny – and how and why? Tying these questions to the other themes in the book, it is also necessary to ask when and where particular discourses are used. In doing so, we believe that discourse opens up analytical space for new and innovative accounts of a range of work-related and employment-related issues.

INTEGRATING TIME, SPACE AND DISCOURSE

We also recognise that the categories of time, space and discourse should not be artificially polarised or advocated, even if some proponents make sweeping claims on behalf of their analytical preference. Herod (2002: 14) claims that social life is fundamentally spatial and has an ontological status: 'an active component in structuring social life' and 'a material product of human struggles to shape the spaceeconomy and the geographical relationships between various industrial relations actors'. These views echo claims made in an influential text by Somers & Gibson (1998) about the links between narrative and identity: that 'social life is storied' and 'narrative is an ontological condition of social life'. They argue that narrative is fundamentally significant to all expressions of life, that experience and identity is constituted through narrative: 'people are guided to act in certain ways, and not others, on the basis of the projections, expectations, and memories derived from a multiple but ultimately limited repertoire of available social, public and cultural narratives' (Somers & Gibson 1998: 38–40). Similarly, others stake universal territory for organisational discourse: 'Organisations exist only in so far as their members create them through discourse', although these same writers partly qualify this broad assertion (Grant et al. 2004: 3).

Herod (2002: 14–15) goes on to implicitly link space, time and discourse. Technology, he argues, has sped up work production and information flows and restructured geographic relationships. Herod seems to tacitly concede that the category of space that he champions so strenuously (he challenges 'anyone' to disprove that social life is fundamentally spatial) is in fact inherently tied to a relationship both to time and indeed to 'information flows' – that is, discourse.

We seek to encourage research that explores the links and relationships between the temporal, spatial and discursive dimensions of work analysis. For instance, the discourse in studies of the employment relationship which evokes 'globalisation' in their argument is essentially a spatialised discourse that reconstructs the space in which work now takes place; the different spaces in which work is performed are affected by considerations of time as some individuals struggle to balance their work and non-work time; and how time as an object is understood and used in work and employment relations can be discursively constructed.

While the categories of time, space and discourse each require more rigorous analysis in their relationship with work, and cannot be simply added, as Herod says of space, to the explanatory mix as an afterthought, we acknowledge that research that constructs tight disciplinary boundaries may create barriers to a penetrating analysis of work. Time, space and discourse are interdependent categories, and chapters in *Rethinking Work* explicitly draw out or suggest the connections. Cooper & Ellem focus on the way the new jobs of the information age fragment work across time and space; Hearn & Knowles follow the national narrative of work as it was reshaped across time.

We are also concerned to avoid a perception that our employment of time, space and discourse is too theoretically abstract or rarefied. Each chapter is grounded in empirical research and many chapters draw attention to compelling issues of public policy. The pragmatic and contested nature of work and employment relations brings time, space and discourse back to a real-world context. Cutcher & van den Broek provide a powerful insight into the stresses imposed on customer service workers, and their efforts to control the terms of their employment; Baird argues that it is time to address seriously the gender agenda, which would include the development of a national system of paid maternity leave; and Michelson & Wailes show that organisations are still principally guided by the pursuit of shareholder value in spite of attempts to make some 'space' for corporate social responsibility in their strategic decision-making.

Privileging time, space and discourse does not depoliticise the analysis of work. In contrast, politics is everywhere in *Rethinking Work*, just as it infiltrates workplace relations and public policy more generally. Chapters on gender, migrants and labour law stress emancipation and workplace rights; space is contested terrain for employers, unions and workers; the discourse of work invariably draws out underlying and disputed values that have shaped the discrete codes of human resource management, the identity of workers in general, and negative stereotyping of older workers in particular. In many respects, *Rethinking Work* is an argument for policy intervention to promote workplace fairness and equity, employing time, space and discourse to uncover the politics embedded in work practice and policy.

This book demonstrates that our categories and methodologies to explain work, work relations and the employment relationship in the 21st century require rigorous assessment and scrutiny as we employ them in relation to interrogating and understanding the world of work. We maintain that *Rethinking Work* points the way towards a more sophisticated integration of our analytical categories for scholars, students and practitioners.

CONCLUSION

This book reflects a significant moment in the history of Work and Organisational Studies as it seeks to encapsulate a distinct and unique identity for a 'Sydney School' approach to work and employment relations. In doing so, it demonstrates a conscious attempt to participate in and to lead debates both nationally and internationally. This desire is consistent with the view 'that the past and the future are connected to the present' (George & Jones 2000: 659). The three analytical themes of time, space and discourse together suggest that our understanding of work can be interpreted both subjectively and objectively, and that there are enduring conflicts and struggles in how work is experienced, managed and resisted.

In 2003 the discipline celebrated the fiftieth anniversary of teaching and researching industrial relations at the University of Sydney as changes continued to unfold to its teaching and research profile, while its status as a key contributor to the analysis of the world of work also continued to develop. WOS is responsible for editing the two most prestigious and longstanding Australian journals in the field: *Labour History* and the *Journal of Industrial Relations*. Members of WOS are involved in the International Centre for Research on Organisational Discourse, Strategy and Change (ICRODSC), which connects the discipline with colleagues in Australia, Canada, Sweden, the UK and the USA. Recently, the Business and Labour History Group was established within the School of Business to stimulate new research in this field, and WOS scholars play a leading role in this Group.

Industrial relations, human resource management and organisation studies are important and well-established areas of research and teaching. WOS collectively aims to provide students with a well-rounded understanding of all aspects of work and the employment relationship. The skills and content derived from these courses provide a vital foundation not only for careers in traditional industrial relations institutions such as unions, employer bodies and government, but also in human resource management, research, policy development, consultancy work, industrial law and many aspects of private and public sector management, reflecting the intrinsic role and value of work in the life of the community and the nation. The innovative and heterogeneous contributions to *Rethinking Work* reflect that the study of work must itself be capable of adaptation to the profound changes reshaping this most powerful expression of human relationships and experience.

References

ACIRRT (Australian Centre for Industrial Relations Research and Training) 1999, *Australia at Work: Just Managing?*, Sydney: Prentice Hall.

Ackers, P. & Wilkinson, A. (eds) 2003, *Understanding Work and Employment: Industrial Relations in Transition*, Oxford: Oxford University Press.

Adam, B. 1990, *Time and Social Theory*, Cambridge: Polity Press.

Adam, B. 1995, *Timewatch: The Social Analysis of Time*, Cambridge: Polity Press.

Baldry, C. 1999, 'Space: the final frontier', *Sociology* 33(3): 535–53.

Bluedorn, A.C. 2002, *The Human Organization of Time: Temporal Realities and Experience*, Stanford University Press.

Callus, R. & Lansbury, R. D. (eds) 2002, *Working Futures: The Changing Nature of Work and Employment Relations in Australia*, Sydney: Federation Press.

Dabscheck, B. 2001, 'The slow and agonising death of the Australian experiment with conciliation and arbitration', *Journal of Industrial Relations* 43(3): 277–93.

Deery, S. & Mitchell, R. (eds) 1999, *Employment Relations: Individualisation and Union Exclusion*, Sydney: Federation Press.

Ellem, B. & Shields, J. 1999, 'Rethinking "regional industrial relations": space, place and the social relations of work', *Journal of Industrial Relations* 41(4): 536–60.

Epstein, C.F. & Kalleberg, A.L. (eds) 2004, *Rethinking Time at Work*, University of Chicago Press.

Ewing, K. (ed.) 1996, *Working Life: A New Perspective on Labour Law*, London: Lawrence & Wishart.

Fairclough, N. 1995, *Critical Discourse Analysis: The Critical Study of Language*, London: Longman.

Felstead, A., Jewson, N. & Walters, S. 2005, 'The shifting locations of work: new statistical evidence on the spaces and places of employment', *Work, Employment and Society* 19(2): 415–31.

George, J.M. & Jones, G.R. 2000, 'The role of time in theory and theory building', *Journal of Management* 26(4): 657–84.

Giles, A. 2000, 'Industrial relations at the millennium: beyond employment?', *Labour/Le Travail*, 46: 37–67.

Gollan, P., Markey, R. & Ross, I. (eds) 2002, *Works Councils in Australia: Future Prospects and Possibilities*, Sydney: Federation Press.

Gollan, P. & Patmore, G. (eds) 2003, *Partnership at Work: The Challenge of Employee Democracy*, Sydney: Pluto Press.

Grant, D. & Hardy, C. 2003, 'Introduction: struggles with organizational discourse', *Organization Studies* 25(1): 5–13.

Grant, D., Hardy, C., Oswick, C. & Putnam, L. (eds) 2004, *The Handbook of Organisational Discourse*, London: Sage.

Hardy, C., Palmer, I. & Phillips, N. 2000, 'Discourse as a strategic resource', *Human Relations* 53(9): 1227–48.

Hearn, M. & Lansbury, R. 2005, 'Reworking citizenship: renewing workplace rights and social citizenship in Australia', in M. Baird, R. Cooper & M. Westcott (eds) *Reworking Work*, Proceedings of the 19th AIRAANZ Conference, vol. 1, Sydney, pp. 257–64.

Hearn, M. & Patmore, G. (eds) 2001, *Working the Nation: Working Life and Federation, 1890–1914*, Sydney: Pluto Press.

Herod, A. 2002, 'Towards a more productive engagement: industrial relations and economic geography meet', *Labour and Industry* 13(2): 5–17.

Herod, A., Peck, J. & Wills, J. 2003, 'Geography and industrial relations', in P. Ackers & A. Wilkinson (eds) *Understanding Work and Employment: Industrial Relations in Transition*, Oxford: Oxford University Press, pp. 176–92.

Kaufman, B.E. (ed.) 2004, *Theoretical Perspectives on Work and the Employment Relationship*, IRRA series, Ithaca, N.Y.: Cornell University Press.

Kitay, J. & Lansbury, R.D. (eds) 1997, *Changing Employment Relations in Australia*, Melbourne: Oxford University Press.

Lansbury, R.D. & Michelson, G. 2003, 'Industrial relations in Australia', in P. Ackers & A. Wilkinson (eds) *Understanding Work and Employment: Industrial Relations in Transition*, Oxford: Oxford University Press, pp. 227–41.

Lansbury, R.D. & Michelson, G. 2005, 'Industrial relations as a field in Australia: the implications of a decentralized labor market', in D. Lewin & B.E. Kaufman (eds) *Advances in Industrial and Labor Relations*, vol. 14, New York: Elsevier, pp. 301–23.

Michelson, G. & Kramar, R. 2003, 'The state of HRM in Australia: progress and prospects', *Asia Pacific Journal of Human Resources* 41(2): 133–48.

Morris, J. 2004, 'The future of work: organizational and international perspectives', *International Journal of Human Resource Management* 15(2): 263–75.

Peetz, D. 1998, *Unions in a Contrary World: The Future of the Australian Trade Union Movement*, Cambridge University Press.

Pocock, B. 2003, *The Work/Life Collision: What Work is Doing to Australians and What to Do About it*, Sydney: Federation Press.

Rehn, A. 2002, 'Time and management as a morality tale, or "what's wrong with linear time, damn it?"', in R. Whipp, B. Adam & I. Sabelis (eds) *Making Time: Time and Management in Modern Organizations*, Oxford: Oxford University Press, pp. 77–85.

Richardson, S. (ed.) 1999, *Reshaping the Labour Market: Regulation, Efficiency and Equality in Australia*, Cambridge University Press.

Sheldon, P. & Thornthwaite, L. (eds) 1999, *Employer Associations and Industrial Relations Change: Catalysts or Captives?* Sydney: Allen & Unwin.

Somers, M.R. & Gibson, G.D. 1998, 'Reclaiming the epistemological "other": narrative and the social constitution of identity', in C. Calhoun (ed.) *Social Theory and the Politics of Identity*, Oxford: Blackwells, pp. 37–99.

Sturges, J. 2004, 'Making time for work? An exploration of the meaning of work time to young professionals and its relationship to long hours'. Paper presented to the 20th European Group for Organizational Studies (EGOS) conference, Ljubljana, Slovenia, 1–3 July.

Thompson, E.P. 1967, 'Time, work-discipline and industrial capitalism', *Past and Present* 38: 56–97.

Warhurst, C. & Thompson, P. 1998, 'Hands, hearts and minds: changing work and workers at the end of the century', in P. Thompson & C. Warhurst (eds) *Workplaces of the Future*, Basingstoke: Macmillan Business, pp. 1–24.

Watson, I., Buchanan, J., Campbell, I. & Briggs, C. 2003, *Fragmented Futures: New Challenges in Working Life*, Sydney: Federation Press.

Williams, C. 1992, *Beyond Industrial Sociology: The Work of Men and Women*, Sydney: Allen & Unwin.

PART ONE

TIME

Mark Hearn and Grant Michelson

How are we to understand the relationship between time and work, at an historical moment when work has placed ever more intense demands on our time, often demands of simultaneous strictness and flexibility? Epstein & Kalleberg capture a sense of these complexities and contradictions, and our subjective relationship with time, when they propose that 'time, far from being a finite resource, is interpreted, manipulated, and perceived in ways that expedite or impede people's lives'. New technologies have allowed work to consume our time: 'even going home, employees are wired to the workplace'. Employees may at once feel more autonomous in their performance of work, yet electronically chained to work by email; they may remain 'highly supervised' while away from the office, the work/non-work time divide blurred and compromised (Epstein & Kalleberg 2001: 13–14).

The relationship between time and work may also function in insidiously non-linear patterns. Time may be shaped at work to construct identity and reflect the subjectivity of the individual: race, class or gender may determine the ability of the individual to control their work time. A woman asked to perform overtime, 'whose identity is lodged in her family roles', may feel a greater sense of 'conflict and personal denial' about this request than another woman whose identity is focused around her work. Time may function as a 'container of meaning' that reflects social or cultural roles – roles that must often be managed against the time-persistent demands of work (Epstein & Kalleberg 2001: 8–12).

Bluedorn also emphasises our conditional and subjective reading of time: the 'concepts and values we hold about time are the products of human interaction'. Human time is an elaborate social construction, geared to our values and needs (Bluedorn 2002: 14). No human need is more privileged than the compulsion to work and to subordinate our time to its performance. Amateur clocksmith Henry Ford imagined an assembly line elegantly geared like 'the absolutely regular movements' of a clock; and indeed he was praised for creating 'a giant moving time-piece' that regulated his workforce to the requirements of production, both on the job and in the home – or so Ford briefly attempted, initiating a short-lived experiment to send investigators into his workers' homes to ensure that 'they used their leisure time properly' (Bluedorn 2002: 12–13). Ford anticipated a range of management strategies in order to have work colonise their employees' private values and time.

Like Bluedorn, Greg Patmore contemplates what Braudel (1980) described as the *longue durée* of human experience, highlighting time and work as a dialogue between past and present values of time, as 'work–time' undergoes a fundamental period of redefinition. Patmore brings an historian's perception to an exploration of the 'temporal dimensions of work': its boundaries and content – the boundaries that divide work from leisure and paid work from unpaid work; and its temporal content – work organised on a temporal basis. What is the speed of work? How do workers overcome a perception of slow-moving time at work? Patmore also interrogates the three temporal frames of reference, past, present and future, which he explores through a trinity of intellectual demarcations – historicism, presentism and futurism – cutting through the scholarly boundaries to assert the fundamental interdependence of our time-frames.

Marian Baird's focus on the 'gender agenda' may be read as an argument on behalf of the need to establish what Epstein & Kalleberg (2002: 12) describe as an 'identity-affirming' definition of work time, including entitlements that promote workplace harmony over patterns of conflict. Using contemporary debates about the introduction of paid maternity leave in Australia, Baird considers the way in which industrial relations, both as a disciplinary area of study and as an issue of public policy, have been characterised by a gendered agenda over the past 50 years. The consequence has been an exclusion of women's particular interests and issues from industrial relations scholarship and policy. A clear example is Australia's lack of national paid maternity leave provisions. Baird reviews the contemporary debate about paid maternity leave, tracking the development of this key entitlement for working women and their families in industrial relations and public policy, and considers the emerging debate about the related issues of parental and carer's leave. Time is the key value of these entitlements, establishing not only an industrial right to withdraw from and return to work, but also asserting the intrinsic value of an identity – and time – beyond work.

Suzanne Jamieson applies a 'reflexive lens' to the historical development of Australian labour law. She explores notions of regulation, deregulation and reregulation in the light of Guenther Teubner's theory of the three-stage historical development of law: from an initial period of rule-oriented resolution of individual disputes, through a period identified with the welfare state and heavy intervention by the state in market relations, to a final period of reflexive rationality which idealises self-regulation. Jamieson's chapter brings an important theoretical dimension to the analysis of labour law and its development over time. Jamieson argues that Australian labour law has generally lacked theory, partly because Australia's indigenous conciliation and arbitration system was seen as so idiosyncratic but also because 'theorising is not something that legal writers in Australia have been comfortable in doing'. Jamieson surveys legal theory from Europe and North America in the light of globalisation and the apparent retreat by the nation-state in an era of neo-liberal hegemony.

The focus on time in Chapter 5 by Jim Kitay and Russell Lansbury centres on the debate over the nature and regulation of work in Australia that flourished in the late 1980s and early 1990s – the emergent era of neo-liberal hegemony. Some accounts of change are dichotomous and linear; Kitay & Lansbury challenge the view that changes in work and employment relations have progressed from an 'old' to 'new' model during recent decades. They focus on two major industries, automobile manufacturing and retail banking, exploring the extent to which new working arrangements can be found, the forms they take and their consequences. They conclude that while there have undoubtedly been major changes over time, these have not all been unidirectional. There has been considerable diversity in the forms of work and its regulation, the nature of the changes that have occurred, the means by which these work changes have been introduced and the probable trajectories of change for the future.

Leanne Cutcher and Diane van den Broek shift the analytical focus to customer service in telecommunications and banking. They conclude that nowhere is the subjectivity and elasticity of time more

19

evident than in service work, because the very characteristics of service work render concrete notions of time redundant. Cutcher & van den Broek identify key attributes evident in 'interactive' service work, where the service 'product' is produced and consumed at the same time (perishability, simultaneous consumption and production) and is formed in part by individual customers' perceptions of the service (intangibility, variability and inseparability). These attributes highlight not only the distinctive nature of service work but also its temporal dimension. Notions of time are implicit within all these attributes, they argue, not time as fixed and measurable but time as variable and highly contested.

Social constructions are invariably political constructs. The varieties of work time and its regulation elaborated in these chapters all point to a contested dimension of human experience and identity. The challenge of analysing work and time is a challenge to recognise, as Rose (1999: 31) argues, that time, in human organisation, is a technology of power: time discipline geared to the governance of 'productive subjects . . . the beeping wrist watch, the courses in time management and the like inscribe the particular temporalities into the comportment of free citizens as a matter of self-control'. Referring time-disciplined self-control to free citizens is not, however, a one-way exchange. Some, such as Cutcher & van den Broek, reject the notion that customer service employees have become 'self-disciplined subjects' merely conforming to the temporal demands of management. They argue that the elasticity and subjectivity of the service exchange allow spaces in which employees can attempt to reclaim time, either for themselves or in combination with customers. Service employees may resist management attempts to control the service interaction by making choices about how to perform their work – with enthusiasm, detachment or indifference. Our analysis of time and work must identify the tense negotiations between control and freedom, seeking to privilege the power and play of free citizens.

References

Bluedorn, A.C. 2002, *The Human Organization of Time: Temporal Realties and Experience*, Stanford University Press.

Braudel, F. 1980, *On History*, University of Chicago Press.

Epstein, C. & Kalleberg, A. 2001, 'Time and the sociology of work: issues and implications', *Work and Occupations* 28(1): 5–16.

Rose, N.S. 1999, *Powers of Freedom: Reframing Political Thought*, Cambridge University Press.

CHAPTER TWO

TIME AND WORK

Greg Patmore

The cry is heard among many from different walks of life that we do not have enough time to do everything we want. There are the pressures of paid work and the need of many to juggle employment with household demands, volunteer work and leisure. We are witnessing an intense 'space-time compression' (Harvey 1989: 285) due to faster transportation, the internet, communication satellites and the increasing speed of money markets. Against the background of these concerns, this chapter explores the issues of time and work. Time can described 'as a non-spatial dimension in which events occur in apparently irreversible succession from the past through the present to the future' (Ancona et al. 2001: 514). There are many different types of time and humanity has shaped the perception of time. People designed the hours, days and months. Historians also classify past time into eras.

The chapter emphasises the need to consider time when dealing with the issues related to the world of work. There are two temporal dimensions of work: temporal boundary and temporal content. The temporal boundaries of work are the lines that divide work from leisure and paid work from unpaid work. How many hours or days do we work for payment in a week? How much annual leave and how many holidays? How much unpaid work at home is divided on the basis of gender and class? The temporal content of work is the way in which work is organised on a temporal basis. What is the speed of work? How do workers overcome a perception of slow-moving time at work?

Finally, the chapter explores temporal frames of reference. There is a focus on the past, present and future – historicism, presentism and futurism. At its worst, historicism is antiquarianism, which focuses on history for its own sake and denies any link to the present or future concerns. Historians can also ignore the context in which events occur. Similarly, presentism denies the relevance of the past, while futurism can be pure fantasy with no grounding in past or present experiences. Despite these divisions, the three temporal frames of reference are linked. The chapter ends with a concrete example of how temporal frames of reference impact on issues in the world of work – employee democracy.

THE MEANING OF TIME

When we think of time, it appears to be moving forward without any variation. However, while physicists have shown that you cannot reverse time, it does vary as it moves forward according to the relative velocity of objects (Hawking 1988: 35–6; Mainzer 2002: xiii). There is also psychological literature that notes that perceptions of the speed of time may vary between individuals and groups. A longstanding belief is that time goes faster as we get older. Another saying is 'that time goes faster when you're having fun'. There is evidence that the greater the stimuli, the faster individuals perceive time passing. Older people have more memories to draw upon and greater responsibilities than younger people (Starkey 1989: 37–43).

Ancona et al. (2001: 514–16) note five types of time. There is clock-time, the most common way of describing time in the Western world. It is a continuum that can be divided into quantifiable units such as seconds, days and minutes. There is cyclical time, which is linked to phenomena such as night and day or the four seasons. Time can also be viewed as life cycle, where human life follows the predictable pattern of birth, childhood, adulthood, old age and death. Time can be constructed around particular events that provide a reference point for the past and future. Event time can be unpredictable and predictable. Examples of the former include earthquakes and examples of the latter include socially constructed festivals in Judaeo-Christian societies such as Christmas, Easter and Passover.

Human agency plays a role even in the construction of clock-time. The notion of a day divided into 24 hours of 60 minutes and 60 seconds per minute comes from the Babylonians, whose mathematical system was based on powers of 60 instead of 10 (Mainzer 2002: 2–3). This was unsuccessfully challenged by the French Revolution, which sought to decimalise time with days divided into 10 hours of 100 minutes of 100 seconds each (Adler 2004: 150). The calendar changes of the last few hundred years are better known. Pope Gregory issued a papal decree replacing the Julian calendar with a new calendar in 1582 because the old calendar diverged from the solar calendar. The papal decree cancelled ten consecutive days in October 1582 and reduced the number of leap years. While many Catholic countries immediately adopted the changes, Protestant England and its colonies did not do so until 1752. There were even greater delays in Eastern Orthodox countries, with the Imperial Russian team arriving at the 1908 London Olympic Games ten days late because it relied on the Julian rather than the Gregorian calendar (Bluedorn 2002: 160–3).

The growth of railways, telegraphs and telephones in the 19th century highlighted the need to standardise time within countries and between nations. Each town had its own time depending on solar time and the vagaries of the town's timepieces. Until the enactment of standard time in Australia in 1895, Melbourne clocks ran 25 minutes slower than Sydney and 32 minutes slower than Brisbane (Davison 1993: 50–65). Similar problems led to the passage of legislation to standardise time in Great Britain in 1880 and the USA and Canada in 1918 (Thrift 1990: 120–8; Bluedorn 2002: 163–4). The planet-wide system of 24 time zones based on Greenwich meridian as the zero longitude meridian was initiated at the International Meridian Conference in Washington DC on October 1884, but only gradually adopted throughout the world (Landes 2000: 304).

A more recent attempt to regulate time is daylight saving time (DST). By shifting clocks forward one hour during spring and turning them back in autumn, a number of benefits were gained for energy conservation and leisure activities. DST was first introduced by the Australian, British, German and US governments during the First World War to conserve energy but was abandoned with the end of hostilities. Most Australian States adopted DST in the 1970s, in the face of strong opposition from groups such as farmers and shift workers, who disliked working and travelling to work perpetually in the dark. Overlooking the human construction of time, some objectors claimed that DST violated God's natural law. Recent evidence has suggested that the benefits of DST may be outweighed by the costs. The benefits for energy conservation, for instance, have been exaggerated. There are also concerns about the psychological costs arising from the loss of sleep as DST commences, which can be manifested in increased traffic accidents and even a decline in share market prices. There have been calls for the practice of DST to be discontinued as a result of these negative research findings (Davison 1993: 114–21; Bluedorn 2002: 206–12).

Historians also divide the human experience according to temporal periods: the Dark Ages, the Age of Industrialisation, or Post-Industrialism for example. More specific periods in Australian history would be the 1890s and 1930s Depressions. Historians debate the characteristics and dates that begin and end these periods, but they do provide the context for the particular research being done within the period. The periods may also be compared. In the USA one can compare the retreat from Progressive social engineering to laissez-faire in the 1920s with the impact of Reaganomics on the welfare state in the 1980s (Haydu 1998: 339–40). Comparisons can also be made between different countries in different periods. The period from 1890 to 1914 is seen as a critical juncture in Australia with Federation, compulsory arbitration, tariffs and the rise of the Labor Party. Similarly, the 1930s Depression provided a 'critical juncture' in the USA through the 'New Deal' and the Wagner Act. Comparative historians focus on these critical junctures to explain why different choices were made in particular countries. Why was compulsory arbitration adopted in Australia and rejected in the USA, for instance? (Strauss 1998: 187).

While there are different types of time and humans have attempted to measure and organise it in various ways, time is also a sequence of events in the past, the present and into the future. Events may not necessarily generate a sequence and have any implications for the future. Some events may be forgotten or not communicated beyond a very small group. Individuals can carry their experiences over lengthy periods. In the USA older skilled workers brought their memories of shop-floor militancy during the First World War into the organising campaigns for the new industrial unions of semi-skilled factory workers in the 1930s (Haydu 1998: 351). The significance of particular events may not be understood or have meaning unless linked to a plot or story or greater whole (Bluedorn 2002: 186–7). At one extreme, the attack on the World Trade Center in New York in September 2001 was seen as it happened by many people throughout the world by satellite television. Not only was such a horrific event etched on people's memories but has been reinforced through the US-led 'war on terror' and continued public investigation. This event and earlier events such as the Paris upheavals of May 1968 have a 'social meaning', whereby time becomes a 'medium through which we co-ordinate and reproduce everyday affairs'

(Hassard 1990: 14–15). At the other extreme, individual experiences such as dropping a pencil at work may be soon forgotten by the individual and unseen by others. Some apparently insignificant events may accumulate. A supervisor swearing at a worker may not be acted on, but if there are a number of repeated instances the events may accumulate and lead to violence, a formal complaint about bullying or resignation.

Most theories are based on fairly simple assumptions that X influences Y and ignore the temporal dimension. When did X occur and when did Y occur? What was the lag between the two? X and Y could also change over time during this lag. What is the rate of change? While X is impacting on Y, Y in the meantime could also impact on X. Mitchell & James (2001: 532–5) have suggested at least eight possible configurations of causality between X and Y when one introduces four periods and two other different variables on which X may have an impact. Mitchell & James (2001: 537) also ask when does one measure X or Y? If relationships are cyclical, then when one measures X or Y could be crucial. One might measure X at the peak of the season and measure Y at the trough.

Time has many facets and is 'an interdisciplinary concept *par excellence*, in which the natural and social sciences and humanities complement and rely on each other' (Mainzer 2002: x). Time is not absolute but relative in the natural sciences, social sciences and humanities. There are various types of time and it is shaped by human agency, whether through the measurement of time or the periodisation of history. The neglect of time in understanding causality in theoretical models is a significant omission. This chapter will now examine the implications of time for work, focusing on the temporal boundaries and temporal content of work.

TIME AND WORK

With the rise of industrial capitalism, there were two implications for time and work. Thompson (1967) argued that the rise of industrial capitalism was associated with the shift from task-based work to time-based work. The clock, which had become more accurate and widespread, became an important means by which employers controlled and disciplined their workers. Second, time also become a commodity which workers exchanged for wages. Clock-time provided for work 'an invariable, standardised measure that can be applied universally regardless of context' (Adam 1990: 112). As time was commodified it

25

became a scarce and valuable resource. This necessitated management maximising productivity through either the lengthening of the work day or the intensification of work in the time available (Blyton et al. 1989: 2–4). These are the two dimensions of work time: the 'temporal boundary' (Hassard 1990: 12) and the 'temporal content' of work.

In a recent study, Glucksmann (1998: 243) broadened the conception of work by challenging the assumption that time can only be exchanged for wages. When exploring the shift of women's labour from the household economy to the formal wage economy that accompanied the rise of mass production and mass consumption in the UK, Glucksmann argues that all labour activity can be regarded as work. She refers to the 'total social organisation of labour', which is 'all of the labour undertaken in a society irrespective of who it is taken by, in which institutions, under what conditions, and how'. This enables us to examine the connections between paid labour, unpaid domestic labour, volunteer labour, caring and other forms of labour. Glucksmann's broader view of work allows her 'economy of time' to include work that has no financial rewards, such as volunteer labour.

While people's sense of time is founded on the biology of the human body, individuals experience the process of 'temporal socialisation' before commencing work. Social constraints determine the correct times for infants to feed, drink, play and sleep. Education provides the child with an even more rigid temporal discipline. The school day is divided into periods with breaks for play and meals. The school even extends its temporal discipline beyond its physical boundaries through the assignment of homework, which must meet certain deadlines (Hassard 1996: 590). From the earliest days of industrialisation there were ideas that encouraged the internalisation of temporal discipline. While Puritan, Methodist and Evangelical clerics urged their flocks to 'redeem time' by spending it 'wholly in way of duty', Benjamin Franklin coined the term 'time is money' for the secular industrialist (Thompson 1967: 86–9).

Formal work organisation represents the 'final stage in conditioning the individual to an "organised" time consciousness' (Hassard 1996: 590). Here workers and managers had to deal with the temporal boundaries of paid work. Managers wanted to get maximum productivity by extending hours of work, while workers wanted sufficient time to spend with families, to rest and pursue other interests. Initially one major issue was who interpreted clock-time at work, particularly when workers commenced and completed paid work. Other issues that developed

26

included weekly hours of work, holidays, overtime, shift work, short-time working and retirement (Blyton 1989: 110–29).

Watches were expensive at first and workers had to rely on clock-time provided by employers. During industrialisation in the UK there were examples of employers manipulating clocks to force workers to work longer hours and dismissing workers for having watches in the work-place (Thompson 1967: 85–6). In industrial communities the rhythms of life were determined by bells, steam whistles and electric sirens that notified the beginning and end of shifts. At the Sunshine Harvester plant of H.V. McKay near Melbourne, Australia during the 1920s, the first whistle at 6.30 a.m. woke workers, the second at 7.15 reminded them that they should be on their way and the third at 7.30 signalled the commencement of work. In Australia the arrival of the cheap wrist-watch after the First World War 'democratised time-telling' across class, gender and age and ended the employer dominance of workplace time-keeping (Davison 1993: 41, 107–9).

From the 18th century, workers in Great Britain dealt with the time-discipline of industrialisation by demanding shorter hours. British work-ers achieved the *Ten Hours Act* in 1847, and by 1875 the 54-hour week was widespread (Thompson 1967: 85; Blyton 1989: 108). In Australia, stonemasons in Sydney and Melbourne gained the eight-hour day in 1856. Workers believed that if the British practice of the 10-hour day was followed their health would deteriorate in the warmer Australian climate. But despite the early successes, the eight-hour day spread slowly in Australia. Metal tradesmen and their labourers in the NSW Government Railways workshops won the shorter hours in 1873, but the eight-hour day was not universal in that industry until 1916. Most Australian workers who gained the eight-hour day did not, in prac-tice, work these hours. They worked eight and three-quarter hours for five days, and four and a quarter hours on Saturday. The eight-hour day movement meant a half-day holiday on Saturday. In New South Wales, after several attempts, workers finally gained the 44-hour week in 1933 and the 40-hour week through State legislation in 1948. Some workers were ultimately able to obtain a 35-hour week, such as New South Wales electricity utility workers in 1979 (Patmore 1991: 57–8, 2003a: 24, 30; Fraser 2003: 224). During the 1990s, however, there was a deterioration in the working hours of Australian workers due to management's desire to cut costs and increase worker flexibil-ity. The number of Australians working more than 48 hours a week increased from 30.2 per cent in 1990 to 33.3 per cent in 2000. By comparison, the number of workers on the standard hours between 35 and 40 hours a week declined from 36.6 per cent to 30.5 per cent. One consequence of these longer hours is stress and possible complications for health (Callus & Lansbury 2002: 244–5; Wooden 2002: 61–3).

Another way of limiting the temporal boundaries of paid employment is through annual leave or paid holidays. In Australia this has been further extended through the concept of long service leave. The proponents of annual leave argued that the break from the 'monotony of work' was beneficial for workers' health and productivity. Initially annual leave was viewed as a privilege for white-collar workers and public servants. State railway employees in New South Wales gained one week's annual leave in 1916 and two weeks' annual leave in 1941. NSW Parliament legislated for two weeks' annual leave in 1944 and three weeks in 1958 for all State award employees. The precedent for long service can be found in the Australian public service. Both Victoria and South Australia passed legislation in 1861 allowing civil servants long service leave to go on sabbaticals to Europe after a minimum of 10 years' service. Commonwealth public servants gained this benefit in 1901. The NSW government enacted the first Australian legislation for long service leave of three months for every 20 years in 1951. The three major arguments for long service leave were a reduction in labour turnover, a reward for loyalty, and worker health. The NSW legislation for annual leave and long service set the pace for Australian industrial jurisdictions. The Australian standard ultimately became four weeks' paid annual leave with New South Wales providing two months' paid long service leave for every 10 years of employment (Patmore 2003b). By comparison within the European Union, in 2003 statutory minimum annual leave ranged from 20 days in the UK to 22 days in Spain to 25 days in France (Eiroline 2003). There are other forms of paid and unpaid leave which allow workers to deal with issues such as maternity, paternity, care-giving, sickness and bereavement.

Other significant issues relating to the temporal boundaries of paid work include overtime, shift work, short-time working, retirement and work-time flexibility. There has been a long history of union resistance to compulsory overtime, which is time worked in excess of standard hours, on the grounds that it affects workers' leisure and increases unemployment during recessions. Unions have obtained penalty rates, such as time and a half, to discourage overtime. Overtime can be very resistant to economic conditions, remaining high during both booms and recessions. Management relies on overtime to counter short-term extraordinary circumstances that relate to labour supply. There is also systematic overtime where overtime is regularly incorporated into the work schedule. Management may prefer to use overtime as an alternative to the recruitment of new labour to avoid non-wage labour costs and the training of inexperienced staff. Shift work is another way of extending the working day and allowing the workplace to operate 24 hours a day. This is important for continuous process industries and essential services such as police and hospitals. Shift work also allows management to maximise its investment on any capital outlay (Blyton 1989: 114–19). Night shift work, which was assisted by the development of artificial light, is more disruptive to family life, social life and physiological rhythms such as sleep than other shifts (Bluedorn 2002: 205–6). While shift work and overtime extend the length of the working day, short-time working reduces it, particularly during periods of economic downturn. It allows management to retain experienced staff rather than lose them through retrenchment. The level of short-time working tends to be highest at the onset of an economic downturn when it is unclear if retrenchments will be necessary. Retirement sets the limit to the paid working lifetime. Early retirement is offered by management as an alternative to redundancy. The timing of retirement is also influenced by the generosity of pensions available through the social welfare system and superannuation schemes offered in the private and public sectors. Since the 1970s there have been calls for greater worktime flexibility through the greater use of part-time and casual labour. There has been a push for 'flexible rostering' whereby the fixed eight-hour day is abandoned and replaced by rosters of between seven and nine hours to allow the matching of work time and operational needs (Blyton 1989: 121–9). There has also been an interest in 'flexitime', which allows workers to come and go to work earlier or later. Workers can link work hours to family needs, such as picking up children from school (Hochschild 1997: 26–7).

In the household, gender and class provide the basis for the temporal boundary of unpaid work. There is a blurring of the line between paid work and housework. With mobile or cell phones, workers can be interrupted at home by work issues and interrupted at work by family members. Computers allow people to work at home, while watching children. There is also the growth of a 'time famine' or 'time poverty', particularly when workers are in paid employment and have a 'second shift' (Hochschild 1989) with responsibilities for caring for others. Mothers in full-time employment with children and sole parents with children work the longest number of unpaid hours. Australian evidence from a national survey conducted in 1996–97 found that men worked nine hours a week on housework, while women worked 24 hours a week. While women have reduced the time they spend on household work, their partners have not increased their share of it. The drop in women's household work arises from the purchase of market-produced goods and services. Women continue to be primarily responsible for childcare even if they are undertaking paid employment. The ageing of the Australian population has contributed to the family responsibilities, and the growth in hours of paid work has further 'squeezed' the time available for family activities (Cass 2002: 145–9). Research in the UK also argues that class is a significant factor in the distribution of household time for dual-earning couples. Middle-class couples were more likely to share or have the man do washing and ironing, while working-class couples were more likely to share or have the man undertake childcare responsibilities. This was particularly notable with working-class couples where women worked days and the men worked nights. For these couples, 60 per cent shared childcare compared with 36 per cent for other couples. Despite the more enlightened view of these couples towards childcare, the other household tasks remained female-dominated (Warren 2003). There is a range of options that can 'ease the squeeze' on family time, such as strengthening all forms of leave that provide for greater time with family. These include not only parental, sick, family and maternity leave, but also recreational leave such as annual leave and long service leave that allow for leisure and rest. There is a greater need for 'family-friendly' workplaces, which provide, for example, greater flexibility in starting and finishing times. Finally, the growth in working hours has to be checked to allow greater integration of family time and employment time (Cass 2002: 157–8; Morehead 2002).

While there are issues relating to the temporal boundary of work, there are also questions relating to the temporal content of work. In paid employment the pace of work is a major issue. Management has attempted to increase this pace by various means. Piecework payment systems linked payment to output in a specified period. Ford's assembly line or mass production relied on machinery to force the pace of production. Scientific management or Taylorism, with its emphasis on time and motion studies with a stopwatch, linked clock-time to minute components of human movement at work in order to increase efficiency. Problems with time and motion studies resulted in the development of Predetermined Motion Time Systems (PMTS), of which MTM (Methods-Time-Management) was the most popular in Australia during the postwar economic boom. MTM reduced the need for the direct observation of workers with a stopwatch. Experts in the USA and the UK had already determined the standard time for each motion by various means including photography. This method of study provided the basis for 'scientific' incentive schemes, which provided bonuses for workers who exceeded set times. During the 1980s the Japanese new production concept of Just-in-Time was widely publicised in Australia. Work was only done as needed in response to immediate market needs and inventories were reduced to the bare minimum. The impact of computer technology in areas such as data-processing increased the pace of work. These innovations were not without worker resistance. One example is the 'darg', where workers restricted the amount of output to spread the amount of work and restrict competition among them. The appearance of the stopwatch in the Australian metal trades could provoke strikes and even violence (Patmore 1991: 140, 152–3; Wright 1995: 74–8, 169–74).

While workers resisted efforts to increase the pace of work, some workers played 'games' to deal with the monotony of work. Roy's (1960) classic study of machine shop employees highlights how they put meaning into monotonous work and perceived time as going faster irrespective of clock-time. Workers constructed times for each day such as 'banana time', where one worker would 'steal' a banana from another and there would follow a verbal interaction. Instead of a long boring day the workers transformed it into a series of regular social activities.

Other studies have noted that perceptions of time vary between management and workers and according to the type of work being done. Management may be preoccupied with the linearity of clock-time, while workers may develop a set of strategies or rituals to deal with the pace of work and to manipulate time. Individual workers deal with the passing of time by eating, singing and day-dreaming. Organisational time varies according to each day of the week. Monday may be a good day because workers are fresh and interested in catching up on the weekend's news, but Friday is a slow day with everyone looking forward to the weekend. The rhythm of organisations can also vary. Firms in the fashion industry have different cycles based on the design of the new season's fashions and then the marketing of the new fashions. There are higher levels of expectation in the former than the latter, and time may be perceived as going faster in the design stage (Hassard 1996: 586–9).

31

TEMPORAL FRAMES OF REFERENCE

When dealing with issues in the world of work such as the impact of time, we bring together perspectives based on the past, present and future. There are three temporal frames of reference based on the past, present and future. They are historicism, 'presentism' and futurism. At its worst, historicism is antiquarianism, which focuses on history for its own sake and denies any link to the present or future concerns. Historians can also ignore the context in which events occur. At its best, historicism allows the generation and testing of theories. For example, historians have tested and challenged Braverman's deskilling hypothesis. History provides researchers with a long-term perspective, allowing them to avoid the pitfalls of the snapshot. It focuses on process and allows researchers to develop dynamic rather than static theoretical frameworks. Theoretical perspectives that fail to take account of a changing economic, political and social climate have limited explanatory power (Patmore 2002: 27). 'Presentism' denies the relevance of the past and claims that history, unlike the natural or social sciences, is idiographic in that it explores details of unique and non-reproducible events. It ignores the fact that historians can develop long-term theoretical perspectives (Mainzer 2002: 138–44). The most extreme example of futurism can be found in the 'deep time research' undertaken by the US government. It asked a panel of experts to predict what the USA would be like in 10 000 years, including questions concerning what language would be spoken and whether the USA would still exist. This arose from safety concerns over the nuclear waste stored in a facility near Carlsbad, New Mexico, which would take 10 000 years to decay safely (Bluedorn 2002: 136–7). Despite sophisticated econometric models and supercomputers, it is difficult to predict the future. As physicists have noted in the world of quantum mechanics, systems can become chaotic. There is also a 'butterfly effect' where the smallest local change or event could have national and even international implications (Mainzer 2002: 100). An isolated strike could unexpectedly cascade into a full-blown revolution and the overthrow of a government. Despite these divisions, the three temporal frames of reference are linked.

The past and future are embedded in the present and the three fuse into a 'flux' in the human mind (Jacques 1990: 25). The present is traditionally represented on the time axis in which the past and present come infinitely close. However, since time can vary because of differing psychological perceptions of the passage of time, the present may flow sluggishly or elapse instantaneously. The past preconditions the present through memory, while the future is based in the present in terms of expectations and hopes (Mainzer 2002: 127–8). Present concerns can also shape how we see the past and the questions we can ask about it. Futurism can become pure fantasy if it is not grounded in past or present experiences. Indeed the 'deep time' Carlsbad project required the team to think what things were like 10 000 years in the past in order to understand what they might be like 10 000 years in the future. As Bluedorn (2002: 138) notes, the past 'served as metaphor for the future: deep-past metaphors for deep-future concerns'.

TEMPORAL FRAMES OF REFERENCE AND EMPLOYEE DEMOCRACY

The role of temporal frames of reference can be seen in both practical and theoretical debates on employee democracy. When management attempt to introduce participatory practices, the past behaviour of management and employee expectations will influence whether the participatory practices will be successfully introduced. They are less likely to succeed if management in the past have acted autocratically rather than democratically. If employees anticipate that the new participatory practices are temporary and that management will revert to autocratic behaviour, they will be more hostile. They will be more favourable if they believe that there are increasing opportunities to participate in the future (George & Jones 2000: 669–70).

The recent decline in trade union membership in many Western countries has rekindled interest in schemes of employee democracy as a hope for the future. Scholars emphasise that workers without union representation no longer have a voice in the management of their workplaces. This 'representation gap' reduces the potential of workers to contribute to improving productivity and the quality of working life. The gap can be overcome by encouraging collectivist but non-union mechanisms such as works councils or joint consultative committees. The advocates of these forms of representation argue that they complement the call for 'high performance workplaces' 'or mutual gain enterprises' in an era of heightened global and domestic competition by encouraging decentralised decision-making, team forms of production and a climate of cooperation and trust (Kaufman & Taras 2000: 4; Gollan & Hamberger 2002: 24–5; Mizrahi 2002).

The problem with this debate in Australia is that it is 'presentist'. There is a 'public policy amnesia' (Patmore 2002: 36), where previous experiments in employee democracy are overlooked (see Gollan et al. 2002). In Australia there have been at least three waves of interest in employee democracy before the present wave. Two major approaches use a 'historicist approach' to explain this recurrent interest in employee democracy. Ramsay (1980) in the UK and Wright (1995) in Australia noted that employers have adopted a cyclical approach to employee participation driven by threats to managerial authority. The 'favourable conjunctures' thesis rejects the inevitability of cycles and is more focused on factors that help explain the rise of industrial democracy. This approach acknowledges a 'broad long-term trend towards greater experimentation and richness of forms' of industrial democracy; it also recognises 'a discontinuous historical pattern, in which the main forms of industrial democracy have varied substantially in their incidence and impact at distinctive points in time'. It takes an optimistic view of the progress of employee democracy (Poole et al. 2001: 23). Both the cyclical and 'favourable conjectures' theses highlight that there is a long history of prior experimentation with industrial democracy to draw on in evaluating the success or failure of contemporary proposals.

In the USA and Canada, academics interested in overcoming the 'representation gap' have explored their historical traditions, particularly in regard to the Rockefeller Plan or Employee Representation Plans (ERP) before the outbreak of the Second World War (Kaufman 2000a; McDowell 2000). The plan formed the foundation of a movement that spread throughout the USA and covered 2.5 million workers in various industries by 1935. Critics condemned these plans as 'sham organisations' that impeded labour organisation and they were outlawed in the 1935 *National Labor Relations Act* (Kaufman 2000a: 22–9). Despite this, Fairris (1995: 524) argued that in the 1920s these schemes 'marked a definite improvement for the worker as well as the firm' by reducing labour turnover, fostering worker loyalty and allowing workers a voice in determining shop floor conditions. Kaufman (2000b: 55) claimed that the ERP movement was on the whole 'a constructive positive development for improved industrial relations'. While the willingness of these scholars to undertake a historicist approach is welcome, one of the problems with these interpretations is a reluctance to explore the full historical context of the ERPs, particularly at the workplace level. At the Colorado Fuel and Iron Company, for example, the 'progressive' ERP during the 1920s sat alongside a tradition of management spying on labour activities (Rees 2004).

CONCLUSION

Time is not an absolute dimension but is shaped by human intervention. The Babylonians shaped the hours and minutes, while the rise of railways and telegraphs forced the need for standard time. Clock-time is only one of many different types of time, and time can vary according to human perception. Time is also a sequence of events. Some events are of major significance, while others have no impact. Theoretical models based on causality that do not integrate time weaken our understanding of the world.

During the industrial revolution the clock helped management to discipline workers and commodified time. Management maximised productivity through either the lengthening of the work day or the intensification of work in the time available. These are the two dimensions of work time: the 'temporal boundary' and the 'temporal content' of work. Issues concerning the temporal boundaries of paid work include hours of work and holidays. The temporal boundaries of unpaid housework are determined by factors such as gender and class. An important question relating to the temporal content of work is the pace of work. Management has tried ideas such as scientific management and MTM to obtain precise measurements of tasks so that work can be performed quickly and efficiently. Workers have resisted management's efforts to increase the pace of the line. They also have their own perceptions of time at work that conflict with management's emphasis on clock-time. The workplace can be temporally mapped out on the basis of different constructions of time.

There are different temporal frames of reference based on the past, present and future. These are historicism, presentism and futurism. Historicism allows us to ask the simple question whether the conditions that led to failure in the past are still present. Historical analysis enables one to subject 'dominant paradigms' to closer scrutiny and question claims of 'transformation'. Historians, however, can also ignore the context in which events occur to justify a point being made in contemporary debates. The discourse on employee democracy highlights a major problem with presentism. If you are only focused on the present you may miss long-term trends and make unsubstantiated claims about 'transformation'. As ideas such as 'chaos theory' and the 'butterfly effect' show, it is extremely difficult to predict the future. This problem is further exacerbated by a failure to ground the future in either the present or the past. The past, present and future are linked and to deny the relevance of any temporal dimension is problematic.

References

Adam, B. 1990, *Time and Social Theory*, Cambridge: Polity Press.

Adler, K. 2004, *The Measure of All Things: The Seven-Year-Odyssey that Transformed the World*, London: Abacus.

Ancona, D.G., Okhuysena, G.A. & Perlow, L.A. 2001, 'Taking time to integrate temporal research', *Academy of Management Review* 26(4): 512–29.

Bluedorn, A.C. 2002, *The Human Organization of Time: Temporal Realities and Experience*, Stanford University Press.

Blyton, P. 1989, 'Time and labour relations', in Blyton et al., *Time, Work and Organization*, pp. 105–31.

Blyton, P., Hassard, J., Hill, S. & Starkey, K. 1989, *Time, Work and Organization*, London: Routledge.

Callus, R. & Lansbury, R.D. 2002, 'Working futures: Australia in a global context', in R. Callus & R.D. Lansbury (eds) *Working Futures: The Changing Nature of Work and Employment Relations in Australia*, Sydney: Federation Press, pp. 233–50.

Cass, B. 2002, 'Employment time and family time: the intersections of labour market transformations and family responsibilities in Australia', in Callus & Lansbury (eds) *Working Futures*, pp. 142–62.

Davison, G. 1993, *The Unforgiving Minute: How Australia Learned to Tell the Time*, Oxford University Press.

Eiroline, 2003. http://www.eiro.eurofound.eu.int/2004/03/update/tn0403104u.html

Fairris, D. 1995, 'From exit to voice in shopfloor governance: the case of company unions', *Business History Review* 69(4): 493–529.

Fraser, A. 2003, 'Alexander Craig Beattie, 1966–1981', in G. Patmore (ed.) *Laying the Foundations of Industrial Justice: The Presidents of the Industrial Relations Commission of NSW 1902–1998*, Sydney: Federation Press, pp. 81–102.

George, J.M. & Jones, G.R. 2000, 'The role of time in theory and theory building', *Journal of Management* 26(4): 657–84.

Glucksmann, M.A. 1998, '"What a difference the day makes": a theoretical and historical exploration of temporality and gender', *Sociology* 32(2): 239–58.

Gollan, P.J. & Hamberger, J. 2002, 'Enterprise-based employee representation in Australia: employer strategies and future options', in Gollan, Markey & Ross (eds) *Works Councils in Australia*, pp. 24–36.

Gollan, P.J., Markey, R. & Ross, I. (eds) 2002, *Works Councils in Australia: Future Prospects and Possibilities*, Sydney: Federation Press.

Hassard, J. 1990, 'Introduction: the sociological study of time', in J. Hassard (ed.) *The Sociology of Time*, London: Macmillan, pp. 1–18.

Hassard, J. 1996, 'Images of time in work and organization', in S.R. Clegg, C. Hardy & W.R. Nord (eds) *Handbook of Organization Studies*, London: Sage, pp. 581–98.

Harvey, D. 1989, *The Condition of Postmodernity*, Oxford: Blackwells.

Hawking, S. 1988, *A Brief History of Time: From the Big Bang to Black Holes*, London: Bantam Books.

Haydu, J. 1998, 'Making use of the past: time periods as cases to compare and as sequences of problem solving', *American Journal of Sociology* 104(2): 339–71.

Hochschild, A.R. 1989, *The Second Shift*, New York: Avon.

Hochschild, A.R. 1997, *The Time Bind: When Work Becomes Home and Home Becomes Work*, New York: Metropolitan Books.

Jacques, E. 1990, 'The enigma of time', in J. Hassard (ed.) *The Sociology of Time*, London: Macmillan, pp. 21–34.

Kaufman, B.E. 2000a, 'Accomplishments and shortcomings of nonunion employee representation in the pre-Wagner Act years: a reassessment', in B.E. Kaufman & D.G. Taras (eds) *Non-Union Employee Representation: History, Contemporary Practice and Policy*, Armonk, NY: M.E. Sharpe, pp. 21–60.

Kaufman, B.E. 2000b, 'The case for the company union', *Labor History* 41(3): 321–51.

Kaufman, B.E. & Taras, D.G. 2000, 'Introduction', in B.E. Kaufman & D.G. Taras (eds) *Non-Union Employee Representation*, Armonk, NY: M.E. Sharpe, pp. 3–18.

Landes, D.S. 2000, *Revolution in Time*, rev. edn, Cambridge, Mass.: Belknap Press.

Mainzer, K. 2002, *The Little Book of Time*, New York: Copernicus Books.

McDowell, L.S. 2000, 'Company unionism in Canada, 1915–1948', in Kaufman & Taras (eds) *Non-Union Employee Representation*, pp. 96–120.

Mitchell, T.R. & James, L.R. 2001, 'Building better theory: time and the specification of when things happen', *Academy of Management Review* 26(4): 530–47.

Mizrahi, S. 2000, 'Workers' participation in decision-making process and firm stability', *British Journal of Industrial Relations* 40(4): 689–708.

Morehead, A. 2002, 'Commentary: employment time and family time', in Callus & Lansbury (eds) *Working Futures*, pp. 168–74.

Patmore, G. 1991, *Australian Labour History*, Melbourne: Longman Cheshire.

Patmore, G. 2002, 'Changes in the nature of work and employment relations: an historical perspective', in Callus & Lansbury (eds) *Working Futures*, pp. 27–38.

Patmore, G. 2003a, 'Industrial conciliation and arbitration in New South Wales before 1998', in G. Patmore (ed.) *Laying the Foundations of Industrial Justice: The Presidents of the Industrial Relations Commission of NSW 1902–1998*, Sydney: Federation Press, pp. 5–66.

Patmore, G. 2003b, 'Legislating for benefits: NSW 1941–1958', *Australian Bulletin of Labour* 29(1): 14–30.

Poole, M., Lansbury, R. & Wailes, N. 2001, 'Participation and industrial democracy revisited: a theoretical perspective', in R. Markey, P. Gollan, A. Hodgkinson, A. Chouraqui & U. Veersma (eds) *Models of Employee Participation in a Changing Global Environment: Diversity and Participation*, Aldershot: Ashgate, pp. 23–34.

Ramsay, H. 1980, 'Cycles of control: worker participation in sociological and historical perspective', in P. Boreham & G. Dow (eds) *Work and Inequality: Ideology and Control in the Capitalist Labour Process*, Melbourne: Macmillan, pp. 104–29.

Rees, J. 2004, '"X," "XX" and "X-3": labor spy reports from the Colorado Fuel and Iron Company archives', *Colorado Heritage*, 28–41.

Roy, D.F. 1960, 'Banana time: job satisfaction and informal interaction', *Human Organization* 18(4): 156–68.

Starkey, K. 1989. 'Time and work: a psychological perspective', in Blyton et al., *Time, Work and Organization*, pp. 35–56.

Strauss, G. 1998, 'Comparative international industrial relations', in K. Whitfield & G. Strauss (eds) *Researching the World of Work: Strategies and Methods in Studying Industrial Relations*, Ithaca, NY: Cornell University Press, pp. 175–92.

Thompson, E.P. 1967, 'Time, work-discipline, and industrial capitalism', *Past and Present* 38: 56–97.

Thrift, N. 1990, 'The making of a capitalist time consciousness', in J. Hassard (ed.) *The Sociology of Time*, London: Macmillan, pp. 105–29.

Warren, T. 2003, 'Class- and gender-based working time? Time poverty and the division of domestic labour', *Sociology* 37(4): 733–52.

Wooden, M. 2002, 'The changing labour market and its impact on work and employment relations', in Callus & Lansbury (eds) *Working Futures*, pp. 51–69.

Wright, C. 1995, *The Management of Labour: A History of Australian Employers*, Melbourne: Oxford University Press.

CHAPTER THREE

THE GENDER AGENDA
Women, Work and Maternity Leave

Marian Baird

At the beginning of the 21st century, women constitute close to half the paid workforce and represent over 40 per cent of trade union membership in Australia. Like men, they are 'breadwinners', contributing to household incomes, organisational profits and the national economy; but they continue, disproportionately, to be also the 'breadmakers', combining the domestic responsibilities of mothering and caring with paid work and careers. There is a clear gendered distribution of time in the household, with repercussions in the workplace (HREOC 2005). For women in particular, the changes in workforce participation have increased the stresses on the allocation of time between work, family, leisure and other activities.

In Australia, these changing social patterns have not been recognised with commensurate changes in policy or adequate re-evaluation of women's contribution to the paid workforce. There are clear policy lags and inequities in the distribution of wages and entitlements (Burgess & Baird 2003), and one area in particular shows that women do not receive adequate recognition for their multiple work and family roles. This is the availability of paid maternity leave. Although there has been considerable discussion and debate about the choices and constraints on women's ability to take time out of their working lives to bear and raise children, Australia remains one of only two industrialised nations (the other is the USA) without statutory paid maternity leave for working women.

This chapter is premised on the argument that while time is widely recognised as a socially constructed phenomenon (see Patmore, this volume), when combined with the concept of paid work, it is also highly gendered. The notional construction of the many time-based concepts associated with work, for instance the standard working day, the working week, overtime, clocking on and clocking off, lifetime employment and the career, are all predicated on traditional male patterns of workforce participation. Even though these are currently undergoing extensive change and are highly contested, there remains an underlying assumption of working time that suits men – or at least the 'ideal' male employee – who, in turn, is reliant on female support in the private sphere (Rapoport et al. 2002). Witness, for instance, the prevalence of extended working hours and the resistance to introducing quality part-time work and employee control over rostering, or the demise of a genuine interest in job sharing and a reluctance to engage properly with new job design that would allow job splitting and different job sizes. Although some countries such as France, Holland and Denmark have experimented with more novel constructions of working time, Australia, on the whole, has not. Instead, like the USA, Australia has arguably embraced a long-hours work culture rather than an innovative one, placing many employees in a difficult and irreconcilable 'time bind' where there is not enough time for either home or work (Hochschild 1997).

As a result of this failure to construct working time in a more female-friendly (or family-friendly) way, debates about the distribution of time between work and family and the value placed on time in each of these spheres remain unresolved and this becomes particularly evident with regard to paid maternity leave. Following from the concept of working time being socially constructed by and for men, time becomes an important concept in the debate about paid maternity leave. The essential argument in the policy debate is that while paid maternity leave can never replace the time a woman must take out of paid work to bear children, this time should at least be valued appropriately. Since it is recognised that 'time is money', women on maternity leave should be compensated for the time they are out of the workforce. This is why paid maternity leave is defined as income replacement to compensate for the leave from paid employment necessary around childbirth (Earle 1999: 211; HREOC 2002a: 13). Maternity leave is distinct from parental leave, which is a broader concept that includes leave for fathers, and it is an entitlement related to women's participation in the paid workforce, affirming women's roles as workers as well as mothers. It is also distinct from a welfare payment, which bears no relationship to work-force participation.

Furthermore, in the debate in Australia about paid maternity leave there is a sense of 'time' in terms of urgency, change and trajectories. It is argued in this chapter that it is time to attend to women's work and it is time that the gender agenda becomes a recognised and main-streamed part of industrial relations theory, policy and practice. There is also a need to recognise 'time' in terms of change. Over the last century women's participation in paid work has changed markedly, highlight-ing the dissonance between women's life cycles and the normative male cycles of work and life, as well as the growing tensions between pub-lic and organisational policies and worker's experiences. Finally, there is a need to understand policy over 'time' in terms of a linear trajec-tory. Maternity leave policies in Australia tend to display a conservative pattern. Coupled with a discernible shift in industrial relations policy away from national and industry standards to enterprise standards, these policies have impacted directly on paid maternity leave outcomes and resulted in an uneven and inadequate distribution of the entitlement.

The chapter begins with a brief discussion of the gendered agenda in mainstream industrial relations theory and practice. This is followed by a section outlining the changing workforce participation of women in Australia. The core of the chapter analyses the different orientations to paid maternity leave. The two orientations most closely associated with the industrial relations agenda – the bargaining and business orientations – are examined both conceptually and empirically. The evidence shows that many working women are still excluded from receiving benefits that enable them reasonably and equitably to com-bine family and work. The chapter focuses on maternity leave (rather than the more generic parental leave) because of Australia's unusual position in the industrialised world in not providing paid maternity leave. Furthermore, and significantly for this 'time' section of the book, this situation highlights the somewhat laggard policy and time-warped position of working women in Australia.

THE GENDER AGENDA

The exclusion of a statutory paid maternity leave scheme from Aus-tralian industrial relations and public policy is very surprising to many observers, especially given Australia's record as a workers' welfare state

41

and as a 'working man's paradise'. Yet this latter phrase highlights the core of the problem: the dominance of the male view, a view which has tended to exclude women's issues from the industrial agendas of unions, employers and governments. The clearest manifestation of the gendered agenda in industrial relations is in the perpetuation – metaphorically and practically – of the male breadwinner model. Not confined to Australia, however, debates about the relevance of the male breadwinner concept are taking place in most English-speaking countries.

In Australia, this traditional view of the male in full-time employment and the female as the full-time housewife and carer was epitomised in the Harvester decision of 1907 (*Commonwealth v. McKay* 6 CLR 41) in which Justice Higgins of the Commonwealth Court of Conciliation and Arbitration determined the living wage of a male with a dependent wife and three children. While the historical context of the time may have deemed this appropriate, this is no longer the typical family model in Australia.

By 2002, the traditional male breadwinner model was the least common pattern in Australia, with only 28 per cent of couple families with dependants fitting this model (ABS 2003). There are two contenders for the new norm: either the full-time working male and part-time working female, or the dual career couple with both in full-time employment (Bittman & Rice 2002). This traditional view of family and work fed the notion that the ideal worker was 'care-less' (Pocock 2003), generally male and unencumbered by caring responsibilities. Women as mothers, with many caring responsibilities, are therefore not ideal workers.

To date, and reflecting the dominance of this idealised Harvester world and the distribution of paid working time between men and women, the employment arrangements and benefits that accrue to workers have consequently been shaped by men's needs rather than women's. Although pay equity remains elusive (Todd & Eveline 2005), the gendered outcomes of the Australian industrial relations system are not restricted to pay. In the area of non-wage benefits and entitlements, gendered outcomes are also pronounced. The standard employment benefits, covering three-quarters of the full-time workforce, include superannuation, paid holiday leave, paid sick leave and long service leave. Apart from superannuation, for which there is national legislation, women have less access to these benefits (Burgess & Baird 2003). Furthermore, these standard benefits are not only historically specific (Patmore 2003) but also gender-specific, introduced to support a male breadwinner's work cycle and not the broken, intermittent cycle of women's work-life experience. In Australia for instance, women's employment pattern is distinguished by the 'extent to which mothers exit the labour market with the birth of children and the concentration of mothers in part-time work' (Whitehouse 2005: 403).

As childbirth and the taking of maternity leave sit at the very intersection of women's working and domestic lives, the issue is therefore one that straddles both industrial and welfare policies. Whitehouse argues that Australia's historical decision not to introduce a contributory pension system to provide family-based entitlements, such as most other countries have, but to rely on the industrial state, has made the introduction of benefits like maternity leave more problematic (Whitehouse 2005). That is, it is not easy to locate the responsibility for providing paid maternity leave in a country that has so clearly differentiated between the two spheres of the male industrial world and the female-focused domestic world.

Interestingly, the most recent attempt to address the lack of paid maternity leave in Australia came not from the traditional industrial relations actors but the Human Rights and Equal Opportunity Commission (HREOC). In 2002, following a lengthy consultative process and public debate, HREOC recommended federal government funding for 14 weeks' maternity leave, paid at the federal minimum wage for women in paid work for 40 weeks over the previous year, including casual, permanent and self-employed women (HREOC 2002b). This recommendation, which met the International Labour Organisation's recommendation (ILO Convention 183), was ultimately rejected by the federal government. Instead, a welfare-style maternity allowance was introduced. By so doing, the specific issue of a paid maternity leave entitlement was cast firmly back into the industrial relations arena, contingent on the power of bargaining or the discretion of employers. These conflicting approaches, or orientations, are examined further below.

While industrial relations practice has clearly reflected the male agenda, industrial relations scholarship has similarly been consumed with the study of the determination and regulation of work and working conditions by and for men (Baird 2003). While the call for change and for the inclusion of a more balanced gender approach in industrial relations has increased (Forrest 1993; Pocock 1997), there is considerable room for improvement. The industrial relations concerns of the present day – the precariousness of work and of entitlements, the expansion and extension of working hours, the pursuit of living wages, work and family tensions – are women's issues as much as men's, and it is time to refocus industrial relations and to genuinely include women workers, their work and their interests in the discipline.

WOMEN IN THE WORKFORCE

The participation rates of women in the Australian labour market have changed dramatically over time, especially since the 1960s and 1970s and particularly among married women. This trend contributed to a long-term overall increase in Australia's workforce. At the beginning of the 20th century approximately 20 per cent of women were in paid work, increasing to about a quarter of the female working-age population in 1950. By 1970 the female participation rate was 37 per cent. It was almost 45 per cent in 1983 and now stands at close to 60 per cent (ABS 2004; Whitehouse 2005). By contrast, male participation rates in the labour market are declining. Between 1983 and 2003 they fell from 76.7 per cent to 71.6 per cent (ABS 2004).

Women now constitute approximately 47 per cent of the total workforce and 42 per cent of the unionised workforce. Importantly for the issue of maternity leave, 71 per cent of women in the prime child-bearing years (25–34) are in paid work; this represents a 31 per cent increase over the past 20 years (ABS 2005: 165). More broadly, the significant increase in mothers entering the workforce increases the need to understand the interlocking of work and family agendas. Almost 50 per cent of mothers are in paid work and women with children under five years of age are now more likely to be in paid work than at any other time in Australia's history (ABS 2003).

In the period 1986 to 2001, the proportion of women aged 15–24 years who were studying also increased, from 36 per cent to 56 per cent (ABS 2003), suggesting that women's interests in pursuing paid work and careers will continue to rise rather than abate. Additionally, as the total population ages, the need of the Australian labour market for more female workers grows (Commonwealth of Australia 2004).

In terms of employment patterns, however, there is still a marked gender difference between men and women, with most of the increase in women's labour force participation rate being in part-time and casual work. For instance, in the year 2000 in couple families with children, only 26 per cent of wives were in full-time work compared with 85 per cent for husbands (Whitehouse 2005: 403). Whitehouse argues that these figures suggest both a contemporary variant of the breadwinner model and continuing gender inequity.

These brief statistical overviews of the gender agenda and of women's working experiences in Australia highlight contradictory tendencies over time. On the one hand, a significant change in women's participation in paid work has occurred, but on the other hand there has been little change in achieving an equitable distribution of work and, as the discussion below will highlight, a concomitant inequity in the provision of employment benefits. This is especially so in the case of the one benefit that most affects the competing pulls on women's time, between work and family – paid maternity leave.

SHIFTING ORIENTATIONS TO MATERNITY LEAVE

Using a framework of 'orientations to paid maternity leave' (Baird 2004), I now turn to trace the various constructions of maternity leave (paid and unpaid) that have been used over time in Australia. Each orientation encapsulates certain characteristics that define the different approaches to maternity leave and the consequent outcomes. These include the 'dominant discourse', which highlights the language and rhetoric used about maternity leave; a 'principal agency', which is the party or group mainly responsible for conveying the message, advocating the particular approach and having carriage of the issue; a 'primary mechanism' by which the policy is introduced and codified; and finally, a set of 'expected outcomes' that can be recognised and anticipated as a result of the specific orientation.

By using this framework we are able to make more sense of the differing and somewhat confusing ways in which paid maternity leave has been approached. Three orientations are initially identified and are called 'welfare orientation', 'bargaining orientation' and 'business orientation'. While each of these has influenced policy, none has hitherto delivered an outcome that provides universal access to paid maternity leave for working women that would enable them to balance their time in and out of the labour force without undue financial or career penalty.

The current approach to maternity allowances and maternity leave in Australia is somewhat confusing, with competing and overlapping orientations operating simultaneously. In addition to a welfare-style maternity allowance, there are potentially a variety of other sources of paid maternity leave under current Australian industrial relations and public policy. These include industrial tribunal test case decisions, industrial awards, enterprise agreements, company policies and legislation.

The only paid maternity leave legislation that exists in Australia covers public sector employees. As far back as 1973 the then federal Labor government introduced legislation providing 12 weeks' paid maternity leave for federal public servants. This has remained the most enduring standard and benchmark in Australia. However, there has been little movement beyond this in over 30 years, and many State governments have only recently amended their own legislation. For instance, in 2005 Queensland and Western Australia still only provided six weeks for their public servants; Tasmania provided 12 weeks and New South Wales has just introduced 14 weeks. Victoria, the Australian Capital Territory and the Northern Territory had introduced 14 weeks' paid maternity leave for public sector employees a few years earlier.

Paid maternity leave: the welfare orientation

The analysis begins with an examination of the 'welfare orientation' to maternity allowances in Australia, an orientation that has dominated Australian public policy over the past century and continues to influence the Australian government's policy-making agenda. There have been various forms of maternity allowance in Australia, but none has taken the form of paid maternity leave as defined above. This distinction between a maternity allowance and paid maternity leave goes to the heart of how women's time and efforts are valued in Australia. The distinction is about whether or not women are recognised only for their time in one role, that of mother, or for their time spent in dual roles, combining paid work with motherhood.

The 'welfare orientation' tends to accept uncritically the traditional male-breadwinner model, and its corollary, the female dependent on her male partner for economic security, with additional support from the state if necessary. Such an orientation is based on the notion of women's 'maternal citizenship' (Eveline 2001): that women's primary (and almost exclusive) role in society is reproduction, care-giving and domestic service for the good of children, the family unit and the community. It is not surprising that the dominant discourse in this orientation uses the language of domesticity and dependence, motherhood, child welfare, family and fertility. In the welfare orientation, the primary agency for promoting a maternal discourse is the government, generally of a paternalist and protectionist persuasion, and the primary mechanism for providing maternity-related welfare payments is legislation. It is generally recognised that the main objective of maternity allowance schemes is to encourage fertility and traditional home-based roles for women. They are not intended to encourage women's ongoing attachment to the paid workforce or to compensate working women for income or career forgone as a result of time out of the workforce due to childbirth.

The first maternity allowance introduced in 1912, for example, was a payment designed to protect the health and well-being of mothers and babies (Lake 1999: 75) and was also directed towards the population growth of white Australia, an issue of major concern to the government of the day. Falling birth rates over the last 20 years have once again focused government attention on women's breeding capacities and it is significant that the introduction of another maternity allowance in 2002 (dubbed the 'Baby Bonus') occurred in the context of Australia's birth rate declining to 1.7, well below replacement rates. The 'Baby Bonus' was widely criticised for also being overly complex and favouring stay-at-home mothers by financially penalising women who returned to work. In mid-2004, it was replaced by yet another maternity allowance that provided mothers with a non-taxable lump sum payment of $3042 (rising to $5000 in 2008), irrespective of income or asset level. Unlike a genuine paid maternity leave scheme, however, this payment does not guarantee a right of return to work, does not equate with income replacement, and does not refer to women's labour market participation.

Paid maternity leave: the bargaining orientation

In contrast to a 'welfare orientation' and a maternity allowance, the 'bargaining orientation' associates paid maternity leave directly with employment in the paid workforce. Considered in this way, paid maternity leave is a potential, though contested, outcome of the industrial relations processes of a particular country and may be gained through bargaining, negotiation, arbitration or other joint regulatory processes between unions and employers. In a bargaining orientation, the proponents for paid maternity leave are generally unions, with the response or reaction emanating from employers. The language of the bargaining orientation is rich in terms of bargaining claims, entitlements, fairness, equity, trade-offs, worker rights, employer obligations and so on, and the outcomes are contingent on factors such as bargaining power, union strength, employer resistance or acquiescence, labour market power and economic conditions. The outcomes are usually codified or enshrined in industrial agreements or contracts, and importantly, any change to these necessitates further bargaining between the parties. By placing the responsibility for paid maternity leave directly with the parties to the industrial relationship, the bargaining orientation allows governments to withdraw. Consequently, a further outcome of a bargaining orientation is that there is no perceived need for a legislative or statutory provision of paid maternity leave.

In Australia, the bargaining orientation to maternity leave has played out in different ways over time, including test case arbitration by federal industrial relations tribunals and industry-level award bargaining. But the favoured means of the current federal government for allocating paid maternity leave is individual or enterprise-based bargaining. Combined with an ongoing welfare orientation to maternity allowances such as was discussed above, this situation has resulted in somewhat episodic and uneven outcomes. For instance, while mothers are entitled to an allowance on the birth of a baby and while Australia has provided *unpaid* parental leave for some time, approximately 40 per cent of women workers in Australia still do not have access to any *paid* maternity leave (Baird & Litwin 2005).

The availability of unpaid maternity leave in Australia dates back to the Maternity Leave test case of 1979 (218 CAR 120). In this case the Australian Council of Trade Unions (ACTU) brought a case before the main industrial relations tribunal, the Australian Industrial Relations Commission (AIRC), for a period of between 12 and 78 weeks' unpaid maternity leave for employees in the private sector. In its decision on the case, the Commission recognised the changing times: 'The claim was advanced principally by reference to the changed social and economic role of women within Australia and to their significant participation in, and contribution to, the Australian workforce' (218 CAR 120 at 121).

The Commission subsequently awarded women working in either full-time or permanent part-time jobs the right to 52 weeks' unpaid maternity leave. In the decision the Full Bench noted, with a sense of surprise, the 'limited extent' to which federal awards at the time dealt with maternity leave. The decision was heralded as a 'breakthrough' by the ACTU's first female advocate, Jan Marsh (Martin 1979). It did award a comparatively long period of leave (by international standards) with the right to job protection, but it still was not paid leave. The

ACTU had not argued for paid maternity leave and the Commission, having arbitral but not statutory authority, therefore could not award it, even if they had a mind to do so. To date, relatively few federal awards make reference to paid maternity leave.

The situation is not very different in the State jurisdictions, For example, as of April 2005 a search of the NSW Industrial Gazettes showed that paid maternity leave appears in just 60 current New South Wales awards. It is most commonly found in the awards for employees of the crown, employees of the Catholic Church (teachers, health), and employees in local government and utilities. Again, like the federal sphere, these are all in the public sector or, one might say, under the influence of the NSW public sector, and replicate State legislation. The most common entitlement in these 60 awards is for nine weeks' paid maternity leave (43 awards offer this amount), reflecting State public service conditions. However, this is expected to change once the 14 weeks' ministerial directive for crown employees of 1 January 2005 flows through to awards.

Perhaps the opportunity to provide paid maternity leave in a widespread fashion through Australia's industrial award system was lost forever in 1979 because, although women continued to enter the workforce in increasing numbers, the economic and business contexts soon changed, as did the philosophies underpinning the industrial parties. In 1969 and 1972 the Commission had made equal pay decisions and after these, and in 1974 the Commission abandoned the concept of the family wage for men. Whitehouse (2005: 409) argues that this latter decision formalised the separation of the wages and welfare systems between the industrial parties and government, respectively. If this is the case, here was another obstacle to paid maternity leave: governments had difficulty separating it from a welfare payment and the Commission required a claim for paid maternity leave to be made. This was not forthcoming from the union movement.

It would seem that when the concept of the 'family wage' was abandoned in the 1970s, the prospects for gaining paid maternity leave were doomed. Although the original maternity leave decision recognised the 'special industrial interests of women', the equal pay decisions, which preceded it by only a few years, meant that women were now to be treated equally – at least in theory. These decisions reflected the Commission's difficulties and quandaries in dealing with women workers and their working lives under a male paradigm. Thus, in terms of wages, women were to be treated equally, that is in the same way as men; but in terms of leave, they were to be treated differently, that is, as mothers and carers, and with the leave granted for bearing children receiving no monetary compensation.

Subsequent test cases altered and extended the unpaid leave provision. In 1985 maternity leave was broadened to include adoption leave (298 CAR 321). However, in its decision and again emphasising its changing role, the Commission stressed that it was not an agent of 'social welfare reform'. The next significant change came in 1990 when, as a result of a claim from the ACTU that the maternity leave provisions were 'outdated' and 'discriminatory', the Commission awarded men the equivalent right to unpaid paternity leave if they were the primary carer. At this time the discourse surrounding the leave became known as parental leave, not maternity leave.

The AIRC's decisions and the ACTU's arguments in these cases reflected the changing times, especially the changes in social attitudes (if not behaviours) regarding parenting, as well as the changes in the business climate. The 1990 decision allowed fathers access to the existing 52 weeks of unpaid leave, but it was not in addition to the mother's right to 52 weeks' leave. Reviewing this decision through a critical gender lens, it might now be argued that by expanding the coverage to include men, women were forced to share their leave and consequently lost their right to the full 52 weeks' leave. This did not necessarily improve the situation for women. Furthermore, the change in terminology to 'parental leave' meant that women no longer received 'special treatment' for their role as mothers as well as workers. The leave had effectively been de-gendered.

The quest for more unpaid parental leave has continued right through to the present day. In the 2005 Family Provisions test case decision, the AIRC awarded employees the right to request an extension of 52 weeks' unpaid parental leave. Again, the union movement had not argued for the introduction of paid leave. While they had their own reasons for this position, it has continued the tribunal's emphasis on unpaid, rather than paid, maternity leave.

In 1993, the parental leave provision was included in the *Industrial Relations Reform Act*, giving all working parents (rather than just award-covered employees) in permanent full-time jobs access to 52 weeks' unpaid parental leave. The same provision was subsequently included in the *Workplace Relations Act 1996*. Women, however, continue to utilise the leave more than men (Baird & Litwin 2005). As MacDermott (1996) argues, while this leave remains unpaid, women not only bear the child but also disproportionately bear the economic cost of children, losing career and income continuity and security, and affecting their long-term incomes, superannuation and promotion prospects.

While the claims over unpaid maternity and parental leave were being pursued by the ACTU at the national scale, the issue of paid maternity leave was, with a few exceptions, largely ignored by the major industrial relations actors at the workplace level.

It was not until 2000 that paid maternity leave firmly made it onto the bargaining agenda of unions. The catalysts for the shift included the publicity surrounding the International Labour Organisation's revised Maternity Convention recommending 14 weeks' paid maternity leave in 2000; the Australian Catholic University's introduction of 12 weeks on full pay and 40 weeks at 60 per cent of pay in 2001, and in 2002, HREOC's inquiry into proposals for a paid maternity leave scheme for Australia. This decision sparked a round of enterprise bargaining claims for large increases in maternity and paternity leave in the tertiary sector and began to set new social standards. We return to these examples below.

The evidence from bargaining

As we have seen, right up to the turn of the 21st century, paid maternity leave improvements were slow in coming (see Baird et al. 2002) and despite increased attention in the past five years, progress remains patchy. For example, in studying the incidence (not the length) of paid maternity leave, we see that just below 8 per cent of enterprise agreements in the federal jurisdiction in 2000 included a clause providing for some paid maternity leave; by 2004, the comparable figure was just 10 per cent. In the State jurisdictions there has been more movement, albeit from a lower base of 3 per cent of agreements with a paid maternity leave clause in 2000 to 9 per cent in 2004 (2002 data: WAD, DEWR and ADAM, ACIRRT Sydney; 2004 data: ADAM, ACIRRT, Sydney).

While improvements in the aggregate have been slow, the distinction between the public, private and not-for-profit sectors shows an even clearer picture of where change in paid maternity leave has, and has not, occurred. While approximately 57 per cent of public sector and government enterprise agreements include paid maternity leave, a little under 7 per cent of current private sector enterprise agreements have paid maternity leave (see Table 3.1).

Table 3.1 *Paid maternity leave in enterprise agreements by sector, May 2004 (%)*

Public enterprise	25.8
Government/business enterprise	31.0
Non-profit enterprises	16.6
Private enterprise	6.8

Source: ADAM, ACIRRT, Sydney

As the data show, access to paid maternity leave through bargaining is still significantly related to public sector employment. More recent research shows that other variables of significance include union membership, income and size of organisation, and that the likelihood of access to paid maternity leave for a female employee in the public sector is more than twice that of an employee in the private sector (Baird & Litwin 2005). In summary, what these figures unfortunately reveal about the incidence of paid maternity leave is that there has been very little change in 30 years, that there has been little cross-fertilisation from the public sector to the private sector, and that there is no widespread evidence of private sector bargaining introducing paid maternity leave.

As important as the frequency of paid maternity leave clauses in enterprise agreements is the period of paid time available for maternity leave. On this issue there has been considerable discussion but marginal change in practice. In 2000 the ILO set a recommended benchmark of 14 weeks, but this is still rarely achieved in Australian enterprise agreements. Six weeks and 12 weeks are now the most common outcomes. The most notable shift between 2000 and 2004 was a decline in the proportion of agreements with a two-week paid maternity leave period and an increase in the proportion of agreements with six weeks' paid maternity leave (DEWR and ADAM data sets, 2000 and 2004), reflecting the introduction of six weeks' leave for Western Australian public servants in 2003 and some increases from two to six weeks in finance sector agreements.

Some of the most recent outcomes in paid maternity leave under enterprise bargaining (which are not yet included in the datasets used above) indicate further improvements in the duration of leave and the return-to-work options, for example in higher education and for New South Wales public servants. The new University of Sydney agreement provides for a total of 36 weeks' paid maternity leave for employees with two continuous years of service. This includes 14 weeks at full pay and the equivalent of another 22 weeks' paid leave, which may be taken as paid leave or as a return-to-work program providing for research funding, access to conference leave or staff development. The NSW Public Service Association also recently achieved an increase from nine to 14 weeks' paid maternity leave for public servants (PSA 2004).

Therefore, it seems that there is some movement to the ILO standard, but it has been a long time coming. It is a long time since the old public sector standard of 12 weeks' paid leave was set in 1973 by the Whitlam federal Labor government, and even that, as we have seen, has remained largely restricted to the public sector. It must be stressed that these improvements, while beneficial, are restricted to certain sectors of the economy where there has typically been more active union involvement.

The outcomes of a bargaining approach to paid maternity leave are contingent on the bargaining agenda and bargaining power of the parties. Consequently, since women's needs have not been given the same priority as men's over time, the reality is that under bargaining there are limited and highly variable provisions. Furthermore, access to the entitlement is restricted to those covered by the enterprise agreement, providing only partial coverage for women at work. For some other women, paid maternity leave is enshrined in neither awards nor agreements, but is provided through managerial discretion, goodwill or company policy. This leads us to consider the third orientation to paid maternity leave.

Paid maternity leave: the business orientation

Within the 'business orientation', women's employment in the paid workforce is recognised and affirmed, so paid maternity leave is connected with employment rather than welfare. This is similar to the 'bargaining orientation', but with the important distinction that in the 'business orientation', provisions such as paid maternity leave are associated with company or business needs rather than with the employee's needs. Therefore, when paid maternity leave is approached from a business orientation, it is not automatically regarded as an industrial right of women and must instead be argued for on other grounds, most typically in terms of business case arguments.

A 'business case' argument is the dominant discourse in this orientation and the rhetoric most commonly includes phrases such as becoming an 'employer of choice', improving the bottom line, investment in human resources or capital, and diversity management. Business case arguments suggest that the benefits to the employer or business of introducing paid maternity leave can be shown to outweigh the costs of paying employees while on leave. These benefits include improved motivation, morale and productivity, reduced recruitment and training costs, increased retention rates and return to work rates of highly skilled employees, reduced sickness and improved organisational efficiency through the benefits of long service, institutional memory, industry knowledge, networks and contacts (EOWA 2003).

However, the business case provides justification for paid maternity leave only for those with high or unique skill levels and qualifications. Although the Equal Opportunity in the Workplace Agency (EOWA) suggests that more employers are now adopting a business case rationale to provide paid maternity leave, the OECD has noted that in the past 'such considerations have not been sufficient to lead to extensive use of maternity pay in Australia' (OECD 2002). As it is regarded as a prerogative and responsibility of the company, it follows that the state should be absent from responsibility for providing paid maternity leave. Accordingly, when the business orientation dominates debate and policy thinking, it is unlikely that national legislation will be enacted to provide for paid maternity leave.

When included in a suite of company policies, paid maternity leave is more often than not associated with diversity management, work and family or work–life policies and practices rather than equal employment opportunity or affirmative action policies, potentially further weakening women's special need for, and claims to, the entitlement. Although women's participation at work is accepted and even sought in a 'business orientation', women's unique combination of roles is not necessarily explicitly recognised and when combined with other diversity or work-family policies, the distinctiveness of women's dual roles is further obscured. As noted above, the special needs of business (rather than of women) are of primary concern in the 'business orientation'.

Dickens (1994, 1995) argues that where there has been an ascendancy of the business case approach in recent decades, such as in the UK and the USA, there has been a general reluctance by the state to act in the promotion of equality issues. This has also been the case in Australia where the government has only reluctantly considered the question of paid maternity leave in the last five years after considerable social and community pressure. Yet, probably partly driven by the wider debate and partly by the tightening of the labour market, there have been some notable examples of paid maternity leave policies unilaterally introduced by employers.

Examples of changes in business case outcomes over time

It might be argued that a clear and discernible shift from the parliament to the bargaining table to the boardroom has occurred in relation to the provision of paid maternity leave in Australia (Baird et al. 2002). Now all three orientations or domains appear to be in use, with different results and quite divergent outcomes. In the private sector, maternity leave policy changes are not necessarily negotiated and may come through as new company policies, introduced as the prerogative of management. In terms of research, it is only in the last one or two years that movement in company policy has become more pronounced, and definitely more noteworthy. A sample of these new policies is presented in Table 3.2 below.

Noting the recency of these changes and the small selection provided, one can only speculate at this stage about the patterns emerging in contemporary company policy, but some tentative comments may be offered. The first is that since the HREOC reports in 2002, there has been some movement in company policy towards women and paid maternity leave. The second is that new policies usually attract a lot of positive media attention, reflecting the still rather novel status of paid maternity (and parental) leave in Australia, most notably in the private sector. The third is that the changes do appear to be related to certain industries, indicating some cascading of policies among employers; for example, many of the recent improvements appear to be emerging in the finance sector. A fourth characteristic of the changes in company policy is that there is more focus on non-gendered entitlements, such as parental leave and carers' leave. Finally, the varied and diverse nature of company policies is becoming more apparent.

CONCLUSION

Like many storylines, the development of women's work and maternity leave in Australia is structured by time: time in a chronological sense, in this case with a linear and gender-specific trajectory; timing in terms of decision-making, with unevenness and delays; time as distribution, as it is defined around changing and balancing work and family duties.

Table 3.2 *Sample of recent changes in company policies (introduced without union bargaining)*

Date	Company	Entitlement	Industry
December 2002	Holden Ltd	14 weeks paid maternity leave for employees with 2 years' service.	Car manufacturing
December 2003	Colonial First State (CBA)	12 weeks paid maternity leave for primary caregiver.	Finance
January 2004	ING Administration	8 weeks paid parental leave for primary caregiver; 1 week for secondary care giver.	Finance
January 2004	GE Capital	1 week paid paternity leave.	Finance
February 2004	Allianz	6 weeks paid parental leave for primary caregiver. 1 week paid leave for secondary care giver – for employees with 12 months' service.	Insurance
March 2004	IBM	12 weeks paid parental leave for primary caregiver.	Information Technology

Source: Compiled from *Workplace Express*, 2002–04.

Over the past century, women's (and especially mothers') participation in paid work has changed so significantly that the normative male-breadwinner model is threatened, yet work entitlements and arrangements have not altered accordingly. The Harvester model is at once out of time and enduringly influential. There is now severe institutional and policy lag, and Australia (with the USA) is far behind other industrialised countries in affirming women's multiple work roles and identities. This is particularly evident in relation to the absence of comprehensive paid maternity leave policies.

In Australia, public policies derived from the paternalistic 'welfare orientation' continue to affirm women's maternal role through various permutations of maternity allowances. As we have seen, such policies continue right through to the present day. These maternity allowances are not equivalent to paid maternity leave as they bear no relation to labour market position; they do not equate to income and they provide no job protection. Women are barely understood as citizens, certainly not as workers.

In addition to maternity allowances, however, there is also scope for the 'bargaining orientation' to operate. In this way women's workforce participation has been episodically recognised, mainly through test case decisions which have followed a linear development of unpaid maternity (and parental) leave. The attention to unpaid maternity leave in Australian industrial relations since the late 1970s arguably marginalised the need for paid maternity leave to be on the agenda of the major industrial parties. So, while the gains in unpaid leave for women were a 'breakthrough' in one respect, recognising women's labour market role and protecting job status, they also compromised arguments for paid leave. Furthermore and somewhat ironically, the effect of the equal pay decisions and abolition of the family wage, both also a product of the 1970s, had the effect of invalidating arguments grounded in the 'special' industrial needs of women. Women were to be treated as equal to men. Hence arguments in favour of extending to men the same unpaid leave as women received held sway and continue to do so in current claims, despite the evidence that men do not contribute to unpaid caring to the same extent as women.

Not until recently has paid maternity leave been seriously considered as integral to the industrial relations agenda. Yet despite the fanfare the HREOC campaign generated, paid maternity leave remains a fairly marginal issue, highly contested and far more firmly embedded in public sector thinking than private sector experience. The business case, which is dominant in the private sector, provides for only limited and contingent paid maternity leave outcomes.

The uncertain and difficult path to paid maternity leave in Australia outlined in this chapter tells us that it is now time to address seriously the gender agenda in industrial relations and public policy. None of the existing orientations referred to, that is, neither the 'welfare', 'bargaining' nor 'business' orientations, has delivered universal access to paid maternity leave for working women in Australia. It seems all too obvious that a new approach, an orientation based on 'social equity' (Baird 2004), is required. Such an orientation would allow women's difference from men (in terms of child-bearing and child-raising), as well as their need for equality with men (in terms of their personal work and economic interests), to be affirmed and legitimated. It would also acknowledge that time is itself a gendered idea, with women's and men's understanding of time arguably also quite different. In moving to a social equity orientation, agenda-setters in industrial relations and public policy would then logically include gender concerns, such as the need for paid maternity leave, in their claims. By so doing, the tensions in policy-making about gender, work and family that now exist might begin to be addressed.

References

ABS 2003, *Australian Social Trends, Family and Community – Family Functioning: Balancing Family and Work*, Canberra: ABS.

ABS 2004, Labour Force Survey, Australia, Detailed-Electronic Delivery, Cat. No. 6291.0.55.001, accessed 17 January 2005.

ABS 2005, Year Book Australia, No. 87, Canberra, Cat. No., 1301.0.

ACTU 2004, Work and Family Test Case Information Material, http://www.actu.asn.au/public/papers/famikit.html, accessed 5 February 2005.

Baird, M. 2003, 'Paid maternity leave: the good, the bad, the ugly', *Australian Bulletin of Labour* 29(1): 97–109.

Baird, M. 2003, 'Re-conceiving industrial relations: 2003 AIRAANZ presidential address', *Labour and Industry* 14(1): 107–15.

Baird, M. 2004, 'Orientations to paid maternity leave: understanding the Australian debate', *Journal of Industrial Relations* 46(3): 259–74.

Baird, M., Brennan, D. & Cutcher, L. 2002, 'A pregnant pause: paid maternity leave in Australia', *Labour and Industry* 13(1): 1–19.

Baird, M. & Litwin, A.S. 2005, 'Rethinking work and family policy: the making and taking of parental leave in Australia', *International Review of Psychiatry*, 17(5): 385–400.

Bittman, M. & Rice, J. 2002, 'The spectre of overwork: an analysis of trends between 1974 and 1997 using Australian time-use diaries', *Labour and Industry* 13(1): 91–110.

Burgess, J. & Baird, M. 2003, 'Employment entitlements: development, access, flexibility and protection', *Australian Bulletin of Labour* 29(1): 1–13.

Commonwealth of Australia 2004, *Australia's Demographic Challenges*. Discussion paper.

Dickens, L. 1994, 'The business case for women's equality: is the carrot better than the stick?', *Employee Relations* 16(8): 5–18.

Dickens, L. 1999, 'Beyond the business case: a three pronged approach to equality action', *Human Resource Management Journal* 9(1): 9–19.

Earle, J. 1999, 'The International Labour Organisation and maternity rights: evaluating the potential for progress', *Economic and Labour Relations Review* 10(2): 203–20.

EOWA (Equal Opportunities in the Workplace Agency) 2003, Benefits of providing paid maternity leave. Available at http://www.eowa.gov. au/About_Equal_Opportunity/Key_Agenda_Items/Work_Life_Balance/ Paid_Maternity_Leave.asp

Eveline, J. 2001, 'Feminism, racism and citizenship in twentieth-century Australia', in P. Crawford & P. Maddern (eds) Women as Australian Citizens, Melbourne University Press, pp. 141–252.

Forrest, A. 1993, 'Women and industrial relations theory', Relations Industrielles, 48(3): 409–38.

Hochschild, A.R. 1997, The Time Bind, New York: Henry Holt & Co.

HREOC (Human Rights and Equal Opportunity Commission) 2002a, 'Valuing parenthood: options for paid maternity leave: interim paper', Sydney: HREOC.

HREOC 2002b, 'A time to value a proposal for a national paid maternity leave scheme', Sydney: HREOC.

HREOC 2005, 'Striking the balance: women, men, work and family', Sydney: HREOC.

Lake, M. 1999, Getting Equal: The History of Australian Feminism, Sydney: Allen & Unwin.

MacDermott, T. 1996, 'Who's rocking the cradle? Maternity rights in Australia', Alternative Law Journal 21(5): 207–12.

Martin, K. 1979, 'Win for working mothers', Sydney Morning Herald, 10 March, p. 1.

OECD (Organisation for Economic Cooperation and Development) 2002, Bosses and Babies: Reconciling Work and Family Life, vol. 1, Australia, Denmark, Netherlands.

Patmore, G. 2003, 'Legislating for benefits: NSW 1941–1958', Australian Bulletin of Labour 29(1): 1–13.

Pocock, B. 1997, 'Gender and Australian industrial relations theory and research practice', Labour and Industry 8(1): 1–19.

Pocock, B. 2003, The Work/Life Collision: What Work is Doing to Australians and What to Do About it, Sydney: Federation Press.

Rapoport, R., Bailyn, L., Fletcher, J. & Pruitt, B. 2002, Beyond Work-Life Balance: Advancing Gender Equity and Work Performance, San Francisco: Jossey-Bass.

PSA 2004, Women@Work, Women's unit, Public Service Association of NSW, September–December.

Todd, P. & Eveline J. 2005, 'The gender pay gap: reviewed, researched, will it be resolved?' in M. Baird, R. Cooper & M. Westcott (eds) Reworking Work, Proceedings of the 19th AIRAANZ Conference, Sydney, pp. 235–43.

Whitehouse, G. 2005, 'From family wage to parental leave: the changing relationship between arbitration and the family', Journal of Industrial Relations 46(4): 400–12.

CHAPTER FOUR

REGULATION AND DEREGULATION IN AUSTRALIAN LABOUR LAW

Through a Reflexive Lens

Suzanne Jamieson

Theory is about explaining the present and predicting the future. In a period of what may prove to be epochal change in Australian labour law, I shall argue in this chapter that students of labour law need some extra tools to enable them to make sense of what is happening and to analyse these changes in some kind of coherent historical continuum. This might prove to be problematical as Australian legal writers have never shown a great deal of interest in theory, although as will be shown below, some labour law writers are beginning to use overtly theoretical frameworks to explain and to influence political opinion, and other writers are using regulation theory to analyse events. In an era when regulation and deregulation are contentious topics for academics, policy-makers and practitioners, however, a lack of interest in theory continues to dominate. But this is not to suggest that most labour law writers are what the undergraduate jurisprudence textbook writers would describe as 'black letter enthusiasts' or even that their writing is without a frame of reference. Interestingly, significant writing exists in the area of feminist and feminist-inspired Australasian labour law writing (for example Bennett 1988; Hunter 1992; Owens 1993; Wilson 1994; MacDermott 1996). Just why Australian (and New Zealand) writers have taken up feminist theory with such apparent gusto but not other kinds of theory is beyond the scope of this chapter.

Here it is argued that most academic labour law writing is written in the context of a liberal view of the world where the state largely operates through the remnants of the arbitration arrangements to provide

protection for workers and their interests. Until fairly recently, industrial relations scholars have been more or less obsessed by arbitration, as
have academic labour lawyers. Both groups of writers have shown limited interest in the wider issues of the nature of regulation and deregulation. The current way in which academic productivity is rewarded by
privileging the production of refereed journal articles over books does
not encourage 'big picture' thinking or writing where theory might con-
veniently be discussed or developed. What is sketched below looks at
overseas theory on deregulation and self-regulation which, it is argued,
has something to add to our understanding of what has happened in
the past and what we might expect in the future. Most importantly, it
attempts to explain the development of law in terms of a rational series
of identifiable historical periods and is concerned with the question of
why things (here read change in labour law) happen when they do. This
is about time in its historical sense and an attempt to understand legal
change within the broad sweep of history.

This chapter is part of a wider project which is attempting to test
theory developed overseas against the Australian reality. Testing overseas theories in the cognate industrial relations area has not often met
with success (see Dunlop's work in the 1950s and its more recent iter-
ation by Dabscheck [1995] and the pungent critique of that work by
Michelson & Westcott [2001]). The most recent major attempt followed this pattern (Kitay & Lansbury 1997). This chapter is not built
on the premise that the 'local is bad' and 'overseas is good' or better. It
is an attempt to explore whether frameworks developed overseas have
any relevant explanatory power in Australia. Care is taken to avoid
what the late Professor Kahn-Freund (1974) would have criticised as
being work that attempted to use comparative method for local ideological purposes. It is useful to remember that Teubner, whose work is
used extensively below, comes out of the European (continental) civil
law tradition based on the Roman and Napoleonic approaches. That
legal tradition bears no close relationship at all to the British (or rather
English) common law tradition which, like the British Empire, has left
its mark in all of the cricket-playing nations and in most of Canada and
all of the USA. And while Australia is joined umbilically to the other
common law nations, it has shared its peculiar conciliation and arbitration system governing the regulation of labour with no other country
except New Zealand (Barry & Wailes 2004; Isaac & Macintyre 2004).
What follows is an examination of a few ideas about some overseas

theory with an emphasis on the work of Teubner but with asides to some British and North American writers. This discussion will be followed by matching overseas theory to the case of Australia and some conclusions will be offered as to why this has occurred.

REFLEXIVE LABOUR LAW THEORY

Reflexive labour law and the other positions put forward by Teubner below provide a lens through which the social experience of labour regulation may be viewed. The reflexive approach attempts to enhance explanations of the way in which labour law in all advanced economies is changing and the way in which it is finding increasing difficulty in dealing with atypical employment and the development of flexible work patterns. The reflexive approach attempts to deal with increasing calls for less intervention by a protective state just at a time when trade unions in Australia and in the other developed nations are finding it increasingly difficult to protect their members. There are ongoing debates between those who want increased regulation and those who insist this constitutes a burden on business (Rogowski & Wilthagen 1994: 3). Globalisation itself will eventually pose additional questions for national systems of labour law (Twining 2000; Conaghan et al. 2002). Labour law itself is said to be under threat as a field of study (Collins 1989; Rogowski & Wilthagen 1994). The latter two writers assert that reflexive labour law

> assesses the role of labour within society in a fundamentally new way which is in line with the recent paradigm shift in the theory of social systems. Labour law, like any other social system, is conceived as a communication system whose main elements are not actors or social actions, not even interactions, but communications. Self-reference of communications constitutes the autopoietic basis of reflexive labour law, on which it then relates to the wider legal system, the industrial relations system, and the economic system. (Rogowski & Wilthagen 1994: 8)

Building on this essentially post-structuralist and postmodern view of labour law in which 'labour law systems or discourses are characterised by self-reference of labour law communications which generate new labour law communications' (Rogowski & Wilthagen 1994: 8), regulation occurs through the self-regulation of the labour law system by itself. This evolutionary approach owes much to the work of Habermas and also of Selznick (see Teubner's extensive bibliography [1983]) and is overtly sociological in nature.

Building on this approach, Teubner presents a three-stage historical development of law which begins with the appearance of modern capital: from an initial period of rule-oriented resolution of individual disputes, through a period identified with the welfare state and the heavy intervention by the state in market relations, to a final period of reflexive rationality which idealises self-regulation. Teubner's separate stages of development are triggered generally by crisis (Hyde 1994: 179), although Hyde points out that the major changes instigated in Thatcher's Britain did not follow this pattern, and a similar point is made below in relation to Australian labour law. Hyde further points out that in the USA labour law is well overdue for reform and that rewriting with no apparent crisis on the horizon is likely to trigger the change that would mark it as a mature labour law system.

Teubner's first stage of legal development is characterised by its reference to the values of individualism attendant on the appearance of the capitalist state, and it is very concerned with the resource issues associated with a developing market society. The second stage of legal development is associated with the emergence of the welfare state and its attempts to moderate some of the inequities that arose from the untrammelled operation of the market. In this stage there is a heavy emphasis on regulation, with government agencies devoted to compliance matters. The third stage of legal development is concerned with setting up a superstructure that will support self-regulatory processes. In effect, law begins to set up the procedures under which this self-regulation will take place, rather than engaging itself in directing particular outcomes (Teubner 1983: 275). While it is interested in procedural matters, it is not by definition a law without content. Hyde (1994: 178–80) notes that labour legislation can also have a symbolic effect and can be passed with a number of outcomes in mind that may include the political elites in making political points of their own or creating legislation in response to symbolic conflict. Perhaps for the student of law, the most important point Teubner makes is that the legal system as a whole should be seen as a 'system-in-an-environment' and not separate from that environment (Teubner 1983: 280). We now turn to an examination of how Teubner's three-stage development theory may help to explain what has happened in the history of the development of Australian labour law and how to account for what is happening now and what might happen in the very near future.

AUSTRALIAN LABOUR LAW AND THEORY

Among other things, this chapter is interested in why labour law in Australia has, over time, largely followed a non-theoretical approach to writing when its very close social science cousin, industrial relations (or employment relations as it is often called, or even human resource management), has always attempted to engage with theory (although not always well or comprehensively) in the same way that all the other social sciences do. Part of this can be explained by the fact that law has never seen itself as mainstream social science. Moreover, the argument that labour law has been largely written without an obvious attachment to theory probably also applies to British (in its widest possible meaning) labour law writing as well.

Law defines itself as separate and special. And obviously law is only part of the social sciences for the purposes of organising university libraries, university administrative structures and bureaucratic arrangements for the dispersal of government research funding. Certainly the research methods employed by most academic legal writers do not have much relationship to those followed by their colleagues in the other social sciences. Close reading of judicial decisions is the essential method employed by lawyers of all persuasions. Mass surveys, open-ended or highly structured interviewing, regression analysis or other quantitative methods used in the other social sciences are typically eschewed by most lawyers. Law is about authority and it is the job of the judges to declare what the law is (as far as they can based on precedent and whatever it was that the parliament thought it was doing) and for the academic lawyers to argue over just what it is that the judges meant.

The authority of the courts emphasises the view of the law as special. And it is also apparent that the way in which judicial decisions are made has had a significant effect on the way in which labour law writing has evolved. Legal writing, if it is to have authority, so goes the theory, whether by academics or judges, is about the law, not about politics. It is probably also true to suggest that this apparent writing without a theoretical framework clearly articulated at the outset is common across most legal writing. That characterisation excludes the broad area of socio-legal scholarship, which in my mind also includes the critical legal writers and their supporters (Kelman 1987). Could it be that most labour law writers are caught in the no-man's-land between the ugly Scylla of the 'black letter' descriptive accounts and the equally unappealing (for many at least) Charybdis of the critical legal scholars?

Before moving on to sketch the main themes in the writing of labour law in Australia over the last 100 years or so, it needs to be made clear that in talking about the overt lack of discussion of theory in labour law writing I am not talking about the so-called point-of-viewlessness that is often the hallmark of the 'black letter' or positivist approach. This approach appears to be without any theory at all but is in fact intensely conservative in making law appear as if it has been handed down from God (or a similarly unassailable source) ready-made for use by humankind. It essentially says that the law is what it says it is, without reference to economics, politics or society. Most Australian labour law writing is not like this at all. I argue that most academic labour law writing in Australia in the 20th century (or more particularly the last 30 years in which I have been reading this work) is written in a broadly pro-worker, pro-union framework. It is almost universally written in an unacknowledged institutionalist or liberal framework. Kennedy (1997) would call this 'writing with ideology' or with a political underpinning because that is what law is about. To imagine labour law writing in a 'black letter' mode where, for example, the great power imbalance between workers and employers is not acknowledged in some way would be nonsense. In the arena of labour law in particular, law is very much about politics.

Perhaps some of the writers who are mentioned below would not be happy to be categorised like this by Kennedy of all people. But when McCallum (1998, 2005) writes about industrial citizenship he is using mainstream 18th-century liberal calls to revolution which in the context of the early 21st century should not frighten the horses! In using this kind of language McCallum is attempting to make an argument of wide appeal, as some British labour lawyers have done (cf. the rather longer journey undertaken by Collins [1982, 2002]). He is using classical mainstream liberal theory to give authority to his call for the protection of workers' rights. He does this because he (correctly) thinks workers' rights are under or about to be under attack and he wants to alert us to action. He is using the well-accepted rhetoric that most people in Australia can share, irrespective of their particular party politics. Here it is argued that this analysis applies equally well to most of the other writers whom I consider to be the major contributors in this tradition over the past 30 years in particular (for example Adrian Brooks, Brian Brooks, Breen Creighton, William Ford, Harry Glasbeek, Richard Johnstone, Richard Mitchell, Richard Naughton, Andrew Stewart and Philippa Weeks). Some of these writers have allowed themselves to write in a more obviously political way towards the end of their careers and I believe Glasbeek (2002) is perhaps the best example of this. Older age confers a certain freedom, not least of which is freedom from promotion scrutiny inside the academy.

On occasion, major writers have referred to non-mainstream theory, such as Cooney & Mitchell (2002) on reflexive labour law, in the East Asian context. A small number of other writers (see the comprehensive literature survey by Howe 2005) have taken up the application of regulatory theory (see below) led by Gunningham & Johnstone (1999) in the arena of occupational health and safety law. To generalise, most of the remainder of the writing is about a legal response or explication of public policy developments, and of course there has been no lack of these since 1983; no doubt we are in for some more in the very near future. In the earlier period we saw a concentration on the shape of the system so-called, with this tradition going back to some of the earlier overseas commentators such as Foenander and Perlman (see Dabscheck 1998). In the context of an intellectual obsession with intervention by the state, it is perhaps odd that there has been almost no attempt to look at theories of the state or to develop any new ones based on the arbitration experience. Is theorising something only foreigners and women do?

SOME CAUTIONARY WORDS ABOUT DEFINITIONS

It is very easy to use words that seem fashionable without looking closely at what they actually mean. It is, for example, common to read about the increasing decentralisation and increased deregulation of Australian labour law that has occurred over the past 15 years. It is certainly true that there has been increased decentralisation occurring in the system: we have seen the decreased ability of the Australian Industrial Relations Commission after 1996 to intervene in disputes to the extent it once did (Creighton & Stewart 2005), and we note the significant capacity for decentralised enterprise bargaining available to the parties since the passage of the *Industrial Relations Reform Act 1993*, which wrought so many changes to the *Industrial Relations Act 1988* and its successor *Workplace Relations Act 1996*. But it is useful to remember that the terms 'decentralisation' and 'deregulation' are not the same.

There has been much rhetoric about deregulation, in particular by the current conservative government under the prime ministership of John Howard, although the previous Labor government was also very keen to link deregulation with international competitiveness. Closer inspection, however, probably reveals not a removal of regulation in total but a shift in that regulation towards the workplace and by definition towards greater regulation and control by employers (Buchanan & Callus 1993). This approach has been recently taken up by Howe in scrutinising the so-called deregulation of the building industry, which is clearly about adding to regulation or, in Buchanan & Callus' terms, re-regulating the system. All of these deregulatory legislative changes must of course also be seen in the light of the dramatically falling union membership that characterised the 1990s. A better term to describe the shift from external regulation by the state through the machinery of conciliation and arbitration towards greater internal regulation of workplace relationships is 're-regulation'. Ayres & Braithwaite (1992: 7) call this a period of 'regulatory flux'. Some other writers call this a re-regulation of the markets in favour of capital and a re-regulation of social life that sees citizenship subordinated to the needs of big corporations (Anderson 1999).

Deregulation, like talk of lower levels of taxation, is a term that has a positive aura in the public mind, but it is always instructive to look closely at the degree of rhetoric or 'spin' that might be associated with the use of the words. Certainly a cursory look at the way in which the sheer size of the federal industrial relations legislation has physically ballooned over the past 15 years would not suggest a diminution in regulation but a shift in the focus of that regulation. Complexity in the nature of that regulation is something that has only recently gained any attention at all from legal academics. Fetter & Mitchell (2004) point out that the imposition of Australian Workplace Agreements (AWAs) on an already crowded terrain of awards, company HRM policies and the older concept of a contract of employment adds unnecessary complexity to the understanding of employment regulation. That increased complexity for the layperson may also have contributed to the relatively slow rate at which the AWAs have been taken up by private enterprise. Another example of obvious complexity is to be found in the procedures surrounding the making of an award (ss.143–155) and the certification procedures involving the Commission, the relevant trade unions and the employers in the establishment of a certified agreement (also often called an enterprise agreement or an enterprise bargaining agreement) outlined in ss.170L–170NH of the *Workplace Relations Act 1996*.

The AWAs constitute an obvious way in which Australian labour law might be said to be increasingly individualised, and more particularly how the regulation of the work of non-executive employees has been individualised. Senior management have always had their terms and conditions of employment determined in an individualised way and expressed in an individual contract of employment. Some States have even developed a jurisdiction to deal with these matters, such as the NSW Unfair Contracts provisions in the *Industrial Relations Act 1996* (see Part 9, ss.105–116). While these provisions had their origins in a political desire to protect the working conditions of truck owner-drivers and other 'non-employees' rather than the high-flying television stars who now appear in these cases, this provides interesting evidence of the fact that the collectivist tribunals based on conciliation and arbitration (Kirby & Creighton 2004) always had an eye on individual expressions of work contracts that were not necessarily about the paradigm case of the ordinary employee engaged on a 'contract of service'. The allegedly inflexible structure of conciliation and arbitration has always had some flexibility within it (Jamieson 1990; Howe 2005). The regulation of labour in Australia has for a long time also had another very important area of individualised operation in the equal opportunity laws which – except for the so-called federal affirmative action laws which only ever applied to women (see *Affirmative Action (Equal Opportunity for Women) Act 1986* and its successor *Equal Opportunity for Women in the Workplace Act 1999*) – operate on the basis of individual complaints. The complicated matrix of State and federal legislation in this area adds another dimension to the regulation of Australian labour.

All of this, of course, is to put the cart before the horse as the whole issue of regulation is very rarely looked at carefully in either the industrial relations or labour law literatures. Regulation itself is now the subject of a huge body of work (note, for example, the bibliographies in Ayres & Braithwaite 1992 and in Gunningham & Johnstone 1999) and in an era of so-called retreat by the state and galloping technological development, how regulation of important resources may be maintained (the natural environment is an obvious example here) is an important ongoing political debate. Ayres & Braithwaite (1992) sought to avoid the intellectual stalemate created between the proponents of state regulation and the band of deregulators by looking towards a symbiosis between state regulation and self-regulation. An obvious example of this in Australian labour law is in the regulation of occupational health and safety which, since the adoption of the British Robens-style reforms (*Occupational Health and Safety Act 1983* and its successor *Occupational Health and Safety Act 2000* from New South Wales), operate on a largely self-regulatory model at the workplace, supported by a system of inspection and compliance enforcement by means of state-initiated criminal prosecutions.

Kahn-Freund (1972: 5) famously defined labour law as having as a principal purpose 'to regulate, to support, and to restrain the power of management and the power of organized labour'. If labour law is still about the regulation of the relative power of the workplace parties, it is presumably about balancing the powers of the parties, vis-à-vis each other and the public good. So regulation is about intervention by the state with the purpose of maintaining a particular balance. And of course the accepted history of these matters in Australia is that the state has intervened to give some weight to the side of the workers and their trade unions in order to counterbalance the power of capital and the markets. That balance, however, is not immutable and the proposed changes, which are likely to go ahead after July 2005 when the incumbent conservative government assumes control of both houses of parliament, reflect a further retreat by the state and a further shifting of power towards employers. While some element of deregulation is contained within these changes, it is more accurate to speak of them in terms of re-regulation.

TIME, HISTORY AND THEORY IN LABOUR LAW

Periodisation of history itself poses problems (Haydu 1998: 340). As Katherine Stone (2004: x) points out, reality is ambiguous and our attempts to categorise periods of time, especially during times of great change, can be skewed by the influence of small detail. To engage for the purposes of this chapter in gross applications of theory to reality, there may be some agreement that Teubner's three-stage historical explanation could have some resonance in Australian industrial history if we see the pre-arbitral period as roughly constituting Teubner's first period. This period saw the supremacy of the *Master and Servant Acts*, which were very much based on the rule-oriented resolution of individual disputes, where the master literally held the whip-hand and trade unions had either no role at all or did not yet exist. The second period might be constituted by the period of arbitration and dates from 1904, or from 1901 if you come from New South Wales.

The problem in applying Teubner's approach is to decide if the third period he defined has actually begun, or to put it the other way, if the second period has actually ended. Might it be that one period segues into another rather than simply beginning on an identifiable day? This reveals one problem in attempting to sequence time into discrete phases. A good example of this might be the date of commencement of a new piece of legislation, or, more dramatically, the arrival of a whole new legal order such as that experienced by the English in 1066 on the day after the Battle of Hastings. We might be less certain in assigning a particular date for the beginning of a much broader historical period such as the Italian Renaissance. Characterising events can be difficult. Single events, like broader history, are always capable of more than one interpretation. If we look at the very recent *Electrolux* decision in the High Court (*Electrolux Home Products P/L v. Australian Workers Union* [2004] High Court of Australia 40) we might say that it looks on the surface like added regulation from a trade union point of view in that it seems seriously to limit the kind of industrial action that can be engaged in at a certain time in the negotiation cycle. On the other hand it could be viewed as a freeing up of business from possible trade union interference. Is it about Teubner's self-regulation? What kind of internal (that is, internal to labour law) communication is the High Court's decision in *Electrolux*? Is it about regulation by means of self-regulation? One thing is certain: in spite of the rhetorical debate of the past 20 years it is not a communication about deregulation even if the rhetoric around it says so. Perhaps other debates (such as those revolving around occupational health and safety) could be characterised more easily in terms of self-regulation, but might the communication of this approach be about deregulation when we think in terms of Teubner's so-called trilemma? This trilemma is said to arise from the lack of response by the regulated field, the legalisation of the regulated field and the politicisation of law in that arena.

REFLEXIVE APPROACHES AND AUSTRALIAN LABOUR LAW

We now move to an application of Teubner's bold attempt to divide the history of labour law into three periods to the nature of state regulation in Australian history since the coming of the Europeans in 1788. As will be demonstrated, the first two periods seem to fit well, but the application of the third seems to call for more time to evaluate its relevance.

Teubner's first period of legal development in Australian labour law

The records of labour law left to us by writers in the 19th century reveal a law based very much on the individual operating as a commercial entity. The other characteristic that would most surprise modern students of Australian labour law is the extent to which the general law was relied on. By this we mean in particular the law of contract, the criminal law and the law of admiralty (that is, the sea). This is not because there was no specific labour law (see *Masters and Servants Act 1828* [NSW] and its successors) but because the statutes were simply not very comprehensive and merely sought to exert certain kinds of controls on workers by their employers. Industrial action such as strikes was not regarded in a very positive light and, in the case of ships' crews, could be regarded as mutiny, for which the death penalty could ensue (see *R. v. Anderson, Davis and ors* 1832 in the Macquarie Law School website given after the reference list). In the *Anderson* case, in finding the men guilty and sentencing them to death, Justice Dowling in the NSW Supreme Court made it quite clear that he thought the punishment would be a salutary lesson for the accused (with which the present writer must humbly agree) and, no doubt, for any others who thought they might engage in the same behaviour. Similar situations are to be found in the cases *R. v. Fox and ors* 1825 and *R. v. Firth and ors* 1832, although in *Fox* the defendants were found guilty only of conspiracy, which did not attract the death penalty (see Macquarie website). The cases gathered in the Macquarie Law School collection would suggest that significant industrial unrest occurred in the maritime industry in the first part of the 19th century. The gravity of the seafarers' situation is underscored by the possible penalties their industrial action could attract at sea.

Many of the cases involving the law of master and servant on land are concerned with servants absconding before their terms expired (see *Australian Agricultural Company v. Adams* 1827) or with attempts by the servant to recover wages (see *Cullen v. Crawford* 1829; *Lee v. Macqueen* 1832; *Patterson v. Hughes* 1833; *Johnstone v. Wright* 1833). The wage recovery cases in particular are conducted like ordinary contract/debt cases and suggest that the master-and-servant legislation provided protection in only one direction.

Access to justice is something that should exercise a labour lawyer's mind and it is not clear from these cases how ordinary workers secured legal representation in an era where legal aid and representation by one's union did not exist. In this context it is useful to remember that trade union membership was still illegal in the UK (and in New South Wales by extension) until the passage of the *Combination Laws Repeal Act* in 1825, and that as late as 1834 the 'Tolpuddle Martyrs' were sentenced to seven years' transportation to Australia for swearing an oath in support of their trade union in rural Dorset. In short, the cases as a whole suggest a close compliance with Teubner's first period of legal development, depending as they do on the rule-oriented resolution of individual disputes, and wherever the individual law of contract does not provide appropriate avenues of resolution, the criminal law is available. The collective regulation of labour is completely absent and the individual disputes between master and servant underscore the dramatic power imbalances between the two industrial parties. The rise of Australian trade unions in the period immediately after the conduct of the cases outlined above does not, therefore, seem so surprising.

Teubner's second period of legal development in Australian labour law

Teubner's second period of legal development might be said to have begun with the adoption by the new Commonwealth Parliament of a scheme of conciliation and arbitration in 1904. New Zealand had already adopted such a scheme in 1894 in its *Industrial Conciliation and Arbitration Act*, as had New South Wales in its *Industrial Arbitration Act* in 1901. While it is usually argued that the UK did not really enter the world of the welfare state until the implementation of the Beveridge Report after the Second World War, it is useful to think of state welfarism beginning in Australia at the outset of Federation because of the establishment of the conciliation and arbitration system and because significant steps were taken towards the institution of social welfare schemes that were in advance of the rest of the world, if not New Zealand. The atmosphere of social and political progress was strengthened by the very early adoption of universal adult suffrage in both countries – universal, that is, if we don't count the Australian Aborigines.

The emphasis in the Australian conciliation and arbitration system on the quick resolution of industrial disputes no doubt owed something to the enormous disruption that had occurred in Australia in the first half of the 1890s (see Macintyre & Mitchell 1989) when substantial industrial action successively engulfed the maritime, shearing and mining industries. The interstate nature of these disputes, that is, the fact that they did not respect the existing colonial borders, led to the adoption of a curiously limited federal industrial relations power in the Constitution. That power recognised the existing industrial jurisdictions of the colonial governments (which became States on the commencement of Federation) while keeping for itself the regulation of certain industries that appeared to have some national character. The so-called Federation settlement was a three-pronged affair with the adoption of conciliation and arbitration (which went on to be central to the establishment of enforceable national industry minima in wages and conditions for union members and non-members alike) in tandem with adherence to protectionism for the nascent Australian manufacturing industries and an overtly racist White Australia policy which not only protected the 'purity' of the White race, but also ensured that the arbitrated industrial wins by the trade unions would not be undercut by unscrupulous employers bringing in demonstrably cheaper coloured labour.

As early as 1907, the new Commonwealth Court of Conciliation and Arbitration heard what was in effect a national wage case in the Harvester case (*Re H.V. McKay* [1907] 2 CAR 1). This not only set the level of a living wage that was to support an unskilled labourer and his wife and three children, but also set the tone for what was essentially a 'breadwinner' approach to national wage-setting that did not admit to women being primary breadwinners (Bennett 1988). For the next 80 years many Australian workers had their minimum working conditions established by means of industrial awards to which registered trade unions were primary parties, along with single employers or employers grouped together in employer associations. As mentioned above, these industrial awards could legally cover non-union members in the establishments and industries covered by the particular industrial award. This system has subsequently been criticised as giving rise to inflexibility (see Howe 2005), but no doubt it also gave employers some certainty in competitive markets that they could not be undercut by other employers paying cheaper wages. Trade unions were central to the system and did not have to engage in the ugly recognition battles so familiar to unions in the USA (Creighton & Stewart 2005: 483–532). Similar schemes of conciliation and arbitration operated in most Australian States (Creighton & Stewart 2005: 468–73), providing industrial coverage for other workers outside the strictly defined boundaries of the federal system. Those strict boundaries of jurisdiction were established and monitored by the High Court of Australia acting as a constitutional court, aided and abetted until 1986 by the Privy

Council in London, which acted as a court of final appeal. Throughout most of the 20th century the conciliation and arbitration tribunals
presided over not just the function of preventing and settling industrial
disputes but of being central to the Australian state's intervention in,
and mediation of, the operation of the market. McCallum (1998) has
fretted that the tribunals have never had the recognition in public life
that they deserve (cf. Howe 2005), and while that may be true, they
have been enormously influential and central to the collective regulation of labour in Australia throughout the 20th century.

As was noted above, even during the period of close collective regulation of labour by the Australian state throughout the 20th century,
using the institutions of conciliation and arbitration, individual regulation through the equal opportunity laws began to emerge in the 1970s
with the appearance of anti-discrimination statutes at both State and
federal levels. All of these laws were based on an individual complaint
model with the exception of the affirmative action laws, which were
program-based. This is just one form of individualisation of labour regulation. These laws are not closely enforced by the state for various reasons and nor are they enforced through the existing industrial tribunals.
In retrospect, in many ways they look very much like the individual
cases in labour law from the 19th century that we examined above,
and therefore closely fitting Teubner's definition of his first period of
legal development; they might also be characterised as belonging to
Teubner's third period of reflexive law because they are about self-
regulation with very little intervention by the state. This non-
intervention by the state is underscored by the apparent loss of interest
in both State and federal governments of all political persuasions in
human rights matters in the later 1990s and beyond. This loss of interest has been expressed in the conscious de-funding of the agencies at
a State and federal level (for example the Human Rights and Equal
Opportunity Commission in 1996 and the NSW Anti-Discrimination
Board in 2003). These individual complaint-based laws were clearly not
intended by their framers to have any large effect on the operation of
the wider market but were meant to provide some redress for individuals
whose workplace human rights had been abrogated.

Further individualisation of the once entirely collective labour laws
occurred in 1996, with the passage of the *Workplace Relations Act*. A
partial retreat from the strictly union-based industrial award system had
occurred federally in 1993 under the Keating Labor government with
the amendments to the *Industrial Relations Act 1988*, which formally

made enterprise bargaining possible. Further non-union bargaining appeared in the 1996 legislation, which was also described as deregulationist. Earlier we saw that this is itself open to some doubt, although it could clearly be described as re-regulation. Under the 1996 statute, annual living wage cases are still conducted to provide updated wage minima for the lowest paid, and must be seen in the light of the welfare state tradition established back in 1907 in the Harvester decision. It is not clear, however, that this will continue from 2006.

Teubner's third period of legal development in Australian labour law

Has this period even begun? I have already outlined significant evidence that the balance of regulation in Australian labour law has been shifting since the amendments to the federal statute in 1993 under the last Labor government. Re-regulation (see Buchanan & Callus 1993; Howe 2005) has certainly occurred and is probably about to occur again. However, it is not clear that the system established in 1904 and mirrored in most of the States has morphed into the self-reflexive and self-regulated legal order described by Teubner. It is also not clear that this is about to happen under the proposed pro-employer changes that the federal government is planning to bring about after July 2005. As we saw above, there is some evidence that occupational health and safety matters might well fall into Teubner's third period of self-reflexive law and may have done so since the inception of the Robens-style legislation going back to the early 1980s. Added to our conclusion that the operation of the equal opportunity laws seems to owe more than a little to Teubner's characterisation of the first period of legal development, are we faced merely with a period of transition or regulatory flux (to adopt Ayres & Braithwaite's term, 1992: 7) or does more than one temporal period operate at once? Might it be that this is always going to be the case because very rarely does a whole new legal regime replace another and remnants of the earlier arrangements will always survive in some form?

CONCLUSION

Teubner's three-stage theory of the historical development of law seems to fit more or less comfortably with the first two periods in Australian labour law history as I have chosen to characterise them here for the sake of argument. The application of the third stage of reflexive rationality as idealising self-regulation is not entirely convincing. Re-regulation is simply not the same thing as self-regulation. There are, however, some small hints that it might be in an inchoate stage and that the proposed changes to be debated in the federal parliament from July 2005 may eventually be characterised as self-regulatory. As the system stands, however, it looks very much like regulation morphing into other forms of regulation, and in the case of the building industry changes described and analysed by Howe (2005), it looks very much like considerably more regulation of the old kind. Alone, only occupational health and safety law seems to be clearly entering the third period (Ayres & Braithwaite 1992; Gunningham & Johnstone 1999) of reflexive or responsive self-regulation.

Perhaps this pattern can be explained away. On the other hand, as Hyde (1994: 174) argues, perhaps it is simply not helpful to think like this because of the inability of theorists and theories to cross international boundaries. But I stand by my view that Australian labour law deserves a little more theorisation than it has hitherto attracted. If Hyde is right it is time to create some Australian theories of our own.

References

Anderson, T. 1999, 'The meaning of deregulation', *Journal of Australian Political Economy* 44: 5–21.

Ayres, I. & Braithwaite, J. 1992, *Responsive Regulation: Transcending the Deregulation Debate*, New York: Oxford University Press.

Barry, M. & Wailes, N. 2004, 'Contrasting systems? 100 years of arbitration in Australia and New Zealand', *Journal of Industrial Relations* 46(4): 430–47.

Bennett, L. 1988, 'Equal pay and comparable worth in the Australian Conciliation and Arbitration Commission', *Journal of Industrial Relations* 30(4): 533–45.

Buchanan, J. & Callus, R. 1993, 'Efficiency and equity at work: the need for labour market regulation in Australia', *Journal of Industrial Relations* 35(4): 515–37.

Collins, H. 1982, *Marxism and Law*, New York: Oxford University Press.

Collins, H. 1989, 'Labour law as a vocation', *Law Quarterly Review* 105: 468–84.

Collins, H. 2002, 'Is there a third way in labour law?', in Conaghan, Fischl & Klare (eds) *Labour Law in an Era of Globalization*, pp. 449–70.

Conaghan, J., Fischl, R.M. & Klare, K. (eds) 2002, *Labour Law in an Era of Globalization: Transformative Practices and Possibilities*, Oxford: Oxford University Press.

Cooney, S. & Mitchell, R. 2002, 'What is labour law doing in East Asia', in Cooney et al. (eds) *Law and Labour Market Regulation in East Asia*, pp. 246–75.

Cooney, S., Lindsey, T., Mitchell, R. & Zhu, Y. (eds) 2002, *Law and Labour Market Regulation in East Asia*, London: Routledge.

Creighton, B. & Stewart, A. 2005, *Labour Law*, 4th edn, Sydney: Federation Press.

Dabscheck, B. 1995, *The Struggle for Australian Industrial Relations*, Melbourne: Oxford University Press.

Dabscheck, B. 1998, 'Orwell de Foenander: Australia's first labour law scholar', *Australian Journal of Labour Law* 11(1): 1–23.

Fetter, J. & Mitchell, R. 2004, 'The legal complexity of workplace regulation and its impact upon functional flexibility in Australian workplaces', *Australian Journal of Labour Law* 17(3): 276–305.

Glasbeek, H.J. 2002, *Wealth by Stealth: Corporate Crime, Corporate Law, and the Perversion of Democracy*, Toronto: Between the Lines.

Gunningham, N. & Johnstone, R. 1999, *Regulating Workplace Safety: Systems and Sanctions*, Oxford: Oxford University Press.

Haydu, J. 1998, 'Making use of the past: time periods as cases to compare and as sequences of problem solving', *American Journal of Sociology* 104(2): 339–71.

Howe, J. 2005, '*Deregulation of labour relations in Australia: toward command and control*', Working Paper No. 34, Centre for Employment and Labour Relations Law, University of Melbourne.

Hunter, R. 1992, *Indirect Discrimination in the Workplace*, Sydney: Federation Press.

Hyde, A. 1994, 'Labor law as political symbol: a critical model of labor legislation', in R. Rogowski & T. Wilthagen (eds) *Reflexive Labour Law*, Dordrecht: Kluwer, pp. 173–82.

Isaac, J. & Macintyre, S. (eds) 2004, *The New Province for Law and Order: 100 Years of Australian Industrial Conciliation and Arbitration*, Cambridge University Press.

Jamieson, S. 1990, 'Enterprise bargaining: the approach of the Business Council of Australia', *Australian Journal of Labour Law* 3(1): 77–82.

Johnstone, R. & Mitchell, R. 2004, 'Regulating work' in C. Parker, C. Scott, N. Lacey & J. Braithwaite (eds) *Regulating Law*, Oxford: Oxford University Press, pp. 101–21.

Kahn-Freund, O. 1972, *Labour and the Law*, London: Stevens.

Kahn-Freund, O. 1974, 'On uses and misuses of comparative law', *Modern Law Review* 37(1): 1–27.

Kelman, M. 1987, *A Guide to Critical Legal Studies*, Cambridge, Mass.: Harvard University Press.

Kennedy, D. 1997, *A Critique of Adjudication: Fin de Siècle*, Cambridge, Mass.: Harvard University Press.

Kirby, M. & Creighton, B. 2004, 'The law of conciliation and arbitration', in J. Isaac & S. Macintyre (eds), *The New Province for Law and Order: 100 Years of Australian Industrial Conciliation and Arbitration*, Cambridge University Press, pp. 98–138.

Kitay, J. and Lansbury, R. (eds) 1997, *Changing Employment Relations in Australia*, Melbourne: Oxford University Press.

McCallum, R. 1998, 'Collective labour law, citizenship and the future', *Melbourne University Law Review* 22(1): 42–61.

McCallum, R. 2005, '*Justice at work: industrial citizenship and the corporatisation of Australian labour law*', Kingsley Laffer Memorial Lecture, University of Sydney, 11 April.

MacDermott, T. 1996, 'Who's rocking the cradle? Maternity rights in Australia', *Alternative Law Journal* 21(5): 207–12.

Macintyre, S. and Mitchell, R. (eds) 1989, *Foundations of Arbitration: The Origins and Effects of State Compulsory Arbitration 1890–1914*, Melbourne: Oxford University Press.

Michelson, G. & Westcott, M. 2001, 'Heading into orbit? Braham Dabscheck and industrial relations theory', *Journal of Industrial Relations* 43(3): 308–29.

Owens, R. 1993, 'Women, "atypical" work relationships and the law', *Melbourne University Law Review* 19(2): 399–430.

Parker, C. 2002, *The Open Corporation: Effective Self-regulation and Democracy*, Cambridge University Press.

Parker, C., Scott, C., Lacey, N. & Braithwaite, J. (eds) 2004, *Regulating Law*, Oxford: Oxford University Press.

Rogowski, R. & Wilthagen, T. (eds) 1994, *Reflexive Labour Law*, Dordrecht: Kluwer.

Stone, K. 2004, *From Widgets to Digits: Employment Regulation for the Changing Workplace*, Cambridge University Press.

Teubner, G. 1983, 'Substantive and reflexive elements in modern law', *Law and Society Review* 17: 239–85.

Twining, W.L. 2000, *Globalisation and Legal Theory*, London: Butterworths.

Wilson, M. 1994, 'Contractualism and the Employment Contracts Act 1991: can they deliver equality for women?', *New Zealand Journal of Industrial Relations* 19(3): 256–74.

The following website has been developed at Macquarie Law School. The cases are available in the Law Reports as well but this website constitutes a very convenient and interesting resource: www.law.mq.edu.au/scnsw/.

CHAPTER FIVE

DIVERSITY AND CHANGE IN WORK AND EMPLOYMENT RELATIONS

Jim Kitay and Russell Lansbury

The changing nature of work and employment relations is often discussed in a linear fashion so that 'old' systems are portrayed as changing over time into 'new' systems. Work and employment relations in Australia have sometimes been conceptualised in terms of an 'old' Fordist system, based on mass production, and characterised by adversarial relations between management and unions. While accounts vary, the old system of work and employment relations was characterised as repetitious, fragmented, low-skilled, poorly paid, with low trust between managers and workers and underpinned by highly centralised wage determination processes. According to some accounts, this has been replaced by a 'new' system based on more flexible forms of work and employment practices which is characterised as either 'post-Fordist' or 'neo-Fordist', depending respectively on the degree of optimism or pessimism with which the commentator regards the new developments.

The focus on 'time' in this chapter examines a debate over the nature and regulation of work in Australia that flourished in the late 1980s and early 1990s. Some accounts of change are dichotomous and linear, and we seek to challenge the view that changes in work and employment relations have progressed from an 'old' to a 'new' model during recent decades. While there have undoubtedly been major changes over time, these have not all been unidirectional and we suggest that there has been considerable diversity in the forms of work and its regulation, the nature of the changes that have occurred, the means by which these changes have been introduced, and the probable trajectories of change for the future. The assumptions on which discussions about changes over time are based need to be scrutinised and subjected to empirical assessment. A number of important questions must be addressed. Was there an 'old' model of work and employment relations which achieved paradigmatic influence at an earlier point in time? Is there an identifiable 'new' model that is now the prevailing norm or is in the process of being introduced? If so, where and how? To the extent that new working arrangements can be found, what forms do they take, what are their effects and how have they changed over time?

The first section of the chapter briefly examines debates regarding the nature of 'transformed' workplaces. The second section outlines the background of the project and the nature of the research design. The third section presents the findings from case studies in the automobile and retail banking industries with reference to changes in work and employment relations practices. We conclude that some models of workplace change overstate the degree of consistency that prevailed in the past and underestimate the extent to which diversity is likely to continue in the foreseeable future. In other words the way in which 'time' has been, and continues to be, experienced is different in automobiles and retail banking.

MODELS OF CHANGE AFTER FORDISM

Many contributions to the Australian debate on changing employment and work relations in the late 1980s and early 1990s addressed change in terms of a shift away from some version of a Fordist model along one of two pathways, either neo-Fordism or post-Fordism (Bramble 1988; Badham & Mathews 1989; Boreham 1992; Harley 1994; to some extent Hampson et al. 1994). The debate emerged through engagement with overseas theoretical developments in the mid-1980s, including the French regulation school (Boyer 1988), the German 'new production concepts' approach (Kern & Schumann 1987) and American flexible specialisation theory (Piore & Sabel 1984). The debate took on a distinctive antipodean character, however, particularly in its policy prescriptions for award restructuring, workplace change and the future of trade unionism.

Other terms have been proposed, such as lean production versus socio-technical production (Mathews 1994) or profitability-oriented versus productivity-oriented strategies (Boreham et al. 1996), but

the details suggest that we are dealing with two alternatives arising from a common Fordist paradigm. Post-Fordists are cautiously
optimistic about the direction of change while neo-Fordists are pessimistic (Phillimore 1989). Change is usually attributed to increasingly
turbulent markets, which make Fordism untenable due to its supposed
rigidity, as well as to new technologies which allow the introduction
of more flexible production systems (Piore & Sabel 1984). Institutions
(Streeck 1987) and management strategy (Kochan et al. 1986) affect
the speed and direction of change.

We have sought to distil some of the key elements of Fordism, post-
Fordism and neo-Fordism from these writings, which are summarised in
Table 5.1.

The attributes of classic Fordism emphasise low-cost, high-volume
production (Meyer 1981). Functional flexibility is low and numerical flexibility is limited to hiring and firing full-time employees to
meet demand. Most jobs are routine, performed by unskilled employees with little prospect of career advancement, and, not surprisingly,
little attachment to the enterprise. Employment relations are centralised and adversarial. Fordism is seen as inflexible and unable to cope
with turbulent markets.

Neo-Fordists and post-Fordists agree that the limitations of Fordism
are not simply technological, but require a change in human resource
management practices as well, particularly greater functional and
numerical flexibility. The two schools of thought differ mainly in the
dominant trends they discern and the motives they ascribe to management.

Post-Fordists argue that managements, preferably with the willing
participation of unions, understand the need to develop a highly skilled
workforce that exercises considerable autonomy (Mathews 1989).
They advocate work reorganisation that requires multi-skilling and
teamwork, allowing employees to work 'smarter rather than harder'.
Increased numerical flexibility can be accomplished through decentralised production, and flexibility in working time by consent. There
is high mutual commitment within enterprises, and the opportunity
for 'boundaryless careers' (Arthur & Rousseau 1996) for those workers who choose to pursue opportunities outside the traditional firm.
Post-Fordists typically support the ideals of trade unionism (Mathews
1989), but warn that unless unions break free of an adversarial approach
and accept the need to accommodate progressive managements in the

Table 5.1 *Features of Fordism, Post-Fordism and Neo-Fordism*

	Fordism	Post-Fordism	Neo-Fordism
Job classifications	Many	Reduced	Reduced
Skill requirements	Low	Increased, apart from a few menial jobs	Decreased, apart from a few high-status jobs
Work intensity	High	Working smarter rather than harder	Increased
Functional flexibility	Low	Increased through multi-skilling	Increased through multi-tasking
Numerical flexibility	High staff turnover but limited in other respects	Increased through flexible or decentralised production arrangements	Increased through non-standard employment practices
Staff autonomy	Low	Increased in order to ensure commitment	Low – rhetoric of empowerment viewed as a sham to increase management control
Teamwork	None	Widespread; essential to production	Tenuous, and typically 'management by stress' where it appears.
Career structures	Limited horizons	Either mutual commitment or 'boundaryless' careers	Highly fragmented. Reduced career horizons for non-core staff
Industrial relations	Centralised; adversarial	Decentralised; unitarist or consensual	Decentralised; unitarist or adversarial
Dominant HR strategy	Cost minimisation	Mutual gains	Cost minimisation

development of new working arrangements, they will become irrelevant (Streeck 1987). The focus of union activity should be the workplace, but both unions and managements should be incorporated into wider skill formation structures that encourage skill enhancement and allow mobility. At a general level the human resources strategy adopted by managements can be termed 'mutual gains' (Kochan & Osterman 1994).

Researchers who perceive a neo-Fordist direction of change agree that functional flexibility is increasing, but argue that this is due to multi-tasking rather than multi-skilling (Bramble 1988). Increased levels of numerical flexibility are accompanied by greater job insecurity through casualisation and temporary employment. Flexibility in working time is driven more by the needs of management than of employees, and frequently involves excessive hours of work that are often unpaid. Rather than being 'boundaryless', career opportunities are becoming highly fragmented, with reduced horizons for many. Most importantly, employee empowerment, the centrepiece of the post-Fordist project, is viewed as more rhetoric than reality (Boreham et al. 1996; and especially Bramble 1988). In their view, the post-Fordist scenario applies only to a small, privileged elite of workers, with the remainder subject to a regime of deskilled, intensified work involving greater levels of surveillance by electronic monitoring. Both schools agree, however, that industrial relations are becoming decentralised, but neo-Fordists are sceptical of consensual approaches, viewing them as simplistic and likely to lead to dominance by management and marginalisation of unions.

While most commentators (Bramble 1988; Hampson et al. 1994; Boreham et al. 1996) noted that in practice elements of the models can coexist, and Campbell (1990: 17) argues against couching arguments in terms of 'paradigms', the debate over the direction of change in Australia was effectively polarised between the alternative views of post- and neo-Fordism. Our research has sought to explore the extent to which either perspective sheds light on contemporary and subsequent developments. To the extent that either model is a more adequate portrayal of change over time, we would expect to find a common pattern of 'old' employment relations along Fordist lines giving way to a dominant model along either neo-Fordist or post-Fordist lines.

THE RESEARCH PROJECT

Automobiles and banking were selected for the research that forms the basis of this chapter because the former is a core manufacturing industry while the latter is an example of a major service industry. Much of the theoretical debate over workplace change has arisen from research on manufacturing, and in our view autos and banking provide an interesting comparison. We wish to examine, first, how well concepts such as post- and neo-Fordism apply on their 'home' terrain in a mass production industry; and second, to what extent a major service industry conforms to these models.

The case studies of automobiles and banking were based on industry-level data plus 'narrative histories' of several enterprises at different points in time. Cases were selected on the basis of advice from knowledgeable observers and the authors' understandings of the industries. The enterprises included some of the largest automobile manufacturers and banks in Australia. There were good grounds for believing that 'new' employment relations were more likely to emerge in major enterprises than in small businesses, as small firms typically lack the knowledge, resources and management capability to introduce significant workplace reform (Wright 1995).

The research was conducted primarily using semi-structured interviews at all levels of the enterprises, from senior executives to shopfloor employees. Although special attention was given to specialist industrial relations and HR managers and trade union officials, line managers were interviewed as well. A common range of information was gathered, with specific questions tailored to each industry.

In the case of automobile manufacturing, all four production facilities, owned and operated by Ford, General Motors Holden, Toyota and Mitsubishi, were visited several times over a ten-year period. Interviews were conducted with a wide range of individuals and observations were made on the assembly line of the changing nature of work and organisation. Visits were made to the head offices of each company in Australia as well as the union headquarters to gain interviews and documentary material. In the banking industry, interviews were conducted with employees, managers and union representatives in all four of the major banks: ANZ, Commonwealth Bank, National Australia Bank and Westpac, and one regional bank.

The research was conducted in two phases, the first covering the early 1980s to the mid-1990s, which was chosen to correspond with the period in which significant organisational changes were generally believed to be occurring in developed countries. The second updated the findings from the mid-1990s to 2005. In both automobiles and banking, long-serving or retired employees, employer association and trade union officials were able to reflect back to the early 1980s and beyond, and this information was supplemented by documentary materials.

THE CHANGING ORGANISATION OF WORK AND EMPLOYMENT
RELATIONS IN THE AUTOMOBILE AND BANKING INDUSTRIES

The two industries which are discussed in this chapter experienced significant changes between the early 1980s and 2005. New forms of work
organisation and employment relations were influenced by a range of
factors, some of which related to Australia while others were part of
broader global economic and political developments. Both industries
experienced major changes in product markets, production processes
and the application of new technologies. These developments placed
new demands on management and the workforce in each industry and
altered long-established patterns of employment.

The Australian auto industry has been greatly affected by the growth
of international trade, facilitated not only by the reduction of tariffs
but also by changes in production systems. During the past two decades
the world auto industry began to move away from integrated production
where all parts were sourced in one country towards a global network of
plants which has enabled basic parts to be sourced from lower-cost, less
industrialised countries. The more complex and capital-intensive components (such as engines) were obtained from more advanced industrialised countries. The Australian auto industry was for many years
dependent on a high level of tariff protection, producing relatively small
volumes with inefficient production methods. In 1985, however, the
federal government introduced a plan to reshape the industry. Tariffs
were lowered from 57.5 per cent in 1988 and will reach 5 per cent in
2006. The number of different models produced was greatly reduced and
the number of local manufacturers was reduced to four: Ford, General
Motors Holden, Toyota and Mitsubishi. The market share of locally
manufactured autos fell from 85 per cent in 1987 to 40 per cent in
2002, and total employment in the auto assembly industry declined
from 33 000 in 1989 to 16 000 in 2000. Employment in component suppliers increased during this period but did not offset the decline within
the assembly plants.

The retail banking industry has also been affected by global changes.
In 1983 the federal government liberalised Australia's role in global
financial markets by floating the dollar, abolishing many of the restrictions on capital flows and investment and removing interest rate controls. External deregulation was matched with measures that changed
the competitive character of the industry within Australia. From 1984,
foreign-owned banks were allowed to operate in all areas of the industry

and a number of domestic non-bank financial institutions such as building societies were granted banking licences. A spate of mergers produced significant market concentration in the hands of the four major
retail banks. Deregulation of the industry from the mid-1980s served
to offset any reduction in competition from the mergers, allowing new
entrants to the market, reducing the barriers between sectors of the
finance industry and increasing the exposure to market forces. Privatisation also sharpened the competitiveness of the old government-
owned banks. Finally, new competitive strategies emerged seeking to
increase sales while simultaneously reducing operating expenses. From
1985 to 1990, employment in the banking sector grew rapidly as the
level of business increased, but then declined as several banks, particularly the major banks, experienced financial difficulties and downsized
their workforce. There was also a structural change in the composition
of the workforce as the proportion of part-time employees increased
considerably.

Both the auto manufacturers and the banks have argued that the
changes affecting their industries over the past two decades require
employees to adapt to new forms of work and organisation. In order
to determine the degree to which employment relations have been
'transformed' in these two industries, we have examined changes in
three broad areas: the changing nature of work, the increase in workplace flexibility and the employment and HR strategies that are being
practised.

The changing nature of work

Within auto manufacturing there was a long tradition of highly differentiated job classifications based on the fragmented work performed in
assembly plants. Retail banking differed in that there was strict observation of seniority-based job classifications, but considerable fluidity and
variety in the day-to-day tasks performed by branch-level employees.
Within the auto industry, there was little upward mobility from the shop
floor, whereas in banking there was a strong concept of 'career banker',
although this only applied to males.

There were significant changes in both industries during the 1980s.
With the advent of award restructuring in the auto industry, the number of job classifications was reduced and workers were given opportunities to undertake a wider range of activities. These developments
coincided with changes in production that required a more skilled and

86

flexible workforce. Within retail banking, there were similar changes as job classifications based on seniority were abandoned for broadbanded positions based on job evaluation. New positions such as business and mortgage lending and financial planning specialists appeared, and the content of branch managers' jobs was downgraded to a customer service supervisory role as the role of branches narrowed.

As the types of jobs available in each industry altered, new skills were required. Within the auto industry, most skills had traditionally been obtained through experience on the job without any planned program. As a result of the award restructuring process initiated by the Australian Industrial Relations Commission, a Vehicle Industry Certificate introduced industry-level standards and all new employees were required to undertake formal training in order to acquire the competencies necessary for the performance of their job. It was intended that future career progression in the industry would require workers to undertake a structured program of skills development. However, there has been considerable variation in the speed and extent to which companies have upgraded the skills of their employees. Furthermore, while many workers gained the skills to perform a variety of tasks (multi-tasking), fewer gained genuine multi-skilling across a range of different functions. There is now less of an industry-wide approach to skills development as companies seek to become more differentiated.

In banking, the traditional concept of the 'rounded' career banker described a person who was able to perform most or all of the tasks in a branch depending on experience. This applied more to men than women, whose opportunities to enhance their skills were more limited. In the new era of retail banking, however, branch employees were no longer required to understand back office processing tasks, but were expected to gain selling skills. They were also expected to acquire knowledge about a wider range of products, though roles became further specialised after 2000 and the need for detailed product knowledge on the part of all branch staff diminished. Overall, there was a requirement in branches for a smaller but deeper set of skills than in the past. However, the nature and range of tasks in processing centres and call centres were clearly deskilled in comparison with work in traditional branches, where a full range of banking skills was expected of most staff. By contrast, within regional banks (many of which upgraded from building societies in the 1980s), the widening range of banking activities was dealt with by increasing the range of skills required of employees. The concept of the 'career banker' largely disappeared in the major banks as tertiary-level educational qualifications rather than on-the-job experience was increasingly required for promotion to management. External recruitment above entry-level positions grew rapidly, internal labour markets became segmented and branches were increasingly staffed by a large number of part-time workers with limited career prospects.

The means by which work is performed has also changed in each industry. Work on the auto assembly line has traditionally been arduous, monotonous and repetitive, with workers having little autonomy and management being highly directive. As the auto industry has moved towards more 'lean production' systems, however, there has been greater emphasis on the use of technology to eliminate the most arduous aspects of work. The introduction of teams has given some workers more influence over the way tasks are shared and greater discretion in the performance of tasks. Within Australian auto plants, however, the application of lean production principles has been fairly limited. Tasks on the assembly line remain rather narrowly defined, teamwork is found mainly in off-line areas of production, and in most cases the autonomy of workers and workgroups (or teams) remains circumscribed. Greater emphasis has been given to worker involvement in issues such as quality and continuous improvement, but many of these activities have been spasmodic and short-lived. Due to declining volumes of production, the degree of automation has been low by international standards and levels of productivity and quality have not risen as fast as comparable plants in other countries.

Traditionally, work in retail banks was not onerous and its intensity fluctuated with daily peaks and troughs in front office jobs. While there has always been considerable regulation to ensure fiduciary compliance, branches had considerable autonomy in day-to-day activities. While there was little formal teamwork practised at branch level, there was considerable informal 'helping out'. Hence the nature of work in banking was very different from that in auto assembly plants. Since deregulation, work intensity in branches has increased. Managements have introduced performance targets for all employees that are often difficult to achieve, and the 'goal posts' are continually shifting. The targets are centrally imposed and the work of most staff, and work groups as a whole, can be electronically monitored. The introduction of 'lean' staffing profiles has led to frequent complaints by employees and their union representatives of understaffing, as well as unpaid overtime.

Worker autonomy in branches has declined as control over activities has become increasingly centralised.

The increase in workplace flexibility

Workplace flexibility has become a key concept in changes to work organisation and employment relations. According to Streeck (1987: 287), flexibility has become 'a common denominator of the industrial relations concerns of employers today'. While flexibility is widely viewed as desirable by employers, downward flexibility on wages or employment levels may have negative consequences for an enterprise or industry, particularly if it is seeking to attract high-quality employees. Similarly, while functional flexibility can be positive for employees if it leads to the acquisition of more skills, it may also lead to work intensification, and thereby reduce employee commitment to the employing organisation. In this section, we will focus on functional and numerical flexibility for the purpose of analysing changes in autos and banking.

Retail banking had considerable functional flexibility in the past in that there was much 'learning by doing' among bank employees in order to gain skills so that they could perform a variety of functions in both the front and back office areas of branches. Employees thus became more functionally flexible as they gained experience. Regional banks retained a high degree of such functional flexibility in their branches and used new technology to give front office staff more skills and responsibility as they took on a wider range of banking activities. This has not been the case with the major retail banks, where demarcations within branches and between front and back office staff have become more pronounced.

There was little numerical flexibility in the traditional retail banking system, as almost all employees were full-time, trading hours were restricted, lifetime employment was assured for male employees and there was no outsourcing. Since deregulation there has been a rapid increase in part-time employment that provides flexibility, and information technology, aspects of HRM and some processing tasks have been outsourced. Hours of operation have increased and many lending specialists are expected to see clients outside 'normal' banking hours. Large-scale redundancies in the recession of the early 1990s in some banks heralded the end of lifetime employment. These and other measures now give banks considerable numerical flexibility.

The auto companies have sought, in recent years, to retain workers, particularly those who are more highly skilled, because of the cost of training and the difficulty of recruiting experienced skilled workers. However, due to declining sales of domestically manufactured vehicles as imports have risen, there has been significant downsizing in the industry as well as contracting or outsourcing of work. Unlike banking, there has not been much use of part-time or casual employees, though the ailing Mitsubishi company introduced temporary contract workers on the ground that long-term positions could not be guaranteed. This might mark the beginning of a new trend in the auto industry to seek greater numerical flexibility.

New employment and human resource strategies

In the private sector banks, industrial relations were traditionally adversarial but not militant until the 1970s, while a consensual relationship prevailed in the public sector Commonwealth Bank. Union density was typically around 60 per cent in the major private banks, higher in the Commonwealth Bank and lower in the small regional banks. Most banks were affiliated with the Australian Bankers Association (ABA), which represented them in industry-level negotiations with the Finance Sector Union (FSU). Most private sector employees were covered by a common federal award, the main features of which were incorporated in an agreement in the Commonwealth Bank. A shift towards enterprise-level bargaining began in 1986–87 when the three major private banks introduced company-specific provisions into the industry award to replace the common incremental wage scales.

Since 1987, industrial relations have become less centralised. Separate agreements cover each bank, in many cases further decentralised to business unit or site-specific instruments. However, there remains a distinct element of pattern bargaining, and negotiations are often marked by industrial disputation. Management–union relations in the privatised Commonwealth Bank deteriorated greatly during the process of privatisation and remain antagonistic. The bank made repeated attempts to introduce Australian Workplace Agreements, with the clear intent of reducing the role of the FSU in the enterprise. The National Australia Bank and Westpac, however, attempted to establish management–union partnerships with limited success, though relations remain cordial. Relations between the ANZ Bank and the FSU became strained in the mid-1990s, but have improved to the point of being merely arm's length. No new enterprise agreement has been reached in the ANZ since 1998, with the company paying regular wage increases based on market movements.

The major retail banks have sought to develop a more strategic approach to their HRM practices from the early to mid-1990s with the intention of ensuring high-quality customer service and increased sales. However, this occurred simultaneously with an emphasis on cost reduction, particularly an attempt to channel customers away from face-to-face contact with staff in branches and into lower-cost telephone and electronic services. Hence the banks' traditional paternalist approach to employment relations has given way to an uneasy balance between a 'low road' cost-cutting strategy of downsizing and work intensification and a 'high road' strategy designed to narrow but deepen skills with the intention of identifying sales opportunities and providing a high-quality customer experience.

Industrial relations in the auto industry have a long history of conflict and turbulence. Strikes were numerous and employers were less inclined to resist pressures for wage increases because they were able to use the high tariff protection to absorb increased costs. Closed shop arrangements ensured that the industry was fully unionised. The Vehicle Builders Union organised most of the production workers while other unions had coverage of the skilled trades, clerical and supervisory employees. As a key manufacturing industry, autos were a target for union campaigns to improve wages and conditions.

Industrial disputation declined generally in Australia during the Accord period of the 1980s, and auto companies sought to develop more cooperative relationships with the unions. The Ford Motor Company took the initiative in the early 1980s with a program of employee involvement, and similar programs were introduced by other auto companies. The Australian Manufacturing Workers Union (AMWU) then became the dominant union from the mid-1990s through an amalgamation of several unions in the auto industry, including the Vehicle Builders Union. The main trend in the 1990s, however, was towards enterprise-level bargaining whereby each company conducted separate negotiations in order to conclude specific agreements. Although there were variations in the content and timing of these agreements, there remained a high degree of similarity between them. Hence although there is no longer an industry-wide award, there has developed a form of pattern bargaining whereby the unions have been able to ensure that variation between the company-level agreements is minimised. While industrial relations remain fairly harmonious in the assembly plants, there has been increased disputation within the automotive compo- nents sector. This is due in part to pressures placed on the components sector by the major auto companies to cut costs and increase produc- tivity.

A report by Standard & Poor's (1996) noted that the auto pro- ducers in Australia were generally pessimistic about future growth in the domestic market as well as their chances of winning a greater share of export markets. The report questioned whether the indus- try could remain viable unless it became more integrated into global component sourcing and developed niche export markets. Today, the industry remains focused on survival in the short term through cost-cutting.

DISCUSSION

The evidence from the automobile and retail banking industries pro- vides considerable insight into the main questions that are being addressed: was there a common Fordist model of work and employment relations that dominated Australian enterprises across different indus- tries for much of the latter part of the 20th century, and is there a clear change in the direction of a new dominant model that can be termed either post-Fordist or neo-Fordist? The evidence suggests that not only is there no clear shift towards a new common model, but also that the view that Fordism – understood in terms of a specific set of practices – was the paradigmatic model for work organisation and employment relations through much of the latter 20th century is greatly overstated. What we observe when we compare automobile manufacturing and retail banking is diversity. While there are enough similarities to iden- tify 'old' and 'new' models within industries, even this must be qualified, for example the differences between major and regional banks and the divergent industrial relations policies of some of the major banks. The inter-industry differences, however, are compelling, and we believe that it is inaccurate to refer globally to 'old' and 'new' national models of work and employment relations. We note that both autos and banking have changed greatly over time, but not necessarily in the same way. We compare the models from Table 5.1 to our findings.

A standard model of work and employment relations generally pre- vailed in the automobile industry until recently, which not surprisingly conformed in many respects to the classic model of Fordism, with no Australian counterparts to innovative plants such as General Motors'

Saturn or Volvo's Uddevalla (see Berggren 1992). This was not the case, however, in retail banks. Central to this difference was the concept of the rounded 'career banker', who was expected gradually to gain all of the skills necessary to work in a bank branch. In the course of a long career, there was a great deal of 'learning by doing' as employees helped out informally in a range of activities that were outside their assigned tasks, as well as undergoing extensive formal training. For most men, at least, a job in a bank was a 'job for life', in contrast to the 'minimum interaction' model (Davis cited in Littler 1982: 56) characteristic of Fordism. Although many work practices in banks were strictly controlled by regulations designed to ensure the probity of employees and accuracy in handling financial transactions, individual bank branches had a great deal of autonomy in their everyday activities, and many were allowed considerable discretion in performing their work. If many banking tasks were routine, it would be difficult to argue that banking work was deskilled, even in lower-echelon positions. Industrial relations in both industries were centralised, as well as adversarial, with the notable exception of the Commonwealth Bank, but disputation within banking was typically channelled into the formal procedures of the federal industrial tribunal and seldom appeared as overt conflict. Finally, the HR strategies of banks were generally benevolent. Even the private banks were not cost minimisers; indeed, far from it, as one would expect of Fordist enterprises. It is possible, therefore, to identify a range of 'old' patterns typical of industries or sections of industries, but there was not a standard 'old' pattern of work and employment relations applicable to all industries, and in the case of a major industry like banking, the dominant pattern clearly was not Fordist in many essentials.

Turning to the current situation in automobiles and banking, it is clear that post-Fordism fares little better today than Fordism did earlier as a general model common to major Australian industries. Only in the number of job classifications and numerical flexibility does post-Fordism adequately predict our findings, and there is some question even with these. The number of job classifications in automobiles has clearly dropped, but in banking this has changed from an age- and seniority-based system in which classifications bore little relation to the work that was performed, to a model based on job evaluation that is not really comparable to the old system. Numerical flexibility has definitely increased, but in different ways in each industry. Both industries have experienced downsizing, but banking has made considerable use of part-time employment, whereas autos has not. The automobile industry has made more use of outsourcing, though this practice is rapidly growing in banking. In effect, by redefining themselves as sales-based rather than transaction-based organisations, processing is less likely to be seen as part of the core business. There has been some increase in functional flexibility in autos, as could be expected under post-Fordism, but this is more multi-tasking than multi-skilling, and there has been a clear drop in functional flexibility in banks with the introduction of a sharp divide between front and back office activities.

The changes to skills are more difficult to assess from a post-Fordist perspective. There has been an increase in skills development in autos, but the extent of upskilling is somewhat limited. In banks, the task range of work in branches has narrowed with the removal of many processing tasks, but arguably deepened with the introduction of sales skills. However, work for the back office processing workers has unquestionably been deskilled, as the task range has been reduced with no compensating changes such as the development of customer service skills. For this reason, the evidence fails to support the expectations of a post-Fordist model. The evidence in banking alone is sufficient to contradict post-Fordism in the areas of careers, autonomy, teamwork and work intensity. For many employees, work in banks is now 'just a job' rather than part of an organisational career. Vertical career horizons have been sharply curtailed for many, and there is also less horizontal mobility with the sharp demarcation between front and back office work and call centres. The level of mutual commitment has plummeted in banks, and banking careers are far from the concept of 'boundaryless-ness'. Work intensity has increased almost universally, genuine teamwork has been fragmentary and generally short lived, and the autonomy enjoyed even by fairly senior employees in branches has been reduced with the introduction of technology that constrains decision-making and allows surveillance of activities to take place in real time. Leaving industrial relations aside for later, the mutual gains expectations of post-Fordism in the area of HR strategy are limited.

Neo-Fordism appears to be a more plausible model across a range of dimensions in both industries. The empirical expectations for numerical flexibility and job classifications are similar to those for post-Fordism and are supported, with differences in detail between industries noted above. The evidence for careers, work intensity, teamwork and employee autonomy give some support to neo-Fordism, but with some qualifications concerning the latter two dimensions. There is considerable talk about teamwork and some experimentation in both

industries, with some tentative moves towards greater employee autonomy in autos. While a long way from post-Fordist expectations, we
are nevertheless unconvinced by neo-Fordist arguments that these are
little more than thin facades designed to increase management control.
Based on our interviews, managers genuinely believe in the benefits of
teamwork and empowerment, but have had little success in introducing
them. Functional flexibility in banks has declined, as expected by neo-
Fordism, but this has not been the case in autos, limited though such
developments have been. There is a considerable element of cost minimisation in both industries, as expected of HR strategy by neo-Fordists,
but the constant 'high-commitment' rhetoric and frequent experimentation suggests that viewing managers as nothing more than cost
minimisers is simplistic.

Finally, it is difficult to assess the evidence for industrial relations. Both industries have become more decentralised, though pattern bargaining still prevails. Management–union relations in autos
have become somewhat more consensual, but the situation in banks
varies from company to company. Cautious steps towards a consensus
approach were taken in the National Australia Bank and Westpac at
various points, for example, while relations between management and
unions in the previously consensual Commonwealth Bank deteriorated
markedly from the mid-1990s. It is simply too difficult to generalise at
present, but one can safely say that neither of the patterns predicted by
neo- and post-Fordist writers has clearly emerged across both industries.

We conclude that there was never an 'old' standard model of work
and employment relations in Australia, as the evidence from two major
industries is so divergent. Furthermore, there is not a single 'new' model
emerging. Although autos and banking look more neo-Fordist than
post-Fordist, there are sufficient discrepancies to raise serious doubts
about the descriptive and explanatory power of neo-Fordism as a global
model. Indeed, we would go further and argue that it was incorrect to
elevate Fordism to the paradigmatic status it has enjoyed in much of the
literature in the first place, because the practices of a major employer of
labour such as banking failed to conform in so many respects throughout
the 20th century. We suggest that the mistaken centrality of Fordism
is the result of developing theory almost entirely on the evidence of
manufacturing industry while overlooking the service sector. In our
view, the debate between post- and neo-Fordists is at best limited to
those sections of manufacturing in which Fordism can plausibly be said
to have existed, and more likely is simply misguided.

How might we account for our finding that diversity, rather than the development of a paradigmatic model, characterises workplace change? There is a high degree of consensus between post- and neo-Fordists that the changes we are witnessing in work and employment relations are primarily due to changes in product markets, in interaction with new technology. The post-Fordists in particular emphasise that managers perceive a need to increase quality, variety and customer service, while both schools agree on the importance of greater flexibility. There are various post-Fordist scenarios, but all stress the need for highly skilled employees exercising discretion over their work, which will enable firms to compete on quality and variety rather than price. Neo-Fordists are sceptical, however, and focus on the negative side of flexibility associated with a cost-cutting strategy.

The problem with these either/or scenarios is that both are right to a limited extent. In our view, the post- and neo-Fordist positions correctly point to the importance of product markets and new technology, but overemphasise them to the exclusion of the influence of capital markets. The work of Useem (1993, 1996) and Williams and his colleagues (Williams et al. 1987; Froud et al. 1998, 2000), for example, shows how the structure of capital markets and the demands of shareholders affect organisational decision-making in ways that have profound consequences for work and employment relations.

Chief executive officers and boards of directors are strongly influenced by 'the market', a reification that refers to large and small investors, market analysts and the financial media. Even the rumour of reduced profits or losses is likely to be reflected almost immediately in falling share prices, which raises a clamour for remedial action. Profitability can be raised in one of two ways – by increasing revenue or cutting costs. The former is usually a long-term proposition, while the latter can often be effected swiftly. There is no reason, however, why managements cannot attempt to do both at once, and often they do.

Increasing revenue typically involves the 'high road' scenario prescribed by the post-Fordists. High quality and innovation can, indeed, be enhanced by a workforce of highly skilled and dedicated employees (Ichniowski et al. 1996). However, investing in HR involves a long-term commitment, the outcome of which is very difficult to measure. Because 'capital markets and financial institutions are structured in ways that place great emphasis on short-term profits, costs and movements in stock prices and relatively less value on long-term investments' (Kochan & Osterman 1994: 112), a strategy of high investment in HR involves considerable patience on the part of investors.

Kochan & Osterman (1994: 45) point to a 'remarkable consensus' on the benefits of the post-Fordist model, yet they and others such as Storey & Sisson (1990) note the widespread failure to do more than timidly implement fragmentary features of the model, which has been borne out by more recent work in Australia (ACIRRT 1999; Watson et al. 2003) and overseas (Thompson 2003). Levine (1995) demonstrates theoretically how vulnerable post-Fordism is to competition from cost-cutting enterprises, and the fragility of such prescriptions as employee involvement and competency-based career progression is entirely unsurprising. Structural and business cycle differences between industries, institutional differences between nations and industries, and the history and competitive position of individual enterprises make it unlikely that there will be a uniform temporal response to global forces such as growing competition and turbulent product markets (Kochan et al. 1986; Rubery 1994; Williams et al. 1994; Hall & Soskice 2001).

Our expectation, therefore, is that work and employment relations will be characterised by a diverse range of models rather than a single dominant tendency. Our interviews reveal that managers are well aware of the benefits that are widely believed to result from 'high road' initiatives, and new programs are regularly introduced with the best of intentions. To accept the neo-Fordist argument without qualification would suggest that managers are either naive in introducing practices that have no hope of success, or entirely cynical in seeking to dupe the workforce. In our experience few managers fall into either category, and we think that the most accurate explanation for diversity is that managers continually seek to innovate with a desire to pursue 'high road' strategies, but that their intentions are continually compromised by the pressure to cut costs. These compromises, combined with institutional differences between industries and enterprises, lead to diverse outcomes. Thus post- and neo-Fordism point towards one or the other of the different ways to deal with the pressures that arise from product and capital markets, but are inadequate as explanations for current developments in work and employment relations because they grossly underestimate the contradictions inherent in these pressures.

Our view of the diversity of patterns of work and employment relations is shared by postmodernists such as Crook and colleagues (1992), but we disagree with their view that capitalist industrial societies are increasingly driven by consumption rather than production. Societies such as Australia are still 'modern' in the sense of the dominance of production, large enterprises, and instrumental-rational thought. Diversity in work and employment relations has typified these societies throughout the 20th century, and our argument suggests that this will continue to be the case.

CONCLUSION

This chapter has adopted a linear view of time to understand the changing nature of employment relations in the automobile and banking industries in Australia in order to determine the nature and extent of change from 'old' to 'new' or transformed patterns. Three areas in particular were examined: the organisation of work, the growth of flexibility, and industrial relations and HRM strategies. It was found that both autos and banking had changed considerably, but not necessarily in the same way. Banking diverged in many respects from the classic model of Fordism, and neither industry conformed to the models of post-Fordism or neo-Fordism. Although more elements of neo-Fordism than post-Fordism appeared in both industries, they incorporated aspects of both. Our conclusion is that the search for dichotomies – 'old' versus 'new' or post-Fordism versus neo-Fordism – is unhelpful as a model of workplace change, as none of these categories fully capture the variety of differences that we observed within and between the auto and banking industries.

We argue that work and employment relations have been and remain characterised by a diverse range of models rather than a single tendency. The focus on a diverse range of contingent possibilities better describes the nature of change than neo-Fordism or post-Fordism. This suggests that how linear 'time' is experienced is different across different industry sectors, a point seldom made explicit in previous studies of workplace change. We expect that new forms of work and employment relations will continue to evolve, not only as a result of changes in the Australian economy but also as part of global economic and political developments. These developments will place new demands on both management and the workforce and result in new patterns of work and employment relations. However, the timing of such demands and patterns will vary between and within industries.

References

ACIRRT (Australian Centre for Industrial Relations Research and Training) 1999, *Australia at Work: Just Managing?* Sydney: Prentice-Hall.

Arthur, M. & Rousseau, D. (eds) 1996, *The Boundaryless Career: A New Employment Principle for a New Organizational Era*, New York: Oxford University Press.

Badham, R. & Mathews, J. 1989, 'The new production systems debate', *Labour and Industry* 2(2): 194–246.

Berggren, C. 1992, *Alternatives to Lean Production: Work Organization in the Swedish Auto Industry*, Ithaca, N.Y.: Cornell University Press.

Boreham, P. 1992, 'The myth of Post-Fordist management: work organization and employee discretion in seven countries', *Employee Relations* 14(2): 13–24.

Boreham, P., Hall, R. & Harley, B. 1996, 'Two paths to prosperity? Work organisation and industrial relations decentralisation in Australia', *Work, Employment and Society* 10(3): 449–68.

Boyer, R. (ed.) 1988, *The Search for Labour Market Flexibility*, Oxford: Clarendon.

Bramble, T. 1988, 'The flexibility debate: industrial relations and new management production practices', *Labour and Industry* 1(2): 187–209.

Campbell, I. 1990, 'The Australian trade union movement and post-Fordism', *Journal of Australian Political Economy* 26: 1–26.

Crook, S., Pakulski, J. & Waters, M. 1992, *Postmodernization: Change in Advanced Society*, London: Sage.

Davis, E.M. & Lansbury, R.D. 1998, 'Australian employment relations', in G.J. Bamber & R.D. Lansbury (eds) *International and Comparative Employment Relations*, Sydney: Allen & Unwin, pp. 110–43.

Froud, J., Haslam, C., Johal, S. & Williams K. 2000, 'Shareholder value and financialization: consultancy promises, management moves', *Economy and Society* 29(1): 80–110.

Froud, J., Williams, K., Haslam, C., Johal, S. & Williams, J. 1998, 'Caterpillar: two stories and an argument', *Accounting, Organizations and Society* 23(7): 685–708.

Hall, P. & Soskice, D. 2001, *Varieties of Capitalism*, Oxford: Oxford University Press.

Hampson, I., Ewer, P. & Smith, M. 1994, 'Post-Fordism and workplace change: towards a critical research agenda', *Journal of Industrial Relations* 36(2): 231–57.

Harley, B. 1994, 'Post-Fordist theory, labour process and flexibility and autonomy in Australian workplaces', *Labour and Industry* 6(1): 107–29.

Ichniowski, C., Kochan, T.A., Levine, D., Olson, C. & Strauss, G. 1996, 'What works at work: overview and assessment', *Industrial Relations* 35(3): 299–333.

Katz, H. (ed.) 1997, *Telecommunications: Restructuring Work and Employment Relations Worldwide*, Ithaca, N.Y.: ILR Press.

Kern, H. & Schumann, M. 1987, 'Limits of the division of labour: new production and employment concepts in West German industry', *Economic and Industrial Democracy* 8(2): 151–70.

Kochan, T., Katz, H. & McKersie, R. 1986, *The Transformation of American Industrial Relations*, New York: Basic Books.

Kochan, T., Lansbury, R. & MacDuffie, J. (eds) 1997, *After Lean Production: Evolving Employment Practices in the World Auto Industry*. Ithaca, N.Y.: Cornell University Press.

Kochan, T. & Osterman, P. 1994, *The Mutual Gains Enterprise*, Boston, Mass.: Harvard Business School Press.

KPMG 1994, *Financial Institutions Performance Survey*, Sydney: KPMG.

Legge, K. 1995, *Human Resource Management: Rhetorics and Realities*, London: Macmillan.

Levine, D. 1995, *Reinventing the Workplace: How Business and Employees Can Both Win*, Washington, DC: Brookings Institution.

Littler, C. 1982, *The Development of the Labour Process in Capitalist Society*, London: Heinemann.

Locke, R., Kochan, T. & Piore, M. (eds) 1995, *Employment Relations in a Changing World Economy*, Cambridge, Mass.: MIT Press.

Mathews, J. 1989, *Tools of Change*, Sydney: Pluto.

Mathews, J. 1994, *Catching the Wave: Workplace Reform in Australia*, Sydney: Allen & Unwin.

Meyer, S. 1981, *The Five Dollar Day: Labor Management and Social Control in the Ford Motor Company, 1908–1921*, Albany, N.Y.: State University of New York Press.

Phillimore, A. 1989, 'Flexible specialisation, work organisation and skills: approaching the second industrial divide', *New Technology, Work and Employment* 4(2): 79–91.

Piore, M. & Sabel, C. 1984, *The Second Industrial Divide*, New York: Basic Books.

Regini, M., Kitay, J. & Baethge, M. (eds) 1999, *From Tellers to Sellers: Changing Employment Relations in Banks*, Cambridge, Mass.: MIT Press.

Rubery, J. 1994, 'The British production regime: a societal-specific system?', *Economy and Society* 23(3): 335–54.

Standard & Poor's, 1996, *Industry Profiles: Automotive Australia*, Melbourne: Standard & Poor's.

Storey, J. & Sisson, K. 1990, 'Limits to transformation: human resource management in the British context', *Industrial Relations Journal* 21(2): 60–5.

Streeck, W. 1987, 'The uncertainties of management in the management of uncertainty: employers, labor relations and industrial uncertainty in the 1980s', *Work, Employment and Society* 1(3): 281–308.

Thompson, P. 2003, 'Disconnected capitalism: or why employers can't keep their side of the bargain', *Work, Employment and Society* 17(2): 359–78.

Useem, M. 1993, *Executive Defense: Shareholder Power and Corporate Reorganization*, Cambridge, Mass.: Harvard University Press.

Useem, M. 1996, *Investor Capitalism: How Money Managers Are Changing the Face of Corporate America*, New York: Basic Books.

Watson, I., Buchanan, J., Campbell, I. & Briggs, C. 2003, *Fragmented Futures: New Challenges in Working Life*, Sydney: Federation Press.

Williams, K., Cutler, T., Williams, J. & Haslem, C. 1987, 'The end of mass production?', *Economy and Society* 16(3): 405–39.

Williams, K., Haslam, C., Johal, S. & Williams, J. 1994, *Cars: Analysis, History, Cases*, Providence: Berghahn.

Wright, C. 1995, *The Management of Labour: A History of Australian Employers*, Melbourne: Oxford University Press.

CHAPTER SIX

TRANSACTIONS IN TIME
The Temporal Dimensions of Customer Service Work

Leanne Cutcher and Diane van den Broek

By the late 1990s, service industries had come to dominate economic activity in most OECD countries including the USA, France, Denmark and Belgium. In 2001 in Australia, services accounted for more than 70 per cent of economic activity and more than three-quarters ($419 billion) of the total output of the economy. Indeed service industries employed 7.4 million of the 9 million (or four out of five) people in paid employment in Australia in 2001 (McLachlan et al. 2002). While service work covers an increasingly diverse range of occupations, many service jobs involve daily interaction with customers. In these jobs, which Leidner (1993) has called interactive service work, the customer is not one step removed from the organisation but enters into the workplace through direct contact with employees. Customers bring their own expectations about what constitutes 'good' customer service and it is the role of customer service employees to deliver according to these expectations as well as those set by management. In recent years researchers from a broad range of disciplines have sought a better understanding of the nature of these three-way interactions. This chapter contributes to this growing body of literature by highlighting the temporal dimensions of customer service work.

In particular, this chapter outlines the way that contemporary retail banking organisations have, in part, used technological service options to limit the unpredictability and uncertainty of routine service exchanges. In a number of service industries including banking, many customer service exchanges have moved from an interaction between customer and worker to a service interaction between customer and machine and, most recently, to a virtual customer service interaction in cyberspace. However, technology cannot entirely replace the need for human interaction. Here we describe the impact of technology and changing conceptions of time for customer service employees in retail bank branches and in call centres. The chapter begins by highlighting the temporal dimensions embedded in competing concepts of customer service. We then outline the way in which technological innovation has impacted on service delivery in retail banking and the implications of this for bank branch employees. Because of the increasing reliance by retail banks on service delivery through call centre operations, the remainder of the chapter explores how call centre management seek to measure and quantify employee performance amid uncertain and unpredictable service encounters. This is followed by a brief discussion of the ways in which call centre employees reappropriate time and resist the constraints placed on them by the managerial emphasis on absolute time and quantifiable targets.

CUSTOMER TIME IN SERVICE WORK

Interactive service exchanges are often referred to as the 'moment of truth' – the point when lasting impressions about organisations are formed (Frenkel et al. 1999: 6). While this phrase alludes to the temporal dimension implicit in the service exchange, it does not reflect the complexity of that 'moment' in which shifting and competing temporal expectations develop. As already indicated, service work brings an important third actor into the workplace, the customer, and customers have their own temporal subjectivities and expectations about quality customer service. Of course customer expectations may vary depending on the nature and purpose of the interaction and the context in which it is embedded. In certain settings customer service may rely on rapid and standardised exchanges underpinned by a customer desire for speed and efficiency. In less routine service interactions there may be more need for taking time to listen, for not hastening the service exchange (Batt 2000).

Similarly, managerial control strategies designed to discipline labour have long relied on technologies that measure time. Many of these strategies, however, assume a notion of time as absolute and objective, when in fact time is elastic and subjective (Mainemelis 2001). It is not only an external stimulus (for example the clock on the wall) that determines a person's notion of time; time also depends on internal characteristics of the observer. As Mainemelis observes, time is determined by inner duration – it can appear to slow down, run or stop, depending on one's emotional state. Clark (1990) comments that the notion of a single, unitary form of time which is absolute and objective is massively inhibiting and says we need to recognise that organisational members hold different senses of time. He argues that in any organisation there will be a complex fabric of chronological codes, some focusing on time as unfolding and regular, others holding more heterogeneous conceptions of time where interpretations of pace and duration are socially constructed (Clark 1990: 155). In line with this, Fitzpatrick (2004) calls for a need to distinguish between measurable or absolute time, which is linear and independent of things bound within it; relative time, which is shaped by objects and subjects within it; and relational time, which is inhabited by social actors that are subject to struggle and contestation. He argues that the trick of capital or capitalism is to fill 'the social with absolutist contents', a kind of temporal commodification (Fitzpatrick 2004: 201). However, management cannot hope to control time entirely, because, as Burrell (1992) suggests, time is made uncertain by human intervention. In service work it is customers who add a further element of uncertainty and unpredictability to the service exchange.

Nowhere is the subjectivity and elasticity of time more evident than in service work because the very characteristics of this work render concrete notions of time redundant. Korczynski (2002: 6–7) identifies five attributes that help us think about the important differences between services and manufacturing work: intangibility, perishability, variability, simultaneous production and consumption, and inseparability. These five attributes are particularly evident in 'interactive' service work, where the service 'product' is produced and consumed at the same time (perishability, simultaneous production and consumption) and is formed in part by individual customers' perceptions of the service (intangibility, variability and inseparability). These attributes highlight not only the distinctive nature of service work but also its temporal dimension. Notions of time are implicit within all five attributes, however, not time as fixed and measurable but time as variable and contested.

As such we suggest that the variable and contested notions of time in service work are indelibly related to competing notions of the customer. For instance, Korczynski and colleagues (2000: 671) argue that in seeking to achieve the dual goals of 'customer-orientation and efficiency, management will prefer employees to identify with a collective, disembodied concept of the customer'. Conversely, employees 'may be more likely to identify with an embodied, individual customer, for service employees interactions with specific customers may be an important arena for meaning and satisfaction in work'. The issue here is that these two conceptualisations of the customer are underpinned by conflicting temporal fabrics. A concept of service that relies on 24-hour availability is centred on a notion of a collective, disembodied customer. As indicated below, such an instrumental approach to customer service is associated with measurable interactions that are standardised, predictable and efficient, with an emphasis on speed.

This is not to suggest, as some have, that customer service employees have become 'self-disciplined subjects' conforming to the temporal demands of management (Knights et al. 1999: 19; Aleroff & Knights 2000: 12). Rather, the elasticity and subjectivity of the service exchange allow spaces in which employees can attempt to reclaim time, either for themselves or in combination with customers. Service employees may resist management attempts to control the service interaction 'simply by making choices about how to perform their allotted work – for instance, with enthusiasm, detachment or indifference' (Knights & McCabe 1998: 192).

To explore the changing temporal dimension of service work, this chapter draws on findings from two large qualitative research studies, covering call centre operations and retail banking, conducted between 1994 and 2003. While the research into call centres was carried out across a range of sites, it is relevant to our discussion of retail banking because it is the finance sector that dominates the call centre industry both in Australia and overseas (Barnes 2001; Kessler 2002; Rose 2002). Together the two studies provide a rich source of data drawn from a total of 150 semi-structured interviews with management, employees, union officials and consumer advocates. This interview data is also supported by information gathered from analysis of a range of primary and secondary documentation including company literature, brochures, PR information, customer newsletters, media reports and government inquiries.

TIME, TECHNOLOGY AND SERVICE IN RETAIL BANKING

Retail bank management in Australia have moved away from providing face-to-face service in branch outlets and now 'encourage' customers to carry out their banking via an automatic teller machine (ATM), over the phone or the internet. The service interaction in retail banking is now very often between the customer and a machine and the banks have introduced fee incentives to discourage customers from conducting their personal banking in branches. The introduction of ATMs and electronic funds transfer at point of sale (EFTPOS) has given rise to the concept of self-service in retail banking. Since 1993, the number of ATMs throughout Australia has almost tripled to 14 714, outnumbering bank branches by three to one, and the number of EFTPOS terminals has increased from 30 486 in 1993 to 40 084 in 2002 (APRA 2002).

New technologies have also expanded to enable customers to do a large amount of their banking from home, either by telephone or over the internet. When retail bank customers need to discuss banking options they are directed to phone banking. As one customer service officer (CSO) in an Australian and New Zealand Banking Corporation (ANZ) bank branch explained, 'customers are told to ring call centres or other business districts rather than talk to the branches; even our phone number is not in the phone book any more'. In 2001, the Commonwealth Bank of Australia's (CBA) NetBank had more than 550 000 customers banking online (Johnston 2001). A bank spokesperson also noted that:

> The CBA has chosen to approach online banking as an internal improvement strategy, using its service to lower the cost of managing accounts and improve service levels. The services the bank branch provides move onto a centrally controlled internet site, but the costs involved in running a branch, such as staff and building costs, all but disappear. (Johnston 2001: 5)

Automated self-service options have enabled retail bank managers to give customers access to their money at any time of the day. These new technologies co-opt customers as a 'co-producer' of the retail banking service and in this way, 'economies may be achieved by getting or educating customers to perform some of the labour themselves' (Sturdy 2001: 7).

The uptake of these new service options by retail bank customers is the result of several factors. The flexibility and convenience offered by these new technologies has undoubtedly suited the changing lifestyles of many retail banking customers. Longer working hours and the increasing participation of women in the workforce made accessing branches in bank hours increasingly difficult.

Table 6.1 *Bank charges in the four major Australian retail banks, 2005*

Bank	Over the counter	Own bank ATM	EFTPOS	Phone	Internet
ANZ	$2.50	50c	50c	50c	Free
CBA	$2.00	50c	30c	30c	30c
NAB	$3.00	60c	60c	60c	20c
Westpac	$2.50	65c	50c	40c	25c

Source: Bank websites, accessed 1 February 2005

But it is not purely lifestyle choices that have driven the adoption of self-service options. The large banks have used fee increases to 'encourage' people to adopt technological service options and avoid over-the-counter transactions. Table 6.1 indicates price disincentive comparisons associated with over-the-counter transactions for personal banking on basic savings accounts once a customer has exceeded the nominated number of free transactions per month. Such additional over-the-counter penalties have been very effective in shaping customer behaviour. In evidence to a federal parliamentary committee on fees for electronic banking, the CBA reported that it had raised the proportion of its transactions performed electronically to 80 per cent of total transactions, and in the three years to 2001, the ANZ had reduced the proportion of branch-based transactions from 20 per cent to 12 per cent (Gittins 2001).

The large-scale closure of retail bank branches over the past 20 years has also made accessing over-the-counter services more difficult. In 1980, Australia had 11 760 bank branches but by June 2000 the number had fallen to 4728 (APRA 2002). Between 1990 and 1999 the finance industry (principally the retail banks) shed over 24 per cent of its workforce, a total of 54 600 jobs (Probert et al. 2000: 11).

Where branches have remained in place the functions they perform have changed significantly over the past decade. The major banks have moved away from branch-based banking, where virtually all tasks were performed at branch level, and have centralised many of the back room functions, leaving the branches that remain with a predominantly sales function. In this way Australia is following a trend that began in the USA in the 1980s. Pollard (1999: 62) explains that these changes first occurred in California, where, since the early 1980s, 'retail bank branches once designed as microcosms of an entire bank have gradually relinquished their role in the transaction handling aspects of operations and lending and have been adapted to function as sales outlets'. In the Australian context, the adoption of these retail innovations has transformed customer relations strategy and practice in the banking industry: '[Whereas] previously, the focus of activities was on processing large numbers of standard transactions quickly and accurately, with a prevailing culture of providing good service to customers, banks now view transactions with customers less in terms of processing and service than as "sales opportunities"' (Kitay 2002: 137).

While retail bank customers may go into a bank branch with a view to being provided with a service, bank management require that the front-line service officer attending them takes the opportunity to try to sell them a banking product. Korczynski (2002: 105) argues that in this way 'sales work tends to prioritise the role of the firm, and its front-line sales workers, in constituting the "real" interests of the customer, and to marginalise the role of the customer in this process'. The customer may be looking for friendly, reliable service but the emphasis on selling reminds them that the bank sees them in a much more instrumental way: as a source of further profits. In short, 'there is less emphasis on the customer *per se*, and more emphasis on getting the customer's money' (Korczynski 2002: 116).

As well as selling customers financial products, customer service staff in branches are required to try and shift customers away from over-the-counter transactions to the self-service technological options. A CBA branch manager explained, 'My staff have targets for the number of people we have to move out onto Netbank and electronic methods of banking.' Bank management have argued that encouraging people to use electronic banking is 'not about closing bank branches, it is about providing a mix of services and that offering on-line services is part of providing what they call a relationship mix for customers' (Johnston 2001: 5). Built into the CBA's internet banking website is a 'customer relationship monitor' aimed at providing the bank with information on what its customers want.

Despite the move to automated, phone and internet banking, there is evidence that many bank customers still desire service through face-to-face contact. For instance, a Deloitte Research study charted responses to a telephone survey of 2000 banking consumers in 10 countries and compared these with responses of 133 senior financial services executives in 17 countries. The results indicate an incongruity between the meaning attached to customer service offered by the customers and that offered by executives:

> Although financial services executives agree on the critical importance of customer service, they often mean such issues as 24-hour access, increased convenience, and one-stop shopping. Consumers, on the other hand, are more concerned with the quality of their interactions with their financial services providers, so-called 'moments of truth'. Is information provided quickly? Is it easy to resolve problems? Are personnel friendly and eager to help? Am I recognised? Do they remember my last call? (Deloitte Research 2000: 7)

The survey showed that many customers expect personal, responsive attention and that branches remain highly relevant (Deloitte Research 2000: 4). In short, this survey indicates that customers want customer service officers who have time to serve them. So while management are emphasising fast and predictable service encounters that fit with their preference for an interaction with a collective, disembodied customer, customers indicate that they still want to be recognised as an embodied individual.

This mirrors findings drawn from interviews with customer service officers in a range of retail banks indicating that there is also a pronounced mismatch between retail bank employees' ethic of customer service and senior management's expectations about the level and type of service that should be provided (Cutcher 2004a,b). As one branch manager remarked: '[The] interaction that they have with this person on the other side of the counter is important. It is important for that person and you do get a confusion in your head about what is real and what is not and the way the bank perceives how that interaction should occur and how it really does occur.' All CSOs interviewed indicated that the contact with the customers was the most rewarding aspect of their work. One CSO remarked: 'It is the people that come in, you get to know them all on a name basis, and you get to know all about their life stories and everything.' Another commented that the most rewarding aspect of the work was 'to have people be happy, smile at you and call you by your name and you the same, to know that they are satisfied'. There is a clear temporal dimension to this type of customer service: caring about and relating to customers takes time.

While the range of service options available to customers in retail banking has greatly expanded over the past two decades, allowing customers to bank anywhere, any time, there is also evidence of a disconnection between the instrumental sales relationship being promoted by retail bank management and the desire of both customers and employees for a relationship of empathy and identification.

TIME, TECHNOLOGY AND SERVICE IN CALL CENTRES

Nowhere is this mismatch between the managerial preference for the concept of a collective, disembodied customer and the employees' desire to relate to an individual, embodied customer more apparent than in relation to routine call centre work. Unlike internet and ATM technology where customers 'self-serve', routine call centre operations are highly centralised, rationalised and closely managed (Holtgrewe et al. 2002).

While call centre operations vary widely in terms of size, industry location, labour market and the types of labour management policies and practices they implement, some generic similarities can be identified. For instance, emotional labour underpins much of the call centre labour process as customers interact with customer service representatives (CSRs) who provide detailed product or service information. However, such emotions are expressed within particularly constrained technological and physical environments. Among the most dominating visual features of the call centre workplace are motivational mobiles encouraging teamwork, commitment and quality performance displaying messages such as 'MOMENTS OF TRUTH'. Along with the mobiles are large suspended display boards that measure whether this expectation is realised. Electronic boards, for instance, indicate various statistics, including the number of calls feeding through the automated call distribution (ACD) system, production targets and queue times (van den Broek 2002).

Employees working with ACD systems face constant call queues where staff are required to enter a code outlining the reason for any absence from their workstations. Various expectations about performance are established. In many cases staff are expected to answer over 80 per cent of calls within 12 seconds and abandoned calls are benchmarked at around 3 per cent. 'Talk-time' represents the amount of time spent conversing directly with customers on the phone, and 'wrap-time' describes the amount of time for completing administrative tasks after the customer has hung up. In order to maximise talk time and deal with waiting customers, extended wrap-time is strongly discouraged.

The ACD technology, pervasive in most call centre operations, predicts the number of employees required to process customer demands each day. It facilitates the allocation of workloads and charts future workloads based on employee performance. The system allows management to measure performance and to recognise achievement and respond to under-achievement by assigning responsibility and accountability (van den Broek 2002). Each stage of the call is monitored, producing statistics that measure quantifiable aspects of each call. Qualitative aspects are also measured through remote call taping and review of call content. Results for sales campaigns, adherence to scripts and set procedure and call completion times are then displayed on whiteboards visible to managers and other CSRs. Such elaborate technology allows for continuous workflows that increase the speed and efficiency of the system and allows management to allocate time for tasks and set the overall pace of work. In short, the technology allows management to monitor the quantity as well as the quality of employee output (Taylor & Bain 1999).

Much of this monitoring relates to the temporal expectations placed on quick service and is facilitated by tight employee scripting. Central factors determining the quality of a call are disaggregated into three areas of verbal expression including how calls are opened, the manner in which the body of the call is performed, and how the call is finalised. The basic call requirements include assessment of phone manner, the attempt to build rapport, and courtesy to customers. Again, the emphasis is on certainty and predictability. While statistics measure both qualitative and quantitative factors, the latter often dominates. Pressure to get through calls quickly stems in part from the fact that a CSR's statistics influence his or her remuneration and promotional prospects within the firm. For instance, one interviewed CSR believed that the two team leaders and manager who interviewed him for promotion were looking mainly for quantitative productivity achievements.

The monitoring technology rotates around expectations about how time is allocated: the length of customer waiting time, time allocation per call including the time it takes to answer a call, time spent on the call, time taken to finalise issues off the phone and time spent away from workstations. Such technological sophistication intensifies the various tensions that take place during routine service interactions. For instance, customers don't like being kept waiting on the phone line and once calls are answered, they don't want to feel they are being hurried off the call. Yet for the call centre operator, dealing with each call quickly is a measure of good performance. Indeed key performance indicators (KPIs) are temporally significant. Call centre work shows how office technology has extended the time-frame in which a service can be delivered to retail bank customers; however, it has also reduced the length of the actual customer interaction while also facilitating the firm's ability to measure and control the labour process.

Existing research indicates that call centre recruitment gives preference to enthusiastic employees capable of building good customer rapport (Callaghan & Thompson 2002). This is surprising given the lack of time to empathise with customers in high-volume, routine call centre work. Employees recruited for their customer service skills express frustration with the managerial preoccupation with call times rather than completing tasks well in the course of their work. This tension is further highlighted by the customer service training that call centre employees receive. While induction training is used to develop qualitative measures such as customer empathy and rapport, displaying these emotional skills requires time and discretion. But such time and discretion is undermined by the nature and extent of surveillance and quantitative KPIs outlined above. As one respondent in Thompson and associates' (2004: 141) research noted:

> I thought that each customer was supposed to have individual needs, so you've got to give them time. But it's 'we need to bring those down, let's look at bringing your stats in line with everybody else's'. It's on top of you all the time . . . Basically, at the moment I feel like a machine. The personal touches have gone and they need to bring them back.

The undermining of 'personal touches' by managerially enforced output targets is reflected in surveys which reveal that many CSRs generally disliked performance statistics used to measure performance and were concerned with excessive workloads (Taylor & Bain 1999: 10; Deery et al. 2000: 8). CSRs' perception that the introduction of statistics was encouraging a 'worse service' has been reinforced by survey and interview evidence. One Australian call centre study revealed that while 98 per cent of CSRs thought customer service was important, 72 per cent did not believe that management had a high regard for service quality and 66 per cent thought they were inadequately rewarded for customer service (Deery et al. 2000: 12–13).

Clearly the nature of call centre work has in-built temporal dimensions which impact significantly on those who work in the industry and those who use its services. The rationale for call centre operations is based on efficiency and rationalisation and is operationalised through ACD technology, which has revolutionised retail banking services. However, various temporal tensions have been identified here relating to managerially enforced output targets and customer expectations about quality service. As indicated below, these tensions play out in various ways.

RESISTING TIME

High-volume call centre labour processes that primarily compete on cost will always find it difficult to deliver consistently high-quality customer service and to maintain employee morale. But while this picture may appear very bleak, call centre CSRs respond or variously resist many of the temporal constraints embedded in call centre labour processes. Indeed these are not one-way temporal transactions within firms because CSRs construct their own temporal limitations and expectations.

The most obvious negative response to the time pressures in call centre employment is to leave. Across the industry voluntary turnover rates average at around 22 per cent (Taylor & Bain 1999). In individual firms this can be as high as 75 per cent a year (van den Broek 2004). Much of the attrition rate is attributed to the relentless pace of the work and the work intensification facilitated by sophisticated employee monitoring technology described above.

Employees might also attempt to control the pace of their work by engaging in the regular practice of 'flicking'. For instance, employees might hang up on customers, redirect calls to other areas of the corporation or to other firms, or leave customers waiting for lengthy periods. While one response might involve cutting off or otherwise sabotaging customers, other responses could indulge their requests. Employees might exercise their own judgement and undertake additional tasks for customers outside the targets set by management. There are numerous situations where employees try to reclaim time, either for themselves or in combination with customers.

There is often a perception that the contemporary workplace is free of the temporal demands associated with traditional workplaces. Reflecting these sentiments, one call centre manager believed that 'one of the underlying things in this organisation is the youthfulness and the high energy levels. There are no clocks in the place . . . no-one signs in, no-one signs off, and people just work until the job is done.' However, this research suggests that while there may not be visible clocks ticking on the wall 'in this place' or many other workplaces, and while staff may no longer sign in or out, they do most certainly log into technology which has very sophisticated mechanisms for measuring temporal activities. This technology logs or tracks arrival and departure time as well as time spent away from their workstations, including precious time spent in the bathroom. Indeed this research shows that in 'low-skilled' high-volume call centre work, the transaction in temporal demands and expectations between manager and employee and between employee and customer are as strong as they have ever been. There are of course numerous contextual variables here. Call centre workflows and customer segmentation have a significant influence on the nature of employee discretion and time allocation, so that while low-skilled operators retain little control over workflows, other more skilled operators undertaking more complex tasks are more likely to control the pace and nature of their daily workflows (Batt 2000).

CONCLUSION

The research presented in this chapter contributes to our understanding of service work by highlighting the competing temporal dimensions of customer service in the retail banking industry. It shows that technological innovation in the banking sector has reinforced the idea that time thrift, time efficiency and work-time discipline are as much part of the contemporary workplace as they have been in the past. For service employees technological change and the varying temporal expectations and subjectivities of management and customers manifest in specific ways. While the temporal dimension of retail bank service has been extended to allow customers 24-hour access to their bank accounts from any location, for front-line service employees in bank branches and call centres, technological innovation has had various negative temporal consequences.

For bank branch employees, the shift from over-the-counter transactions with an emphasis on customer service to a highly rationalised and centralised sales culture emphasises the instrumental nature of the customer relationship and shows up a mismatch between managerial concepts of customer service and customers' expectations. Customer service employees can be caught between the temporal expectations of management, the customers they serve, and their own conceptions of 'timely' customer service. Whereas management might promote or hold to objective notions of time centred on a 'disembodied customer' (Korczynski 2002), with an emphasis on convenience via technological service options, employees and customers may be more likely to bring to the service interaction competing notions of time built around the concept of an individual, embodied customer.

Many front-line bank branch jobs have been transferred to the call centre industry, where we see a particular emphasis on speed and rationalised efficiency. Such speed and efficiency are reflected in a call centre discourse that evokes the pressures of time, such as 'talk-time' and 'wrap-time'. Indeed in call centres the temporality of service work has been intensified so that the concept of service work as a 'moment of truth' is more likely now to be measured in 'seconds of truth' where employees are continually reminded of the temporal dimension of their work. Within the context of rigid output targets, employees lament their inability to devote the time required to deliver quality customer service and to find ways to overcome such temporal constraints.

Customer service work is underpinned by subjective concepts of time that are not simply a response to external stimuli but arise from internal, emotive perceptions of and expectations about service and time. These internalised notions of time relate to Korczynski's notion of an 'embodied customer' and a desire on the part of both the front-line service employee and the customer for personalised and individualised service. Such a relationship reinforces the suggestion that notions of time and service are conflated and their relationship socially constructed (Epstein & Kalleberg 2001).

This examination of the way that time is constructed in retail banking technology, bank branches and call centres has highlighted the elastic and subjective nature of time (Mainemelis 2001). It has shown how the internal characteristics of the observer (in particular the customer) and the struggle and contest between actors in the service exchange shape notions of time (Fitzpatrick 2004). In customer service work, managerial attempts to control and construct time as absolute and objective are increasingly thwarted as the intervention of, and interactions between, front-line service employees and customers add further uncertainty and unpredictability to the service exchange.

References

Aleroff, C. & Knights, D. 2000, 'Quality time and the beautiful call'. Paper presented to the workshop Are Regimented Forms of Work Organisation Inevitable? Call Centres and the Chances for an Innovative Organisation of Service Work in Europe, Duisburg University, Germany, 2–3 December.

APRA (Australian Prudential Regulation Authority) 2002, *Points of Presence*, 30 June.

Barnes, P.C. 2001, 'People problems in call centres', *Management Services* 45(7): 30–1.

Batt, R. 2000, 'Strategic segmentation and frontline services: matching customers, employees and human resource systems', *International Journal of Human Resource Management* 11(3): 540–61.

Burrell, G. 1992, 'Back to the future: time and organization', in M. Reed & M. Hughes (eds) *Rethinking Organization: New Directions in Organization Theory and Analysis*, London: Sage, pp. 165–83.

Callaghan, G. & Thompson, P. 2002, 'We recruit attitude: the selection and shaping of routine call centre labour', *Journal of Management Studies* 39(2): 233–54.

Clark, P. 1990, 'Chronological codes and organizational analysis', in J. Hassard & D. Pym (eds) *The Theory and Philosophy of Organizations*, New York: Routledge, pp. 137–63.

Cutcher, L. 2004a, Banking on the customer: customer relations, employment relations and worker identity in the Australian retail banking industry. Unpublished PhD thesis, University of Sydney.

Cutcher, L. 2004b, 'The customer as ally: the role of the customer in the Finance Sector Unions' campaigning', *Journal of Industrial Relations* 46(3): 323–36.

Deery, S., Iverson, R. & Walsh, J. 2000, 'Work relationships in telephone call centres: understanding emotional exhaustion and employee withdrawal'. Paper presented to the International Industrial Relations Association Conference, Tokyo, May–June.

Deloitte Research 2000, *Myths vs Reality in Financial Services: What Your Customers Really Want*, pp. 1–38.

Epstein, C.F. & Kalleberg, A.L. 2001, 'Time and the sociology of work: issues and implications', *Work and Occupations* 28(1): 5–16.

Fitzpatrick, T. 2004, 'Social policy and time', *Time and Society* 13(2/3): 197–219.

Frenkel, S.J., Korczynski, M., Shire, K.A. & Tam, M. 1999, *On the Front Line: Organization of Work in the Information Economy*, Ithaca N.Y.: Cornell University Press.

Gittins, R. 2001, 'Bruising time in electronic fee-for-all', *Sydney Morning Herald*, 14 February 2001.

Holtgrewe, U., Kerst, C. & Shire, K. (eds) 2002, *Re-organising Service Work: Call Centres in Germany and Britain*, Aldershot: Ashgate.

Johnston, L. 2001, 'NetBank delivers net worth for CBA', *Australian Financial Review*, 7 March, p. 5.

Kessler, I. 2002, 'Call centres', *People Management* 7 February: 54.

Kitay, J. 2002, 'Continuity and change: employment relations practices in Australian retail banking', *Bulletin of Comparative Labour Relations* 45: 135–51.

Knights, D. & McCabe, D. 1998, 'What happens when the phone goes wild?: Staff, stress and spaces for escape in a BPR telephone banking work regime', *Journal of Management Studies* 35(2): 163–94.

Knights, D., Noble, F., Willmott, H. & Vurdubakis, T. 1999, 'Constituting the CSR: consumption, production and the labour process in call centres'. Paper presented to the 17th Annual International Labour Process Conference, Royal Holloway, University of London, 29–31 March.

Korczynski, M. 2002, *Human Resource Management in Service Work*, Basingstoke: Palgrave.

Korczynski, M., Shire, K., Frenkel, S. & Tam, M. 2000, 'Service work in consumer capitalism: customers, control and contradictions', *Work, Employment and Society* 14(4): 669–87.

Leidner, R. 1993, *Fast Food, Fast Talk: Service Work and the Routinization of Everyday Life*, Berkeley, Calif.: University of California Press.

McLachlan, R., Clark, C. & Monday, I. 2002, *Australia's Service Sector: A Study in Diversity*, Canberra: Productivity Commission.

Mainemelis, C. 2001, 'When the muse takes it all: a model for the experience of timelessness in organizations', *Academy of Management Review* 26(4): 548–66.

Pollard, J. 1999, 'Globalisation, regulation and the changing organisation of retail banking in the United States and Britain', in R. Martin (ed.) *Money and the Space Economy*, Chichester: John Wiley & Sons, pp. 49–70.

Probert, B., Whiting, K., & Ewer, P. 2000, *Pressure from All Sides: Life and Work in the Finance Sector*. Report Commissioned by the Finance Sector Union, Melbourne, pp. 1–58.

Rhodes, D. & Ackland, M. 2002, *Dare to be Different: Opportunities for Action in Financial Services*, Boston: Boston Consulting Group, pp. 1–13.

Rose, E. 2002, 'The labour process and union commitment within a banking services call centre', *Journal of Industrial Relations* 44(1): 40–61.

Sturdy, A. 2001, 'Servicing societies? Colonisation, control, contradiction and contestation', in A. Sturdy, I. Grugulis & H. Willmott (eds) *Customer Service: Empowerment and Entrapment*, Basingstoke: Palgrave, pp. 1–17.

Taylor, P. & Bain, P. 1999, 'An assembly line in the head: work and employee relations in the call centre', *Industrial Relations Journal* 30(2): 101–17.

Thompson, P. & McHugh, D. 1990, *Work Organisations: A Critical Introduction*, London: Macmillan.

Thompson, P., Callaghan, G. & van den Broek, D. 2004, 'Keeping up appearances: recruitment, skills and normative control in call centres', in S. Deery & N. Kinnie (eds) *Call Centres and Human Resource Management: A Cross National Perspective*, Basingstoke: Palgrave Macmillan, pp. 129–52.

van den Broek, D. 2002, 'Monitoring and surveillance in call centres: some responses from Australian employees', *Labour and Industry* 12(3): 43–59.

van den Broek, D. 2004, 'Globalising call centre capital: gender, culture and employee identity', *Labour and Industry* 14(3): 59–75.

PART TWO

SPACE

Mark Hearn and Grant Michelson

Foucault observed that 'time probably only appears as one of the possible games of distribution between the elements that are spread out in space'. Just as we are governed by our subjective constructions of time, we do not live or work in 'homogeneous and empty space', but in space 'laden with qualities' (Foucault 1998: 177). We inhabit social and private space invested with our values and relations of power – space reflecting, as Geertz (1973: 5) realised, the webs of cultural significance that we have spun for ourselves. Work is one of the most contested domains of our social space. As our contributors argue, the nature of union power, the movement of migrant labour, the international organisation of work and the operation of markets all reflect space as a distribution of labour market function and power, and the right of workers, unions and managers to contest these allocations. Just as the distribution of time is not only an operation of power directed down upon subjects, the distribution of space is an exchange between individuals and institutions. Space, Foucault suggested, perhaps best understood as 'relations of emplacement', reflects the negotiation of our place in the realm of work.

Prominent labour geographer Andrew Herod defines workers and capitalists as spatially embedded in their 'material geographies'. Constrained by their embeddedness, workers are nonetheless '*active* social and spatial actors', engaged in 'intense political struggles to structure the geography of capitalism' in service to their rights and needs (Herod 2002). In their chapter, Rae Cooper and Bradon Ellem assert a dynamic role for workers and unions in the contested terrain of the Australian workplace. Drawing on 'the human geographers and the industrial relations researchers who see unions as agents of their own history', they argue that unions are at once geographic and strategic agents that interact with and shape the spaces and institutions around them.

Cooper & Ellem are also alert to the spatial and structural constraints that operate on workers and union strategies. The current 'union crisis' of declining industrial power and falling membership since the 1980s is exacerbated by weaknesses within, and divisions between, union structures as well as the difficulty of securing change within individual unions. 'The geography of union power' in postwar Australia had been specifically embedded in full-time male employment in large workplaces in manufacturing, mining and transport; the new jobs of the knowledge and information age are, by contrast, 'fragmented by time and space: casual work, part-time work, and indeed by jobs in which the legal nature of the employment relationship was unclear, such as outwork, sub-contracting, franchises'. There are now scattered material geographies with little tradition of union coverage, disconnected from the values of solidarity that unionists had once cultivated in shared work space.

In Chapter 8, Dimitria Groutsis argues that labour geographers take us to a deeper analysis of the phenomenon of global migrant labour by focusing on spatial embeddedness. 'Labour geographers suggest that social groups shape the spaces and are party to or participants in negotiating and renegotiating the entry points into particular spaces. That is, workers are central to the creation of labour market spaces and influence the actions of stakeholders as a result of spaces forged.' Yet Groutsis notes that there has been little rigorous analysis of the insights offered by labour geographers on the labour market experience of migrants, although the number of mobile labour force participants has more than doubled in the last 25 years. In 2002, the International Labour Organisation noted that there were approximately 120 million migrant workers globally, 'flowing from different countries and workplaces bound for a myriad countries and workplaces'. Groutsis argues that where human capital theory and labour market segmentation theory focus on labour demand and labour supply in isolation and at the cost of one or the other, 'labour geographers establish how particular spatial arrangements emerge by focusing on political/institutional, material and social forces while drawing our attention explicitly to the importance of space as a defining factor in shaping the labour market outcomes for workers'.

Exploring the spatial perspective of international work and management in Chapter 9, Susan McGrath-Champ takes the example of China to challenge the idea of 'global homogenisation' of work and management that is said to be a characteristic of global capital. A key to this challenge is to understand that geography, our sense of 'place and space', is not an 'optional extra but is integral to, an active element in, all social life and activity'. Referring to a classic expression of global capital in our time – the transfer of manufacturing production from a 'first world' economy to China – McGrath-Champ provides a spatial analysis of an expatriate manager dispatched to China to establish a plant that will supply the manager's home market:

> This 'going to a new place' is spatial. Experiencing a new place and adapting to it (or not) is geographical. The expatriate is a social agent, bringing with him or her attributes and experiences ('culture') from the home environment, and mixing them with the new environment. He or she is also a spatial agent: different places 'meet' through this encounter. Over time there stands to be some change to the receiving and sending localities. There may be some heightened awareness of what things are like in the expatriate's home country plus implementation of some of the ways of doing business that are transferred from there. The expatriate also conveys knowledge of the host country back to the home country – its social, regulatory and institutional milieu, the impediments and opportunities that these entail. A further spatial dimension is evident in the control mechanisms conveyed over distance, as is the sale of goods back into the home market.

'Geography', McGrath-Champ concludes, 'thoroughly permeates organisational, managerial and working life'; and this embeddedness in the *particularity* of spatial experience undermines simplistic notions of global homogenisation, as myriad values and lessons are exchanged between expatriate, host country and home country.

In Chapter 10, Mark Westcott argues that the analysis of work and its relationship with labour, product and financial markets can be significantly enriched by drawing on the research of economic and labour geographers.

> Marshalling the concepts of space and scale can assist in removing determinism and reactivating agency in studies of markets and work relations. Markets are produced in particular spaces and their shape reflects the contingent interaction of processes in that space. The concept of space grounds market development and market influences in particularly material geographies, and perhaps more importantly it provides a nexus between different market spheres.

The 'complex interconnections' of social agents – managers and workers – might also be better understood: 'appreciation of space and scale can also reinforce the social agency of actors and their capacity to structure and restructure market forms and influence market conditions'. Drawing on Jamie Peck's (1996) research, Westcott argues that these complex interconnections must also focus on the particularity of the market. Labour markets 'should be seen as the particular spatial location in which social processes are played out'.

Herod and his colleagues (2003: 188–9) have previously argued that 'conflicts over the fundamental spatial constitution of capitalism are central to how industrial relations are conducted and imagined', although 'the engagement between labour geographers and industrial relations practitioners is still largely waiting to happen'. The contributions in this section of *Rethinking Work* demonstrate the rich analysis that may be developed from an engagement between the value-laden categories of work and space.

References

Foucault, M. 1998, 'Different spaces', in M. Foucault, *Aesthetics, the Essential Works*, vol. 2, London: Penguin, pp. 175–85.

Geertz, C. 1973, *The Interpretation of Cultures*, New York: Basic Books.

Herod, A. 2002, 'Towards a more productive engagement: industrial relations and economic geography meet', *Labour and Industry* 13(2): 5–17.

Herod, A., Peck, J. & Wills, J. 2003, 'Geography and industrial relations', in P. Ackers & A. Wilkinson (eds) *Understanding Work and Employment: Industrial Relations in Transition*, Oxford: Oxford University Press, pp. 176–92.

Peck, J. 1996, *Work-place: The Social Regulation of Labour Markets*, New York: Guilford Press.

CHAPTER SEVEN

UNION POWER
Space, Structure, and Strategy

Rae Cooper and Bradon Ellem

For most of the 'boom years' from soon after the end of the Second World War to the economic crises of the 1970s, Australian unions, like those in so many other market societies, enjoyed high levels of membership and apparently entrenched power. In this world, different from the old capitalism which preceded it and the new one which has followed it, the social institutions that made 'industrial relations' were consolidated after what had been a much less certain period before the war. Collective bargaining and workers' unions were central elements of this world, but today they are both under threat. Membership has collapsed from postwar highs; individualism tramples over collectivism.

This chapter sets out an argument about the present union crisis. Contrary to much orthodoxy, we argue that Australian unionism has undergone immense change in the recent past. Many things point to this: the corporatist Accord with the national Labor government, the rationalisation of unions through amalgamation, the adoption of organising strategies. The membership base has been transformed, such that over 42 per cent of all unionists are women, a figure more or less in line with the gender division of the paid workforce. Unlike other countries, there are no ethnic and racial groups conspicuously excluded from the union movement. Nevertheless, union power and membership remain, quite clearly, in crisis.

The chapter draws on the human geographers and the industrial relations researchers who see unions as agents of their own history and argue that unions themselves hold the key to their survival. As suggested by others in this book (for example Westcott in Chapter 10), most industrial relations research pays little attention to geography: it takes places and scales as given. Geographers, though, emphasise how these concepts have real political purchase, how local labour markets and local regulatory regimes have become more important with globalisation and how workers and unions, like companies and states, find, invent and argue about the scales of action that suit them best (Ellem & Shields 1999; Herod & Wright 2002). In the current environment it is tempting to see unions as the passive victims of external change. But researchers who have looked 'inside' unions have given us a different perspective on workers' organisations. Rather than being predetermined by the union context, a range of forces – both inside and outside unions – shape these strategies (see Cooper 2002a). Drawing these bodies of work together, we argue that unions are at once geographic and strategic agents which interact with and shape the spaces and institutions around them.

In this light, we suggest that the changes that unions are making have, in the main, been at the national scale but that at other scales and sites there has been less change. There are two overlapping elements to our argument. First, we explain it through changes in geographies of work over the last 20 years: both economic globalisation and regulatory decentralism pose strategic and spatial challenges to nationally scaled labour organisations. Second, union crisis is exacerbated by weaknesses within, and divisions between, union structures as well as the difficulty of securing change within individual unions.

We look first at the nature of union power and strategy over the last generation, then examine the dimensions of the current crisis in union power. We then chart changes at the national scale and examine two studies which illustrate some of the more novel developments that are taking place and the obstacles to their success.

POWER AND STRATEGY IN THE BOOM YEARS

The sources of Australian union power were perhaps clearer after the long boom was over than during it. However, the indicators of that power were obvious enough. Aggregate union membership and union density (the proportion of the workforce belonging to a union) grew throughout that boom, despite the failure of the unions' political wing, the Australian Labor Party (ALP), to win national office for 23 years after 1949. Unions were, formally at least, encouraged by the state and recognised by employers as the collective voice of workers.

By 1954, union density was on one count 61 per cent, its all-time high. Membership sometimes fell, in the mid-1950s and early 1960s, but these setbacks merely reflected mild, temporary recessions (Bain & Price 1980: 121–5; Peetz 1998: 24–30). Many things that might have undermined unionism, like prosperity or Cold War factionalism, had no such impact. Weak areas, like the public sector in general and nursing and teaching in particular, became union strongholds – often militant ones (Rawson 1986: 1–29). However, union coverage and power was uneven, fractured across space and between the sexes. For example, when union density was at its national peak in the mid-1950s, Queensland's rate was over 70 per cent (with State legislation delivering 'absolute preference' to unionists); the rate in New South Wales was about the national average and all other States were below. There were also significant gender differences. At the 1954 peak, male density was 65.3 per cent, female, 41.8 per cent. For most of the 20th century, South Australia, Western Australia and Tasmania had much greater differences between male and female rates than was the case in the other States (Bain & Price 1980: 126–8).

Despite some spatial unevenness, national union membership and density were impressive, above those in many similar countries. Observers therefore sought explanations specific to Australia. The obvious place to look was the regulatory framework of compulsory conciliation and arbitration which, for most of the 20th century, required employers to recognise unions and apply a common rule. The best known of these explanations turned the argument about the success of Australian unions on its head. Howard (1977) suggested that Australian unions were not real unions at all but merely 'industrial cosmetics', reliant for their very existence on the state. Union power was more apparent than real. This analysis rightly pointed to the importance of the state in shaping union structure and strategy, but it downplays pre-arbitration union traditions and sustained challenges to arbitration from workplace militants (Sheldon 1993; Cooper 2002b; Cooper & Patmore 2002). Union strategy in fact varied over time and space.

This concentration on the relationship between unions and the state also opened up ways to understand union strategy. Australian unions, like unions elsewhere, drew power from recognition by employers. This of course came at a cost, suppressing militant challenges to workers' subordination (Hyman 1975 has the best summary of this contradiction). With arbitration and recognition, however, the sharp edge of wage competition was blunted, especially in industries and occupations protected by trade restrictions or more natural product market barriers, and unions were more secure than in many other countries.

Accepted wisdom about the period underplays other vital aspects of union–state relations, particularly the full (male) employment that underwrote the 'postwar settlement'. This was not an uncomplicated success for labour. Without the threat of unemployment, employers and the state required legislative and ideological measures to control union militancy and wages. The settlement also locked in arbitration's male breadwinner paradigm, one that with a few notable exceptions male union officials did not challenge (see D'Aprano 2001 for a recent overview). If the gender order was not challenged, much else was. With the influence of the Communist Party at its peak immediately after the war, there was an intense struggle over radical schemes of postwar reconstruction around public ownership and practically every aspect of union strategy, not only in the male blue-collar workforce (Sheridan 1989) but also in many areas of female-dominated employment (Ellem 1999). This struggle, cast by one author as 'arbitrationist' against 'mobilisational', continued throughout the boom between and within unions (Bramble 2001). It must also be remembered that many of the mobilisational unions were concerned with far more than the wages and conditions of 'bread and butter' unionism. They were committed by deed as well as word to the struggles of workers under apartheid and in various colonies, and to anti-war and environmental campaigns (see for example Burgmann & Burgmann 1998; McDonald & McDonald 1998). In short, union strategy was *not* shaped solely by the state.

With arbitration and boom, most unions developed particular geographies of power and strategy, serving the interests of full-time 'breadwinning' males. These unions were typically constructed as national or State-based organisations, rather than local or workplace ones. Historically, unions were structured around crafts, occupations or industries. Changes in the scale of their operations (shifting between State and federal jurisdictions) reflected changes in political structures more broadly, and perceptions of immediate threats and opportunities. But *within* these scalar shifts, union structure remained stable. The workplace was privileged over community, the paid worker over family. There were some exceptions to this, but analysis after analysis pointed to a weak workplace presence (Callus et al. 1991; Peetz 1998). As the world began to change in the 1970s, many union officials were more at home in the lawyer's office and the courtroom than they were in the workplace, let alone with the unorganised workers.

Table 7.1 *Union membership and density, 1976–2003*

Year	Members millions	Density %
1976	2.51	51.0
1982	2.57	49.5
1986	2.59	45.6
1988	2.54	41.6
1990	2.66	40.5
1992	2.51	39.6
1993	2.38	37.6
1994	2.28	35.0
1995	2.25	32.7
1996	2.19	31.1
1997	2.11	30.3
1998	2.04	28.1
1999	1.88	25.7
2000	1.90	24.7
2001	1.90	24.5
2002	1.83	23.1
2003	1.86	23.0

UNDOING UNION POWER

Union membership continued to grow until the early 1990s. By 1992, however, membership was falling. In that year the total dropped to 2 508 800, having been 2 659 600 in 1990 (no figures were collected for 1991). Union *density* had been declining for much longer – on one set of figures, since 1976. In that year it had stood at 51 per cent; by 1992 it was 39.6 per cent. When raw numbers started to fall, density fell precipitously. By 1996 when the conservative coalition of the Liberal and National parties won office, membership was down to 1 943 000 and density was 31.1 per cent. The most recent figures, for August 2003, show membership at 1 866 700 and density at 23 per cent (ABS 1977–96, 1997–2004). Trends were broadly similar between States too, though varying over time due to anti-union legislation at that scale (Peetz 1998: 100–2). In three of the last four years, however, membership totals have actually risen, prompting the suggestion, which the next section explores in detail, that some of the more recent union strategies may at last be biting (ABS 1977–96, 1997–2004; see Table 7.1).

The standard explanations for union decline are familiar enough (for an early overview see Griffin & Svensen 1996; for the most comprehensive analysis see Peetz 1998). Here we outline the major factors – changes in the nature of work and the workforce and a sustained assault by many employers along with legislative change – showing how each posed spatial and strategic problems for union power in Australia, as in so many other countries. Combined, their impact was, and remains, all but crushing, often confounding the changes in strategy and structure that unions do make.

As the structure of work changed, unions took a double hit, losing members as the number of jobs fell in their heartlands of manufacturing, mining and transport. The impact was more than quantitative, for these were often the sites of the most militant unions, those that had been leaders in wage campaigns and in driving radical definitions of union purpose. At the same time, employment grew in areas of union weakness like hospitality, information technologies and the like. More than this, it was clearly the case that the sort of job being lost – the full-time, male variety – was that on which union strategies had been based. The new jobs – casual and part-time work – were fragmented by time and space, and they were jobs such as outwork, subcontracting, franchises in which the nature of the employment relationship was at law unclear. In recent years, the terrain has become still more problematic for unions, with membership also declining in heartland industries and occupations (Cole et al. 2002).

These changes also revealed that the geography of union power in the long boom had been quite specific and showed just how challenging it would be to hold any ground now, far less win any more for labour. It was the larger workplaces that were the most organised and the more likely to remain so (Callus et al. 1991; Morehead et al. 1997; Peetz 1998). Conversely, not only were smaller workplaces less likely to be unionised but there were, it appeared, an ever increasing number of them. As workplaces shrank and as hours of work for full-time employees expanded, the logistical difficulties involved in organising and representing workers only expanded. As the major cities of Sydney and Melbourne grew, so worksites became more fragmented. This was not the geographically concentrated workforce from which unionism had sprung in the 19th century (see Savage 1998 on the geography of organising).

Just as the nature of work has changed, so has the regulation of that work. Employers and governments have constructed arguments in terms of what geographers call the politics of scale, which depict local and national regulatory change as an unavoidable corollary of all-powerful 'globalisation' (Sadler & Fagan 2004). The link between this and the fate of unions lies in regulatory change, 'unmaking' arbitration, tariff protection and the postwar commitment to full employment.

Clothed in the term 'deregulation', successive national governments set out to reduce trade barriers, to open up Australia to global finance – and then to re-regulate the labour market (Callus & Buchanan 1993; Ronfeldt & McCallum 1995; ACIRRT 1999; Watson et al. 2003). The term 'deregulation' was useful to its proponents, fitting snugly with the rhetorical power of unstoppable globalisation and the transformation of other markets, in products, services and finance. Labour market change shifted the geographies of regulation, as the common industrial relations term 'decentralism' suggests and as the term 'individualisation' implies. Since 1996, in particular, these changes have led to the 'decollectivisation' of industrial relations – cause and effect of declining union power.

The relationship between unions and the state began to change in 1987 with the 'managed decentralism' of a two-tier arbitration system, in which major wage increases could be won only by productivity offsets (McDonald & Rimmer 1989). The Business Council of Australia and other employer groups mounted political pressure for new bargaining regimes and for legislative change (Dabscheck 1993). After being put under pressure from all sides, the Australian Industrial Relations Commission introduced the Enterprise Bargaining Principle in the second (October) national wage case of 1991. This was still largely union-based but Labor's *Industrial Relations Reform Act 1993* introduced a (collective) non-union bargaining stream of Enterprise Flexibility Agreements. This is not to say that enterprise bargaining was 'a fait accompli imposed upon trade unions' (Briggs 2001: 27). A number of key unions and the Australian Council of Trade Unions itself now believed that union-based enterprise bargaining could alleviate wage pressures and deliver workplace efficiencies.

After the Coalition Liberal–National parties won power in 1996, however, it was clear that the new government intended to go much further in winding back union power. This kind of government-led anti-unionism was hardly novel. In the USA under President Reagan, the federal government took on the unions, destroying PATCO, the once powerful union of air-traffic controllers, in 1981. In Britain, the National Union of Mineworkers was broken by Thatcher's Conservative government in 1984–85. The print unions suffered a similar fate, all but destroyed by Rupert Murdoch with the full support of the

government. The newly elected Australian government set out to promote not only non-union enterprise bargaining but also individual contracts. The *Workplace Relations Act 1996* introduced heavy fines for
'unprotected' industrial action, stripped back awards to only 20 matters, made union access to workplaces more difficult and reduced the
power of the Commission to settle industrial disputes. Prime Minister
John Howard made it clear that things had changed: 'the goals of meaningful reforms, more jobs and higher wages, cannot be achieved unless
the union monopoly over the bargaining processes in our industrial relations system is dismantled' (quoted in van Barneveld & Nassif 2003).
A century of law and practice which assumed that the collective was
the norm was over.

These changes in legislation have had precisely the impact intended:
the substantial reduction of union power. That power has of course been
fragmented across space – after all, that is what enterprise bargaining
does – at precisely the same time that union resources to control and
unify space has been diminished by lack of resources. The traditional
system of union-based awards declined from 67.6 per cent of all agreements in 1990 to just 23.2 per cent in 2000 (DWR/OEA 2002). Campbell (2001: 19) has used similar figures to argue that at least two-thirds
of Australian workers, a considerably greater proportion in the private
sector, have their wages set by individual arrangements of one sort or
another, what he calls 'management unilateralism'.

With arbitration cut back, unions' ties with the state were frayed.
With the ALP in opposition since 1996, they were thinner still. If
the ALP's national political weakness reduced union power, it also
altered the union movement's internal power relationships. Under the
Accord, the ACTU enjoyed unrivalled power both over and for its affiliates, with the ACTU's structural engagement with the state delivering
unique power to the national peak body (Briggs 2002; see also Brigden
2000).

Power derived from employer recognition also collapsed, although
this trend had begun well before 1996. Many employers sought to control unionism or eradicate it entirely from the workplace. Even in the
1980s, at the height of the national Accord, a series of bitter local disputes savaged unionism, very often in its heartlands. From abattoirs in
the Northern Territory, to manufacturers in Melbourne, plumbers across
Sydney's building sites, and State electricity workers in Queensland and
iron ore miners at Robe River in Western Australia's Pilbara, unions
were besieged.

If the most obvious sources of union power – membership levels, state support and employer recognition – were being eroded, so were expressions of that power. Industrial action, measured by the number of working days lost and the number of workers involved, has declined substantially over the past two decades (ABS 2003). Such disputes as have arisen have tended to be defensive in nature, aiming to minimise defeat, secure entitlements, stop legislative change or ward off specific anti-union approaches of employers (Gorman 1996; Wiseman 1998; Cooper 2003a).

How have the many dimensions of this hostile environment affected unions? David Peetz, the researcher who has done most to explain the collapse of union membership in Australia, has suggested that employer practices were at least as significant a contributor to membership decline as was structural change in the labour market (Peetz 1995). Combined with legislative changes that sought to weaken union influence and decollectivise employment relations, Peetz (1998: 31–4) argues that there has been nothing less than a 'paradigm shift' in the determination of union membership. To this we would add that as the geographies of work and unionism have changed, unions have had the added burden of trying to do ever more with ever fewer resources in the last decade. We now turn to an examination of changes in union strategy.

POWER AND STRATEGY IN CRISIS

It seems an obvious point to make that Australian unions have been slow in responding to the massive environmental changes discussed earlier in the chapter, given that the crisis is ongoing, if not worsening. But it is our contention that if we look closely at union strategies in recent years, there *are* signs of reappraisal of union action, structures and policy. This section presents an analysis of union renewal across a diverse range of workplaces, discussing the activities of unions organising very different workers and implementing strategy at various scales. In so doing we uncover the challenges facing trade unions, the responses of unions to this environment, and the implications that union action has for our understanding of union power and strategy. The cases discussed here demonstrate that both peak union bodies and individual unions have attempted to chart a more autonomous course, making themselves less dependent on the state and employers for their power.

Echoing similar debates across the globe, Australian unionists have since the mid-1990s engaged in a vital debate about the need to shift priorities, to rework structures and to change strategies. The source of these changes lay in the beleaguered union movement in the USA. It was from here, with union density at 15 per cent, that the 'organising model' emerged. The debate in the USA, as elsewhere, hinged on the dichotomy between 'organising' and 'servicing' and the need to adopt one at the expense of the other. In Australia, as in the USA and later in the UK, national peak union bodies have driven an organising agenda. Many unions have now come to accept that 'organising' will provide the spark for union revitalisation. They have argued that the 'transactional' relationship between union members and union organisation engendered in the 'servicing' approach to unionism should be cast off. This approach to unionism is described in a bureaucratic fashion where the role of union officials was as the guardians of union resources, strategies and interests. Unions have been encouraged to adopt the organising mode of operation, which, in contrast to the servicing approach, presents a 'transformational' vision for union activity centred on growing membership, building union workplace activism and enhancing internal democracy. The organising model also calls on unions to forge alliances with particular communities which might in turn sow the seeds of 'community unionism' (Tattersall 2004). These modes of union action hold out the promise of building union power in the 21st century. This is largely because of the focus on the 'internal' resources, in the form of active membership, rather than cooperation with employers or the state. It is here, in the relationships between grassroots communities and national union leaderships, and then in the tensions with governments and capital, that new forms of unionism may emerge.

The Accord between the ACTU and the federal Labor government, which lasted from 1983 to 1996, delivered unprecedented power to the national union federation. However, with the election of the Howard Coalition government, the derived power of the ACTU unravelled very quickly. This, in tandem with the massive changes in the nature and the regulation of work, left the ACTU with a much diminished ability to exert influence for affiliates and their members and a weaker authority to direct affiliate behaviour. In these two very different power contexts the ACTU released two documents, which can be viewed as the signature strategies of, first, Accord unionism and, second, unionism in a decollectivised environment.

In 2003 the ACTU published a document entitled *Future Strategies: Unions Working for a Fairer Australia* (ACTU 2003), which articulated the council's vision for union renewal. The title of this policy paper echoed a contribution of the ACTU some 16 years earlier, in the form of *Future Strategies for the Trade Union Movement* (ACTU 1987). There are certain similarities between the documents, apart from the obvious similarity of their names. Both identify a crisis in the union environment and, in response, argue for an urgent reorientation in union practice, structures and priorities. *Future Strategies (Mk I)* suggests that 'unions cannot ignore the mounting pressure for further change. The question is not whether the movement can adapt and respond but whether it can adapt at a sufficient rate not just to ensure its survival but to promote further growth' (ACTU 1987: 1).

Similarly, the chief premise of *Future Strategies (Mk II)* is that, due to the massive and negative changes in the environment for unionism, fundamental changes in union practice are required. The document seeks, in the words of the ACTU president and secretary, to 'accelerate change and generate policy ideas' (ACTU 2003: 1) for national, State and workplace unionism. Otherwise, the two documents could not be more unlike. One seeks to build union power by restructuring and the provision of services to members, while the other draws on organising by new member organising and member activism as the means to rebuild unionism, shaping new geographies of union power.

Future Strategies (I) set out the ACTU's ambitious plan to restructure unions by a wave of mergers. The amalgamation of the then 326 mainly occupationally based unions into 20 'super unions' was heralded by the ACTU leadership as the means to remove the duplication of union services, organising and research functions which had arisen due to the multiplicity of occupational, industry and craft-based unions. Super-unions, it was argued, would effect economies of scale within the labour movement, free up resources for the better servicing of existing members and release resources to be directed at building membership in poorly organised and non-unionised sectors of the economy (ACTU 1987: 15).

The amalgamation program began in earnest in the early 1990s. In an unprecedented reorganisation of the union movement between 1991 and 1994, over 120 mergers took place. In the five years between June 1989 and June 1994, the number of unions in Australia nearly halved, decreasing from 299 to 157 (ABS 1995). By the end of 1994 the total number had halved and the number of large federally registered unions had fallen from 134 to 52 (ABS 1995); by the mid-1990s, 98 per cent of the members of ACTU affiliates were members of the largest 20 unions (ABS 1995). Considering that union numbers have remained fairly constant throughout the last century, this was a considerable feat (Griffin 1991). These were certainly spectacular results in terms of restructuring the union movement, but they were less impressive on other measures; as a response to declining membership the amalgamations were an abject failure. As detailed earlier, during the period in which amalgamations were in full swing, from 1991, membership decline did not abate, it actually *accelerated*.

Future Strategies (I) advocated that unions pursue strategies for attracting members and maintaining a relationship with them, based on the provision of union services to members. It argued that enhancing the services provided to members was the best way for unions to ensure the viability of the organisation and member relationship, for example: 'members need to have a perception that the union has something to offer in terms of service. For that to happen the union actually needs to have something to offer' (ACTU 1987: 17).

It almost goes without saying that these nationally scaled policies, *Future Strategies (I)*, or Accord unionism more generally, failed to reinvigorate Australian unionism. Once the Labor Party lost office, and in the absence of power sources external to the union movement, it became clear just how vulnerable unions were. In this context the ACTU developed a new strategy, heavily influenced by the debate about 'organising', and in 2003 released *Future Strategies (II)* setting out this strategy.

Whereas its predecessor advocated union restructuring and centralised service provision, *Future Strategies (II)* emphasised activist organising strategies as the key to union power. It would be wrong to suggest that this was the first time that the national peak body advocated 'organising' as the key strategy for renewal. Indeed from 1999 onward the ACTU's secretary had attempted through various initiatives and policy developments to take organising into the 'mainstream' of peak and individual unionism (Cooper 2000, 2003b). *Future Strategies (II)* reiterated this commitment to organising and, crucially, placed workplace organisation centre stage. It argued that an active delegate is the single most important factor affecting union density, activity and effectiveness in the workplace (ACTU 2003: 22).

Accordingly, unions were encouraged to recruit and educate thousands more workplace representatives. In addition, *Future Strategies (II)* advocated that affiliates should devote unprecedented resources to new member organising to involve members in a debate about 'the direction and priority' of their unions and to adopt a more strategic approach to building membership and the execution of union campaigns.

This radically different agenda could not be further from the prescriptions of *Future Strategies (I)*. It holds more promise for unions attempting to build power in the decollectivised industrial relations environment of the mid-2000s. Drawing on the internal resources of an active membership offers more hope for union revival in this context than legislated or negotiated preference, which are unlikely to be forthcoming, or the structural change or service provision strategy of Accord unionism. This strategy represents a fundamental shift in the scale of union action. But it is not without its contradictions. For instance, while *Future Strategies (II)* is a nationally driven strategy, it can only be implemented by unions in their offices and their members' workplaces. Without union action at this local scale, *Future Strategies (II)* remains a symbol of change in the orientation and vision of a weakened ACTU.

What impact has this urging towards change had on the structures, strategies and ideologies of individual affiliate unions to date? How have the national and other scales of action intermeshed? There is certainly evidence of 'institutional sclerosis' in some quarters, with many unions preferring to continue with practices of old (Pocock 1998: 17). Yet some Australian unions have chosen to radically alter their structures, cultures and organising tactics in an attempt to revitalise themselves. What follows is a discussion of the reorientation under way in some unions which provide glimpses of a new form of union power and strategy. We analyse the recent experience of one national union, the Community and Public Sector Union (CPSU) and one local campaign in the de-unionised Pilbara region of Western Australia. These studies focus on different spaces and strategies as unions attempt to build or maintain their power. This allows us to explore two very different union worlds: one is public sector, white-collar, urban; the other, private sector, blue-collar, country.

The CPSU has recently attempted to reinvigorate itself in an extremely hostile environment (this account is drawn from Cooper 2001). Starting from 1997, the union attempted to transform itself from a service-focused organisation to an 'organising union'. After the Howard government was first elected in 1996, the CPSU underwent a period of organisational shock. Massive membership losses resulted from wholesale redundancies in the core area of the union's coverage in the Commonwealth public sector. Management took full advantage of the provisions of the new *Workplace Relations Act 1996* and shut the union out of bargaining, refusing organisers access to workplaces and removing activists' rights to undertake union activity in the workplace. For 18 months the union reeled under the pressure of this changed environment. Organisers described the enormous pressure placed on them to bring new member forms in, stress levels were high, and the union's leadership was forced, due to declining income, to issue redundancy notices to a number of organising staff. In essence the union's staff was doing *more* with *less*, as are so many other unions faced with changes in the nature of work and the scale of regulation.

In this hostile environment, it was extremely difficult for the officers and leaders of the union to come up with strategies to turn the union's fortunes around. In 1997, however, officials decided that moving to adopt organising unionism was the answer. Over the next three years they enacted massive organisational and cultural change. There were three key changes in this process: first, moving away from a 'recruitment' and towards an organising approach to building membership; second, redefining the role of the organiser; and finally, adopting what is dubbed here a more strategic approach to building membership. Each of these changes represented a fundamental strategic reorientation.

The process of replacing recruitment with organising as a means of bringing new members into the CPSU was as much a question of changing ideology as it was of changing campaigning tactics. Recruitment, the traditional means by which Australian unions have built membership, involved a union official convincing an individual non-member of the merits of union membership, in a sales-like manner. Instead, the union chose to adopt a more active organising approach that involved members, rather than officials, recruiting non-members, active campaigning around collective workplace issues, and the nurturing of workplace union organisation. The union's organisers adopted new methods that emphasised activist development.

The role of the organiser within the CPSU was turned on its head. Whereas once an organiser performed mostly servicing functions such as advocacy in industrial tribunal cases and bargaining with employers, in the new regime, the role of the organiser was focused more squarely on organising. Organisers focused more clearly on non-union spaces, while stimulating activism in areas where the union had an established membership base. This shift necessitated a reduction in the large servicing workload of officials, and involved the introduction of State and federal union call centres, staffed by dedicated organisers, to deal with individual grievances as they arose.

This approach to organising also included a radical restructuring of the spatiality of the organisation. Faced with massive change around it, the union moved to reorganise itself such that it mirrored the structures of its members' workplaces. The CPSU moved away from geographically based branches (that is, based in the States), and adopted instead a structure based on national sections in line with designated industry sections. This change is arguably the most radical structural change in any Australian union in the post-amalgamation era. This drove other internal changes, including strategic planning of organising campaigns and new performance management of staff to incorporate the newly defined role of the organiser. As in other unions, the organising model has focused energies at the workplace, but in the CPSU's case, there has also been a reworking of the entire geography of the national structure.

National union strategies, then, led to thoroughgoing institutional change in one union. They have also had profound local implications in particular places. Nowhere is this clearer than in the Pilbara's iron ore mines and ports. In few places are the spatial and logistical challenges to unions greater. For a long time, the Pilbara has been the site of controversial industrial relations. From Robe River in the 1980s to Hamersley Iron in the next decade, it was the site of massive disputes that heralded a wider and sustained attack on unions across the country.

This industry appears quintessentially global: controlled by the planet's two biggest multinational resource companies, BHP-Billiton and Rio Tinto, selling into export markets and raising capital across the world (this account is drawn from Ellem 2003, 2004). But its resource – ore – is locally specific and therefore fixes in place the geography of production. This means that national, State and local forms of politics and regulation are crucial for the managers in these global organisations. The companies appear to have one enduring weakness, their immobility; the domestic places, the communities, around their worksites may come to be as problematical as the worksites, for these spaces are, for workers, not simply mining dormitories, but 'places in which to live, places in which they have considerable individual and collective cultural investment' (Beynon & Hudson 1993: 182). In this setting and with the majority of the industry de-unionised after major struggles earlier, BHP's Iron Ore Division moved to de-unionise its operations in November 1999. The managers sent out offers of individual contracts, contracts that would make union membership of no use to workers.

The unions were divided among themselves and weak on the ground, but they regrouped. This renewal drew on the logistical support and the organising principles of the ACTU as workplace structures were rebuilt, delegates were trained and unions worked together. In some senses, a strategy driven by a peak union that calls for greater powers for local delegates appears inherently contradictory. In this case, however, the contradictions produced a powerful synthesis. Local traditions of activism and community interaction were rekindled. Divisions between unions were buried and a combined union structure emerged. The unions lost nearly half their members straight away but held the line after that. When a new contract offer came along in April 2001, there was practically no take-up. In November, the State Industrial Relations Commission granted award workers a 20 per cent wage increase. The unions had regrouped.

News of these changes leaked back to the Rio Tinto sites elsewhere in the Pilbara, especially those of its wholly owned subsidiary, Hamersley Iron. Changes to State laws saw the company offer its workers a non-union collective agreement under the national *Workplace Relations Act* to replace abolished individual State agreements. But the Hamersley workers voted 'no'. The unions had run a campaign with little time and few resources and now they combined with the ACTU support to build the sort of union the workers had told them they wanted. They wanted a one-union site, with local community issues placed alongside workplace ones. Once again, local traditions, and, most markedly, the overlap of workplace and community issues, were to the fore. In terms of thinking about union changes, this was rather different from what happened in the CPSU. True, there was a national strategy but few foresaw the breadth of the changes, the emergence of a *de facto* single-union form with a strong community focus. This came neither from 'above' nor from 'below', but from the intersection of these scales in a geographically distinct setting.

Thus, in a non-union site, there emerged a new form of unionism, the Pilbara Mineworkers Union (PMU). Building the union from the town into the mine sites, from community as well as work issues, was novel, though slow and, for some unions, too risky. The venture was not to succeed. It was not the contextual issues that we have examined in this chapter – workforce, legislative and employer hostility – that undermined it. They had already done their worst. Just as negotiations began for a State award, the unions' unity cracked. A very familiar kind of (historical) division between unions threatened the PMU plan after one national union, the Australian Workers Union, worked out a deal for a federal award with the Rio management. This gave the PMU nowhere to go with State award coverage. The traditional, nationally scaled arbitration orientation of unions, was not entirely dead and buried – nor was inter-union rivalry. The strategies of the PMU remained intact at BHP, where the local unions, with national unions in agreement, formalised their cooperation by establishing the BHP-PMU.

There are two important elements here. First, this unusual attempt to meld national union strategy (the ACTU's role) with a local focus and a community connection was an example of a more or less explicit response to this changed environment. Second, it provides a good example of how changes in structure and strategy actually do happen. It also shows how obstacles to change endure. This imaginative response to union crisis, one that might well be echoed in a range of settings, did not last, at least in Rio Tinto's operations.

CONCLUSION

Two of the key challenges to organised labour in the 21st century are, as they have been for some time, globalisation of production and distribution and the re-regulation of labour markets. Whatever else they are, these are spatial processes which have reduced union power. To understand unionism today, we must first explain how history and geography shaped union structures and strategies in the past. Over the last two decades, the most obvious sources of union power, membership levels, state support and employer recognition, have been eroded, along with expressions of that power such as industrial action. There is no doubt that unions in Australia are in crisis.

Contrary to the perception of unions as intensely conservative organisations, quite radical changes in union strategy have been enacted in recent years. The changes were most obvious at the national scale. The ACTU's response to union crisis in the late 1980s relied, among other things, on centralising union structures, but by 2003 the ACTU's strategies focused more clearly on organising new members and building activism in workplaces. As important as these changes were, national strategy did not of itself rebuild union power without action in particular unions and at local scales. It is true that some unions have not changed, but the glimpses of union strategy presented here suggest that, at least in some sectors, change in union behaviour since the late 1990s has been more real than rhetorical. Success had occurred when unions drew on new sources of power. Even in these cases, problems remained which by their nature were neither new nor easily overcome. For the CPSU, government anti-union strategies and employer hostility continued unabated. For the PMU, inter-union rivalry was as much a problem as employer antagonism. Unions may make history and space, but not just as they please.

In the last ten years, partly because of the logic of organising unionism, but also because of the changes in state practice and employer orientation, unions have attempted to draw power from sites and sources that they did not rely on for much of the 20th century. They have drawn power from their own members, in the workplace, and have connected with a range of social forces to renew themselves. In so doing, union power itself has been reinterpreted and rebuilt.

References

ABS 1977–96, *Trade Union Members, Australia*, Cat. No. 6325.0, Canberra: ABS.

ABS 1997–2004, *Employee Earnings, Benefits and Trade Union Membership*, Cat. No. 6310.0, Canberra: ABS.

ABS 1995, *Trade Union Statistics, Australia*, Cat. No. 6323.0, Canberra: ABS.

ABS 2003, *Industrial Disputes, Australia*, Cat. No. 6321.0.55.001, Canberra: ABS.

ACIRRT (Australian Centre for Industrial Relations Research and Training) 1999, *Australia at Work: Just Managing?* Sydney: Prentice-Hall.

ACTU (Australian Council of Trade Unions) 1987, *Future Strategies for the Trade Union Movement*, Melbourne: ACTU.

ACTU 2003, *Future Strategies: Unions Working for a Fairer Australia*, Melbourne: ACTU.

Bain, G.S. & Price, R. 1980, *Profiles of Union Growth: A Comparative Statistical Portrait of Eight Countries*, Oxford: Basil Blackwell.

Beynon, H. & Hudson, R. 1993, 'Place and space in contemporary Europe: some lessons and reflections', *Antipode* 25(3): 177–90.

Bramble, T. 2001, 'Union strategy since 1945', *Labour and Industry* 11(3): 1–25.

Brigden, C. 2000, 'Beyond peak body authority: power relations in the THC', *Labour and Industry* 11(2): 59–74.

Briggs, C. 2001, 'Australian exceptionalism: the role of trade unions in the emergence of enterprise bargaining', *Journal of Industrial Relations* 43(1): 27–43.

Briggs, C. 2002, 'The paradox of ACTU hegemony', *Labour and Industry* 12(3): 77–102.

Burgmann, M. & Burgmann, V. 1998, *Green Bans, Red Union: Environmental Activism and the New South Wales Builders Labourers' Federation*, Sydney: UNSW Press.

Callus, R. & Buchanan, J. 1993, 'Efficiency and equity at work: the need for labour market regulation in Australia, *Journal of Industrial Relations* 35(4): 515–37.

Callus, R., Morehead, A., Cully, M. & Buchanan, J. 1991, *Industrial Relations at Work: The Australian Workplace Industrial Relations Survey*, Canberra: Commonwealth Department of Industrial Relations, AGPS.

Campbell, I. 2001, 'Industrial relations and intellectual challenges: reconceptualising the recent changes to labour regulation in Australia'. Paper presented at symposium on 'Future Directions of Industrial Relations as a Field of Inquiry', 14 September.

Cole, M., Briggs, C. & Buchanan, J. 2002, 'Where are the non-members?' Unpublished research paper, Sydney: Australian Centre for Industrial Relations Research and Training.

Cooper, R. 2000, 'Organise, organise, organise! ACTU congress 2000', *Journal of Industrial Relations* 42(4): 582–94.

Cooper, R. 2001, 'Getting organised? A white collar union responds to membership crisis', *Journal of Industrial Relations* 43(4): 422–37.

Cooper, R. 2002a, 'Organising at work: growth strategies in Australian white-collar unions, 1996–2000'. Unpublished PhD thesis, University of Sydney.

Cooper, R. 2002b, 'To organise wherever the necessity exists: a study of the activities of the Organising Committee of the NSW Labor Council 1900–1910, *Labour History* 61: 43–64.

Cooper, R. 2003a, 'Trade unionism 2002', *Journal of Industrial Relations* 45(2): 205–223.

Cooper, R. 2003b, 'Peak council organising at work: ACTU strategy 1994–2000', *Labour and Industry* 14(1): 1–21.

Cooper, R. & Patmore, G. 2002, 'Trade union organising and labour history', *Labour History* 61: 3–18.

D'Aprano, Z. 2001, *Kath Williams: The Unions and the Fight for Equal Pay*, Melbourne: Spinifex Press.

Dabscheck, B. 1993, 'The Coalition's plan to re-regulate industrial relations, *Economic and Labour Relations Review* 4(1): 1–26.

DWR/OEA (Department of Workplace Relations and the Office of the Employment Advocate) 2002, *Agreement Making in Australia under the Workplace Relations Act: 2000 and 2001*, Canberra: DWR.

Ellem, B. 1999, 'Women's rights and industrial relations under the postwar compact in Australia', *International Labor and Working-Class History* 56: 45–64.

Ellem, B. 2003, 'Re-placing the Pilbara's mining unions', *Australian Geographer*, 34(3): 281–96.

Ellem, B. 2004, *Hard Ground: Unions in the Pilbara*, Port Hedland, WA: Pilbara Mineworkers Union.

Ellem, B. & Shields, J. 1999, 'Rethinking "regional industrial relations": space, place and the social relations of work', *Journal of Industrial Relations* 41(4): 536–60.

Gorman, P. 1996, *Weipa: Where Australian Unions Drew Their 'Line in the Sand' with CRA*, Sydney: Weipa Industrial Site Committee with the CFMEU Mining and Energy Division.

Griffin, G. 1991, 'Changing trade union structure', Centre for Industrial Relations and Labour Studies Working Paper no. 61, Melbourne: University of Melbourne.

Griffin, G. & Svensen, S. 1996, 'The decline of Australian union density: a survey of the literature', *Journal of Industrial Relations* 38(4): 505–47.

Herod, A. & Wright, M. 2002, 'Placing scale: an introduction', in A. Herod & M. Wright (eds) *Geographies of Power: Placing Scale*, Malden, Mass.: Blackwell, pp. 1–14.

Howard, W.A. 1977, 'Australian trade unions in the context of union theory', *Journal of Industrial Relations* 19(3): 255–73.

Hyman, R. 1975, *Industrial Relations: A Marxist Introduction*, London: Macmillan.

McDonald, T. & McDonald, A. 1998, *Intimate Unions: Sharing a Revolutionary Life*, Sydney: Pluto Press.

McDonald, T. & Rimmer, M. 1989, 'Award restructuring and wages policy', *Growth* 37: 111–34.

Morehead, A., Steele, M., Alexander, M., Stephen, K. & Duffin, L. 1997, *Changes at Work: The 1995 Australian Workplace Industrial Relations Survey*, Melbourne: Longman.

Peetz, D. 1995, 'Deunionisation', *Proceedings of the 9th Annual AIRAANZ Conference*, Melbourne, February, pp. 357–64.

Peetz, D. 1998, *Unions in a Contrary World: The Future of the Australian Trade Union Movement*, Cambridge University Press.

Pocock, B. 1998, 'Institutional sclerosis: prospects for trade union transformation', *Labour and Industry* 9(1): 17–33.

Rawson, D. 1986, *Unions and Unionists in Australia*, Sydney: Allen & Unwin.

Ronfeldt, P. & McCallum, R. (eds) 1995, *Enterprise Bargaining, Trade Unions and the Law*, Sydney: Federation Press.

Sadler, D. & Fagan, R. 2004, 'Australian trade unions and the politics of scale: re-constructing the spatiality of industrial relations', *Economic Geography* 80(1): 23–43.

Savage, L. 1998, 'Geographies of organizing: justice for janitors in Los Angeles', in A. Herod (ed.) *Organizing the Landscape: Geographical Perspectives on Labor Unionism*, Minneapolis: University of Minnesota Press, pp. 225–52.

Sheldon, P. 1993, 'Arbitration and union growth: building and construction unions in NSW, 1900–1912', *Journal of Industrial Relations* 35(3): 379–97.

Sheridan, T. 1989, *Division of Labour: Industrial Relations in the Chifley Years, 1945–1949*, Melbourne: Oxford University Press.

Tattersall, A. 2004, 'Community unionism: a strategy for union power under neo-liberalism'. Proceedings of the 18th Conference of the Association of Industrial Relations Academics of Australia and New Zealand, Noosa, Qld: AIRAANZ.

van Barneveld, K. & Nassif, R. 2003, 'Motivations for the introduction of workplace agreements', *Labour and Industry* 14(2): 21–38.

Watson, I., Buchanan, J., Campbell, I. & Briggs, C. 2003, *Fragmented Futures: New Challenges in Working Life*, Sydney: Federation Press.

Wiseman, J. 1998, 'Here to stay? The 1997–1998 Australian waterfront dispute and its implications', *Labour and Industry* 9(1): 1–16.

CHAPTER EIGHT

GLOBALISATION AND LABOUR MOBILITY
Migrants Making Spaces, Migrants Changing Spaces

Dimitria Groutsis

Labour mobility is spatially defined both in the country of emigration and in the host or receiving country. That is, migration decisions are influenced by where people are already located in their own labour markets as well as where they think they will be located in the new country. A range of factors including cultural or human capital (or skill endowments) help shape the decision to allow migrants into a host country.

Labour geographers show how key stakeholders (in this case, skilled migrants entering Australia, employers, professional associations, the state and migrant coalitions) interact to shape the labour market spatial arrangements and the movement of potential labour market participants within and between different labour market spaces (Peck 1996). The pressures forged by the interaction between these players, over time, generate the dynamic and evolving labour market landscape. What is brought out in this analysis is how labour markets develop in tandem with social, political and material institutions and function in geographically specific ways, thus challenging the notion that labour markets are determined by universal economic principles alone (Peck 1996). To date, there has been little rigorous analysis of the insights offered by labour geographers on the labour market experience of migrants, be they skilled (Kofman et al. 2000; Ley 2004) or unskilled (Anthias & Lazaridis 2000), male or female (Anthias & Lazaridis 2000; Kofman et al. 2000), temporary or permanent (Khoo et al. 2003), invited by the host country (pull factors), or forced to leave by the country of emigration (push factors). This chapter aims to address the void in the literature.

LABOUR MOBILITY IN AUSTRALIA

New labour market spaces and the reinforcement of pre-existing ones are created by labour migration. Understanding the force of this mobile labour stock has become more urgent as the number of migrants has more than doubled in the last 25 years (United Nations 2002). In 2002, the International Labour Organisation noted that there were approximately 120 million migrant workers globally (Taran & Geronimi 2003). Within this hyper-mobile landscape there are skilled and unskilled male and female labour force participants, flowing from different countries and workplaces bound for myriad countries and workplaces. The implications of labour mobility in shaping and reshaping labour market spaces challenges the analytical power of labour market theories which treat space in general, and nation-states in particular, as given, monolithic and 'obvious' units of analysis.

In recent years, the politics of migration management has given rise to a new group of settler arrivals in Australia and beyond (Hugo 2000; Birrell et al. 2001). Skilled migrants have become the new target group, as motivated by government policies internationally. In Australia the necessity for this targeted focus was summed up by federal Immigration Minister Amanda Vanstone, who recently announced: 'we're competing globally for skilled workers, it is essential that Australian employers have a competitive edge in this area' (Coleman & Wiese Bockmann 2005). The consequence is that the migration landscape is transforming, as is the degree of competition for skilled migrant labour.

Globalisation has transformed the structure of capitalism in both space and time, generating direct implications for workers with the ability to access a range of labour market spaces and for employers to draw on a ready source of labour internationally (Herod 2001a: 407). The Australian government has responded to the call for a more skill-intensive workforce by welcoming settler arrivals who offer greater human capital and are 'job-ready'. This request has been well served by the higher educational attainments of the recent settler arrivals to Australia (Crock 2000; Ruddock 2000; OECD 2001). Tables 8.1 and 8.2 depict how the shifting policy focus is making space for permanent and temporary skilled migration (Ruddock 2003).

Although it is said that labour is integrated into the host country labour market according to their human capital endowments, spatial considerations are a significant yet neglected factor in understanding

Table 8.1 *Temporary skilled migration, 2000–2003*

Country	Workforce	Program	2000	2001	2002
Australia	9.1m	Skilled visa classes	45 669	43 303	48 779

Source: Joint standing committee on Migration Review, March 2004, p. 4.

Table 8.2 *Permanent skilled migration, 2000–2003*

Country	Workforce	Program	2000/1	2001/2	2002/3
Australia	9.1m	General skilled migration	44 730	53 520	66 050

Source: Joint standing committee on Migration Review, March 2004, p. 5.

the movement, experience and implications of the migrant labour market landscape.

To date, there has been no theoretical engagement incorporating labour with other key stakeholders in the labour market such as employers and management, whereby these players act and interact in some ways and not others based on pre-existing spatial arrangements. That is, there has been no theoretical development to show how space influences stakeholder decisions, behaviours and strategies and simultaneously how stakeholder interactions create shifts in labour market spaces (Herod 2001a).

The shifting labour market landscape frames our central concerns. How are we to understand the spaces occupied by this hyper-mobile group and the spaces they create in the labour market of the country from which they exit? How are we to *read* this new hyper-mobile landscape? How is the hyper-mobility of migrants challenging the entry of skilled migrants from particular areas into particular regions? How do we theorise these global circuits of skilled migrant labour?

The Australian literature on migration is replete with empirical studies, with the analysis of skilled migration falling into two camps. The human capital theorists argue that the experience of skilled migrant labour in Australia is largely shaped by their human capital endowments, which include language proficiency, education, training and vocational experience. The second body of work, informed by the labour market segmentation theorists, suggests that pre-existing labour market structures shape labour market outcomes for new (migrant) entrants.

By interrogating the contribution and limitations of both approaches, this chapter shows how labour geographers provide an analytical basis from which to explore the experience of skilled (professional) migrants in the Australian labour market.

Professional practice, for some, means that they are not spatially confined within a regional, national or international labour market. Labour geographers bring to the fore the strategies employed by key stakeholders in the negotiation of space, the various scales of negotiation, and from this emerges our understanding of the way in which this negotiation shapes labour market outcomes within the different scales. For instance, although skilled labour migration places professional practice in a transnational space, the measurement and assessment of human capital endowments continues to be confined to the national or State-based spatial scale and is driven by local employment demands (Groutsis 2006).

OVERSEAS QUALIFIED PROFESSIONALS IN THE AUSTRALIAN LABOUR MARKET

Human capital theory

Human capital theory has come to dominate Australian research and the direction of policy decisions on skilled migrant labour in Australia. Within this model differential labour market outcomes between individuals are based on differences in human capital investment.

The human capital theory suggests that immigrants choose their positions in a rational labour force setting, where the labour market is seen as a competitive arena that treats all potential participants equally, based on their skills, competency and training (Evans 1984: 1087). Kelly & McAllister (1984: 401) conclude that 'immigrants face no disadvantage in competing for jobs or in the earnings they receive for their labour and they get the same jobs and pay as do native born workers with equal skills, knowledge and the like'.

There is an assumption that after a period of downward mobility a process of social integration irons out the spatial differences between groups, with migrant workers soon enjoying the rewards of high-status positions. The onus is on the individual to 'socially integrate' and blame is cast on the individual should they fail to enter core positions in the labour market (Becker 1971).

The Longitudinal Survey of Immigrants to Australia (LSIA1), commissioned by the Department of Immigration and Multicultural and Indigenous Affairs (DIMIA), surveyed migrants who arrived in Australia between September 1993 and August 1995; a second survey (LSIA2) looked at migrants who arrived in Australia between September 1999 and August 2000 (see Cobb-Clark 2000, 2001; VandenHeuvel & Wooden 2000; Richardson et al. 2001, 2002). The quantitative data presented by these surveys show that skilled migrants gain access to the Australian labour market faster than unskilled migrants. This finding is used as justification for the continued policy focus on skilled migration targets. That is, why someone enters an alternative labour market space is explained simply in terms of personal skill endowments and is assumed to be an outcome forged rationally by the migrants themselves, by employers, by professional associations and by the state. It is therefore believed that all stakeholders see 'skill' in the same way.

Although the quantitative findings of both surveys provide compelling evidence for the continued focus on targeting skilled migrant groups, the figures conceal both the labour market spaces that skilled male and female migrants from different countries enter, and the time taken in gaining access to a position representative of skills and qualifications. Furthermore, the figures conceal the variance in the labour market spaces entered by different groups of migrants.

As well as the occupational differences generated by the self-discrimination of the 'rational' labour force participant, some human capital analysts point to the importance of differential outcomes, driven by the actions of employers and licensing bodies. The 'taste for discrimination' thesis suggests that the higher costs involved in screening immigrants, coupled with the 'perception' among employers that these immigrants may return at some future time to their country of origin, also contributes to explaining the different labour market spaces entered by different groups of migrants (Wood 1992). Wood argues that the cost borne by the host or receiving country in adapting the human capital of an overseas-trained professional is central to the acceptance or rejection of particular groups in the labour market. That is, the transformation costs of the overseas skills must be factored into the labour market outcomes and thus the emergent labour market landscape. Wood (1992: 11) claims: 'If economic migrants originate from more able and adaptable segments of the labour market in their country of origin, their rate of investment in human capital will compare favourably with that of the Australian born employed workforce in the post-restoration period.'

The human capital model denies agency to employers and/or licensing bodies and sectional groups. It is assumed that particular groups of skilled labour consciously enter alternative labour market spaces, and as a result become categorised as a supply of low-skilled, low-paid labour. Consequently, employers and licensing bodies act according to stereotypes and treat all members of a particular group as if they share its actual or imaginary characteristics (Arrow 1972; Akerlof & Dickens 1982). Thus the centrality of space in shaping relationships is given no attention. As indicated by Reich and his colleagues (1973: 359), the experience of individuals is aggregated to produce a picture of group experience, and this removes workers from the spatial and social context of their employment.

The emphasis on the human capital endowments of migrants leads the analyst to view the individual as the primary determinant of labour market outcomes (Employment Services Project Report 1992). Consequently, human capital theory fails to acknowledge the effect of spatially and historically constructed labour market barriers.

Compounding this theoretical weakness is the methodological approach employed by human capital theorists, which sets the foundations for the static and descriptive 'snapshot' illustration of occupational spatial differences. For example, data are drawn from census statistics and labour force surveys, at the cost of collecting qualitative data. While the theory does acknowledge occupational difference (Becker 1971; Arrow 1972), it does not and cannot shed light on the heterogeneity of the labour market. The occupation of different labour market spaces by different groups represents a divergent development rather than a convergence to equilibrium as neoclassical economic theory would have it (Vietorisz & Harrison 1973). The failure to acknowledge divergent structures and divergent outcomes in labour market status based on particular characteristics, such as country of training, highlights the inadequacy of the human capital theory. Also, the theory focuses on the domain of labour supply and the players within this space, in this case the migrants themselves. As a consequence, the domain of labour demand and the role of the state are largely neglected.

What emerges from our critique of the human capital model is a theory-driven analysis with no acknowledgment of the role of pre-existing spatial arrangements and the evolving spatial circumstances, factors that are all the more pressing when considering how to understand the hyper-mobile labour landscape. Little attention is given to the labour market spatial arrangements driving the actions and reactions of labour market stakeholders. The logic offered within this model then serves only to rationalise divergent and uneven developments in the labour market, and offers no explanation of why and how labour market spaces are transformed as a result of inflowing labour force participants (Peck 1996).

Labour market segmentation theory

To date, the main alternative to the human capital theory has been the labour market segmentation theory, which looks beyond human capital endowments and the symptomatic focus on the individual to consider structural factors and social attitudes as key determinants of labour market outcomes. This model then focuses on the status of jobs rather than of individuals, and thus draws our attention to the processes of labour market allocation rather than the training and experience of the individual. Labour market segmentation theory goes some way to establishing an understanding of the formal and informal social processes that are relevant in shaping labour market outcomes. Informal structures include, for instance, community networks and the family structure, while formal structures include bodies such as employment agencies and other institutional organisations that are instrumental in linking overseas-qualified professionals to the Australian labour market. These formal and informal processes foster the occupation of different labour market segments by different groups (Campbell et al. 1991: 188).

While the dual labour market theory (Doeringer & Piore 1971; Vietorisz & Harrison 1973) and the radical models (Gordon et al. 1982) established a shift away from the neoclassical approach to labour market differences between groups, the models are not entirely unproblematic. The early labour market segmentation theorists have tended to reduce the complex set of factors involved in market differentiation at the workplace to singular and descriptive factors. The dual labour market theorists have based the development of a segmented labour market on skill-stability requirements, while the radical theorists have focused on managerial control strategies. Additionally, the structure of the analysis in both approaches is taxonomic in nature, which undermines the explanatory force of the theory (Joll et al. 1983: 385–6). Despite these weaknesses, the models are valuable because they locate the analysis of occupational segregation within a wider context, and there is an assumption of divergent development rather than a convergence to equilibrium (Vietorisz & Harrison 1973: 367).

Collins (1991) was one of the first in Australian research on immigrant labour to use the labour market segmentation theory. He developed a typology set within a politico-economic framework, explaining the dynamics forged between the state and the economy and the subsequent impact on labour. By using a fourfold classification structure, Collins set the groundwork for an analysis of immigrant labour, displaying divergence between sectors of the labour market, with each segment corresponding to a particular sector in the labour market from highly skilled professional positions to blue-collar jobs in manufacturing.

Despite the important contribution of this research, the structures of exclusion that have emerged are not analysed in detail (Lever-Tracy & Quinlan 1988; Campbell et al. 1991). Critics also suggest that the hierarchy developed by Collins simply presents 'a typology of workforce segments' (Campbell et al. 1991: 173) that conflates the many differences characterising immigrants entering the labour market. Castles and colleagues (1989) point out that the clear dichotomy within the hierarchy offered by Collins overlooks the groups of women from Egypt, Sri Lanka and Malaysia, for example, who are entering the service industries along with women from English-speaking countries. Furthermore, the informal processes forged by groups establishing social networks once settled in Australia are also missing from the framework (Ho & Alcorso 2004). Thus the potential for renegotiating spatial differences across labour market segments needs to be entered into the framework.

Labour geographers respond to the theoretical void characterising the dominant literature by going beyond the economically driven explanation of how labour market spaces emerge. Peck (1996: 13) argues that particular 'rounds of accumulation . . . tend to be associated with particular geographies'. In the models surveyed thus far, the singular focus on the domains of labour demand or labour supply is a source of qualified weakness given that geographical considerations are overlooked. Labour geographers shift away from the economically driven distinction on either the demand or supply sphere by considering mobile capital and immobile labour within geographically distinct boundaries. The analysis presented in this chapter featuring migrant labour takes this premise one step further and brings to bear the significance of mobile capital and mobile labour in shaping and being shaped by space. Furthermore, the focus on labour demand or labour supply has

151

not in the past included the political/institutional arrangements and the stakeholders within them. The political/institutional sphere is central to shaping the ideologically driven informal and formal processes by which key stakeholders or groups in the labour market must abide, thus shedding light on how 'labour markets are socially regulated in geographically distinct ways' (Peck 1996: 106).

SPACE, SCALE AND SKILLED MIGRATION

Labour geographers establish how particular spatial arrangements emerge by focusing on political/institutional, material and social forces while drawing our attention explicitly to the importance of space as a defining factor in shaping the labour market outcomes for workers. The various groups in the labour market – representing capital (employers), the state, and labour interests (professional associations/migrant coalitions) – each contribute to the development of these forces. (Note that labour geographers do not dissolve the public/private dichotomy between workplaces and home-places in the construction of labour market spaces. Rather, they go deeper to explore labour from the household perspective, as well as in the public sphere through relations between capital, labour and the state. Households and families not only have active interests in the labour market construction but provide for the reproduction of labour, including socialisation – and in the case of outworking, for example, the public/private dichotomy is dissolved altogether. The issues raised at this level of analysis are not covered here.)

By examining the interests forged by key stakeholders in the process of negotiating space, we gain an insight into the relationship between and within spaces in the labour market as labour market behaviour within and between these groups is captured. Thus labour geographers take us to a deeper level of analysis. As Herod (2003: 113) notes,

> the emergent field of *labour geography* argues that workers are not just historical agents but are also geographical ones, that workers' lives are spatially embedded in the landscapes in which they live, that this spatial embeddedness may be enabling and/or constraining of their social praxis and that workers will thus try to shape in particular ways the geographical structures and relationships within which they live their lives.

Skilled labour mobility provides us with a distinct case in point. The current structure of migration, entry, settlement and labour force participation suggests the development of a tiered politico-economic structure at a macro level; and on a micro level, a tiered labour market, with migrants sourced from a 'preferred' group of countries with 'desired' skills. Bauman (1998: 89) notes that in 'the increasingly cosmopolitan, extraterritorial world of global businessmen, global culture managers or global academics, state borders are levelled down, as they are dismantled for the world's commodities, capital and finances'.

Bauman points out that labour market participants experience the unconstrained 'borderless' space of a global labour market differently, a borderless space tempered and shaped by the state, which implements a migration policy to suit, and by employers and professional associations that temper labour demand and labour supply to satisfy their interests. As Clark (1983: 2) observes, 'local labour markets are man-made not natural and are structured according to power, not neutral rules of demand and supply'.

Metaphorically and conceptually, 'spatial considerations' are at the heart of migrant mobility and entry into the labour market. Pre-existing spatial arrangements dictate how labour market spaces are negotiated by migrants, and thus who gains access and who does not in a position representative of skills and qualifications (see Herod 1995, 1997, 2001a, 2001b). In the first instance, understanding the interplay between the macro and micro spatial scales forges the question and directs us towards an understanding of why people migrate and why they enter particular labour market spaces. That is, in the case of migration and settlement, 'space' is not simply a backdrop but constructs the migrant's labour market reality on a macro (broader politico-economic) and micro (labour market) level. As contended by Herod and colleagues (2003: 178), 'rather than simply viewing space as a stage upon which social life is played out . . . we argue that conflicts over the very structuring of the economic and political landscape are central to the strategic calculation of social actors and to the functioning of social systems'. So space influences behaviour and action: that is, whether or not someone leaves or stays in their pre-existing spatial boundary. Spatial concerns significantly shape workers' and employers' actions and behaviours and these actions and behaviours feed into creating the spatial boundaries in the labour market which, according to Herod and his colleagues (2003: 178), 'reflect geographically unique conjectures of labour supply conditions, patterns of labour demand and skills acquisition, regulatory and legal frameworks, social conventions, industrial relations practices and strategies'.

While labour may be defined as 'internationally mobile' in this globalised postcolonial era, nationally and regionally driven demand conditions (that is, demand for labour), trained stocks of available labour, and the assessment of skills and qualifications (regulatory framework), are all considerations that highlight the centrality of space in labour market arrangements and thus in the responses forged by the various stakeholders. In developing an insight into how space shapes stakeholder actions, labour geographers show us how space can be used as a macro and micro analytical tool.

At the macro level we are able to explain and understand why and how labour migration occurs and the importance of space in shaping such behaviour, in terms of the decision to migrate and the human capital endowments gained in the space from which the individual migrates. According to data from DIMIA's two surveys (LSIA1 and LSIA2), the majority of skilled migrants interviewed reported that they migrated to Australia because of the promise of better economic and social conditions. Thus the geographical arrangements in their location before migration and the foreseeable arrangements after it are a significant consideration in the decision to migrate.

Taken one step further, the impetus to migrate comes from pre-existing spatial arrangements in the home country. The move creates new spaces in the home country and new shifts in the spaces in the host country. It is common to have the spatial shifts of skilled migrants examined as 'brain drain' and 'brain gain' and, as a consequence, to examine the concomitant effects on the labour market, in both the home and host countries. Labour geographers provide us with a more complex model at the macro level than simply considering the migration of skilled labour in terms of a balance sheet showing the 'profit' and 'loss' of skilled migration for the home and host countries. That is, the 'brain drain' in the home country does not always translate into a 'brain gain' in the host country. Labour geographers lead us to the importance of social, state-based and economic factors in influencing the nature and shape of the migrant's spatial arrangements (before and after migration) and the behaviour of the various stakeholders in response to such spatial arrangements. Let us now look at the host country labour market and the insights offered by labour geographers.

Although the conceptual tools offered to us by labour geographers are broad in scope, the threefold classification of factors that combine to create the labour market spaces provides us with a structure for analysis. Material, social and institutional/political forces are crucial to the analytical framework as they influence the behaviour of different groups in the labour market. As interdependent factors, these forces combine to contextualise spatial arrangements defining the labour market, and in turn they are shaped and reshaped by social groups or actors. Thus how social actors engage with space is placed at the centre of the analysis (Herod 2002). This point is drawn from Harvey's (1982) notion of 'spatial fix', which highlights the role played by social actors in establishing the geographical boundaries within which material, institutional/political and social actions are played out and thus the dialectical relationship between these forces and spatial arrangements.

The material or capital forces denote business-cycle shifts and are central to the analysis of labour market space. Thus the development of labour market spatial arrangements is perceived as endogenous to the economic structure. Within the labour market, material decisions are conditioned by particular rules, set by management or employers, licensing or professional bodies, and the state. The group or groups shaping the rules and the subsequent structure and degree of labour market closure is unique to the time and space being analysed – in this case the occupational space. Business-cycle shifts shape the decisions made by employers or management in the recruitment process. In order to protect their interests and/or the interests of their members, employers, managements and professional bodies establish protected labour market spaces barring particular groups from entry into certain areas. Consequently, protection from external challenges by new coalitions (for example overseas-trained professionals) attempting to enter the labour market is ensured. Thus the various professional associations and registration boards are a feature of the analysis.

Historically, professional associations have employed the accreditation process as a tool to restrict or grant access to migrants into the Australian labour market – a process that creates the 'spatial fix' of particular groups and the varying spatial scales fragmenting the labour market. The structured accreditation process, established in the 1950s, facilitated the integration of overseas-qualified professionals and other skilled migrants into Australian society. Accreditation had not been a major concern before this because almost all immigrants were from the UK (Moore 1994). Few of these people experienced problems in transferring their qualifications as their training system was deemed to be sufficiently similar to that in Australia. The ease with which British immigrants were integrated into the Australian labour market overshadowed the difficulties experienced by the small group of immigrants from non-English-speaking countries, which remained unaddressed. Research on the employment status of immigrant labour from non-English-speaking countries revealed poor labour force participation outcomes for overseas-trained professionals (Moore 1994). Several factors were regarded as contributing to the high unemployment rates and under-employment of this group. The most significant of these factors were skills, age, length of settlement, and language proficiency.

Despite this emphasis, labour market integration was also clearly shaped by the structure of the accreditation process, which favoured professionals with skills gained in countries with a British system of education. Spatially defined institutional and cultural barriers, rather than poor language skills per se, were apparent features of the fragmented spatial scales defining the Australian labour market.

Notwithstanding the many policy initiatives that emerged throughout the 1970s, 1980s and 1990s, substantial impediments to the integration of migrants from particular regions remain. Settler arrivals from the UK and Ireland, North America and South Africa show consistently favourable rates of recognition. By contrast, settler arrivals from Asian regions display poor rates based on their spatially defined skills and training (Ho 2004; Ho & Alcorso 2004).

Although the most recent shift in the migration program has considerably enhanced labour market opportunities for professional and skilled immigrants (Cobb-Clark 2000, 2001; VandenHeuvel & Wooden 2000; Richardson et al. 2001, 2002), particular groups continue to face obstacles to social, material and institutional/political inclusion in their new space of engagement. While the greater emphasis placed on language proficiency and skill as migrant entry requirements is regarded as enhancing the scope for spatial inclusion, this has tended to redirect attention from addressing entrenched material, institutional and social obstacles that frustrate employment opportunities, resulting in spatial fix or spatial embeddedness.

Material forces thus bring out the spatial implications of the nation-specific differences in skills and how these skills frame the allocation of labour market positions. How material forces are constructed is crucial in shaping the labour market spaces and the interaction between and within labour market groups.

Understanding material forces comprises only part of the model required to arrive at an illustration of the spatial embeddedness and spatial shifts defining the labour market experience of overseas-qualified immigrants (Massey 1984; Herod et al. 2003). The model is thus complemented with an investigation of social processes. The addition of group interests to the theoretical framework shows why and how the different groups within the labour market occupy different power bases, thus forging the spatial divisions of labour. Massey argues that these divisions 'represent whole new spatial patterns of social organisation, new dimensions of inequality and new relations of dominance and dependence. Each new spatial division of labour represents a real and thorough spatial restructuring' (Massey 1984: 7–8).

By introducing social forces, the analysis goes beyond the perspective of capital or material concerns. Labour (social networks) and capital are given equal attention. In contrast to labour market segmentation theory, labour geographers capture the subtle complexity of the emerging labour market spaces. For example, the framework developed by labour geographers reveals that labour force participants in a variety of locations may receive similar wage levels as a result of their position in areas characterised by stability and continuity of employment, or through gains made via union or professional association membership in spite of not working in a position representative of skills and qualifications (Massey 1984, 1997; Herod & Wright 2002). Thus labour geographers make room for the behaviour of individuals denoted by a complex 'weblike' arrangement in contrast to the traditional dichotomy defined by in-group/out-group labour market arrangements. Labour market spatial arrangements are built and renegotiated through the interaction between those within the in-group (such as the locally trained), between those within the out-group (migrants) and of course across groups, that is, between the in-group and the out-group. While the dichotomy is significant in illustrating the spatial scales 'fixing' particular groups to certain areas, labour geographers invite us to consider how networks or coalitions responding to the spatial shifts forge changes to the spatial scales and create spatial arrangements.

The case of overseas-trained doctors in the Australian labour market is a useful case in point. Regional demands for overseas-trained doctors and the historical presence of the Australian Overseas-Trained Doctors' Association, coupled with the more recent representation of the overseas-trained doctors' interests by the Rural Doctors' Association, have generated a shift in entry portals for overseas-trained doctors, especially for those groups traditionally marginalised (Kenny 2004), such as doctors trained in non-English-speaking countries. Thus labour geographers enable us to identify supply-side constraints, as created by particular collective agents or labour coalitions, which shape labour market spaces while at the same time challenging the spatial scales. Labour geographers then draw our attention to how workers shape labour market spaces and are party to or participants in negotiating and renegotiating the entry points into particular spaces (Herod et al. 2003).

Workers have different options open to them depending on their particular circumstances. Labour may choose to exercise different options at different times. This is a politically significant point as it challenges the notion that capital alone makes and remakes the spatial arrangements that emerge, showing that in choosing to engage in one strategy or option, labour plays a defining role in the spatial arrangements or outcomes that transpire (Herod 2001b). We can then establish an understanding of social processes by examining migration, settlement and labour market behaviours. These factors are tempered by the material conditions and pressures facing migrants after settlement in the private sphere, which are directly influenced by material opportunities defining the labour market; they are also tempered by the institutional arrangements with which they must deal – on a state and occupational level. Thus formal and informal social processes that shape labour market outcomes for this group are revealed.

Organised labour (or, in this case, professional associations) controls competition in the labour market to defend, control and extend opportunities for the professional membership they represent. Professional associations are central to the establishment of institutional arrangements and market processes. They generate restrictions by the use of licensing, accreditation and credential requirements. Such methods ensure a degree of insulation from other 'intruders' who are in the labour market (spatially embedded), or external to the labour market (active job-seekers). The 'spatial fix' of particular groups in alternative labour market spaces reinforces the rules of exclusion and establishes the group's sectional position. Disadvantaged groups remain excluded from collective and effective organisation, so they pose no threat. In the case of overseas-qualified doctors this is mainly because they have little bargaining power since their qualifications are seldom recognised locally. The artificially imposed barriers in the recognition of skills and credentials (enforced by professional associations, government policies and labour demand) facilitate the spatial fix defining migrant labour market arrangements. The framework then allows us to see how particular areas are safeguarded from intrusion, as a direct consequence of the interaction between particular players.

Finally, examination of institutional/political forces provides the missing link to the contextual framework and its addition completes the model for analysis. Ideological considerations are the heart of institutional responsibilities. In Australia the state continues to be especially influential ideologically in the formal and informal rules by which the stakeholders must abide (Crock 2000; Hugo 2000). Despite this, the role of the state remains poorly defined in Australian research that examines its role in shaping labour market spaces. In terms of material forces, the state acts either directly by recruiting labour to work within the public service or public works, or indirectly by recruiting skilled or unskilled labour through migration. Most recently the targeted recruitment of skilled labour provides an excellent illustration (Coleman & Wiese Bockmann 2005).

The state also plays an important regulatory role with regard to the supply of labour, to the extent that it sets the conditions for the reproduction of labour power. This cannot be left to capital alone as the aim of capital is short-term maximisation of returns (also see Michelson & Wailes this volume). The labour market would be threatened if the supply of labour was left completely unregulated. Accordingly, the state operates as a kind of 'moral guardian', thus explicitly driving the ideological agenda. The role of the state as moral guardian is to ensure that limited resources such as scarce positions in all labour market spaces are accessible to all potential labour force participants. Throughout the 1990s and into the 2000s, however, the growing acceptance of economic rationalism has shifted the 'agenda of economic policy towards the libertarian non-interventionist end of the spectrum' (Gill 1994: 140), thereby challenging or undermining the state's role as moral guardian. The state's role is then both complex and contradictory, mainly because of the diverse groups and interests to which its policies and practices must appeal.

The material, social and institutional/political processes are not mutually exclusive. Rather, it is the dynamics operating between these forces that determine labour market spatial arrangements and the behaviours and responses to those arrangements by key groups within the labour market. An investigation of the three forces and how the various stakeholders react to the spatial arrangements these forces generate reveals the processes that engender divergent labour market outcomes for particular groups. The emerging pattern for overseas-qualified immigrants is to enter a labour market that has uneven spatial scales where particular groups are either included in, or excluded from, certain areas

(Richardson et al. 2001). Overseas-trained professionals such as doctors challenge their 'spatial fix' through constant attempts at accreditation and registration, retraining and political lobbying through networks and coalitions. In doing so they reshape the pre-existing spatial arrangements (Groutsis 2006).

CONCLUSION

In presenting this general and broad model, it is important to note that the labour market dynamics and the spaces that ensue are determined by many things and depend on the combined influences of material, institutional and social forces. The model emphasises that causation is not linear either in time or space. Space influences the decisions made by labour force participants at the macro and micro levels. In doing so, we see how space is constantly negotiated and renegotiated. In terms of time through an historical lens we can better understand how spatial patterns emerge as a result of the interaction between social, institutional and material forces (see Peck 1996; Pile & Keith 1997; Herod et al. 2003). In time, patterns of labour market behaviour become 'fixed' and thus patterns and processes of labour market behaviour reinforce the pre-existing spatial arrangements before a renegotiation of social, material and institutional forces dislodges the fixed spatial arrangements to generate a new 'spatial fix' and thus produce new divisions of labour.

Viewing the dialectical relationship between social, material, institutional and spatial factors is complex and possibly even slightly cumbersome. Nonetheless, it provides us with an understanding of how and why labour market divisions emerge and how they are fought over to foster a restructuring of labour market spaces. Labour geographers go beyond simply adding space and scale to the mix of factors that contextualise the experience of migrants in the labour market. Rather, the dialectical relationship between migrants and space and between space and migrants shows how labour market spaces are negotiated and renegotiated to create the resultant labour market spaces and the spatial embeddedness of labour force participants. By highlighting the active participation of labour it is shown how these spaces are in a constant state of flux given that the social actors are responding to and shaping different institutional, material and social forces. The response to and control by these forces brings to the fore the presence of power and conflict whereby spaces are 'struggled over' while being reshaped. Labour geographers offer us conceptual and structural insights, providing us with an understanding of processes of inclusion and exclusion, of scale and a conceptual imagery that allows us to visualise the shelters that particular groups form to protect themselves from competition, while others form shelters to bargain with the in-group and to shift pre-existing spatial arrangements.

The theoretical model offered in this chapter is both wide-ranging and dynamic. Its dynamic nature comes into effect when we examine the interaction between various groups operating in different labour market spaces fused by institutional, material and social forces. The model delivers a superior explanatory system providing a conceptual framework that features the irrational nature of the labour market. The approach to divergent labour market spatial arrangements does not simply show that exclusion of particular groups exists. Rather, by locating the analysis within the broader social, material and institutional context it has been demonstrated why such spatial arrangements emerge and how they are brought about. Thus the model captures the complex set of forces that result in divergent spatial arrangements in the labour market.

References

Akerlof, G.A. & Dickens, W.T. 1982, 'The economic consequences of cognitive dissonance', *American Economic Review* 72(3): 307–19.

Anthias, F., & Lazaridis, G. (eds) 2000, *Gender and Migration in Southern Europe: Women on the Move*, Oxford: Berg.

Arrow, K.J. 1972, 'Models of job discrimination', in A.H. Pascal (ed.) *Racial Discrimination in Economic Life*, Lexington, Mass.: D.C. Heath & Co., pp. 83–103.

Bauman, Z. 1998, *Globalisation: The Human Consequences*, Cambridge: Polity Press.

Becker, G. 1971, *The Economics of Discrimination*, 2nd edn, Chicago University Press.

Birrell, B., Dobson, I.R. & Smith, T.F. 2001, *Skilled Labour: Gains and Losses*, Centre for Population and Urban Research, Melbourne: Monash University.

Campbell, I., Fincher, R. & Webber, M. 1991, 'Occupational mobility in segmented labour markets: the experience of immigrant workers in Melbourne', *Australian and New Zealand Journal of Sociology* 27(2): 172–94.

Castles, S., Mitchell, C., Morrissey, M. & Alcorso, C. 1989, *The Recognition of Overseas Trade Qualifications*, Bureau of Immigration Research, Canberra: AGPS.

Clark, G.L. 1983, *Interregional Migration, National Policy and Social Justice*, Totowa, New Jersey: Rowman & Allanheld.

Cobb-Clark, D. 2000, 'Do selection criteria make a difference? Visa category and the labour market status of immigrants to Australia', *Economic Record*, 76(232): 15–31.

Cobb-Clark, D. 2001, 'Settling in: public policy and the labour market adjustment of new immigrants to Australia'. Australian National University, accessed online: http://econrsss.anu.edu.au/-dcclark/docs/papers/lsia_compare_13.pdf.

Coleman, E. & Wiese Bockmann, M. 2005, 'Migrants to rescue on skills', *Australian*, 15 April.

Collins, J. 1991, *Migrant Hands in a Distant Land: Australia's Post-War Immigration*, 2nd edn, Sydney: Pluto Press.

Crock, M.E. 2000, 'Contract or compact: skilled migration and the dictates of politics and ideology'. Paper presented to the National Skilling, Migration Labour and the Law Symposium, 23–24 November, University of Sydney.

Doeringer, P.B. & Piore, M.J. 1971, *Internal Labor Markets and Manpower Analysis*, Lexington, Mass.: D.C. Heath & Co.

Employment Services Project Report 1992, *NESB Women in the Australian Labour Force*, Canberra: AGPS.

Evans, M.D. 1984, 'Immigrant women in Australia: resources, family and work', *International Migration Review* 18(4): 1063–90.

Gill, F. 1994, 'Inequality and the wheel of fortune: systemic causes of economic deprivation', *Australian Economic Papers* 33(62): 139–54.

Gordon, D., Edwards, R. & Reich, M. 1982, *Segmented Work, Divided Workers: The Historical Transformation of Labor in the United States*, Cambridge University Press.

Groutsis, D. 2006, 'Geography and credentialism: the assessment and accreditation of overseas-trained doctors', *Health Sociology Review* 15(2).

Harvey, D. 1982, *The Limits of Capital*, Oxford: Basil Blackwell.

Herod, A. 1995, 'The practice of international labor solidarity and the geography of the global economy', *Economic Geography* 71(4): 341–63.

Herod, A. 1997, 'Labor's spatial praxis and the geography of contract bargaining in the US east coast longshore industry, 1953–1989', *Political Geography* 16(2): 145–69.

Herod, A. 2001a, 'Labour internationalism and the contradictions of globalisation: or, why the local is sometimes still important in a global economy', *Antipode* 33(3): 407–26.

Herod, A. 2001b, *Labor Geographies: Workers and the Landscapes of Capitalism*, New York: Guilford Press.

Herod, A. 2002, 'Towards a more productive engagement: industrial relations and economic geography meet', *Labour and Industry* 13(2): 5–17.

Herod, A. 2003, 'Workers, space and labor geography', *International Labor and Working-Class History* 64: 112–38.

Herod, A., Peck, J. & Wills, J. 2003, 'Geography and industrial relations', in P. Ackers & A. Wilkinson (eds) *Understanding Work and Employment:*

Industrial Relations in Transition, Oxford: Oxford University Press, pp. 176–92.

Herod, A. & Wright, M.W. (eds) 2002, *Geographies of Power: Placing Scale*, Oxford: Blackwell Publishing.

Ho, C. 2004, Migration as feminisation: Chinese women's experiences of work and family on contemporary Australia. Unpublished PhD thesis, University of Sydney.

Ho, C. & Alcorso, C. 2004, 'Migrants and employment: challenging the success story', *Journal of Sociology* 40(3): 237–59.

Hugo, G. 2000, 'Migrants and demography: global and Australian trends and issues for policy makers, business and employers'. Paper presented to the National Skilling, Migration Labour and the Law Symposium, 23–24 November, University of Sydney.

Joll, C., McKenna, C., McNabb, R. & Shorey, J. 1983, *Development in Labour Market Analysis*, London: Allen & Unwin.

Kelly, J. & McAllister, I. 1984, 'Immigrants, socio-economic attainment, and politics in Australia', *British Journal of Sociology* 35(3): 387–405.

Kenny, A. 2004, 'Medical dominance and power: a rural perspective', *Health Sociology Review* 13(2): 158–65.

Khoo, S., Voigt-Graf, C., Hugo, G. & McDonald, P. 2003, 'Temporary skilled migration to Australia: the 457 visa sub-class', *People and Place* 11(4): 27–40.

Kofman, E., Phizacklea, A., Raghuram, A. & Sales, R. 2000, *Gender and International Migration in Europe*, London: Routledge.

Lever-Tracy, C. & Quinlan, M. 1988, *A Divided Working Class: Ethnic Segmentation and Industrial Conflict in Australia*, London: Routledge & Kegan Paul.

Ley, D. 2004, 'Transnational spaces and everyday lives', *Transactions of the Institute of British Geographers* 29(2): 151–64.

Massey, D. 1984, *Spatial Divisions of Labour: Social Structures and the Geography of Production*, London: Macmillan.

Massey, D. 1997, *Capital Culture: Gender at Work in the City*, Oxford: Basil Blackwell.

Moore, R. 1994, *An Administrative History of the Assessment of Skills and Qualifications of Migrants of Non-English Speaking Background and Equal Opportunity, from the Second World War Until 1990*. Working Paper no. 111, Edith Cowan University, Perth.

OECD 2001, *The Employment of Foreigners: Outlook and Issues in OECD Countries*, Paris: OECD.

Peck, J. 1996, *Work-place: The Social Regulation of Labor Markets*, New York: Guilford Press.

Pile, S. & Keith, M. 1997, *Geographies of Resistance*, London: Routledge.

Reich, M., Gordon, D.M. & Edwards, R.C. 1973, 'Dual labor markets: a theory of labor market segmentation', *American Economic Review* 63(2): 359–65.

Richardson, S.F., Robertson, F. & Ilsley, D. 2001, *The Labour Force Experience of New Migrants*, Adelaide: Department of Immigration and Multicultural and Indigenous Affairs.

Richardson, S., Miller-Lewis, L., Ngo, P. & Ilsley, D. 2002, *Life in a New Land: The Experience of Migrants in Wave 1 of LSIA and LSIA 2*. Report to the Department of Immigration and Multicultural and Indigenous Affairs, Canberra: Commonwealth of Australia.

Ruddock, P. 2000, 'Australian immigration: grasping the new reality'. Paper presented to the National Skilling, Migration Labour and the Law Symposium, 23–24 November, University of Sydney.

Ruddock, P. 2003, *Record Numbers of Migrants to Boost Economy*, MPS 46/2003, 10 July, www.minister.immi.gov.au/media_releases/ruddock_media03/r03046.htm

Taran, P. & Geronimi, E. 2003, *Perspectives on Labour Migration 3 E – Globalisation, Labour and Migration: Protection is Paramount*, Geneva: International Labour Office.

United Nations 2002, Population/844 un.org/News/Press/docs/2002/pop844.doc.htm.

VandenHeuvel, A. & Wooden, M. 2000, 'Immigrants' labour market experiences in the early settlement years', *Australian Bulletin of Labour* 26(1): 59–69.

Vietorisz, T. & Harrison. B. 1973, 'Labor market segmentation: positive feedback and divergent development', *American Economic Review* 63(2): 366–76.

Wood, G.A. 1992, 'The depletion of migrants' human capital'. Economic Programme Working Paper no. 70, Murdoch University, Perth.

CHAPTER NINE

A SPATIAL PERSPECTIVE ON INTERNATIONAL WORK AND MANAGEMENT
Illustrations from China

Susan McGrath-Champ

In the current era of global capitalism, the internationalisation of organisations is a spatial and geographical activity, although this phenomenon is seldom acknowledged in the human resource management, industrial relations or management literatures. Over the past decade, however, there has been growing interest across the social sciences and humanities in space and geographical matters. A similar tendency is emerging in scholarship concerning work and labour, witnessed by single papers and chapters plus a growing number of edited collections (*Economic and Industrial Democracy* 2005 special issue; *Labour and Industry* 2002 special issue; Rainnie & Grobbelear 2005).

Geography is not an 'optional extra' but is integral to, 'an active element' in, all social life and activity. This chapter seeks to highlight the role of 'space' in the social activity of work. Specifically, it focuses on international aspects of work and management, drawing on China for illustrative purposes. It approaches this by providing a brief overview of three different approaches to the international study of work and management (cross-cultural, international HRM and comparative studies), drawn largely from existing literature as well as the author's primary research. It identifies the nature and contribution of each approach, outlines the manner in which 'space' is handled in that body of literature, and provides a brief critique of this. Discussion then shifts to the application of geographical concepts from economic or labour geography and the insights that these hold for studies of international work and management.

To underpin the discussion, some basic geographical concepts – place, space and scale – need to be laid out. As a working definition, 'place' can be understood as a society characterised by certain norms of social behaviour. Place has a core location, in which those norms are most generally established. About that core those norms merge into the norms of a nearby place. As discussed below, 'other places' that contribute to defining a given place can, in physical terms, be very distant. This notion of place is distinctive in its emphasis on social, cultural and behavioural factors in delineating the physical dimension of place. 'Space' refers to the organisation of places (internally and externally) and relates to the social distance between those places. 'Scale' is deployed to identify the most appropriate lens through which to think about place and space. There are many different scales – global, macro-regional (the Asia-Pacific), national, subnational regional (New South Wales or New England), urban (Sydney), or local (inner-city Melbourne). Theories of scale concern questions about the lenses that are most relevant to examining particular social processes. Like place and space, scale is also an object of social and political struggle. There is debate and discussion in the geographical literature over these core notions, and while an operational definition is called for, these depictions should be taken as indicative, not incontrovertible. Note that geographers often avoid single-style definition of these concepts, around which there is common understanding as well as much deliberation. Barnes et al. (2004: 331) say that debates about their nature and importance are as old as the sub-discipline of economic geography itself. For further discussion of these core concepts see, for example, Johnson (1991), Peck (1996), Lee & Wills (1997), Herod (1998) and Barnes et al. (2004).

The following section outlines three key approaches to the study of international work and management and identifies the 'missing dimension' – the absence of geographically informed thinking in these literatures. The third section introduces some key discussions from the geographical literature to provide a sense of how geographically informed interpretation can enhance the understanding of work and management in the context of the global organisation of capital. The final section concludes that a dynamic and prominent sense of place, space and scale can contribute to defining new avenues for worker and management praxis in this era of 'globalisation'.

PLACE AND SPACE IN INTERNATIONAL STUDIES OF WORK AND MANAGEMENT

There are at least three broad approaches to the study of work organisation internationally. As indicated by Harris and colleagues (2003), these are: cross-cultural studies, international HRM studies and comparative (country) studies. This section briefly depicts each body of research and its contribution. Indicative rather than exhaustive in nature, the purpose is to portray each of these in turn as a basis for discerning their inherent spatial and geographical dimensions and opportunities. The second subsection on international HRM is more expansive because of HRM's central importance and recent development. It gives attention to two aspects – training and performance management – and draws in part on the author's primary research.

Cross-cultural studies

As Harris and colleagues (2003: 5) indicate, the key premise of cross-cultural research is that every nation has its own unique set of deep-seated values and beliefs, and that these are reflected in the ways that societies operate, in the ways that economies operate, and how people work and are managed at work. That there are cultural differences between nations – differences in national values and attitudes – is a key factor given the internationalisation of employment. It has been further shown that the different values that typify different nationalities affect the way people organise, conduct and manage work.

Scholars in the fields of work and management have endeavoured to translate the insights of social anthropologists into the world of work. In addition to attempting to define culture (a difficult task), cross-cultural studies have been concerned with culture as a shaping process – a process that shapes organisations and behaviour, including behaviour at work. Pioneering research in this area includes the work by Hofstede (1980), which explored the dimensions of power distance, uncertainty avoidance, individualism and masculinity. Trompenaars (1993) also compared cultures using bipolar cultural dimensions (for example individual/group dynamics; small/large power distance) and others have refined and extended such concepts (Lane et al. 1997). Concern about the Western bias among cross-cultural researchers led to an adapted version of Hofstede's questionnaire that included specifically Chinese values related to Confucianism or long-term versus short-term orientation. Reflecting differences in regard to future (versus present) orientation, thrift and persistence, this accounts for why Japanese and other Asian firms commonly adopt a long-term approach to investment, in contrast to Western companies which require much more immediate returns and profit performance.

This has been an abundant field of research, adding significantly to the understanding of observed and prominent contrasts in work and its attributes between different countries. Probably the strongest contributions were the identification of cultural dimensions with hard data, making comparisons across countries possible, and which revealed cultural consequences in managerial behaviours (Romani 2004: 148). Previously, culture was seen as a vague, intangible, 'soft' dimension that could not be quantified or measured and could thus be ignored. The basic insights yielded by this research domain are relevant to studies that focus on particular aspects of international HRM, and of course provide an essential part of the knowledge base for people who work and manage outside their initial national setting.

The cross-cultural approach subsumes space and geography as 'culture', where differences between places are perceived as cultural differences. That is, culture is what makes places different, and vice versa: cultural differences arise from, and are associated with, different places. Neither way of putting it is incorrect, but represents a partial understanding of 'place'. Place is relational, connected with and constituted by other places and cultures. As discussed below, a place (and its culture) involves both what is 'inside' and 'outside' that place.

Some cross-cultural studies of work and management identify 'space' as an element of culture. For example, Adler identifies 'private/public' space and Hall includes 'personal/physical' space (in Harris et al. 2003: 19) – how much distance is needed between people to feel 'comfortable' in conversation. This acknowledges, but confines, space to the microscale of the person or body and perceives it (inadequately) in solely physical terms.

International human resource management studies

International HRM has been defined as 'the HRM issues and problems arising from the internationalisation of business, and the HRM strategies, policies and practices which firms pursue in response to the internationalisation of business' (Scullion 1995 cited in Scullion & Linehan 2005: 4). While the past 25 years have seen a major growth in attention to strategy and HRM, the related field of international HRM is more recent. Nearly two decades ago, Laurent (1986) commented that international HRM was a field in the infancy stage of development and it has been only in the last five to ten years that a more abundant literature has begun to emerge. The establishment of academic journals in this area and a growing number of textbooks, some primarily for teaching purposes and others blending the functions of research and teaching (for example Harris et al. 2003; Dowling & Welch 2004; Scullion & Linehan 2005), suggest that this area is reaching a further stage.

Consistent with HRM, the international HRM field is concerned with the human resource problems of multinational firms and foreign subsidiaries or ventures (such as expatriate management) or, more broadly, with the unfolding HR issues that are associated with the various stages of the internationalisation process. Reflecting evolving business practice, the field now encompasses international human resource activities that are not so typical of 'expatriate' assignments, including short-term and 'virtual' assignments (Fenwick 2004).

Most functional areas of HRM have been examined within the international/multinational context, though not evenly. Training has received considerable attention and links closely with the cross-cultural approach (see above). It has been shown that cross-cultural training helps expatriates to manage 'culture shock', prepares them for the initial and continuous challenges they will face, and reduces the likelihood of premature return (Brewster & Pickard 1994). The specific ways in which poor expatriate preparation impacts on the expatriate, the parent firm and the host company are now clearer (Kealey & Protheroe 1996). It has also been established that systematic design of cross-cultural training programs can enhance cross-cultural interactions and cross-cultural adjustment (Tarique & Caligiuri 2004).

A key limitation (both in research and business practice) is the almost exclusive focus on cross-cultural training before departure. Little attention is given to training that concerns job content or is directed towards ongoing career development, yet it is in these areas that long-lasting and sustained training benefits augment the initial advantages of culturally well-prepared assignees (McGrath-Champ & Yang 2002; Tahvanainen & Suutari 2005). Further, training for host-country nationals is rare even though it stands to enhance the interface between nationals and expatriates (McGrath-Champ & Yang 2002). While the proportion of multinational companies that provide at least one day of training for expatriates has increased from a low 32 per cent in the early 1980s to around 70 per cent 20 years later (Tarique & Caligiuri

2004: 284), 30 per cent of multinational companies still do not provide expatriate training. It appears that among newly internationalised or internationalising organisations (those not designated as 'multinationals') the extent of training is rather lower (McGrath-Champ & Yang 2006).

If pre-departure training is one of the more examined areas of international HRM, performance management is one of the least (Tahvanainen & Suutari 2005). In particular, there is little understanding of how performance management systems in overseas assignments are integrated with training in foreign ventures to enable the ongoing developmental purposes of performance management to be realised. As a strategic tool, performance management can be used as a mechanism to establish alignment (or control) between parent company (or headquarters) goals and the subsidiary (Tahvanainen & Suutari 2005), acting as a 'pipeline' to the local market (Fenwick et al. 1999). A study that explored how cross-cultural training and career development for expatriates are integrated into performance management in Australian ventures in China showed that larger, multinational companies had performance management arrangements but there was an absence of performance management arrangements in small international ventures. Even in larger organisations, links between training and performance management were underdeveloped (McGrath-Champ & Yang 2006).

Unevenness and knowledge gaps are to be expected in a relatively new field of study and this presently typifies the field of international HRM. Significantly, however, international HRM has inserted people management into the realm of multinational business, which has been dominated by trade statistics and foreign direct investment data and focused on international production, international marketing and international strategy. In observing that 'human resource management is of fundamental importance in realising an efficient and effective multinational company', Harzing (2004: 36) indicates that the fundamental *raison d'être* of this field is to enhance the operation of multinational enterprises – the agents of international business. This presents both an important reality and also a point of contention to those who take a critical stance towards globalisation and the agency of multinationals, a point that is explored below.

As in early cross-cultural studies, there has tended to be a Western bias in international HRM, even though non-Western firms are prominent multinationals also. Interestingly, Dowling & Welch (2004) have

170

observed that increasingly, domestic HRM is taking on some of the flavour of international HRM as the former deals more often now with a multicultural workforce. They also note that ways of managing diversity in a single national context may not transfer to a multinational context without modification (or vice versa). While there is some awareness of non-managerial workers in international organisations (usually termed 'host-country nationals'), international managers or expatriates have been, and remain, the dominant focus of studies in international HRM (the inclusion of host-country nationals is usually host-country *managers* and rarely extends to non-managerial host-country workers). There has been criticism that international HRM has been unduly narrow in its focus on expatriates and culture, giving too little attention to other key dimensions. Rubery & Grimshaw (2003: xvii–xviii) comment in regard to this:

> Our particular frustration . . . has been with the subject of international human resource management; texts in this area often define their topic very narrowly, focusing on the management of employment – and primarily managerial employment – within multinationals. The issue of diversity in employment systems is neatly dealt with by the rather abstract but contentious notion of differences in national culture, which absolves students and textbook writers alike from being required to know too much about the actual social and institutional context in which the subsidiaries of multinationals are located. This institution-free approach to human resource management cannot be justified in the light of the now prolific literature on diversity in employment systems.

In international HRM research, the focus is the organisational interface between corporate strategy and the international assignee as an organisational agent – conveying the corporation's values and ways of working and managing to another place. There is little perception in the literature of the reality of the physical or social nature of space, yet effectively the expatriate is a spatial agent.

The 'pipeline' effect (control mechanism between headquarters and a subsidiary) discussed in the literature on international work and management entails an under-recognised dimension of spatial agency: the implementation in one place of organisational goals from another. The international HRM field has given little attention to the places where managers operate, the influence of space on their managerial activities, and so on. This may stem from the limited spatial dimension of international business, a field with which international HRM has close affinity. One of the other key disciplinary influences on HRM, industrial relations, has likewise been noted for its past 'spatial blindness' (McGrath-Champ 1994).

There is a further dimension. Irrespective of what organisation they work for, workers (including expatriate managers) work locally – in a place. Adapting to a new place is the prime focus of research concerned with the expatriate adjustment, which occupies a good share of the international HRM and cross-cultural literatures.

The importance of space, place and notions of geographical scale is evident in even the simplest example. An international assignee (expatriate) takes up an assignment in a new location, say China, and experiences initial difficulty in adapting to the very different culture. The expatriate adapts, overcoming this unease (adequately enough to remain on the assignment), and goes about implementing headquarters' strategy to establish a manufacturing plant which supplies the market in the home country.

This 'going to a new place' is spatial. Experiencing a new place and adapting to it (or not) is geographical. The expatriate is a social agent, bringing with him or her attributes and experiences ('culture') from the home environment, and mixing them with the new environment. He or she is also a spatial agent: different places 'meet' through this encounter. Over time there stands to be some change to the receiving and sending localities. There may be some heightened awareness of what things are like in the expatriate's home country plus implementation of some of the ways of doing business that are transferred from there. The expatriate also conveys knowledge of the host country back to the home country – its social, regulatory and institutional milieu, the impediments and opportunities that these entail. A further spatial dimension is evident in the control mechanisms conveyed over distance, as is the sale of goods back into the home market. This brief illustration shows that geography thoroughly permeates organisational, managerial and working life. These in turn impinge on existing places to shape and alter their nature – though not necessarily with the outcome of creating unstoppable homogeneity throughout the globe, as discussed below.

There is a need to see geography as spatial strategy and to understand the spatiality of working life and managerial activity. Multinationals are vitally concerned with geographical differences, from the basics of physical resource endowments that make one location more attractive over another, through to the variable human landscape – the accretion of institutional, legal, political and knowledge dimensions – which add additional complexity to the determination of competitive advantage. Indeed geography, understood in these terms, is fundamental to the making and remaking of the landscape of capitalism (industry, jobs, institutions, location and work-related flow of people) across the globe. In the literature on work and management this is missed, while in the business literature on multinationals it is generally over-extended, producing distorted stereotypes of 'footloose' firms that can locate, unconstrained, wherever they choose. We now shift to the third approach in the literature concerning international work and management.

Comparative/country studies

Comparative or country studies abound in the field of industrial relations. Although boundaries between industrial relations and HRM are less marked these days, comparative HRM research is much rarer than comparative industrial relations research (Boxall 1995). Comparative texts tend to be one of two types, providing either a series of single-country studies or taking a (fairly narrow) focus on a particular theme or dimension, such as the industrial relations system or the training system and examining this across a number of countries (Rubery & Grimshaw 2003). Many of the detailed country studies are single-country studies rather than comparative, usually leaving it to the reader to do the work of comparison, a characteristic that has evoked criticism (Boxall 1995; Rubery & Grimshaw 2003).

Prominent among comparative/country studies of labour and HRM in China is the work by Malcolm Warner (and colleagues) concerning labour market changes (Lee & Warner 2002); aspects of HRM and development and work practices (Gooda et al. 2004) that are accompanying the massive shift from the former command economy (based around state-owned enterprises or SOEs) to a market-oriented economy with its 'open door' foreign investment policy; accession of China to the World Trade Organisation (Zhu & Warner 2004); and emergence of the 'new Chinese worker'. This is only a small selection of the available studies.

The findings are wide-ranging. Noting regional variations across China that arise from different legal, economic and political environments (Warner 1997), it is evident that workplace reforms affect and are received differently by different types of workers. While many welcome the new workplace reforms, they appear to be less palatable to older and female workers, who are disproportionately bearing the brunt of displacement (Warner 2001). With the decline in importance of the SOEs, the nature of employment in the increasingly important town and village enterprises (TVEs) has also been a focus (Chow & Fu 2000; Ding et al. 2001). The government has been relying on TVEs to increase government revenue, create employment for the massive unskilled labour force in rural areas, and increase average income levels. They have progressed from being a peripheral and unrecognised part of the (centrally planned) economy to a major pillar of the Chinese economy in the current era.

These studies show that although HRM practices in TVEs are primitive compared to SOEs, there have been significant changes in employment practices (particularly in larger TVEs) such as shifts in recruitment mechanisms (from referral to selection), more formalised training (replacing apprenticeships), and the linking of pay to performance and skill level. A key message is that HRM 'with Chinese characteristics' typifies work and employment in this emerging economy, and there is some, limited, 'convergence' with Western HRM arising from the shift to marketisation. Not surprisingly, China is usually included in comparative texts on work, organisation and employment (for example Frenkel 1993; Budhwar & Debrah 2001; Rowley & Benson 2004). From their multi-country review, Rowley & Benson identify both evidence of a shift towards Western HRM practice (in China and throughout Asia) but mixed responses in terms of policy and underlying beliefs and assumptions. From this they infer that such practices have not yet been internalised so that HRM systems are unstable and characterised by experimentation.

Comparative/country studies salute the differences (and similarities) between places. Yet even so, as an analytical device place is implicit rather than explicit in many of these studies. The historical geography of capitalism contributes to contemporary place differences (Herod 2002). More can be known and understood of these differing places, and those who work in different places stand to be empowered if these places, their contrasts and connections are embraced explicitly and consciously. If we recognise these countries, their constituent sub-areas and supranational relations as distinctive places then we may understand them much more. In the 'world of work', there is a pressing need to see the world as a place, to see the placed-ness and spatiality of the social process of work and how it is organised, regulated, used by capital, and the way in which workers shape capital and institutions and engage politically to achieve this.

The case of China highlights the interrelatedness of all three approaches to studying work and management in an international context. The culture of China, one of the most obvious characteristics of this country (at least to those outside China), is a key influence on human resources, management and work. Cross-cultural research (the first approach) established culture as a bona fide influence rather than a 'soft' category. Studies of Chinese labour in China (the country/ comparative, or third approach) interface with studies of how foreign firms manage their expatriate labour (the international HRM or second approach) in the newest form of corporate organisation to be established in this country during this era of growing marketisation of the Chinese economy.

On their own terms the above studies make a very favourable and significant contribution. However, there are difficulties in how place, space and scale are understood and deployed. The studies interface with space but it has been shown that they do not discuss it. In each of these approaches to the international study of work and management, the spatial or geographical aspects are implicit; they are not deliberately ignored but just not acknowledged or examined. It is more helpful to draw out the influence of place instead of its being 'spoken for' by culture or subsumed as institutional or structural differences. It is important to identify the geographical activity of international managers, to understand them and their work as influenced by and exerting influence on space and impacting on place.

THE 'PLACE FOR SPACE': AUGMENTING INTERNATIONAL STUDIES OF WORK AND EMPLOYMENT

This section addresses three themes or ways in which a clearer grasp of place, space and geographical scale enhance the analysis of work and management in the international domain. It discusses the nature of place, the manner in which this enlightens the mistaken notion of global homogenisation, and spatial embeddedness.

Place and work

The social relations of work have a temporal dimension: they occur at a particular point in time. There is also a spatial dimension: work occurs

175

in the circumstances of 'place' at a particular scale which has, associated with it, an accumulation of connections and relations elsewhere, across geographical space. That is, the social relations of work are accompanied by inherent spatial relations of work. An understanding of place is important in all three approaches outlined above, and thus the notion of 'place' is developed below to enable a more robust reworking of international studies of work and management.

In its most useful form, place is fluid and permeable. What makes a place has usually been regarded as what goes on inside, or within, it. But the implicit distinction between 'local' and 'non-local' is not defensible. Increasingly, places are interconnected, even those at great distances from each other. The notion of globalisation has gone some way to capturing this (Castree et al. 2004: 66). Places are also interdependent and permeable. To understand locally situated workers, managers, firms and institutions, it is necessary to look not only within a place but beyond that place.

Instead of places as bounded and undisturbed, it is more accurate to think of place in terms of openness, interconnection and networks (Massey & Jess 1995: 64). 'Places are not given in nature' (Castree et al. 2004: 64) but are socially constructed. Places are shaped and influenced by the local environment and circumstances, but it is the sedimentation of these practices over time that gives these places their distinctiveness (Massey 1984).

Massey (1994: 152–4) elaborates on 'place' in a manner that provides the foundation for insight into the connection of place and work. Kilburn, her home suburb, a 'pretty ordinary place' north-west of the centre of London, is a cosmopolitan place with people originating from many countries, who bring to that place varied cultures – from Ireland, the Middle East, India and elsewhere. The blending of these cultures, she observes, gives Kilburn 'a character of its own', one that is not static, nor one that is perceived or experienced the same from one person to the next. Kilburn is not introverted, and it is impossible to think about Kilburn without 'bringing into play half the world and a considerable amount of British imperialist history'. Kilburn is connected with, and defined by, the near at hand and things far away. It has its own unique and evolving mix of these local and non-local influences, its own 'sense of place'.

Much the same applies to less (or seemingly un-) changing places – there being simply a different blend of the internal and external, of stasis and change. Depicting place as fluid, as constituted by what is both 'within' and 'outside' a place, a spatial moment in ever-changing social relations, provokes a really 'global sense of place' (Massey 1994: 154). It is certainly a more accurate sense of place.

Similar insights apply to the world of work. Understanding place in this manner enables discernment of how global forces affecting employment intermingle with local, regional and national structures, histories, and patterns of work to produce new patterns and 'new' places that are different from before. It also allows us to understand how local, regional and national events and processes pertaining to work and management connect with, and penetrate, the global realm. For the past 15 years in Australia, there has been growing individualisation of work and deregulation of industrial relations institutions. There is a growing likeness between aspects of Australian industrial relations and those of the USA, which was foreshadowed earlier (Niland 1989). In China, on the other hand, work and human resource practices are being shaped and influenced by the practices and activities conveyed by multinationals, though, as noted above, with 'Chinese characteristics' still quite evident.

Some might call this 'homogenisation'. But the outcomes (transformed characteristics, processes and institutions of work) will be different from those in the places of origin, because of the distinct and unique nature of what they are being blended with (Australian work and industrial relations traditions in the former instance, or the Chinese legacy of work and industry in the latter). Conversely, one might wonder whether 'Chinese characteristics' such as *guanxi* (which refers to building connections or relationships) will become a more common influence on managerial and work relations outside Asia as an outcome of this interface. This is the 'remaking' of place, or the making of 'new' places, the transformation of work, management, employment; the blending of social influences from different places that changes and recreates those places.

A further instance of geographical subtlety concerns the role of language (one of the cornerstones of culture) in shaping corporate organisational structures. Deploying an international HRM (that is, a second) approach, a study of the impact of language on communication in large and geographically dispersed multinationals identified language as a 'shadow structure' – a structure that lies behind the organisational arrangements of the company and recasts the formal control mechanisms, coordination and command arrangements (Marschan-Peikkari et al. 1999). Marschan-Peikkari and colleagues found that 'language

177

distance' (the closeness of relation between the subsidiary and parent company that derives from fluency of subsidiary personnel in the language/s used within the parent company) recasts the formal configuration of companies. In the case of the Finnish corporation Kone, Mexico linked more closely with Spain and Italy (through the Spanish–Italian language affinity) than the physically nearer North America (USA and Canada), with implications for the exercise of power within the multinational. This demonstrates how language constructs a geography that is different from the physical geography which is presumed in standard organisational management arrangements (and depicted in organisational charts). This can only be seen if a physical sense of space and place is discarded in favour of the more relevant sense of geography in fluid social terms.

Global homogenisation?

As indicated above, management and human resources within multinationals are key focuses of the international HRM literature. Discussion of multinationals leads to a consideration of globalisation. The debated and contested nature of 'globalisation' (for example Giddens 1990; Ohmae 1990; Hill 2003) is widely known and will not be reiterated here. One of the myths of globalisation is that everywhere is becoming similar (Castree et al. 2004), that some grand homogenisation of the world is under way, and that in due course differences will be diluted to the extent that places which are presently distinct will become largely the same. Not surprisingly, this evokes a good deal of concern, but it is largely unfounded. While a seemingly 'shrinking globe' and hastening of social interaction between places is a reasonable perception, geographers have argued strongly and successfully against the erroneous belief that this means that places are losing their distinctiveness and becoming similar (Massey & Jess 1995; Bryson et al. 1999). There has been a qualitative change in the economic environment affecting workers and managers throughout the world. But globalisation does not mean the homogenisation of social and economic relations across space (Bryson et al. 1999). It does not mean 'the death of distance' but entails a heightened integration of all places and scales with each other, with an accompanying increase in the complexity of interaction of various scales.

The extent of 'sameness' between different places that may emerge is unlikely to obliterate the distinctiveness of those places, the difference of cultures, work and management in different places. With places constituted as what is 'in' them and their relations elsewhere (what is 'outside' them), globalisation highlights the interconnectedness and interdependence of places, people and work.

In geography, since the pioneering work of Massey (1984), it has become common to depict places (including the influence exerted by capitalist forces and the resulting forms, institutions and processes of work and management) as being an accretion of influences over time that are 'laid down', built upon and transformed further as new influences exert themselves in a 'sedimentary' manner. The similarity with observations concerning the making of industrial relations is striking. Boxall (1995: 12, citing Poole 1986) comments that:

> strategic choices become 'deeply layered' or 'sedimented' through processes of institutionalisation . . . Then, at critical historical junctures, fundamental decisions on appropriate industrial relations forms are taken that gradually become embedded in particular societies and are transmitted from one generation to the next through institutions.

All that is missing here is the notion that just as industrial relations forms become 'sedimented' in different societies, they also become embedded spatially – in different places. Further, that transmission occurs not just through time (from generation to generation) but also across space, through the agency of both management and labour, and the evolution of the capitalist landscape.

Spatial embeddedness and the scaling of work and management

A further myth concerns the relative mobility of workers and organisations – the notion that in this globalised world, firms are now hypermobile but workers remain hopelessly place-bound. The focus of international HRM (the second approach) on multinational corporations and the attention given in comparative/country studies (the third approach) to the interaction of developed and developing countries' employment and HR practices is founded on this myth but largely omits exploration of it. 'Firms are seen as being increasingly able to "play-off" workers one against the other in a geographical divide-and-rule strategy' (Castree et al. 2004), even more so in an era of declining trade barriers. Associated with this is the idea that firms, driven by labour cost, have the capacity to, and commonly will, opt for places with cheap labour. This is understood as creating a 'race to the bottom' whereby,

179

under threat of firm closure or relocation, workers are compelled to accept reduced wages and conditions, knowing that cheaper workers elsewhere could do their work.

Although there are seeds of reality in this (like most myths), a well-established line of argument is that the obsession with the seemingly 'placeless' nature of modern capitalism is unwarranted and that multinationals are only relatively footloose (for example Dicken 2003; Castree et al. 2004). Large national and multinational companies have the capacity to search the globe for the most amenable combination of production and regulatory factors (including labour), but they must ultimately commit to specific places. There are enormous sunk costs (for example workplace facilities, training investments, costs of creating relationships with trade unions) involved in 'connecting with the local' to enable production to occur, and in developing rapport once new product/service destinations or suppliers are sought out in new places (Clark & Wrigley 1997). Further, the preoccupation with multinational capital's capacity to disregard 'place' overlooks the multitude of small and medium-sized enterprises which worldwide constitute the vast majority of total businesses and share of employment (Hayter 1997 cited in Castree et al. 2004: 77). Smaller firms are very much locally embedded, though not unaffected by the competitive activity of firms that have a wider spatial purview.

Harvey (2004: 456) observes that the diminution of spatial barriers heightens the importance of place and space:

> The more spatial barriers disintegrate, so more rather than less of the world's population clings to place and neighbourhood or to nation, region, ethnic grouping, or religious belief as specific marks of identity . . . The diminution of spatial barriers has provoked an increasing sense of nationalism and localism . . . The reduction of spatial barriers has an equally powerful opposite effect: small-scale and finely graded differences between the qualities of places (their labor supply, their infrastructures and political receptivity, their resource mixes, their market niches, etc.) become even more important because multinational capital is in a better position to exploit them. Places, by the same token, become much more concerned about their 'good business climate' and inter-place competition for development becomes much more finely-tuned.

The notion of scale (which we think about in terms such as local, regional, national, international, global) is fundamental to grasping the interface of labour with global capital. Scale, or the processes,

institutions and relationships at different scales, connect with processes, institutions and relationships at other scales. Thus, as Herod
& Wright (2002) emphasise, scales are not discrete and separate rungs
on a ladder by which one climbs up and down, but interwoven, interdependent, dialectical (Howitt 1993: 8) and mutually constitutive. It
is important not to privilege the global scale or to diminish work and
workers as purely 'local'. Rather it is necessary to engage all scales and to
recognise them as interconnected, interwoven, interdependent. Each of
the three approaches to international work and management is characterised by limited scalar engagement. The cross-cultural approach
emphasises the distinctiveness of local and national culture, the international HRM approach is preoccupied with the global activity of
multinationals, and the comparative/country approach is lodged principally at the national scale. Rarely in such studies is there an adequate
embrace of the multi-scalar dimensions of work and management.

An overemphasis on the mobility of capital neglects the fact that
locational decisions of firms are vastly more complex than simply
searching out cheap labour. Skills, compliance, initiatives and productivity are crucial, along with the broader regulatory environment
for labour. Non-labour dimensions may be more important. Another
dimension of this changing 'spatial division of labour' (Massey 1984) is
the effect on low-wage workers. China is arguably the most prominent
low-wage labour source at present, superseding other South-East Asian
countries where wages have climbed over the past two or three decades.
Chan (2001) points out that abuse and exploitation also accompanies
the 'new Chinese economy'. The 'new' Chinese worker is a long way
from universal and it is no surprise that the 'Chinese worker faces a
highly uncertain future in the age of globalization' (Warner 2001: 141).

Associated with discussion of the mobility of capital is the idea that
for workers to resist the spatial manipulations of capital they must 'up-
scale' their activities to match and deflect the translocal influences
that are undermining their well-being. 'The idea here is that if workers in different places [internationally] join together they can act to
prevent firms or certain regulatory authorities playing them off against
each other' (Castree et al. 2004: 21). A range of literature on emerging forms of cross-national organising (Herod 1998; Taylor & Mathers
2004), and the re-emergence of 'new' labour internationalism (Lambert
& Webster 2001; Waterman & Wills 2001) documents and explores
such action, which is exerting increasing influence on union organisation and strategy. In Australia, an example is the Maritime Union of

Australia, which successfully sought international union support during the waterfront dispute of 1998 to extend union activity at the national and local scales to the international scale (Sadler & Fagan 2004).

'Up-scaling' workers' struggles beyond the national scale can be an effective way to improve their livelihoods. However, Herod (2003) and Castree and colleagues (2004) warn that an uncritical celebration of labour trans-nationalism is naive and could be damaging to the interests of some workers. There are three reasons for this. First, the promotion of global union action is sometimes accompanied by an implicit or explicit devaluing of the importance of local worker and union action. Action at all or various scales is usually the most effective, and to presume that a new scale of action should supplant another is unwise. Second, some acts of transnational solidarity are exclusive and include one set of workers by defining their relevant constituency against a set of other workers. 'So the socio-geographic divisions within the global "working class" do not just exist at the local scale but occur translocally too' (Castree et al. 2004: 227). Third, the motives of workers initiating international solidarity campaigns may not always be altruistic. A campaign supported by workers in one country that contributes in another country to raising wages or achieving the right to unionise without employer interference may make these workers less attractive to capital relocation (because of their higher wages or union rights). This may discourage or deny capital investment that would benefit workers in the second country (Johns & Vural 2000 cited in Herod 2003: 513). A grasp of scalar interdependence of worker action is vital to evaluating the impact and implications of such activity, and to enhancing research on international work and management.

CONCLUSION

This chapter has shown that international studies of work and management entail much that is spatial and geographical; moreover, that this study of work and organisation *is* a study of place and space and requires an understanding of geographical scale. From a review of three different approaches in this field, the chapter outlined how a spatial perspective renders international studies of work, management and organisation more subtle, sophisticated and powerful. Analyses of work and management are made more robust by a fluid and relational sense of place, a grasp of the spatial embeddedness of work, and an understanding that the time-space 'shrinking' effect of globalisation entails intensified integration of activity (work) at different scales. The purpose of articulating a spatial perspective corresponds with Herod's comment that thinking about global capital and processes of globalisation as an 'explicitly geographical process (as well as an economic, political, and cultural one) allows us to ponder how the different parts of the planet are being rewired together and how this process of spatial reorganization may close off some avenues of praxis for workers but may yet open others' (Herod 2003: 215). Undoubtedly it also reveals avenues of managerial praxis.

Throughout earlier periods, and now in an era of economic globalisation, with the agency of multinational firms, one of the key goals has been the conquering of space by various organisational means. From this subjugation of space, capital has been able to benefit from the labour of workers and refashion the geographical landscape in its own image (Harvey 2000). But space, just like time and discourse, cannot be eradicated, and remains a major influence in capitalist activity and on the lives of workers and management. This is certainly the case even with the marketisation of China. In rethinking international work, more attention needs to be given to place, space and scale.

References

Barnes, T.J., Peck, J., Sheppard, E. & Tickell, A. (eds) 2004, *Reading Economic Geography*, Oxford: Blackwell.

Boxall, P. 1995, 'Building the theory of comparative HRM', *Human Resource Management Journal* 5(5): 5–17.

Brewster, C. & Pickard, J. 1994, 'Evaluating expatriate training', *International Studies of Management and Organizations* 24(3): 18–35.

Bryson, J., Henry, N., Keeble, D. & Martin, R. (eds) 1999, *The Economic Geography Reader: Producing and Consuming Global Capitalism*, Chichester, UK: Wiley.

Budhwar, P. & Debrah, Y. (eds) 2001, *Human Resource Management in Developing Countries*, London: Routledge.

Castree, N., Coe, N., Ward, K. & Samers, M. 2004, *Spaces of Work: Global Capitalism and the Geographies of Labour*, London: Sage.

Chan, A. 2001, *China's Workers Under Assault: Exploitation and Abuse in a Globalizing Economy*, Armonk, NY: M.E. Sharpe Inc.

Chow, I.H.S. & Fu, P.P. 2000, 'Change and development in pluralistic settings: an exploration of HR practices in Chinese township and village enterprises', *International Journal of Human Resource Management* 11(4): 822–36.

Clark, G. & Wrigley, N. 1997, 'The spatial configuration of the firm and the management of sunk costs', *Economic Geography*, 73(3): 285–304.

Dicken, P. 2003, *Global Shift: Reshaping the Global Economic Map in the 21st Century*, 4th edn, London: Sage.

Ding, D.Z., Lan, G. & Warner, M. 2001, 'A new form of Chinese human resource management? Personnel and labour-management relations in Chinese township and village enterprises: a case-study approach', *Industrial Relations Journal* 32(4): 328–45.

Dowling, P. & Welch, D. 2004, *International Human Resource Management: Managing People in a Multinational Context*, 4th edn, London: Thomson.

Economic and Industrial Democracy 2005, Special Issue on 'Globalisation's Challenge to Labour', 26(3).

Fenwick, M. 2004, 'On international assignment: is expatriation the only way to go?', *Asia Pacific Journal of Human Resources* 42(3): 365–77.

Fenwick, M., De Cieri, H. & Welch, D. 1999, 'Cultural and bureaucratic control in MNCs: the role of expatriate performance management', *Management International Review* 39: 107–24.

Frenkel, S. (ed.) 1993, *Organized Labor in the Asia-Pacific: A Comparative Study of Trade Unionism in Nine Countries*, Ithaca, NY: ILR Press.

Giddens, A. 1990, *The Consequences of Modernity*, Cambridge: Polity Press.

Gooda, K., Warner, M. & Lang, V. 2004, 'HRD in the People's Republic: the MBA "with Chinese characteristics"', *Journal of World Business* 39(4): 311–23.

Harris, H., Brewster, C. & Sparrow, P. 2003, *International Human Resource Management*, London: Chartered Institute of Personnel and Development.

Harvey, D. 2000, *Spaces of Hope*, Berkeley and Los Angeles: University of California Press.

Harvey, D. 2004, 'Between space and time: reflections on the geographical imagination', in S. Daniels & R. Lee (eds) *Exploring Human Geography*, London: Arnold, pp. 443–66.

Harzing, A.W. 2004, 'Strategy and structure of multinational companies', in A.W. Harzing & J. Van Ruyseveldt (eds) *International Human Resource Management*, London: Sage, pp. 33–64.

Herod, A. (ed.) 1998, *Organizing the Landscape: Geographical Perspectives on Labor Unionism*, Minneapolis: University of Minnesota Press.

Herod, A. 2002, 'Towards a more productive engagement: industrial relations and economic geography meet', *Labour and Industry* 13(2): 5–17.

Herod, A. 2003, 'Geographies of labor internationalism', *Social Science History* 27(4): 501–23.

Herod, A. & Wright, M. (eds) 2002, *Geographies of Power: Placing Scale*, Maldern, Mass.: Blackwell.

Hill, C. 2003, *International Business: Competing in the Global Marketplace*, 4th edn, Boston, Mass.: McGraw-Hill/Irwin.

Hofstede, G. 1980, *Culture's Consequences: International Differences in Work-Related Values*, London: Sage.

Howitt, R. 1993, '"The world in a grain of sand": towards a reconceptualisation of geographical scale', *Australian Geographer* 24(1): 33–44.

Johnson, R.J. 1991, *A Question of Place: Exploring the Practice of Human Geography*, Oxford: Blackwell.

Kealey, D.J. & Protheroe, D.R. 1996, 'The effectiveness of cross-cultural training for expatriates: an assessment of the literature on the issue', *International Journal of Intercultural Relations* 20(2): 141–65.

Labour and Industry 2002, Special Issue on 'Industrial relations meets geography: spatialising the social relations of work', 13(2).

Lambert, R. & Webster, E. 2001, 'Southern unionism and the new labour internationalism', *Antipode* 29(1): 337–63.

Lane, H., DiStefano, J. & Maznevski, J. 1997, *International Management Behavior*, Toronto: Nelson.

Laurent, A. 1986, 'The cross-cultural puzzle of international human resource management', *Human Resource Management* 25(1): 91–103.

Lee, G.O.J. & Warner, M. 2002, 'Labour-market policies in Shanghai and Hong Kong: a study of "one country, two systems" in Greater China', *International Journal of Manpower* 23(6): 505–26.

Lee, R. & Wills, J. (eds) 1997, *Geographies of Economies*, London and New York: Arnold.

McGrath-Champ, S. 1994, 'Integrating industrial geography and industrial relations: a literature review and case study of the Australian coal industry', *Tijdschrift Voor Economische en Sociale Geografie* (Journal of Economic and Social Geography) 85(3): 195–208.

McGrath-Champ, S. & Yang, X. 2002, 'Expatriate management, venture performance and the "New Economy": insights from exploratory Australia–China research' *Proceedings of the Fourth Conference on Multinational Business Economy*, Nanjing, China, 18–21 May.

McGrath-Champ, S. & Yang, X. 2006, 'Developing international management: the performance management-training interface in Australian firms in China', in E. Morgan & F. Fai (eds) *Managerial Issues in International Business*, Basingstoke: Palgrave Macmillan.

Marschan-Peikkari, R., Welch, D. & Welch, L. 1999, 'In the shadow: the impact of language on structure, power and communication in the multinational', *International Business Review* 8(4): 421–40.

Massey, D. 1984, *Spatial Divisions of Labour*, London: Macmillan.

Massey, D. 1994, *Space, Place and Gender*, Cambridge: Polity Press.

Massey, D. & Jess, P. 1995, *A Place in the World? Place, Cultures and Globalization*, Oxford: Oxford University Press.

Niland, J. 1989, *Transforming Industrial Relations in New South Wales: A Green Paper*, Sydney: NSW Government Printing Office.

Ohmae, K. 1990, *The Borderless World*, New York: Free Press.

Peck, J. 1996, *Work-place: The Social Regulation of Labor Markets*, New York: Guilford.

Rainnie, A. & Grobbelaar, M. (eds) 2005, *The New Regionalism in Australia: Prospects and Problems*, Aldershot: Ashgate.

Romani, L. 2004, 'Culture in management: the measurement of differences', in A.W. Harzing & J. Van Ruyseveldt (eds) *International Human Resource Management*, London: Sage, pp. 141–66.

Rowley, C. & Benson, J. (eds) 2004, *The Management of Human Resources in the Asia Pacific Region: Convergence Reconsidered*, London: Frank Cass.

Rubery, J. & Grimshaw, D. 2003, *The Organization of Employment: An International Perspective*, Basingstoke: Palgrave Macmillan.

Sadler, D. & Fagan, R. 2004, 'Australian trade unions and the politics of scale: reconstructing the spatiality of industrial relations', *Economic Geography*, 80(1): 23–44.

Scullion, H. & Linehan, M. (eds) 2005, *International Human Resource Management: A Critical Text*, Basingstoke: Palgrave Macmillan.

Tahvanainen, M. & Suutari, V. 2005, 'Expatriate performance management in MNCs', in H. Scullion & M. Linehan (eds) *International Human Resource Management: A Critical Text*, Basingstoke: Palgrave Macmillan, pp. 91–113.

Tarique, I. & Caligiuri, P. 2004, 'Training and development of international staff', in A.W. Harzing & J. Van Ruyseveldt (eds) *International Human Resource Management*, London: Sage, pp. 283–306.

Taylor, G. & Mathers, A. 2004, 'The European Trade Union Confederation at the crossroads of change? Traversing the variable geometry of European trade unionism', *European Journal of Industrial Relations* 13(4): 267–85.

Trompenaars, F. 1993, *Riding the Waves of Culture: Understanding Cultural Diversity in Business*, London: Economist Books.

Warner, M. 1997, 'Introduction: HRM in Greater China', *International Journal of Human Resource Management* 8(5): 565–68.

Warner, M. 2001, 'The new Chinese worker and the challenge of globalization: an overview', *International Journal of Human Resource Management* 12(1): 134–41.

Waterman, P. & Wills, J. (eds) 2001, *Space, Place and the New Labour Internationalisms*, Oxford: Blackwell.

Zhu, Y. & Warner, M. 2004, 'Changing patterns of human resource management in contemporary China: WTO accession and enterprise responses', *Industrial Relations Journal* 35(4): 449–66.

CHAPTER TEN

MARKETS AND THE SPATIAL ORGANISATION OF WORK

Mark Westcott

Industrial relations as an area of study developed, to a large extent, in response to marginalist economic analysis of markets. Marsden (1982: 236–8) has argued that the origins of industrial relations as a focus of inquiry lies in the inability of orthodox economics to explain labour supply. Kaufman (1993) makes a similar claim, charting the growth of institutional labour economics in the USA as the forerunner of the development of industrial relations in that country. Notwithstanding this genesis, the concept of a 'labour market' has been embedded in analyses of industrial relations phenomena from its very beginnings. For many industrial relations writers the operation of the labour market, far from being the competitive one depicted by orthodoxy, is shaped by the agency of buyers and sellers. This agency is expressed through institutional forms and more often than not is constrained or facilitated by the prevailing conditions around labour markets. While much industrial relations analysis empirically challenges the operation of the labour market as described by marginalist economics, it has not on the whole challenged the theoretical foundation of abstract market behaviour.

Herein lies the paradox of industrial relations and the study of work. While often cataloguing empirically the construction and reconstruction of labour and product markets, industrial relations has not developed an effective theoretical alternative to mainstream economics. The result is twofold. In much industrial relations analysis the operation and structure of markets is often seen as self-evident, requiring little or no explicit attention. Markets are at times depicted as aggregated entities that are largely homogeneous, and their shape and development are often portrayed as organic. The fractured or segmented nature of markets and how these segments are created or reinforced are inadequately addressed. Second, markets are treated as a contextual variable that influences the development of work relations. Certain types of work relations emerge as a consequence of specific market conditions. There is often a presumed internal competitive logic (market forces) attached to the effect of markets on the behaviour of managers or workers which results in a tendency towards a linear relationship between market conditions and work relations.

Industrial relations scholars are not alone in their concern about the link between market conditions and work. There are strong parallels between economic geography and industrial relations in their attempts to develop an analysis of work relations that is seen as a distinct and valid alternative to orthodox economics. While economic and labour geography have endured substantial paradigmatic change over the last 30 years (Barnes et al. 2004), a major issue for a number of writers in this area has been to develop alternatives to the orthodox economic explanations of industrial development (Peck 2005: 3). Radical economic geographers have shown a theoretical appreciation of the importance of particular temporal and geographical contexts in structuring capital development and consequently industrial landscapes, although it is only fairly recently that the role of workers and organised labour in this process has assumed more importance (Herod 2001: 3–6, 2002: 5–6).

In contrast, industrial relations writers have been interested in worker organisation and to a lesser extent industrial development and have largely ignored the importance of space and scale, at least in theoretical terms (Ellem & Shields 1999: 537). Many industrial relations scholars have tried to generalise about institutional developments and work relations under certain market conditions, with no recognition of spatial diversity. Perhaps industrial relations analysis would be strengthened by a more explicit theoretical recognition of space and scale and how these are constructed and reconstructed by workers and their representative institutions, by capital and by the state. Indeed, these geographical concepts could provide a way for markets to be incorporated into explanations of work relations. Moreover, appreciation of space and scale can also reinforce the social agency of actors and their capacity to structure and restructure market forms and influence market conditions.

This chapter examines the way in which markets, particularly the labour market, have been used as an explanatory device in industrial and work relations. Markets for labour, goods and services are seen as critical to shaping work relations. But these markets have often remained externally produced 'environmental' variables (Grimshaw & Rubbery 2003). By identifying the connections between capital, product and labour markets and locating these in particular spatial and temporal contexts, a more robust approach to explaining work relations can be developed. In short, this chapter shows that 'placing' labour markets is theoretically worthwhile and empirically significant.

INDUSTRIAL RELATIONS AND SPACE

In order to discuss markets, space and industrial relations meaningfully, it is necessary to make some initial observations about the field of industrial relations. Massey's observations about academic geography have some resonance with industrial relations: 'The academic disciplinary division of labour between "substance" and "space" has done harm to both. The "substance laws" of economics and sociology have been spatially blind, while geography has been periodically thrown in paroxysms of self doubt about whether it had a real object of study, and if so, what it was' (Massey 1984: 51).

While being more concerned with substance than with space, industrial relations is characterised by ambiguity (and self-doubt) over its focus of study. This stems largely from the lack of agreement on the substance at the centre of the field. Industrial relations writers have historically not been able to show the uniqueness of the empirical terrain of their area (the substance), or been able to claim a distinctive manner by which they study this terrain (Laffer 1974; Hyman 1975; Adams 1997).

There have been several issues of concern for industrial relations. Early writers focused largely on the growth and function of organised labour and this continues to preoccupy scholars. In the 1950s and 1960s there was a focus by many on unions and the development of collective regulation as well as the form and function of this collective regulation or, as Grimshaw & Rubbery put it, 'job rules' (2003: 48). Many studies in the USA and the UK focused on collective bargaining, although not necessarily in the same way. In Australia there was heavy emphasis on state-influenced regulation, particularly conciliation and arbitration, and how this impacted on unions, employers and wage fixation.

More recently, there has been considerable interest in labour management issues within organisations, the restructuring of employment, the
future of trade unions, and the changing nature of the labour force and
work itself. This changing focus of research reflects much of the prag-
matism associated with industrial relations as an area of study (Poole
1981).

Industrial relations scholars have drawn on many disciplines to study
these phenomena, with geography being notably absent until recently.
How might the notions of space and scale, as used by economic and
labour geographers, provide a better understanding of how work relations are structured? Herod (2002: 6) considers space as 'the material geographies within which people live their lives'. He argues that
industrial relations specialists, labour and social historians have been
inattentive to issues of geography and social praxis. He sees that 'such
scholars have generally tended to view geography in terms of how place
functions as a "context" for social actions rather than in terms of how
space and spatial relations may serve as sources of power and objects of
struggle' (Herod 2001: 2). Ellem & Shields (1999) have further argued
that industrial relations writers have referred to the notion of space,
albeit indirectly by recognising the levels at which work relations are
structured (workplace, industry, region, nation). Herod (2001: 6) refers
to defined levels of space (in terms of social, political and economic
processes) as 'scales'. Using this notion, most industrial relations writers have, when discussing national systems or undertaking industry or
workplace studies, been referring to particular scales of work relations.
In this way space and scale are portrayed as contextual factors against
which work relations are shaped.

Is space more than context? Massey makes a persuasive case for why
space is important. Work relations are part of a larger group of social
processes that shape how people live their lives. These social processes
occur in particular spaces, but space and process are inseparable. Massey
(1984: 52) argues that just as there are no purely spatial processes (for
instance, geography by itself does not account for uneven economic
development) social processes can never be non-spatial. Social processes do not occur 'in an environmentally characterless, neutral and
undifferentiated world'. Moreover,

> substance laws and analyses of social processes might be different were
> they to make integral the fact of their necessarily spatial character. It
> is certainly invalid for geographers to seek to define abstractly spatial

processes without reference to substantive content. But it is equally invalid for those in the substance disciplines to ignore the fact that the relations they study take place over space and in a geographically-differentiated world. (Massey 1984: 53)

How then does space help to shape work relations? Herod is clear that there needs to be an account of the production of space by both capital and labour. While Marxist economic geographers have focused on how capital constructs space in order to achieve accumulation, less attention has been paid to how workers as social agents resist or assist this construction. By recognising space and geographical scale, a less essentialist view of workers can be formed, revealing the geographical and historically contingent interests of workers that influence how they try to construct material geographies (Herod 2001: 6).

Perhaps the most important issue raised by economic geographers in their discussion of space is the connection between space and substance. Space is not just context; the material geography is not a condition that can be held constant in order to analyse social processes. Rather, social processes are important in shaping the material geographies. Using this rationality, a similar argument can be formulated concerning markets. Rather than being contextual and setting the environment in which work relations are developed, work relations impact on the specific nature of markets. Moreover, recognising that markets are empirical entities that have particular features linked to time and place, that they occupy spaces and can be analysed according to different geographical scales, would assist in developing a richer, if differentiated, account of work relations. Space and geographical scale, as long as we recognise that these are constructed by capital and labour, can provide a new way to activate social agency in an analysis of markets and work relations. Markets then become part of the analysis of work relations rather than peripheral to it. Perhaps the most pronounced influence would be an analysis of labour markets and work relations, which are considered in the following section.

THE LABOUR MARKET

'In a subject not noted for its "laws", one of the propositions coming pretty close to a law, first enunciated by Commons (1909), is that the industrial relations system follows developments in the market' (Sisson & Marginson 2002: 197). These two writers capture both the longevity of the concept of markets as an explanatory variable in industrial relations and the line of causation that has generally been invoked when examining the role of markets: regulatory systems of work follow developments in the market. In the light of Marsden's (1982: 23) proposition that the study of industrial relations was a response to the inadequacy of orthodox economic explanations of labour supply, how has the study of work relations remedied this problem? For orthodox economists, labour supply is a matter of atomistic individuals choosing between work and leisure depending on the relative cost of each. Each worker has a particular set of characteristics that can be altered by education and training. Therefore the quantum and the character of labour supplied depend on the price of labour. This model provided an explanation of the pricing of labour (supply and demand) but failed to deal with issues of work performance (quantity and quality). This problematical explanation of labour supply has been extensively critiqued (see, for instance, Offe 1985). Marsden argues that Sidney and Beatrice Webb's discussion of collective bargaining was responsible for the quarantining of this issue in the new area of industrial relations, consequently sidelining discussion of the fundamental flaws in the orthodox model.

Briefly, then, how have scholars in the industrial relations tradition dealt with labour supply? The issues that have most commonly occupied research efforts have been how workers have organised themselves into trade unions (collectivising labour supply) and subsequently how trade unions have attempted to regulate the price of work, but more particularly the way in which work is performed. Clearly some of these explanations are contrary to the axioms of the marginalist model, while others address areas that are outside the scope of this model. While industrial relations writers have often developed a more empirically nuanced view of how workers supply their labour, they have on the whole failed to break the shackles of orthodox economics in explaining these phenomena. It has generally emerged that particular labour market conditions influence institutional arrangements, which in turn develop particular sets of work relations. There are obviously varying levels of sophistication, with some work exploring the complex way in which labour markets and institutional representation influence each other. However, many studies have explicitly located the labour market as an entity external to analysis, and discussion of the form of the labour market has often been reduced to aggregated employment figures.

Early industrial relations analysis was, it seems, concerned with explaining why labour did not supply itself in the manner stipulated by the marginalist economists (particularly with the development of unions) and why labour and management established sets of rules about how work was performed (when, where, how, by whom and for what pecuniary outcomes). Among the most influential of these early writers were Sidney and Beatrice Webb. Their analysis of trade unions and their method of operation influenced thinking in a number of English-speaking countries. They saw trade union development as a consequence of competition in the British labour market during the 19th century. The competitive menace of the free labour markets lay in the form of individual bargaining (Webb & Webb 1965: 560). Indeed, the trade union devices identified by the Webbs were designed to regulate the labour market and diminish the menace of individual bargaining either by controlling supply in the labour market (restriction of numbers) or by taking wages out of competition (common rule).

Clearly the Webbs accepted that there was a labour market and that it operated according to the competitive principles of supply and demand. Trade unions played an important role protecting workers' lives from the effect of competition in the labour market (caused by 'higgling' in the product market) by restricting the supply of labour or altering its price. Unlike the marginalists, the Webbs saw regulation of the labour market as producing benefits for workers and producers alike: the source of competitive pressure came from unregulated industry ('parasitic trades'). Their answer was to raise the standard of living for all workers (Webb & Webb 1965).

The Webbs did not formulate a conceptually different version of the labour market; rather, they modified the existing orthodox principles. Interestingly, their analysis is replete with empirical examples of how workers organised to structure the way they supplied their labour, and it seems clear that they are not discussing the labour market but particular local labour markets for specific occupations. Rather than analysing broad shifts in supply and demand, the Webbs actually note the construction of labour markets by workers (controlling accepted skill and entry requirements) in particular locations at particular times. Indeed, their call for a national minimum was in itself a geographical strategy, although not conceptualised as such. Their empirical analysis of labour markets recognises the social and spatial aspects of how these markets were constructed, but theoretically they were unable to avoid the abstracted, undifferentiated broad categories of supply and demand.

Later attempts to build a framework for the study of work relations have not fundamentally challenged orthodox notions of labour supply. Those from the British 'Oxford School' chose to focus on the procedures for regulating work relations, particularly collective bargaining. As with the Webbs, this led to a focus on the development of regulation around how work was structured and remunerated and the rules surrounding its performance. The labour market was conceptually a contextual variable for writers like Flanders, perhaps more so than for the Webbs. For Flanders the nature of work rules (both procedural and substantive) depended heavily on the prevailing market conditions. The breakdown of the British system of industrial relations in the late 1960s, as he describes it, is due largely to the development of full employment. This had the consequence of changing the distribution of power, encouraging employees to use informal action at a workplace level to alter the regulation of their work (Flanders 1970: 92–113; Flanders & Fox 1970: 257). While being temporally anchored and implicitly set at the national scale, Flanders' studies were essentially aspatial.

In the 1960s interest moved away from how workers structured the supply of their labour and began to focus on how workers, employers and their representatives developed work rules. Markets are cast as context (explicitly in the case of writers such as Dunlop) and the empirical richness of the Webbs, which shows how labour supply in particular was constructed, is replaced by more general statements. These generalisations, in the case of British writers, were based on the particular labour market conditions in specific industries, notably engineering. Work relations in this industry were influenced by employment growth (increasing demand for workers), but the labour market itself was structured in part by workers and their unions. For instance, the strong delegate structure in parts of this industry allowed for the development of job rules that supplied specified working hours and task allocations. These arrangements were often localised and were the result of particular spatial conditions. Indeed, the work of Massey and others who have explored the de-industrialisation of traditional strongholds of British manufacturing shows how geographically distinct many of these industries were. To generalise these labour market conditions across the national economy, or the national scale, is to reinforce the idea that the labour market is an organic and disconnected entity rather than to see it as structured not just by industrial undertakings but more broadly by material geographies.

Institutional studies of work relations have often developed empirically the rich diversity and complexity of labour markets, but arguably theoretical development has not followed. Some outside the industrial relations discipline, notably economic geographers, labour historians and political scientists, have attempted to deconstruct the notion of the labour market and its connection to the development of work relations. Political economists have emphasised the importance of temporal analysis and noted that social structures, institutions and patterns of behaviour are not universal but are produced, exist and are transformed over time (Giles & Murray 1997). Theories of labour market segmentation embrace the notions of uneven development and heterogeneity in labour markets as a consequence of both the supply of and demand for labour (O'Donnell 1984; Peck 1996). The gendered nature of work and the division of labour between paid and domestic work has been explored by feminist writers from various disciplines (O'Donnell 1984; Forrest 1993). These approaches deconstruct the aggregate entity of the labour market and recognise important and persistent segments within the labour force. Moreover, these approaches explain that these fragments are created and reinforced not by abstract market forces but by social actors; while recognising the importance of time, they have been muted on the role of space.

Peck (1996: xv) argues that recognising space is fundamental to an analysis of labour markets. He develops a labour market analysis that is sensitive to institutional embeddedness and geographic differentiation. According to Peck (1996: 86), 'labor markets operate in different ways in different places'. His work on local labour markets is a more definitive rejection of orthodox economic assumptions. He seeks to incorporate space and scale into analysis of labour markets in order to make analysis of local labour markets meaningful. Rather than a focus on labour markets as geographic entities, these should be seen as the particular spatial location in which social processes are played out. These spaces and processes can be linked in particular ways to provide different scales of labour markets. The three broad sets of social processes played out in the labour market are: production imperatives and consequent structuring of labour demand; processes of social reproduction and structuring of labour supply; and forces of regulation, particularly by the state (Peck 1996: 90). Peck further suggests that a critical realist epistemology is more appropriate in explaining labour markets than the positivism of orthodox economics.

Labour markets are the outcome of intersecting social processes. The causes of these social processes are 'conditioned by the *contingent* inter-action of this process with other, *simultaneously operating* processes" (Peck 1996: 92, italics original) such that all labour markets are locally constituted. This does not mean that it is impossible to abstract from concrete labour market situations. Massey argues that the usurping of localised studies in geography by a drive for general laws establishing causation has reduced the reporting of complexity in much research undertaken in the discipline. She argues that the general and particu-lar need to be appreciated together (Massey 1984: 120). For Peck (1996: 96), the social processes in the labour market constitute what he labels as the production/reproduction dialectic; for Massey, the larger social processes revolve around capitalist accumulation. For both writers these processes take a particular spatial form depending on the contingency of interaction with simultaneous processes (for instance processes that construct gender or ethnicity).

Where does this leave an understanding of work relations? It means that far from labour market conditions providing a context for struc-tured work relations (for instance, high rates of employment lead to greater industrial militancy), structured work relations are important in the shaping of labour markets. These markets will take particular forms in time and space. Indeed, the construction of labour supply is not organic and can be actively shaped by state regulatory measures or the productive requirements of capital.

Labour demand, or labour required to fulfil production, is the other important element in the labour market. Economic geographers and political economists have shown a greater consideration of the uneven generation of labour demand than many industrial relations writers. For many industrial relations scholars, labour demand is again treated in aggregated categories. The product market is cast as the source of labour demand, with company and corporate strategies for labour demand following from product market conditions. Nuances concerning the restructuring of jobs and tasks, the demand for different qualities and quantities of labour, have been explored empirically, and more recently there has been recognition of the agency of capital in determining their labour demand. Like the labour market, however, the product market is usually cast as a contextual variable to which capital automatically responds. The next section will discuss the product market in indus-trial relations analysis with consideration of how space and scale may be useful in recasting the competitive environment.

THE PRODUCT MARKET

While the analysis of how workers attempt to structure the labour supply once they were in jobs was important for numerous writers, equally as important for many is how labour demand was shaped. While the activities of employers and managers in shaping labour demand were explored as a reaction to the activities of workers and their representatives, the motives of employers and managers were increasingly explained in terms of the structure of the market for goods and services. There have been several influential treatments of product markets and work relations in the literature.

While the Webbs drew attention to the 'higgling' of the market, Commons was perhaps the first to explore the connection between product market conditions and work relations. Commons saw trade unions as a product of the extension of product markets. The extension of product markets reflected industrial evolution; they were in part a result of the growth of capital markets, which allowed producers to access credit in order to produce inventories of goods for future sale. For Commons (1909: 76) the growth in the market for goods as well as the creation of a market for capital were important preconditions for the development of trade unions by promoting increasing competition in occupational labour markets. An important role for unions then became to establish some regulation of the labour market. His extension of the product market could be interpreted as an expansion in the scale of markets for certain products. Indeed, his history of American shoemakers explores the movement away from isolated local markets for shoes and the development of this market at a different scale as a consequence of the development of economic infrastructure such as transport routes and communications. Commons describes a profoundly spatial process but does not explicitly analyse it in such terms.

If unions and collectively organised labour supply were employee responses to labour market competition, then regulation of work through collective bargaining was a consequence of employers organising in response to their particular market context. John Dunlop was one to formalise such a framework. Dunlop's influential work on industrial relation systems explicitly modelled the role of product markets. His budgetary or market constraints were part of the context faced by the industrial relations actors when interacting to form the web of rules (Dunlop 1958: 10). According to Dunlop, product markets are a decisive factor in shaping the rules established in an industrial relations system, mainly through the pressure of market forces on management hierarchies.

The conditions in product markets have also been argued by some to have a determinative effect on the way in which employers structure themselves for the purposes of collective bargaining. Ingham (1974) emphasised the importance of industrial infrastructure as a determinant of collective bargaining structure, which is itself instrumental in the institutionalisation of industrial conflict. Embedded in the infrastructure argument is the role played by markets, the industrial infrastructure or the material context in facilitating structures of collective bargaining and consequently strike activity. This was not an unproblematic position. Jackson & Sisson contested what they saw as the determinism of Ingham's argument, arguing for the inclusion of processes that mediated the effects of infrastructure on actual behaviour (Jackson & Sisson 1976: 310).

Earlier, Pierson's (1950: 358) discussion of collective bargaining in the USA had contended that multi-employer bargaining is more likely to emerge in very competitive industries faced with unions trying to attain pattern bargaining outcomes. For Pierson the importance of product markets is plain. He argues that 'in explaining the scope of collective bargaining . . . , labor economists generally stress two influences: the nature and extent of unionization and the nature of the product market' (Pierson 1950: 348).

More recently, Traxler and his colleagues have tested whether the nature of product markets explains changes to bargaining structures in OECD countries. Their large and complex study adopts a similar position to earlier research in terms of linking markets and bargaining structure (Traxler et al. 2001: 110). These writers find a degree of institutional embeddedness in collective bargaining structures and argue that this stems in part from the costs associated with altering existing institutional configurations, but that it also suggests the possibility that institutions reflect particular temporal and spatial configurations of social processes rather than particular market structures (Traxler et al. 2001: 141–2).

The prominence of product markets as an explanatory variable in industrial and work relations was perhaps greatest from the latter part of the 1980s with the growth of the strategic choice model and a renewed interest in management agency rather than bargaining structure. Marchington (1990: 111) noted that it had become common to preface reports and texts with a chapter on the competitive pressures

facing management which placed management of employment relations firmly into its corporate context. Rather than being reactive, particularly to union initiatives, management were seen to be strategic,
making choices in response to the competitive position they faced. This
argument was popularised by Kochan and colleagues (1986). These
authors tried to inject management agency (in the form of strategic
choice) into the industrial relations systems model such that 'industrial relations practices and outcomes are shaped by the interactions
of environmental forces *along with* the strategic choices and values of
American managers, union leaders, workers and public policy decision
makers' (Kochan et al. 1986: 5, italics original). For them employers
or managers adjust their competitive business strategies in response to
changes in market conditions. These adjustments are constrained by
both the values of decision-makers and the historical and institutional
structures in which the choices are embedded (Kochan et al. 1986: 12).

In the UK, Gospel developed an alternative model for explaining
labour management which addressed how employers grapple with the
indeterminacy of the employment relationship. His approach 'places
considerable emphasis on the markets within which firms operate, both
labour and also final product markets' (Gospel 1992: 3). How firms
respond to these market conditions is influenced by both their strategy and their structure. Markets remain the most important explanatory factor, with management agency responding to market conditions
(Gospel 1992: 6).

The inability of many industrial relations writers to put forward an
alternative to economic orthodoxy is perhaps more pronounced in their
treatment of product markets than in their approach to labour markets. While the study of work is located in the arena of labour market
activity and is not focused on product markets per se, the way product
markets are conceptualised has important implications for the study of
work relations. Marginalist economics has the same model for all markets, based on the price mechanism producing equilibrium in supply
and demand. Orthodox competitive markets are those characterised
by multiple suppliers, or producers, which seems to be necessary in
order to ensure price elasticity. Economists as well as industrial relations writers have often been reluctant to identify empirically the structures or features that distinguish different actual product market types.
Consequently the conceptual model of a competitive market is often
transposed onto a concrete empirical entity. These concepts can have
limited empirical value. What is a competitive market? The market

for petroleum products in Australia, for example, is described as competitive as the companies that supply these products compete to maximise market share. But the market itself is characterised by a small number of producers, high barriers to entry and relatively inelastic demand. It is also highly differentiated across Australia due to the material geographies of production and consumption, and there is a high degree of cooperation between oil companies. The label of 'competitive' therefore masks a great deal of diversity within markets that affect how companies determine their demand for labour.

If the issue of what constitutes competition in product markets is not straightforward, what of the relationship between product markets and work relations? Product markets are generally considered as already produced entities; how they are structured by companies or employers rather than by abstract consumers is rarely considered. Clearly, product markets are shaped by social agents. Companies attempt to change the shape and nature of product markets directly through activities such as marketing and advertising. Less directly, companies may use (or misuse) research and development in order to build or maintain markets for their goods. Companies do not merely respond to market changes. The way in which they shape their product market affects the decisions they make about labour demand, for instance where production, management, research and development activities are located (see Massey 1984).

The state also directly affects product markets by regulating the sale of goods and services. The state can change the way goods are made available to the market. For instance, in the UK the Monopolies and Merger Commission report of 1989 resulted in a severing of the tied house arrangement between breweries and public houses (MMC 1989), effectively forcing the major brewers to divest themselves of retail outlets (MMC 1989; Preece et al. 1999). The state can also indirectly alter product markets through changes to taxation and subsidy regimes.

Finally, workers have attempted to influence product markets as consumers. The 'union label' campaigns in the USA have seen unions try to influence conditions in several different product markets. In Australia trade unions have also tried to influence the product market for clothing and textiles through such initiatives as the 'fairwear' campaign (http://www.awatw.org.au/fairwear/index.html). Product markets, like labour markets, are the result of social agency, and to view them as entities important for, but external to, the study of work relations can result in a tendency towards determinism.

Product markets have remained important but relatively under-developed entities in industrial relations. While these markets encourage or constrain managerial agency, the way in which social agents shape the contours of these markets have rarely been examined, excepting perhaps state regulation. Similar to the treatment of labour markets by industrial relations scholars, product markets are viewed as aspatial, perhaps even as transcending space. This is at odds with the empirical studies which explicitly locate product markets temporally and spatially. For instance, Kochan and his colleagues discuss how state regulation has changed the nature of product markets. They develop their thesis through the examination of several industry case studies focused on products for consumption in particular spaces and locations (Kochan et al. 1986). Like the empirical studies of labour markets, this material reinforces that markets are actively structured and restructured rather than developing organically. Labour historians have also proved to be sensitive to the issues of space, or location, and time. For example, Patmore has explored the interaction between local labour markets, local capital and community to explain cross-class conflict and cooperation in Lithgow, New South Wales. In doing so he also draws attention to the different scales in which labour and capital operate (Patmore 2000).

Notwithstanding these contributions, it has again been economic geographers mobilising the concept of space who have moved further in re-examining and dismantling the orthodox economic concept of markets. While industrial relations analysis has empirically recognised the importance of space and location when discussing product markets, this has not translated into a more nuanced theoretical understanding. Gough argues that while marginalist economists see demand as an external constraint, a view the industrial relations writers have found difficult to break with, demand is actually linked to production in particular places at particular times. Demand for goods and services, and consequently the market for products, is shaped in part by 'the incomes and tastes of consumers, derived from locally specific class, gender and other social relations arising from both the production and the reproduction spheres' (Gough 2003: 42). Walsh, too, draws attention to the spatial dimension of product markets and how this can impact upon labour organising strategies. She explains that 'a building that needs to be cleaned cannot be sent to a low-wage state and returned after low-wage workers have performed the task' (Walsh 2000: 1598). Gough's study of the London manufacturing sector reinforces the idea that consumers for goods and services are often other producers or firms. In this way the dynamics of production within firms and the work relations that characterise production regimes affect firm demand and consequently product markets. By locating product markets and recognising their spatial aspects (location and scale) they move from being outside the firm impacting on work relations via the choices of management and labour, to being shaped by these choices and the nature of work relations.

FINANCIAL MARKETS

While Commons recognised the importance of financial capital markets in facilitating different production regimes, it has only been fairly recently that scholars have begun to explore the nexus between financial markets and work relations. This research picks up on the work of Useem (1993) and others who have charted the rise of shareholder power in the form of institutional investors influencing management in firms. Useem argues that the separation between ownership and control in organisations has been reversed, with shareholders seeking corporate structures to serve their interests more closely. This notion of shareholder power has led many writers to consider the connections between how firms are financed and corporate governance. In publicly listed companies the degree to which shareholders are active and can place pressure on management has important implications for work relations. The manner in which firms finance their activities represents another factor that can place pressure on company management. Configurations of passive shareholders and limited external borrowings may provide company management with wider parameters for managing labour and accommodating trade unions and collective bargaining.

Some have sought to generalise about how national financial markets can influence labour management regimes. Christopherson argues that different investment rules in different countries are an important factor in explaining divergences in labour market practices. She contends that 'because they produce different pressures, risks and adaptive strategies, market rules governing investment across and within firms should be a central reference point in interpreting firms' decisions with respect to the demand for and deployment of labour' (Christopherson 2002: 4).

Gospel & Pendleton (2003, 2005) have also addressed issues of national financial markets and labour management. They have argued that those actors who have a financial claim against a firm will seek to acquire a role in the governance of that firm, including influencing issues of labour management (see Gospel & Pendleton 2003: 559). Consequently, the way in which firms are financed (whether through debt, internal financing or equity) will be important for structuring the relationship between creditors and the company, which in turn will impose certain constraints on how companies are managed. In terms of labour management, this affects the support given by management to the interests of capital and labour, the time-frame for returns to investors, the nature of business strategies, the importance of financial factors in decision-making, how employee commitment is secured, and the extent of cooperation with other firms (Gospel & Pendleton 2003: 565). There is plainly a strong spatial component to the analysis as the discussion of financial markets is pitched at the scale of the nation, but once again the elements of space and how these are produced are not recognised using such terms. Particular national legal and institutional regimes combine to create distinctive financial markets in different countries. In contrast to the literature on product markets, there is recognition that financial markets are socially constructed (Gospel & Pendleton 2003: 574–5). Gospel & Pendleton (2005: 18) argue that the causal link between finance, governance and labour management runs both ways, with organised labour having the capacity to shape governance structures and consequently the financing of companies.

The recent work on financial markets and labour management is of particular importance for explanations of work relations. Despite the recognition that the financing of firms simultaneously constrains and facilitates management activity, there is an appreciation that financial markets reflect structural and institutional configurations, mainly at a national scale. Financial markets could represent a more elusive category for analysis. These markets have the capacity to operate transnationally and could more closely resemble economic orthodoxy. Unlike labour markets that take a distinctive spatial form due to the relatively fixed character of workers, or even product markets that depend on consumption in a particular place, financial capital is perceived as relatively mobile. Indeed, the comparative under-analysis of financial markets has seen industrial relations analysis overly influenced by the discourse surrounding globalisation. While globalisation is seen as encompassing several features, perhaps the most important of these is the mobility of financial capital (Wade 1996). At its worst this rhetoric portrays globalisation as 'an all-determining, omnipresent and unstoppable force' (Peck & Yeung 2003: 12). Indeed, the ubiquity and perceived mobility of financial capital and its search for maximum returns can be seen as a major plank in the convergence thesis, around which there has been much debate (Katz & Darbishire 1999; Giles 2000). Recognising that financial markets are a product of particular, usually nation-specific, sets of structural and institutional configuration allows a richer understanding not only of systems of labour management, but also of the complexity of global capitalism itself.

Studies in economic geography have illustrated the spatial concentration of investment flows and the uneven nature of globalisation. They have done so by studying the connections between capital and labour markets at particular scales. For instance, financial capital is situated as an empirical rather than an abstract entity. A more complex appreciation of the effects of economic development on industrial and work relations can follow. Peck & Yeung (2003: 12), referring to the work of Dicken, argue that:

> Nation states remain key players in the structuring and regulation of the global economy; transnational corporations, more than simply bearers of market logic, are engaged in dynamic path dependent and organizationally contingent processes of strategic development; global investment flows are not free-floating extra terrestrial phenomena, but are embedded in networks and regulatory systems; globalization is a complex and uneven process, not a unilinear trend toward unified international markets.

Many economic geographers have been influenced by the work of David Harvey, who draws out the mobility dilemma of capital, including financial capital. He argues that there is a tension between the mobility of financial capital and the requirement of immobility in order to protect the cost of credit and consequently returns to financial capital (Harvey 1982: 385–7). To ensure the viability of credit, nation-states attempt to secure the monetary basis of currency; this is usually achieved by restricting the free flow of financial capital of different forms (Harvey 1982: 387). Harvey outlines the contradictions and complementarities between the mobility of labour (variable capital) and capital (productive and financial). Attention is drawn to the requirements of different factions of capital, namely productive and financial, and the role played by the state in financing and infrastructure to ensure accumulation. With the underlying object of accumulation, capitalist production creates and requires particular social and physical geographies. Dialectical forces then manifest around the mobility of capital and labour.

The threat and counter threat of movement also becomes a major weapon in the war between capital and labour . . . It is not always easy for capital to move in response [to worker movements]. Though the mobility of credit money and runaway shops are formidable weapons, they cannot always be employed without destroying the values which other factions of capital have embedded in physical and social infrastructures. (Harvey 1982: 412)

It is for this reason that capital must create 'spatial fixes' in order for accumulation to occur (Herod 2001: 27). These fixes result in particular material geographies at specific times. The constructions of work relations may reflect broader material and social agendas of capital and labour, but their form represents the conjunction of social processes in particular spaces and scales.

CONCLUSION

This chapter has sought to explore how markets have been used to account for the development of work relations. It has shown that markets have been an important explanatory variable in much industrial relations analysis. It has also identified several limitations to the way in which markets have been incorporated into this analysis. In breaking away from orthodox economics, early industrial relations writers attempted to explain empirically observable labour market institutions. While these writers displayed a keen empirical appreciation of labour markets, they failed to engage in an epistemological exchange over the concept of the labour market. Many of the conceptual building blocks of the orthodox model remained part of the frameworks developed by these writers. This is also evident in the way in which the impact of product markets has been explored. There is a conceptual space left by orthodox economists in their failure to develop an encompassing theory of the firm.

While industrial relations scholars have successfully developed frameworks of management activity emphasising managerial agency, these have been tempered by an underlying acceptance that this activity is strongly shaped by product markets. Writers have developed complex empirical studies of product markets, but there has been little conceptual examination of product markets and how they are structured. Perhaps of most importance, the discussion of markets and their influence on work relations has remained aspatial. This is quite remarkable given the recognition of space and scale evident in empirical studies.

Consequently, an enduring weakness in the way markets are treated in the industrial relations literature lies in a tendency for markets to exhibit an overly deterministic effect on work relations that transcends time and space. While markets may be the structure that constrains the agency of industrial parties, the agency of the parties impacts on the development, nature and shape of these structures. Arguably a more robust explanation of work relations would arise from exploring the totality of work relations and formally recognising the collinear relationships between markets and work relations.

Economic and labour geographers have displayed an interest in issues relating to locating work and labour organisation (Peck 2005). Their contribution has been to mobilise the notions of space and scale when explaining economic development and labour organisation. These concepts locate social agency and break down artificial barriers between context and social processes, providing a better understanding of social processes such as the structuring of work relations. Marshalling the concepts of space and scale can assist in removing determinism and reactivating agency in studies of markets and work relations. Markets are produced in particular spaces and their shape reflects the contingent interaction of processes in that space. The concept of space grounds market development and market influences in material geographies in particular, and perhaps more importantly it provides a nexus between different market spheres. Space tempers the mobility of producers and consumers in all markets. By allowing for an explicit recognition of connection between labour, product and capital markets, it is argued that the complex connections between social agents can be better understood. By deconstructing market operations in terms of space an increasingly nuanced, complex but concurrently also less determinative understanding of work relations might emerge.

References

Adams, R. 1997, 'Integrating disparate strands: an elaborated version of systems theory as a framework for organizing the field of industrial relations', in J. Barbash & N. Meltz (eds) *Theorizing in Industrial Relations*, Sydney: ACIRRT, pp. 29–56.

Barnes, T., Tickell, A., Peck, J. & Sheppard, E. 2004, 'Editors' introduction: paradigms lost', in T. Barnes, A. Tickell, J. Peck & E. Sheppard (eds) *Reading Economic Geography*, Oxford: Blackwells, pp. 13–18.

Castree, N., Coe, N., Ward, K. & Samers, M. 2004, *Spaces of Work: Global Capitalism and the Geographies of Labour*, London: Sage.

Christopherson, S. 2002, 'Why do national labor market practices continue to diverge in the global economy? The missing link of investment rules', *Economic Geography* 78(1): 1–20.

Clegg, H. 1990, 'The Oxford School'. Warwick Papers in Industrial Relations no. 31, University of Warwick, Coventry, UK.

Commons, J. 1909, 'American shoemakers, 1648–1895: a sketch of industrial evolution', *Quarterly Journal of Economics* 24(1): 39–84.

Dunlop, J.T. 1958, *Industrial Relations Systems*, New York: Holt & Co.

Ellem, B. & Shields, J. 1999, 'Rethinking "regional industrial relations": space, place and the social relations of work', *Journal of Industrial Relations* 41(4): 536–60.

Flanders, A. 1970, 'Industrial relations: what is wrong with the system?' in A. Flanders (ed.) *Management and Unions: The Theory and Reform of Industrial Relations*, London: Faber & Faber, pp. 83–128.

Flanders, A. & Fox, A. 1970, 'Collective bargaining: from Donovan to Durkheim', in A. Flanders (ed.) *Management and Unions: The Theory and Reform of Industrial Relations*, London: Faber & Faber, pp. 241–76.

Forrest, A. 1993, 'Women and industrial relations theory', *Relations Industrielles* 48(3): 409–38.

Giles, A. 2000, 'Globalisation and industrial relations theory', *Journal of Industrial Relations* 42(2): 173–94.

Giles, A. & Murray, G. 1997, 'Industrial relations theory and critical political economy', in J. Barbash & N. Meltz (eds) *Theorizing in Industrial Relations*, Sydney: ACIRRT, pp. 77–120.

Gospel, H. 1992, *Markets, Firms and the Management of Labour in Modern Britain*, Cambridge University Press.

Gospel, H. & Pendleton, A. 2003, 'Finance, corporate governance and the management of labour: a conceptual and comparative analysis', *British Journal of Industrial Relations* 41(3): 557–83.

Gospel, H. & Pendleton, A. 2005, *Corporate Governance and Labour Management: An International Comparison*, Oxford: Oxford University Press.

Gough, J. 2003, *Work, Locality and the Rhythms of Capital: The Labour Process Reconsidered*, London and New York: Continuum.

Grimshaw, D. & Rubbery, J. 2003, 'Economics and industrial relations', in P. Ackers & A. Wilkinson (eds) *Understanding Work and Employment: Industrial Relations in Transition*, Oxford: Oxford University Press, pp. 43–70.

Harvey, D. 1982, *The Limits to Capitalism*, Oxford: Basil Blackwell.

Herod, A. 2001, *Labor Geographies: Workers and Landscapes of Capitalism*, New York: Guilford Press.

Herod, A. 2002, 'Towards a more productive engagement: industrial relations and economic geography meet', *Labour and Industry* 13(2): 5–17.

Herod, A., Peck, J. & Wills, J. 'Geography and Industrial Relations', in P. Ackers & A. Wilkinson (eds) *Understanding Work and Employment: Industrial Relations in Transition*, Oxford: Oxford University Press, pp. 176–92.

Hyman, R. 1975, *Industrial Relations: A Marxist Introduction*, London: Macmillan.

Hyman, R. 1978, 'Pluralism, procedural consensus and collective bargaining', *British Journal of Industrial Relations* 16(1): 16–40.

Ingham, G. 1974, *Strikes and Industrial Conflict*, London: Macmillan.

Jackson P. & Sisson K. 1976, 'Employer confederation in Sweden and the U.K. and the significance of industrial infrastructure', *British Journal of Industrial Relations* 14(3): 306–23.

Katz, H. & Darbishire, O. 1999, *Converging Divergences: Worldwide Changes in Employment Systems*, Ithaca, NY: ILR Press.

Kaufman, B. 1993, *The Origins and Evolution of the Field of Industrial Relations in the United States*, Ithaca, NY: ILR Press.

Kochan, T., Katz, H. & McKersie, R. 1986, *The Transformation of American Industrial Relations*, New York: Basic Books.

Laffer, K. 1974, 'Is industrial relations an academic discipline?' *Journal of Industrial Relations* 16(1): 62–73.

Larson, S. & Nissen, B. (eds) 1987, *Theories of the Labor Movement*, Detroit, Mich.: Wayne State University Press.

Marchington, M. 1990, 'Analysing the links between product markets and the management of employee relations', *Journal of Management Studies* 27(2): 111–32.

Marsden, R. 1982, 'Industrial relations: a critique of empiricism', *Sociology* 16(2): 232–50.

Massey, D. 1984, *Spatial Divisions of Labour: Social Structures and the Geography of Production*, New York: Methuen.

MMC (Monopolies and Mergers Commission) 1989, *The Supply of Beer*, London: MMC.

O'Donnell, C. 1984, 'Major theories of the labour market and women's place within it', *Journal of Industrial Relations* 26(2): 147–65.

Offe, C. 1985, *Disorganized Capitalism: Contemporary Transformations of Work and Politics*, Cambridge: Polity Press.

Osterman, P., Kochan, T., Locke, R. & Piore, M. 2001, *Working in America*, Cambridge, Mass.: MIT Press.

Patmore, G. 2000, 'Localism and labour: Lithgow 1869–1932', *Labour History* 78: 53–70.

Peck, J. 1996, *Work-place: The Social Regulation of Labour Markets*, New York: Guilford Press.

Peck, J. 2005, 'Economic sociologies in space', *Economic Geography* 81(2): 129–75.

Peck, J. & Yeung, H.W. 2003, *Remaking the Global Economy: Economic-Geographical Perspectives*, London: Sage.

Pierson, F. 1950, 'Prospects for industry-wide bargaining', *Industrial and Labor Relations Review* 3(3): 341–61.

Poole, M. 1981, *Theories of Trade Unionism*, London: Routledge & Kegan Paul.

Preece, D., Steven, G. & Steven, G. 1999, *Work Change and Competition: Managing for Bass*, London: Routledge.

Roche, W. 1986, 'Systems analysis and industrial relations: double paradox in the development of American and British industrial relations theory', *Economic and Industrial Democracy* 7(1): 3–28.

Shalev, M. 1985, 'Labor relations and class conflict: a critical survey of John R. Commons', in D. Lipsky (ed.) *Advances in Industrial and Labor Relations*, vol. 2, Greenwich, Conn.: JAI Press, pp. 319–63.

Sisson, K. 1987, *The Management of Collective Bargaining: An International Comparison*, Oxford: Blackwell.

Sisson, K. & Marginson, P. 2002, 'Co-ordinated bargaining: a process for our times?', *British Journal of Industrial Relations* 40(2): 197–220.

Traxler, F., Blaschke, S. & Kittel, B. 2001, *National Labour Relations in Internationalized Markets: A Comparative Study of Institutions, Change, and Performance*, Oxford: Oxford University Press.

Useem, M. 1993, *Executive Defense: Shareholder Power and Corporate Reorganization*, Cambridge, Mass.: Harvard University Press.

Wade, R. 1996, 'Globalisation and its limits: reports of the death of the national economy are greatly exaggerated', in S. Berger & R. Dore (eds) *National Diversity and Global Capitalism*, Ithaca, NY: Cornell University Press, pp. 60–88.

Walsh, J. 2000, 'Organising the scale of labor regulation in the United States: service sector activism in the city', *Environment and Planning A* 32(9): 1593–610.

Webb, S. & Webb, B. 1965, *Industrial Democracy*, New York: Kelley.

Wood, S., Wagner, A., Armstrong, E.G.A., Goodman, J.F.B. & Davis, J.E. 1975, 'The "industrial relations system" as a basis for theory in industrial relations', *British Journal of Industrial Relations* 13(3): 291–308.

PART THREE

DISCOURSE

Mark Hearn and Grant Michelson

The relationship between time, space and discourse flows from their common source as expressions of our value constructions, expressed in the metaphorical distribution of time and space and our construction of discourse. Our metaphors are our lives written into meaning, validating or challenging our chosen forms of behaviour and organisation. Discourse analysis and narrative theory have evolved from various influences to uncover the values encoded in speech and document, from Barthes' structural analysis to Ricoeur's focus on the relationships between time, narrative and identity (see Ricoeur 1992; Barthes 2000). In the analysis of work discourse, Foucault's stress on the operation of power, and its elaboration in discursive formations, has proved enduring (Foucault 2003). Following Foucault, McKenna has recently asserted that Critical Discourse Analysis seeks to uncover the relationship between discourse, power, dominance and social equality, and must rededicate itself to this politicised enquiry, with work as a key site of struggle. 'Given the neo-liberal ascendancy, the consumer-identity culture . . . and brutal economic displacements, the issues of identity, agency, social fragmentation and the workplace must be an important focus of study' (McKenna 2004: 10–11, 21). The chapters in this section reflect a commitment to that aim, the force of the analysis driven not only by theory but by the experience of men and women in work and the influence exerted by the narratives that structure work, management strategy and ethics.

There is reference in these chapters (which begin from a more macro perspective and become more micro-focused) to concepts of both narrative and discourse analysis. Narrative here is intended to convey a sense of the broad metaphors of work and national identity generated over historical time, which have also been described as 'meta-narratives' (Somers 1997); discourse analysis is the interrogation of talk and text, through a form of analysis that often reflects a dialogue between the discrete expressions of value and organisation and their relationship with the enduring narratives that have shaped these values and institutional behaviours. Mark Hearn and Harry Knowles explore this relationship in Chapter 11, analysing the links between narratives of work organisation and nation-building in 20th-century Australia from a concern with justifying strict, top-down workplace, union and managerial hierarchies to the post-1980s advocacy of decentralised strategies. The national narrative, expressed and rehearsed in diverse forums and media, in speeches, reports and tracts, sought legitimacy for managerial and workplace disciplines in nation-building goals. 'Nation-building' was also stressed as a rationale for the behavioural changes required of workers to accommodate the post-1980s paradigm of work – a neo-liberal 'enterprise culture' advocated by business and the federal Howard government.

As Grant and colleagues (2004) demonstrate, discourse analysis has played an increasingly vital role in the study of work organisations, though it has made relatively little contribution to analysing the ethical values of business. In Chapter 12, Grant Michelson and Nick Wailes analyse the tension between the discourses of shareholder and corporate social responsibility (CSR). The rational, economic notion of shareholder value sees the interests of the shareholder as paramount and encourages managers to privilege only those strategies and decisions that directly benefit shareholders in the short term. The discourse of corporate social responsibility speaks of a range of legitimate claims on the organisation and suggests that social, ethical and moral considerations ought to play a more significant role in corporate strategic planning and decision-making processes. Using insights from discourse analysis, Michelson & Wailes question the outcome suggested by the 'instrumental' perspective of CSR that firms will adopt socially responsible objectives, as well as the underlying assumption that a greater focus on CSR within organisations is likely to become widespread. 'In spite of the assumed benefits of CSR for business, firms at the present time are generally reluctant to embrace and integrate social objectives within their operations. The organisational modus operandi remains the more rational economic one of maximising shareholder value.'

Ethical values are also a central concern of Susan Ainsworth and Richard Hall's reconsideration of the role and purpose of human resource management. In Chapter 13, Ainsworth & Hall reconsider the ethics of HRM in the context of the tension between the business partnership and employee advocacy roles implicit in strategic HRM theory and practice. Subjecting HR practitioner literature to Critical Discourse Analysis – 'how power relations are reproduced and exercised in discourse' – the authors conclude that while employee advocacy and a concern with the welfare of workers is recognised as part of the HR mandate, '[they tend] to be consistently backgrounded after being initially recognised . . . There was typically little credence granted to the idea that employee welfare might be a key HR value in its own right.' The business partnership role, central to the contemporary rhetoric surrounding strategic HRM, generally received much greater attention in the texts analysed, although the discourse of strategic HRM revealed 'a profound ambivalence and uncertainty . . . insecurity as to whether HR, as an essentially ancillary function, really deserves its place in (strategic) management'. The power relationships embedded in HR practitioner discourse are also revealed in the HR professional's attitudes towards employees: 'To the extent that employees are seen as something more than resources, they tend to be constructed as emotional, potentially fraudulent or prone to industrial militancy. In general the discourse constructs employees as a source of difficulty and disruption for strategic HR executives.'

McKenna (2004: 23) has argued that in the new 'corporate culture' of neo-liberalism the subject worker becomes infused with the logic and ethic of corporations. 'By linking the individual worker to the enterprise, the interests of capitalism are better served because workers align personal goals with ideals of individualism, rather than with those of group solidarity as worker.' David Grant and John Shields address this dilemma in Chapter 14. Rather than interpreting the subject worker as a passive recipient of power, they argue that worker identity under HRM is best understood as 'a socially constructed reality in which workers, managers and a range of other discursive subjects are actively implicated'. Worker identity is produced from 'negotiated meaning around competing discourses in particular contexts'. The key challenge, they assert, 'will be to transcend the longstanding habit of perceiving workers as research objects and to recognise and respect them as whole subjects more than capable of "saving" themselves'.

Discourse analysis offers a range of potentially important methods and techniques for exploring the construction of work-based identities and examining the categories and concepts on which much labour market research and policy are based. In Chapter 15, Susan Ainsworth explores the construction of work-based identities through the example of 'older workers'. There is little consensus on 'who' an older worker is; age identity is ambiguous, fluid and highly contingent on context. 'Age is a cultural construction', Ainsworth argues, elaborated in discourse. 'Much of the commentary on older workers constructs older people as "problematic" and a current and future burden on the rest of society.' Drawing on analysis of a public parliamentary inquiry into the older unemployed, she reveals how multiple versions of older worker identity were constructed, what implications that had for labour market policy, and how ageism was reproduced in discursive practice, even by those intentionally attempting to combat it.

In a well-known work, *The Subject and Power*, Foucault was concerned to explain how individuals are made subjects. Power 'categorizes the individual, marks him by his own individuality, attaches him to his own identity, imposes a law of truth on him which he must recognise and which others have to recognize in him' (Foucault 2001: 331). These five chapters uncover the codes of 'truth' elaborated in the discourse of nation, identity, work organisation, and management purpose and strategy. They not only reveal how subjects are made and characterised; in the act of discovery they suggest the transformation of these codes and the subjectivities they create, fulfilling the ethical project at the heart of any truly critical discourse analysis.

References

Barthes, R. 2000, 'The structural analysis of narratives', in R. Barthes (ed.) A *Barthes Reader*, London: Vintage, pp. 251–95.

Foucault, M. 2001, 'The subject and power', in M. Foucault (ed.) *Power: The Essential Works* vol. 3, London: Penguin, pp. 326–48.

Foucault, M. 2003, *The Archeology of Knowledge*, London: Routledge.

Grant, D., Hardy, C., Oswick, C. & Putnam, L. (eds) 2004, *The Handbook of Organisational Discourse*, London: Sage.

McKenna, B. 2004, 'Critical discourse studies: where to from here?', *Critical Discourse Studies* 1(1): 9–39.

Ricoeur, P. 1992, *Oneself as Another*, University of Chicago Press.

Somers, M.R. 1997, 'Deconstructing and reconstructing class formation theory: narrativity, relational analysis, and social theory', in J.R. Hall (ed.) *Reworking Class*, Ithaca, N.Y.: Cornell University Press.

CHAPTER ELEVEN

THE NATIONAL NARRATIVE OF WORK

Mark Hearn and Harry Knowles

How should the Australian Labor Party, reeling from an unexpectedly decisive defeat in the October 2004 federal elections, rebuild credible economic and workplace relations policies? For the nation's leading business daily, the *Australian Financial Review*, it was a question of language. In November 2004 the AFR editorialised that Labor's 'institutional links' with the trade union movement and the union 'veto' over party policy left Labor lagging behind the re-elected Howard Government's successful advocacy of an 'entrepreneurial culture'. Labor was out of touch with a new constituency of workers – a growing, independent and self-reliant army of contractors, consultants, franchisees and small business people. To appeal to this new constituency, Labor's revised economic policies must 'encourage flexibility, enterprise and upward mobility . . . Labor's leaders risk being trapped in a rhetorical costume drama with a shrinking audience if they can't shrug off the party's historical baggage and speak the language of 21st century workers and entrepreneurs' (*AFR* 3 November 2004).

How has the language of '21st century workers and entrepreneurs' evolved from previous forms of work and managerial language across the 20th century? This chapter explores the close relationship between nation-building and workplace relations that has developed since the Federation of the Australian colonies in 1901. The national narrative of work was expressed and rehearsed in diverse forums and media, in speeches, reports and tracts. The dominant narrative sought legitimacy for managerial and workplace disciplines in nation-building goals; in turn, it has generated forms of renovation and resistance, counter-narratives that have asserted greater rights for workers and unions and disputed the claims – productive or patriotic – of either employers or the state.

From Federation, the advocates of the national narrative were able to bring the weight of the state and the claims of nation-building to their demands for workplace discipline. In 1903 Attorney-General Alfred Deakin introduced the Conciliation and Arbitration bill in the Commonwealth Parliament. The bill brought disputing parties of workers, unions and employers before a formally constituted court of compulsory arbitration, an innovation virtually unique among Western nations. Significantly, the bill's benefits were not restricted to workplace relations. Deakin asserted that the bill would establish 'the people's peace', creating an institution that would 'cement . . . social justice' by uniting the interests of the struggling worker with that vague but idealised conception of social harmony and common civic purpose – the nation. Workers and their families would willingly submit to their 'lot', as Deakin described their disciplined participation in the paid and unpaid workforce, in workplaces and homes, on behalf of the productive development of the young nation (CPD 30 July 1903: 264, 268).

Nineteenth-century liberalism, which defined the values Deakin presented to Parliament, reflected a tension between restraining the role of government while conceding some role for the state in ensuring that the maximum number of citizens enjoyed the benefits of national productivity – in turn stifling demands for the drastic reconstruction of the state and society (Melleuish 2001; Roberts 2001). Australian workplace relations have always developed in the context of wider national goals; the Conciliation and Arbitration Act 1904 was one of the outstanding achievements of the liberal post-Federation 'Australian Settlement', characterised in the early 20th century by protection of both economic and industrial life through tariffs on imports to facilitate the development of a manufacturing industry, compulsory arbitration to spread some of the benefits of economic development to workers and their families, and cultural protection of the broader commonwealth of Australian society, most significantly exercised through the restriction of non-Anglo-Celtic immigration through the Immigration Restriction Act – the White Australia policy (Melleuish 1995; Hearn & Knowles 1996: 12–14).

Nation-building was also stressed as a rationale for the behavioural changes required of workers to accommodate the post-1980s paradigm of work and the apparently radical reduction in the role of the state in workplace relations. The organic and contested nature of the narrative of work, its inherent relationship with the nation and the significance of political leadership in redefining its terms was captured in a snapshot from July 2004, as Prime Minister John Howard appealed to the Australian people, setting out his re-election agenda: 'Who is best-equipped to deliver a secure nation, a strong and prosperous economy, a fair and decent society, a sustainable continent, and an enterprise culture' (AFR 9 July 2004).

Howard's success in transforming workplace relations did not arise from inventing the language of an enterprise culture. Howard's appeal echoed the Thatcherite model that preceded it in the 1980s and tapped into a narrative already circulating in the wider culture of Australian politics, work and management. Keat & Abercrombie (1991: 1) show that Prime Minister Margaret Thatcher skilfully led a self-styled revival of British 'enterprise and initiative' as both policy and dominant political discourse; in Australia there can be little doubt that Howard's advocacy lent the narrative of reform and enterprise new force and credibility.

By contrast, to be left 'trapped in a rhetorical costume drama with a shrinking audience' conjured a striking image of Labor's federal front-benchers as players in a dull theatrical, whose outmoded forms and rhetorical strategies have long lost popular appeal. That is the impression that the AFR wanted to *share* with its readers: the AFR editorial writers very likely assumed that they exchanged a dialogue with its business audience framed around wider and mutual conceptions of work and national progress. *The National Narrative of Work* locates managerial and labour narratives in their social and cultural context, emphasising that they evolved and were expressed in the context of what Somers (1997: 86) has identified as the wider 'meta-narratives' of progress, capital, culture and nationalism. Narrative theory, and the discrete interrogation of text and values provided by discourse analysis, intensifies the critique of work narratives and their assimilation of the values of national progress and identity (Phillips & Hardy 2002: 4–5). Critical discourse analysis clarifies the class and power relations embedded in the language of the national narrative – 'efficiency', a 'fair and reasonable' wage, worker–management 'consultation', 'freedom', 'enterprise culture', and the ideologies represented by these terms. Wasson (2004: 180, 185, 194) outlines the transfer of 'enterprise ideology' between individual, enterprise and nation, and the 'diffuse, unplanned' spread of enterprise language, a transfer reflected in both explicit and inferential value-laden exchanges encouraged by Howard and the *AFR* in their propagation of enterprise values.

Fairclough (1995: 1–2, 19) observes that 'critical discourse analysts sometimes fail adequately to *historicize* their data'. Here we explore the relationship between language and the historical context that shaped it. The symbolic terms of the evolving national narrative reveal the contested dialogue between self, workplace and nation that constituted the narrative and was pursued in war, depression and prosperity. As Somers (1997: 82, 84–5) argues, it is through narrative that 'we come to know, understand, and make sense of the social world, and through which we constitute our social identities'. These 'ontological narratives' structure the individual's 'activities, consciousness, and beliefs' as they engage with the wider public narratives of the workplace, church, government and nation. Anderson (1991: 6–7) argues in his influential study of nationalism that the nation is not a fixed entity with fixed values: it is a community based on a shared identification of values, and cultural, social and often racial traits; the terms of their communion are rehearsed, revised and contested.

White has explored the values of the Australian national story and concludes: 'There is no real Australia waiting to be uncovered. A national identity is an invention' (White 1981: vii). Melleuish (1995: 7–10) has challenged White's equation of an invented national identity with artificiality and 'falsehood'; White leaves an impression of Australians as 'a great mass of manipulated fools'. Melleuish has stressed the evolving tradition of cultural liberalism in Australia, in which Australians played an active role in creating for themselves – as a basis for social and economic progress, and shaping a sense of national identity. Yet the advocates of cultural liberalism – who indeed exerted a powerful influence on the narratives of Australian national identity and work – often assumed that it was their task to guide the great mass of Australians to a reconciliation with their 'lot' as productive subjects of the state and servants of the economy. Rowse has analysed how Australian liberalism attempted to reconcile 'social responsibility' and material 'acquisitiveness' as it sought to shape the national character (Rowse 1978: 21–2). Rose has followed liberalism's immense capacity for adaptation and renewal. The 'advanced liberalism' of the late 20th century abandoned traditional forms of state intervention in economic life to promote the 'freedom' of the 'autonomous individual': employees should become entrepreneurs, an aspiration enthusiastically embraced in Howard's enterprise culture (Rose 1999: 84, 156). Power is always present in the formation of individual and social identity, and we must analyse the expressions and motives of the national narrative of work, asking 'what their function is, whose creation they are, and whose interest they serve' (White 1981: vii).

ETHICS AND ECONOMICS: COMPULSORY ARBITRATION AND NATIONAL EFFICIENCY, 1901–1929

> The Australians have always disliked scientific economics and (still more) scientific economists. They are fond of ideals and impatient of technique. Their sentiments quickly find phrases, and their phrases find prompt expression in policies. (Hancock 1930: 86)

Historian Keith Hancock made this observation in his *Australia* (1930), concluding a discussion of 'the emotional and ideological flavour' of the Australian protectionism that had developed since Federation (Hancock 1930: 82). One of the defining phrases of Australian economic and cultural protectionism was Justice Henry Bournes Higgins' conception of a 'fair and reasonable' living or basic wage. In the 1907 Harvester judgment, his first as the president of the Commonwealth Conciliation and Arbitration Court, Higgins sought to provide for 'the normal needs of the average employee, regarded as a human being living in a civilized community' by setting a national minimum wage of seven shillings a day (1907 CAR vol. 2: 2). Hancock (1930: 82–3, 177) clarified the link between wage policy and nationalism, describing how 'fair and reasonable' became 'the popular refrain of Australian democracy': a democracy parochial, idealistic and nationalist, attempting 'to fashion a new community free from the hereditary oppressions' of old Europe, and aggressively proud of its superior 'standard of living'. This peculiar blend of idealistic parochialism produced the White Australia policy and a national wage structure suited to the needs of protection and justice. A liberal 'realist', Hancock identified a need to break with parochialism while understanding its appeal: Australians were willing to privilege the 'ethical' standard of 'fair and reasonable' over economics – or at least to 'entangle' ethics and economics through the principle of wage justice, as Hancock shrewdly observed (Hancock 1930: 85–6; Rowse 1978: 122; Melluish 1995: 125–6).

Conceiving of the male basic wage as a family wage, Higgins conformed to the wider social meta-narrative of appropriate gender roles. Marriage was after all, as Higgins observed, 'the normal fate of a normal man' (Higgins 1924: 9). Women should focus their lives on the home and rearing children, and Higgins actively discouraged the participation of women in the paid workforce, a form of gender discrimination that he defended as in the national interest. 'It is better for society' if men were preferred in employment before women, Higgins argued in an influential 1919 judgment which set the rate of women's wages at 54 per cent of the male basic wage (13 CAR 701–2). The ruling established 'the customary minimum in Commonwealth awards', a minimum that remained in force until 1950, when it was increased to 75 per cent of the male basic wage. Higgins' precedent was followed in the State jurisdictions (Patmore 1991: 170–6).

In 1922 Higgins published the aptly titled A New Province for Law and Order, which set out 33 'principles of action' which framed his judgments and reflected his liberal protectionist values. Higgins' province was governed by the quest for 'industrial peace', a key phrase in his narrative code, and an elusive quality of industrial harmony that might quell class divisions. Employers, unions and workers would obtain the benefits of arbitration if they maintained the peace in the interests of national productivity and progress. Unions, Higgins believed, had a crucial role to play in maintaining industrial law and order; he did not believe that the arbitration system could function without their strategic role in disciplining worker demands and smothering militancy. 'From the point of view of the Court and of the public, it is fair to state that in nearly every case . . . the influence of union leaders has always been in the direction of peace.' Nonetheless, Higgins consistently refused to grant preference to unionists when making industrial awards; that would constrain the right of the employer to employ 'the best man available, unionist or not'. Higgins was also a firm defender of managerial prerogative – a refusal to intervene in management's right to govern the workplace – so long as management maintained industrial peace in service to the nation (Higgins 1922: 16–17, 18; 4 CAR 18).

A tension between social harmony and the productive needs of the economy also characterised the advocates of 'efficiency' and innovative productivity practices who exerted an influence on the narrative of work in the early 20th century. Among these were the liberal progressive academics R.F. Irvine, professor of economics at the University of Sydney, and Meredith Atkinson, president of the Workers Educational Association (WEA), a liberal project for the education of adult workers developed in Britain and transplanted to Australia in 1913 (Taksa

1997). A 1915 conference revealed the gulf between the idealistic progressives and the workers they sought to summon to a more efficient standard of union organisation – one better adapted to the needs of the nation. Irvine argued that unionists should be 'deeply concerned' with the question of 'productive efficiency', which unions, preoccupied with the pursuit of higher wages and shorter hours, had largely left to employers to resolve. Unions responded to efficiency initiatives such as scientific management with unnecessary hostility. Streamlining work practices and bonus payments should not be opposed by 'sensible workmen'. Unions should give priority to the nation, and 'the general welfare and civilisation of the community'. In the ensuing discussion Kate Dwyer, a key Labor organiser of women workers, cut through the platitudes of national consensus rising over class consciousness so beloved by the efficiency enthusiasts. 'He could scoff at the half-seasoned planks in the Labor platform. In her opinion, some of them had been shouldered by the working-class so long that they had become worm-eaten' (Atkinson 1915: 31, 33–5, 39). The gap between the liberal progressives of the WEA and the labour movement widened during the later years of the war, as class divisions and home-front industrial unrest intensified (Taksa 1997: 29).

By the First World War the Industrial Workers of the World (IWW) arose to challenge the gospel of workplace efficiency. The IWW urged workers to subvert the prevailing work narrative of thrift, efficiency and intensified productivity by resisting management production 'speed-ups' and embracing the international brotherhood of the working class. If the boss paid a thrifty wage, 'be thrifty with your work, work slower' (Burgmann 1995: 138). Despite a modest membership, IWW ideas infiltrated resistance to the attempts by the NSW Rail and Tram Service to impose some scientific management practices, developed by its American pioneer Frederick Winslow Taylor, in its workplaces in 1916–17. The resulting 'Great Strike' of 1917 saw a profound defeat for industrial radicalism (Patmore 1988). The challenge posed to the prevailing narrative of work by the IWW and the Communist Party formed in 1920 was often framed in specific repudiation of traditional work and capitalist relations. The One Big Union (OBU) movement of 1918–23 proposed to draw Australia's over 700 unions into one powerful industrial organisation in a radical challenge to capitalism. The OBU foundered in inter-union rivalry and the reformism favoured by the labour movement. Radicals were often vilified as 'un-Australian', by both labour movement figures and employers, for spreading 'insidious propaganda of foreign origin', as the NSW Chamber of Manufactures darkly warned in its 1926 annual report, reflecting the instinctive racial nationalism of the narrative of work. By the late 1920s left-radicalism remained highly marginalised in Australia.

The advocates of efficiency and scientific management made little impression with their predominantly American-influenced reforms. Some employers dabbled with innovative practices such as scientific management (Patmore 1988; Taksa 1995). In 1927 the NSW Chamber of Manufactures (1928 report: 5) supported the establishment of the Institute of Industrial Psychology, which developed tests and procedures for job selection, factory organisation and distribution procedures. The Chamber was sensitive to claims that Australian manufacturing was inefficient. In its 1926 report it blamed State and federal regulations, 'defective transportation', lack of population, distance from 'world centres' and the time-wasting 'quasi legal business of arbitration procedure' for Australia's industrial inefficiency – all factors apparently beyond the manufacturers' control. By the late 1920s the Bruce Nationalist government responded to employer grievances over the arbitration system and union militancy. The 1929 election was fought over the government's intention to scrap the Commonwealth Arbitration Court, and resulted in the government losing office. The Australian Mines and Metals Association (AMMA), representing employers in metalliferous mining, lamented that the single issue of arbitration could so dominate national affairs, an outcome 'inconceivable . . . in any other English-speaking country'. 'The conclusion cannot be avoided that the incubus of the system of compulsory arbitration, as we know it in Australia, is a serious handicap to national development and prosperity' (AMMA 1930: 1). The AMMA implicitly conceded that the debate about this 'incubus' (an evil spirit or nightmare) was in fact a debate not only about the arbitration system's infiltration of the workplace but about the national imagination. By 1930 the national narrative of work firmly reflected the values of the Australian Settlement. In Hancock's mordant view, the settlement's seductive potion of ethics and economics produced a form of state paternalism, and through the arbitration system – with its stress on 'corporate' applications from employers and unions and its discouragement of individual submissions – a paternalistic workplace culture 'bitterly hostile to individualistic diversity'. 'The ultimate authority over Australian industry', Hancock tartly concluded, 'now belonged to judges' (Hancock 1930: 118, 140, 181).

RECONSTRUCTING AUSTRALIA, 1930–49

In 1930 the Scullin federal Labor government implemented longstanding plans to amend the *Commonwealth Conciliation and Arbitration Act*. Labor proposed to strip the Arbitration Court's legalistic framework by limiting the need for the parties to engage counsel, and shifting the emphasis from arbitration to conciliation – increasing the number and powers of conciliation commissioners, who were not judges – to facilitate informal, private and compulsory negotiations between the parties to resolve their disputes. Labor's aims foundered in the opposition-controlled Senate; a much amended bill passed into law at the end of the year (Crisp 1963: 47–9).

Employers bitterly opposed the reforms as another unwarranted intrusion of third parties into the employer–employee relationship, constraining the employers' 'freedom' to manage. Despite its complaints of the court's 'quasi-legalism', the Chamber of Manufactures believed the new Act 'turns over the management of all the factories to the Conciliation Commissioners', and to the shop committees of worker and union delegates that developed in the wake of the OBU. The Chamber argued that the rapidly developing economic depression would lend renewed impetus to the abolition of compulsory arbitration. Australia's high levels of indebtedness to mainly London banks and its exposure to collapsing commodity prices resulted in profound economic distress and an unemployment rate that peaked at around 30 per cent of the workforce in the Great Depression of 1929–33. The Chamber complained that these conditions and the loss of workplace control represented by the new Act exacerbated the 'curse to industry' represented by 'parasitical' unionism, discouraging investment and reducing profitability (*Australian Manufacturer* 6 December 1930).

The Depression was not profitable for workers. In January 1931 the Commonwealth Arbitration Court reduced wages by 10 per cent. Working hours were also increased from 44 to 48 hours a week and pension and social service payments were cut. The slashed expenditures fulfilled the arguments of the leading advocates of the Premiers' Plan – Sir Robert Gibson, the powerful Governor of the Commonwealth Bank, and Sir Otto Niemeyer, summoned to offer his advice as the representative of the Bank of England, Australia's chief creditor. They drew upon a compelling tradition of disciplined *economy*, a rhetoric of thrift and frugal hard work to push through a deflationary strategy to reduce 'wages, salaries and allowances, pensions, social benefits of all kinds', which Gibson virtually instructed the Scullin Government to implement (*SMH* 14 February 1931). Niemeyer declared that Australia's 'standard of living' was unsustainable. Productivity lagged well behind its major trading partners: Australians would have to work harder to remain competitive (*SMH* 22 August 1930). In 1932 Lloyd Ross, a socialist and WEA tutor, echoed Hancock's *Australia* when he observed that 'the religion of Australia is its standard of living' (Ross 1932: 208). Niemeyer's cool analysis provoked an often fiery response from labour movement leaders, and 'no passage in [Niemeyer's] statement evoked so much criticism' as his 'attack' on Australia's relatively high standard of living – the distribution of the benefits of work (*SMH* 13 February 1931). Australians were proud of building a new world of opportunity in the southern hemisphere, free of 'old world' wrongs: to witness 'the Premiers of the great Australian nation sitting like a class of schoolboys to be lectured by an emissary of British moneylenders', as *Worker* editor Henry Boote lamented, was a humiliating acknowledgment of the nation's continued dependency on the mother country, leaving Australian workers and their families in 'heartrending distress' while 'Britain's wealthiest loafers may . . . wallow still more grossly in sybaritic excess' (*Australian Worker* 27 August 1930). Criticising Australian productivity and living standards, Niemeyer intensified labour movement nationalism.

A decade later, Labor Prime Minister John Curtin outlined the principles that guided Labor's postwar reconstruction plans. The outbreak of the Second World War required workforce reorganisation to meet the national emergency. Coming to office in 1941, Labor was determined that the sacrifices of war, unlike those of the Depression, should stimulate working-class opportunity and living standards. In his 1943 election speech Curtin promised that Labor

> shall not tolerate an uncontrolled, speculative post-war boom which dissolves into the prolonged depression of ruined hopes and wasted lives . . . We are determined to develop this country and its resources to assure to every Australian a national minimum standard of income and social services which will leave him in no envy of any other country. (Curtin 1943)

As publicity director for the Department of Post-War Reconstruction 1943–49, Lloyd Ross was strategically placed to define a program that would restore Australia's once enviable standard of living and its national pride. Work and nation-building formed a central theme of the reconstruction narrative Ross produced in a stream of speeches, articles and pamphlets. Ross acknowledged that Australian workers were 'breaking records of production' in service to the needs of the war economy: 'You are proud of that job – and rightly so.' The war ushered in 'great industrial changes', with unprecedented numbers of women 'impatient to join the services or industry', taking jobs in munitions and aircraft production and a wide range of traditional male occupations. Ross's idealistic conception of reconstruction did not acknowledge that pay discrimination persisted throughout the war; it was not until 1945 that the federal government legislated to increase women's wages to 75 per cent of male wages (Patmore 1991: 173–4). Australians had accepted 'war-time restraints' – rationing, conscription, manpower controls – to protect 'our liberty as a nation'; workers would only be guaranteed postwar prosperity by planning to secure full employment, and a sense of economic security lost in the Depression years (Ross 1944a: 5, 9, 43–4).

Ross the planner was an advocate of government controls and initiatives to guarantee full employment and reduce strikes. In 1942–43 he toured workplaces in the USA and returned as a champion of 'joint consultation' involving workers, management and government (Ross 1944b). Like earlier efficiency advocates, he wanted a better class of worker, with enhanced morale to overcome 'apathy or hostility' and respond to 'the appeal for increasing production'. Consultation encouraged the worker to realise 'his social responsibility' and better understand 'economic processes', so that he would willingly 'take into account the needs of the Government before he takes individual action'. Service to the nation would strengthen 'the Australian working class and Australian democracy' (Ross 1949: 59, 64, 67). Rowse observes that Ross and Labor, committed as they were to 'reconstructing capitalism', strove 'to consolidate the war-time social contract between the working class and the capitalist state' (Rowse 1978: 132, 169). Labor had little choice but to pursue its objectives; undemocratic communism was not, as Ross argued, a valid alternative. Labor, with its roots in Australian experience, was 'the only possible instrument of socialistic change in Australia' (Hearn 1992: 32). Attempting to cultivate worker self-perception as 'a citizen in a productive society', Labor also legitimated a liberal-nationalist ideology suited to the postwar production requirements of business – and Labor's political opponents.

As Labor's reconstruction narrative evolved, a counter-narrative of enterprise and freedom rose to contest it. The Chamber of

Manufactures (1944 Presidential Address: 6–7) was suspicious of the 'Rule by Regulation' it saw in Labor's reconstruction plans, hindering business operations. The extension of wartime industry controls into the peace was 'intolerable'. Private enterprise would have to carry the burden of reconstruction and must operate freely if it was to compete in domestic and international markets. In 1943 the Institute of Public Affairs emerged to promote the values of 'the free society and free enterprise'. Solving postwar industrial and social problems 'will depend upon the renascence of individual enterprise and courage'. Unions had to abandon 'go slow' tactics, and workers had to realise that 'it is only through hard work efficiently applied to the end of greater production that a better standard of life will be possible'. The IPA warned that a planned economy 'leads to totalitarianism', hyperbole lent some credence by the intense Cold War rivalries of the late 1940s. Ross's insistence that planning would create 'liberty' though the security of full employment was a message obscured in Labor's struggles with communist-controlled unions (Ross 1944a: 43, 88). Employers rejected the 'socialisation' of industry and welcomed Labor's 'purge' of the 'un-Australian' and 'alien' presence of communists from key unions, who had plotted production chaos in the crucial coal and transport industries (NSW Chamber of Manufactures 1949 report: 2; 1950 report: 4; AMMA 1949 report: 2). Failing to nationalise the banks and exhausted by the labour movement divisions of the bitter 1949 coal strike and the defeat of the communist-controlled Miners Federation, Labor lost office to the recently established Liberal Party of Australia led by Robert Menzies, who campaigned on the theme 'Socialism or Freedom?' The Post-War Reconstruction Department was scrapped. Employers dismissed 'peace in industry' initiatives involving consultation with unions or government. 'The maintenance of good relationships between management and men in industry is a day to day task better left to industry itself' (NSW Chamber of Manufactures 1951 report: 4).

WORKING TOGETHER, 1950–82

The artwork on the cover of the 1950 *Australasian Manufacturer Annual* served as a tribute to emergent postwar modernism, conceived in 'the machine age of planning, industrialism and limited model production lines' (Dingle & O'Hanlon 1997: 34). In vibrant colour, a machine-tooled, cog-toothed steel archway framed Australia's industrial future. Its centrepiece was a representation of a modernist high-rise factory building flying the Australian flag. At its feet sat sleek-lined electrically powered turbines bordering a large, glistening steel generator. No better image could capture the *Annual*'s subtitle: 'The March of Australia's Industrial Progress'.

The image symbolised the need for Australian industry to continue to modernise and build on the technological and operational advances and industrial discipline achieved during the war. Later, in the foreword to the 1953 *Annual*, Prime Minister Robert Menzies reminded Australian manufacturing that 'watching its costs and efficiency' was one of its 'national duties' if Australia was to become 'a large supplier of manufactured goods to the markets of the world'. Menzies asserted that this goal required 'teamwork' and that 'we must all play in the team if we are to be true and good Australians' (*Australasian Manufacturer Annual* 6 June 1953). Menzies' expectations were little different from the liberal progressive notions of cooperation – subordinating class divisions in service to the nation – so eloquently advocated by the intellectuals of the WEA some 40 years earlier. Brett (1992: 60–1) has argued that in his 1954 election policy speech Menzies unsuccessfully attempted to capture working-class appeal from Labor as he had identified the Liberal Party with the aspirations of the middle class, claiming 'we are the true workers' party'.

The notion of increased worker efficiency was reinforced throughout the 1950s and 1960s. Commenting on a report into industry efficiency by the Commonwealth Labour Advisory Council in 1956, the *Australasian Manufacturer* (17 March) considered that 'the needs of the hour are good leadership, discipline and worker co-operation'. Workers must also appreciate '*their* responsibilities, an understanding of the extent to which the nation is dependent on their skills, their working the full 40-hour week, and their continuity of operations'. The appeal to national pride was an undisguised element of the developing national narrative of work. The Institute of Public Affairs emphasised the economic value of national pride by pointing to the American worker's 'belief in America' as a key factor in American economic achievement (Alomes 1988: 148–9). Harold Holt, Menzies' Minister for Labour and National Service, appealed to Australian workers to realise that their welfare was inextricably linked with that of their employer and to accept, as American workers had done, that they will 'benefit personally from an increased production performance' (Holt 1953: 80).

Notions of productivity and efficiency found some cautious support in the labour movement. Senior ACTU officials were represented on

the Commonwealth Labour Advisory Council. Lloyd Ross (a union secretary from 1952), ACTU President Albert Monk and A.B. Thompson
of the Australasian Society of Engineers each contributed chapters in
the Australian Institute of Political Science 1957 publication *Productivity and Progress*. Both Monk and Thompson questioned whether workers would receive their fair share under employee incentive schemes,
while Ross adopted a more positive position, advocating the value of
joint consultation.

Union wariness may have been well founded; the *Australian Journal
of Productivity and Management* thought national productivity increases
required the 'right' attitude from workers: 'supervisors must be able to
achieve a high degree of integration, welding their particular people
into a team and then integrating them into the whole of the workforce'
(Anon. 1957: 36). The Institute of Public Affairs (1967: 10) promoted
the establishment of a National Productivity Council – providing it
was controlled by a combination of government representatives and
business interests, without any role for the labour movement or worker
representation.

The quest for increased workplace efficiency and productivity continued into the 1970s. Clyde Cameron, Minister for Labour in the
reformist Whitlam Labor Government (1972–75), championed the
need to 'humanise the work-place'. Convinced that management and
unions must cooperate and that 'the increasing flow of literature on the
various behavioural techniques . . . may provide the key to making work
more meaningful', Cameron instructed his Department to investigate
international research in relation to job enrichment, job satisfaction
and attitudes to work. Cameron (1974: 3–7) believed that highly motivated workers would 'contribute towards higher productivity on the one
hand and satisfaction and good mental health on the other'.

In a 1973 speech on the Conciliation and Arbitration Bill, Cameron
announced the establishment of an inquiry to examine the viability
of voluntary mediation, plant-level employer–employee relations and
worker participation schemes (Bentley 1973: 265). Like many of its
initiatives, the inquiry fell victim to the chronic political problems
that increasingly beset the government. Nonetheless, Whitlam also
helped overturn decades of discrimination by supporting the case in
the Commonwealth Arbitration Commission for equal pay for women
in 1974. The government ensured that the decision flowed promptly
to Commonwealth public servants; in other sectors the decision took
much longer to take effect. Whitlam also established the national Trade

Union Training Authority, rectifying 'the absurd situation whereby Australia's trade unionists, comprising 53 per cent of all wage and salary earners, were without any facilities for the training of [union] management' (Whitlam 1985: 287, 517).

The election of the Fraser Liberal Government in the mid-1970s marked the beginnings 'of a campaign which would attribute all economic ills to the costs of government, to trade unions, high wages and strikes, and would offer the panaceas of smaller government, individual initiative and harder work by employees' (Alomes 1988: 266). Prime Minister Malcolm Fraser was an early convert to this 'new rhetoric' to which he gave credence in his 'life was not meant to be easy' view of the world. This rhetoric of sacrifice recalled the 1930s, and was taken up by conservative politicians, think-tanks such as the Centre for Independent Studies, and business bodies such as Enterprise Australia.

Enterprise Australia (EA) was financed by six major Australian corporations and was expected to be crucial 'in the propaganda warfare for capitalism'. EA produced and distributed films for television, radio advertising slogans and videos for schools and conducted courses in 'economic education' for employees. It also brought a succession of economic educators from the USA to Australia to provide guidance. The organisation's first chief executive officer, Jack Keavney, toured the USA on a number of occasions, giving progress reports to the US Chamber of Commerce and the National Association of Manufacturers (Carey 1987: 10–11). Opening EA's Enterprise Week in 1977, Fraser championed free enterprise: the 'entire community benefits from an efficient and prosperous private sector . . . the most efficient economic system available . . . [and] the most efficient provider of the resources required to produce a better life for all Australians' (White & Kemp 1986: 121–2).

Fraser's championship of free enterprise proved problematic in practice. In 1982 regular wage increases through 'indexation', introduced under the previous Labor administration in 1975 to compensate workers for rapid increases in the cost of living, were abandoned. Bowing to Fraser's opposition to full indexation, the Arbitration Commission's decisions from 1977 had been confined to partial indexation, leading to considerable worker unrest and increased industrial disputation, and finally a chaotic return to direct bargaining. Losing control of industrial relations, the government was perceived as losing control of the economy. Fraser's failure generated a narrative of national renewal from Labor, and 'a Radical Liberal Alternative' from within his own party, calling for a 'free market' philosophy and deregulation of the labour market (Crowley 1986: 313, 398; Kelly 1992: 52).

THE ACCORD AND AFTER

In March 1983 Labor returned to federal office under the leadership of the former ACTU president Bob Hawke. Elected as Australia struggled with economic recession and rejecting Fraser's divisive politics, Hawke promised to lead a government committed to 'reconciliation, recovery and reconstruction'. Through the Prices and Incomes Accord, Labor and the unions would join in the process of economic recovery and social development. In April 1983 Hawke's consensus politics drew the parties, together with business leaders, to a National Economic Summit. The delegates approved a strategy of modest wage increases through a restored centralised wage-fixing system and non-wage initiatives to reward workers for increased productivity and wage restraint – a national superannuation scheme and the promotion of industrial democracy in the workplace (Statement of Accord by the Australian Labor Party and the Australian Council of Trade Unions Regarding Economic Policy, February 1983).

The Accord represented one of the most significant expressions since Federation of the identification with nation-building that had characterised the labour movement's intervention in national politics. Hawke's predisposition to consensus instinctively led him to appeal to the broad community of Australians rather than dwell on the 'Labor ideology of class conflict' (Kelly 1992: 272), an ideology that Labor had in fact often put aside to appeal to the nation. Hawke's consensus nationalism was perhaps a little more obvious; in his opening address to the Summit, Hawke 'was so determined to put the imprimatur of the nation on the summit that he managed to say "people of Australia" or "Australian people" six times in the first ten sentences'. Hawke cast Australia's economic 'crisis' as the worst since the Depression, requiring a spirit of community sacrifice comparable with that displayed during the Second World War, and he invoked a 1942 Curtin speech urging Australians to display their 'inherent quality' to meet the national emergency (SMH 12 April 1983). Echoing 1940s Labor, Hawke established the Economic Planning Advisory Council which 'institutionalised co-operation' between the Accord partners (Hawke 1994: 183).

The corporatist nature of the Accord, with its structural discipline of wage restraint through arbitration, successively fulfilled the aims of economic recovery. The Accord proved less successful in fulfilling price restraint – which would only be monitored, not regulated – and in promoting industrial democracy; little was accomplished beyond the production of a discussion paper (Department of Employment and Industrial Relations 1986). Women workers felt excluded from the male-dominated institutions of Accord corporatism and its focus on masculine work skills and organisation, which 'stress[ed] the needs of the male manufacturing sector over the female community and service sector'. The sole dissenter to approving the Accord was a woman unionist representing nurses, who saw little benefit for her members; among the 100 Summit delegates there was only one woman, who observed that its debates would reflect and perpetuate gender discrimination (Schofield 1989: 9, 11).

From 1986, as Australia's trade deficit worsened, the Accord found renewed purpose in 'facilitating the transition to a more competitive economy' (Kelly 1992: 271). Unions struggled with the transition to competitive deregulation, and through various renegotiations of the Accord sought to manage the terms of workplace reform. In 1987 they supported a two-tier wage system, providing wage increases in exchange for reformed work practices; awards were restructured in another round of reforms. In 1988 Labor replaced the 1904 *Conciliation and Arbitration Act* with the *Industrial Relations Act* and were soon to introduce enterprise bargaining. The ACTU encouraged this shift, partly in frustration with the revamped Australian Industrial Relations Commission, but increasingly unions found that, impelled by the narrative of deregulation, they could no longer control the terms of reform.

From 1986 the 'New Right' posed an aggressive reaction to what it derisively characterised as the 'Industrial Relations Club' of government, unions and arbitration. The New Right was distinguished by its radical economic and industrial rationalism, couched in a confrontational polarisation of values. The New Right organised through the H.R. Nicholls Society, adopting an arbitration dissident who had challenged Higgins' 'political' judgments as its role model for attacking Accord wage increases which 'threaten Australia's living standards' (*Arbitration in Contempt* 1986: 11, 69). Employers in the mining and rural sectors dominated the New Right and encapsulated its defensive and alienated ethos: attacking 'union power', mining executive Hugh Morgan described 'Australia's export industries battling . . . on an economic Kokoda trail'. Yet unlike the wartime diggers, while 'the farmers and miners' struggled on behalf of the nation and its poor terms of trade, they felt 'the rest of the country regards their present struggle with unconcern' (*Arbitration in Contempt* 1986: 16). The New Right challenge was also manifest in the workplace: at its Robe River mine Peko Wallsend confronted union power and a culture of restrictive work practices in 1986. Managing director Charles Copeman acknowledged – and sought to subvert – the link between work and consensus politics represented by the Accord: he described the dispute as an 'essentially political' challenge (Hearn & Knowles 1996: 329).

Responding to business and market reform pressures as the economy collapsed into recession, in 1991 the Hawke government issued a major economic statement, 'Building a Competitive Australia', revealing its assimilation of the narrative of competition and deregulation. Tariff protection would be substantially reduced and a range of labour market reforms introduced. 'We are freeing up our transport systems', Hawke declared, 'we are creating more efficient workplaces; we are injecting competition where for too long Australian firms and public sector enterprises have been content with the quiet life' (Department of Prime Minister and Cabinet 1991: 1, 10). In 1994 the Keating Labor government introduced non-union enterprise bargaining, driven by a recognition of declining union influence in the workplace: union membership fell from 56 per cent of the workforce in 1983 to 35 per cent in 1994 (Peetz 1998: 26). In *Future Strategies for the Trade Union Movement*, ACTU secretary Bill Kelty, a key Accord advocate and strategist, urged Australia's over 300 unions to amalgamate as 20 'large and efficient' organisations to meet the challenges posed by the New Right and declining membership – a process still only partially achieved, with mixed efficiency results and continuing decline in membership (see Cooper & Ellem this volume). Kelty conceded that unions must rely on the institutions of the state and its political ties to Labor if they were to advance their members' interests. 'If the union movement in Australia fails to accept its responsibility to preserve and advance the system of social regulations on behalf of all workers then the free market strategy of the New Right will ultimately prevail' (ACTU 1987: 8–10).

In 1996 Labor lost office and unions substantially lost their ability to influence the national narrative of work. The Howard government moved quickly to fulfil the narrative of deregulation through the *Workplace Relations Act*. The Act reflected Howard's broad support of the New Right agenda, refocusing industrial relations on direct employer–employee enterprise bargaining by restricting the Australian Industrial Relations Commission to administering awards with only 20 'allowable matters' – the provision of wage rates and basic entitlements. The Act also established the Office of the Employment Advocate to oversee a new system of individual contracts – Australian Workplace Agreements or AWAs, which were directly negotiated between employers and employees without the interference of 'third parties' – unions (Birmingham 1997).

Since 1984 Howard had argued that employers and employees should have the 'freedom' to enter into 'voluntary work contracts' in order to boost employment and productivity (Kelly 1992: 119). In Howard's neo-liberalism, freedom should not be governed by state intervention but by the discrete relationships between employers and employees. As Rose suggests, this reconstructed narrative of freedom does not see the needs of the nation disappear into the background, even in the context of globalised economic relations: 'it now appears that one can best fulfil one's obligations to one's nation by most effectively pursuing the enhancement of the economic well-being of oneself, one's family, one's firm, business or organisation', enhancing 'national economic health at the same time as [generating] individual freedom' (Rose 1999: 145).

Rose adds that the retreat of traditional government interventionism is not a politics of 'abstention'. 'Politics must actively intervene in order to create the organisational and subjective conditions for entrepreneurship', particularly the 'minimisation of rigidities in the labour market', and stimulating 'the attitudes and aspirations necessary to become an entrepreneur of oneself' (Rose 1999: 144). Since the mid-1990s, business and deregulation evangelists have urged renewed government intervention. In 2001 the Business Council of Australia (2001: 4, 17) argued that it was in Australia's 'national interest' to pursue further labour market reform; 50 chief executives agreed that 'the focus of employment relations in Australia will increasingly be the role of the individual in the enterprise'. The Institute of Private Enterprise urged the government to adopt new forms of intervention favourable to business and the market: a removal of the right to strike, removal of 'union privileges' to picket or enter workplaces, and removal of most of the 'absurd' 20 allowable matters from wage awards, including regulation of working hours, pay rates and a range of leave entitlements (*AFR* 12 October 2004). In 2004 Howard responded to these calls with his advocacy of an 'enterprise culture', and state intervention calculated to guide the individual to self-managed initiative and productivity in service to the enterprise and hence the nation: measures to encourage the use of AWAs, restricting union access to the workplace and requiring secret ballots prior to industrial action, and easing restrictions on dismissing employees. By contrast, Labor's proposed 'reregulation' would diminish living standards and impede 'choice and flexibility for employers and employees' ('Workplace reform equals more jobs and higher wages', Media Release from the Minister for Employment and Workplace Relations, 28 September 2004).

CONCLUSION

> Language has been made the machine of business and politics in the information age. (Watson 2004: 3)

Change Management. Customer focus. Stakeholders. Knowledge Manager. Human Resource Management. Key Performance Indicator. Team player. 24/7. World's Best Practice. Watson says that many of the entries in *Weasel Words*, his dictionary of contemporary 'cant and management jargon', were drawn from the language of companies and government departments: from the realm of work, where the linguistic – and therefore the imaginative – horizons have shrivelled, suppressing the development of an alternative language to that of the prevailing managerial ethos. 'The frustration of the people who work in [companies and government departments], the sense they have that this language is stupid and oppressive and that it denies them a fundamental right', was an inspiration for *Weasel Words*. Watson's reference to rights acknowledges the relationship between language and power (Watson 2004: 6–7, 10). As Wasson's workplace research demonstrated, the spread of enterprise language and ideology, communicated through 'marketplace metaphors', bestowed 'symbolic capital' on employees who embraced this metaphorical language while other co-workers 'lose face by refusing to frame their work processes within the terms of the enterprise language' – a 'disempowering' loss of face that led to negative evaluation by their peers (Wasson 2004: 176, 178–9, 181).

Enterprise language has also proved a valuable political weapon when strategically employed in a wider national discourse of hard work, plain speaking and reward. The Howard government is engaged in an 'ongoing dialogue', to employ a weasel phrase, with business to entrench in the minds and the language of the community the ideological hegemony vital for political success and workplace control, as the *AFR* editorial quoted at the beginning of this chapter demonstrates. Howard's appropriation of 'battlers' as footsoldiers of the enterprise culture; his creation of an imagined realm of us and them, disparaging 'elites' and 'political correctness'; and his ability to present Labor as opposed to a 'fair and decent' enterprise culture are all aspects of the narrative of national politics that bear directly on the narrative of work, and an intention to harness aspiration to the demands of productive enterprise (Watson 2004: 39, 114, 254).

Kroskrity (2000: 23) observes that 'language . . . has long served as the key to naturalizing the boundaries of social groups'. The language of the enterprise culture has largely succeeded in appearing non-political and non-ideological, the machine language of the apparently 'natural' progress of the economy and the nation, to which the workforce should be enthusiastically committed. At the 2004 federal election Labor defied this trend, advocating a defence of collective industrial relations, protection of employee rights and entitlements, and abolition of AWAs (*SMH* 30 August 2004). Labor's comprehensive defeat resulted in a rapid policy reappraisal; within a month of the election Labor hinted that it would support AWAs (*Australian* 8 December 2004). Out of apparent political necessity, Labor allowed the neo-liberal narrative of work and freedom to colonise its values. Echoing the advice offered by the *AFR* a few weeks earlier (and quoted above), in late November 2004 Mark Latham advocated 'flexibility with fairness'. Labor must accept the 'decentralised economy' and 'champion' its 'army of contractors, consultants, franchisees and entrepreneurs', who represented 'new constituencies' to fulfil Labor's dream of a 'fairer Australia' in the spirit of the 'nation building reforms' of the Hawke and Keating governments (Latham 2004). From Federation, Labor had argued that the uniquely Australian mechanisms of state regulation of work would facilitate an inclusive nation-building; in the era of post-Accord globalisation Labor failed to articulate a convincing alternative to neo-liberal deregulation.

John Howard also dreams of a 'fair and decent' Australia, recalling the 'fair and reasonable' aspirations of the Australian Settlement and the arbitration system. To take Hancock's point, has Australia now adopted a different ethical standpoint from which to frame its economics? Howard apparently believes that fair and decent prosperity can be achieved in a liberalised economy of individual entrepreneurs, and has sought to shift the economics of Australian democracy while clinging to the resonant ethical language of an older and more formally regulated Australian nation.

References

ACTU 1987, *Future Strategies for the Trade Union Movement*, Melbourne: ACTU.

Alomes, S. 1988, *A Nation at Last: The Changing Character of Australian Nationalism 1880–1988*, Sydney: Angus & Robertson.

AMMA (Australian Mines and Metals Association) 1930, Directors' Report.

Anderson, B. 1991, *Imagined Communities*, London: Verso.

Anon, 1957, 'Attitudes are important', *Australian Journal of Productivity and Management* 1(2): 36.

Arbitration in Contempt 1986, Melbourne: H.R. Nicholls Society.

Atkinson, M. 1915, *Trade Unionism in Australia*, Sydney: Burrows & Co.

Australian Institute of Political Science 1957, *Productivity and Progress*, Sydney: Angus & Robertson.

Bentley, P. 1973, 'A survey of current issues in Australian industrial relations', *Journal of Industrial Relations* 15(3): 259–80.

Birmingham, A. 1997, 'A guide to the Workplace Relations Act 1996', *Australian Bulletin of Labour* 23(1): 33–47.

Brett, J. 1992, *Robert Menzies' Forgotten People*, Macmillan Australia.

Burgmann, V. 1995, *Revolutionary Industrial Unionism: The Industrial Workers of the World in Australia*, Cambridge University Press.

Business Council of Australia 2001, 'Business in the national interest', Melbourne: BCA.

Cameron, C. 1974, 'Human satisfaction: current social standards and their effect on work, production and productivity'. Paper delivered to Australian Institute of Management Conference Emerging Concepts of Human Relations, South Australia, 24–26 July.

Carey, A. 1987, 'Conspiracy or groundswell?' in K. Coghill (ed.) *The New Right's Australian Fantasy*, Melbourne: McPhee Gribble Penguin Books.'

Crisp, L.F. 1963, *Ben Chifley*, Melbourne: Longmans, Green & Co. Ltd.

Crowley, F. 1986, *Tough Times: Australia in the Seventies*, Melbourne: William Heinemann.

Curtin, J. 1943, 'General Elections 1943: Statement of Policy, 26 July 1943'.

Department of Employment and Industrial Relations 1986, 'Industrial democracy and employee participation', Canberra: DEIR.

Department of Prime Minister and Cabinet 1991, 'Building a competitive Australia', 12 March, Canberra: DPMC.

Dingle, T. & Seamus O'Hanlon, S. 1997, 'Modernism versus domesticity', *Australian Historical Studies* 28(109): 33–48.

Fairclough, N. 1995, *Critical Discourse Analysis*, London: Longman.

Hancock, K. 1930, *Australia*, London: Ernest Benn Ltd.

Hawke, R.J.L. 1994, *The Hawke Memoirs*, Melbourne: William Heinemann.

Hearn, M. 1992, 'Means and ends: the ideology of Dr. Lloyd Ross', *Labour History* 63: 25–42.

Hearn, M. & Knowles, H. 1996, *One Big Union: A History of the Australian Workers Union*, Cambridge University Press.

Higgins, H.B. 1922, *A New Province for Law and Order*, London: Dawsons of Pall Mall.

Higgins, H.B. 1924, 'The Australian Commonwealth Court of Conciliation and Arbitration'. Address to the Oxford University Association for Philosophy, Politics and Economics, 14 June.

H.E. Holt 1953, 'The search for better industrial relations', *Australasian Manufacturer Annual*, June: 80.

Institute of Public Affairs (NSW) 1944, *Looking Forward: A Post-War Policy for Australian Industry*, Institute of Public Affairs, pp. 15, 27, 52.

Institute of Public Affairs (NSW) 1967, 'Does Australia need an active national productivity council?', *Discussion Panel Booklet No. 2*.

Keat, R. & N. Abercrombie (eds) 1991, *Enterprise Culture*, London: Routledge.

Kelly, P. 1992, *The End of Certainty*, Sydney: Allen & Unwin.

Kroskrity, P.V. 2000, 'Regimenting languages: language ideological perspectives', in P.V. Kroskrity (ed.) *Regimes of Language: Ideologies, Politics and Identities*, Santa Fe: School of American Research Press.

Latham, M. 'Modern Labor: a tradition of change'. Speech to the Australian Fabian Society, 19 November 2004.

Melleuish, G. 1995, *Cultural Liberalism in Australia*, Cambridge University Press.

Melleuish, G. 2001, 'Australian liberalism', in J.R. Nethercote (ed.) *Liberalism and the Australian Federation*, Sydney: Federation Press, pp. 28–41.

Patmore, G. 1988, 'Systematic management and bureaucracy: the NSW Railways prior to 1932', *Labour and Industry* 1(2): 306–21.

Patmore, G. 1991, *Australian Labour History*, Melbourne: Longman Cheshire.

Peetz, D. 1998, *Unions in a Contrary World: The Future of the Australian Trade Union Movement*, Cambridge University Press.

Phillips, N. & Hardy, C. 2002, C. *Discourse Analysis: Investigating Processes of Social Construction*, London: Sage.

Roberts, W. 2001, 'Liberalism: the nineteenth century legacy', in J.R. Nethercote (ed.) *Liberalism and the Australian Federation*, Sydney: Federation Press, pp. 42–50.

Rose, N. 1999, *Powers of Freedom: Reframing Political Thought*, Cambridge University Press.

Ross, L. 1932, 'Australian labour and the crisis', *Economic Record* 8(15): 204–22.

Ross, L. 1944a, *You and Your Job, Planning for Employment*, Sydney: Deaton & Spencer.

Ross, L. 1944b, 'Wartime industrial impressions', *Australian Quarterly* 16(2): 33–56.

Ross, L. 1949, 'Labour and production', *Twentieth Century* 4(1): 58–68.

Rowse, T. 1978, *Australian Liberalism and National Character*, Melbourne: Kibble Books.

Schofield, J. 1989, *Freezing History: Women Under the Accord 1983–88*, Industrial Relations Research Centre, University of New South Wales.

Somers, M.R. 1997, 'Deconstructing and reconstructing class formation theory: narrativity, relational analysis, and social theory', in J.R. Hall (ed.), *Reworking Class*, Ithaca N.Y.: Cornell University Press, pp. 73–105.

Taksa, L. 1995, 'The cultural diffusion of scientific management: the United States and New South Wales', *Journal of Industrial Relations* 37(3): 427–61.

Taksa, L. 1997, 'The Workers Education Association and the pursuit of national efficiency in Australia between 1913 and 1923', School of Industrial Relations and Organisational Behaviour, University of New South Wales.

Wasson, C. 2004, 'The paradoxical language of enterprise', *Critical Discourse Studies* 1(2): 175–99.

Watson, D. 2004, *Weasel Words*, Sydney: Knopf.

White, R. 1981, *Inventing Australia*, Sydney: Allen & Unwin.

White, D.M. & Kemp, D.A. (eds) 1986, *Malcolm Fraser on Australia*, Melbourne: Hill of Content.

Whitlam, E.G. 1985, *The Whitlam Government*, Melbourne: Viking.

CHAPTER TWELVE

SHAREHOLDER VALUE AND CORPORATE SOCIAL RESPONSIBILITY IN WORK ORGANISATIONS

Grant Michelson and Nick Wailes

The last couple of decades have seen the interplay of two strong and potentially competing meta-discourses about organisations and the factors that ought to shape their behaviour. The first and more established discourse – associated with the rational, economic notion of 'shareholder value' – sees the interests of the shareholder as paramount and encourages managers to privilege only those strategies and decisions that directly benefit shareholders in the short term. At the same time, a second discourse – 'corporate social responsibility' or CSR – speaks of a range of legitimate claims on the organisation and suggests that social, ethical and moral considerations ought to play a more significant role in corporate strategic planning and decision-making.

The Economist, one of the world's leading business magazines, recently published a major and critical review of corporate social responsibility, noting with alarm that 'if businessmen had a clearer understanding of the CSR mindset and its defects, they would be better at their jobs and everybody else would be more prosperous. Simply put, advocates of CSR work from the [false] premise that unadorned capitalism fails to serve the public interest' (Anon. 2005: 11).

While influential publications such as *The Economist* consider shareholder value and CSR to be conflicting and incompatible views of the organisation, recent literature has downplayed the suggested mutual exclusivity between the two discourses. For instance, there has been a growing tendency to present CSR as helping to serve 'instrumental' organisational purposes (for example Jones 1995; Garriga & Mele 2004). Here, proponents of CSR argue that being socially responsible

239

is 'good for business' since it contributes to firm performance and, ultimately, shareholder value. Thus it has been suggested that evidence of good (and even superior) economic performance by firms that behave in a socially responsible manner will eventually result in more of these organisations adopting a position of CSR (see Orlitzky et al. 2003). By the same token, examples of corporations acting in a manner that maximises shareholder value in the short term but does not necessarily produce desirable outcomes for shareholders in the long term may lead companies to reassess whether a single-minded focus on maximising short-term shareholder wealth is in the best interests of their shareholders (for example Byrne 2002; Blair 2003).

Using insights from discourse analysis, we seek to question the outcome suggested by the 'instrumental' perspective of CSR that firms will adopt socially responsible objectives, as well as the underlying assumption that a greater focus on CSR within organisations is likely to become widespread. Indeed, we argue that in spite of the assumed benefits of CSR for business, firms at the present time are generally reluctant to embrace social objectives and integrate them within their operations. The organisational modus operandi remains the more rational economic one of maximising shareholder value.

Our argument develops in the following way. In the first section we outline briefly how discourses can shape understanding and action in organisations and the potential insights that discourse analysis offers for examining such concepts as 'shareholder value' and 'corporate social responsibility'. The second section then explores the meta-discourses of these two concepts and the relationship between them. It argues that the shareholder value discourse reflects and reinforces a significant shift in power relations inside corporations that has been taking place since the late 1970s. It also argues that CSR was accentuated at the same time and in response to this shift in power relations associated with the rise of shareholder value and, in comparison with other ethical approaches to the firm, is subordinate to the shareholder value discourse. In the third section, we use the well-known concept of 'bounded rationality' to help explain why the dominance of shareholder value might lead managers to refrain from behaving in a socially responsible manner, even in the face of evidence that CSR does not damage shareholder value. Section four uses the case of Enron to illustrate our argument. The recent collapse of Enron, seen to be an exemplar of a firm managed for shareholder value, might not produce any significant shift in corporate managers' decisions about the benefits of maximising shareholder value in the short term. We conclude by arguing that, because of the nature of the current discourses surrounding shareholder value and CSR, perhaps the only way to improve the social actions of organisations is to regulate their behaviour. This is precisely the type of response the discourse of CSR would prefer to avoid.

DISCOURSE ANALYSIS IN ORGANISATIONAL RESEARCH

Discourse analysis is playing an increasing role in the study of work organisations and has been applied to a range of organisational phenomena (Grant et al. 2004). However, it has made relatively little contribution to the areas of business ethics, corporate social responsibility and shareholder value (for some exceptions see de Graaf 2001; Pollach 2003). This chapter attempts to address this situation by illustrating how discourse analysis can be used to understand contemporary developments in these areas.

Discourse refers to the practices of talking and writing, the visual representations and the cultural artefacts that bring organisational objects into being through the production, dissemination and consumption of texts (Grant et al. 2004). Texts can take many forms, such as written documents, verbal reports, spoken words, terminology, pictures, symbols, signs, buildings and so on. Discourse analysis is the systematic study of these texts. It is useful in highlighting work organisations as a socially constructed reality and, in particular, in showing that meaning is created through a negotiated process (Hardy 2001). In other words, and taking language as but one illustration, language does not simply reflect what goes on inside an organisation; it is constitutive of reality itself.

Thus discourse brings an object into being so that it becomes a material reality in the form of the practices it invokes for various interest groups (Hardy 2001). As part of this process, it 'rules in' certain ways of talking that are deemed acceptable, legitimate and intelligible, while at the same time also 'ruling out', limiting and restricting the way these interest groups talk about or conduct themselves. In this sense, discourse can be shown to act as a powerful ordering force (Alvesson & Karreman 2000).

Discourses do not simply start out in possession of meaning. Instead, and in line with their socially constructive effects, their meanings are created, and supported via discursive interactions among key interest groups. This constructive process involves the negotiation of meaning

241

among different groups or stakeholders – typically with different views and interests – and results in the emergence of a dominant meaning that can be seen as a particular discourse. This dominant meaning emerges as alternative discourses are subverted or marginalised and is indicative of the underlying power relationships that might come into play. As Fairclough (1995: 2) explains, the 'power to control discourse is seen as the power to sustain particular discursive practices with particular ideological investments in dominance over other alternative (including oppositional) practices'. In this sense, discourse analysis is helpful in revealing and understanding power relationships in organisational settings.

The construction of meaning for people in organisations results in the emergence of a dominant meaning, the consequence of which is that alternative meanings (or other discourses) are marginalised. We use this interpretation to make our case for the dominance of the 'shareholder value' discourse in work organisations. However, we do not assume that this outcome is deterministic and that once established as dominant, the notion of shareholder value will necessarily remain as such. Such dominance is an ongoing 'struggle' among competing discourses (Hardy 2001; Grant & Hardy 2003) as new texts are continually produced and interpreted in ways that privilege particular interests and goals. The response of proponents of the 'shareholder value' discourse to the collapse of Enron, which is examined in the final section of the chapter, provides an illustration of this discursive struggle.

To understand how and why particular discourses and their meanings are produced, as well as their effects, it is important to understand the contexts in which they arise. This has led to the application of intertextual analyses of discourses (Fairclough 1992, 1995). Such studies identify and analyse specific, micro-level instances of discursive action and then locate them in the context of other macro-level, meta or grand discourses (Alvesson & Karreman 2000). Our chapter draws on this observation by arguing that individual decision-making processes by managers are influenced by meta-discourses which shape what managers regard as the rational aims and purpose of business. In turn, these play a significant role in shaping organisational reality.

THE DISCURSIVE NATURE OF SHAREHOLDER VALUE AND CSR

Given the importance of discourse analysis in shaping organisational decisions, and particularly the connections between micro-level discourses and broader discursive practices, this section will examine some of the salient features of shareholder value and CSR as meta-discourses. We argue that the current discourse of 'shareholder value' is a product of a long-term shift in the power relationships within corporations that has been taking place since the late 1970s. This shift in power relations has privileged certain understandings of the purpose of the organisation, whose interests it represents, and what claims are regarded as legitimate (see, for example, Friedman 1970). In becoming increasingly dominant, the shareholder value discourse has thus marginalised alternative views about the relationship between firms and the societies in which they operate, including those associated with the social responsibilities of the organisation. We therefore argue that the 'instrumental' view of CSR, which treats ethical or social actions as a means of enhancing organisational wealth, can be seen as an attempt to incorporate social responsibility into the shareholder value discourse without questioning the assumptions on which it is based. Thus while CSR appears to offer an alternative conceptualisation of the role of the firm in society (and is a cause for alarm among some proponents of shareholder value), it does so in a partial and contingent way that reflects the extent to which shareholder value is currently the dominant discourse in management decision-making.

It could be claimed that the dominance of shareholder value in part reflects the construction of organisational rationality in ways that favour outcomes over processes. Maximising shareholder wealth appears to be an example of the former, while CSR is concerned with the latter because it refers to a general obligation but does not specifically articulate how this is determined and to whom such responsibilities are directed. In other words, there is some recognition that business organisations have social responsibilities, but the extent of these remains vague. This level of ambiguity is used as a 'discursive resource' (see Hardy et al. 2000) by proponents of shareholder value. For example, in his critique of CSR, Crook (2005: 3) makes the following point: 'it is hazardous to generalize, because CSR takes many different forms and is driven by many different motives.' The implication suggested here is that, in contrast, shareholder value as the 'proper' objective of business is clear, direct and specific.

However, we maintain that the apparent precision and coherence of shareholder value is itself discursively constructed. Shareholder value can be defined as 'the view that corporations should be run for the sole benefit of shareholders, that directors and officers of a corporation are, in fact, the "agents" of the corporation's shareholders, and that, as such, their duties are to maximise shareholder value' (Blair 2003: 886–7). While shareholder value appears to be a very specific notion, and there are a number of consultancies that promote the use of proprietorial financial ratios (for example economic value added) as a way of measuring its value, the precise meaning is in fact quite uncertain. There are myriad ways of calculating shareholder value and the different measures can and often do produce conflicting results (Koslowski 2000). Furthermore, there is little evidence to suggest that there is any relationship between the concept of managing for value and company performance (Froud et al. 2000). As some note, 'Shareholder value is not so much a precisely defined concept . . . as a rhetoric which circulates widely and a thematic which can be invoked as cause, consequence and justification' (Froud et al. 2000: 81). The claims associated with this rhetoric range from an emphasis on the economic efficiency of managing firms and allocating investments, arguments based on moral grounds about the legitimate ownership rights of shareholders, through to views concerned with residual income generated by the firm (Engelen 2002).

Over the past two decades in particular, the ideology of shareholder value has played an increasingly powerful role in shaping debates about the aims and obligations of the corporation and has become the dominant meta-discourse about what types of actions managers should take (see Rappaport 1986). Indeed, some have argued that in spite of more than a hundred years of differences in corporate law across nations, there is now an international consensus on a new 'standard' shareholder-oriented model of organisations. Such a model has the following features:

> Ultimate control should rest with the shareholder class; the managers of the corporation should be charged with the obligation to manage the corporation in the interests of its shareholders; other corporate constituencies, such as creditors, employees, suppliers and customers, should have their interests protected by contractual and regulatory means rather than through participation in corporate governance . . . and the market value of publicly traded firms is the principal measure of shareholders' interests. (Hansmann & Kraakman 2001: 440–1)

While this depiction may exaggerate the extent to which there is a common international model of corporate law (O'Sullivan 2003), concern with shareholder value has a significant impact on management decisions across diverse national settings. For example, in a study of corporate restructuring in three European countries, Edwards found that in spite of continued differences in national business systems, including patterns of corporate governance and industrial relations, 'shareholder value orientation has been a key factor in driving company strategies in general and their approaches to restructuring in particular' (Edwards 2004: 533).

Discourse analysis suggests that shifts in the dominant discourse often reflect and reinforce shifts in underlying power relations. Lazonick & O'Sullivan (2000) provide an historical account of the rise of the ideology of shareholder value in the USA by highlighting various changes in the control of business firms. In the period from the end of the Second World War to the beginning of the 1970s, US firms enjoyed favourable economic conditions and grew rapidly. These favourable conditions made it possible for managers to strike a balance between the interests of shareholders and other interest groups. Thus, for example, Jacoby (1997) argues that this period saw the development of a form of welfare capitalism under which there was an expectation that employees (as one interest group) had a legitimate claim to a share of corporate profits. The declining performance of the US corporate sector during the 1970s, and growing competition from the Japanese in particular, led many to question the extent to which large US firms were being managed in the interests of shareholders.

The intellectual basis for this concern was 'agency theory' – a theory of the firm developed largely by financial economists. At the core of agency theory is the notion that the firm can be reduced to a nexus of contracts between principals (shareholders) and agents (managers) and that these agents and principals have potentially conflicting interests. In the absence of controls, agents/managers might act to further their own interests, rather than those of the principals/shareholders (see Eisenhardt 1989). It was this conceptual model that was used to explain the poor performance of US firms during the 1970s. Agency theorists argued that the lack of shareholder control over managers in large organisations had created a situation where managers had retained the earnings which in their view properly belonged to the shareholders, and built themselves corporate empires that were inefficient. They advocated the introduction of corporate governance reforms, which increased the power of shareholders and the creation of a market for corporate control, making it possible to prune managerial 'deadwood'. They also promoted the idea that managers' remuneration should be more contingent on performance and popularised executive share packages as a way of ensuring that the goals of agents and principals were more closely aligned.

While agency theory provided a powerful critique of management practice and formed a crucial component of the ideology of shareholder value, Lazonick & O'Sullivan (2000: 16) argue that the rise of institutional investors in the late 1970s and 1980s 'made possible the takeovers advocated by agency theorists and gave shareholders much more collective power to influence the yields and market values of the corporate stocks they held'. In theory, while shareholders in the USA have significant legal rights and a number of means at their disposal to control management behaviour, in practice the highly dispersed nature of share ownership meant that historically it was difficult for shareholders to make use of these powers. Recent decades have witnessed a dramatic change in the pattern of share ownership in the USA and other countries. While institutions held less than 20 per cent of US shares in the mid-1960s, by the early 1990s more than 50 per cent of shares in US business firms were held by institutions such as mutual and pension funds (Useem 1998).

There are a number of factors behind this increase in institutional shareholding, including the deregulation of financial markets in the USA during the 1980s and the increasing extent to which private savings for retirement were being funnelled into equity markets. Similar increases in institutional shareholding are observable in Australia and the UK. As Useem notes, this rise in institutional shareholding effectively means that 'company managers almost everywhere, as a result, face not millions of anonymous shareholders but just several thousand identifiable money managers. These institutional owners are more demanding and less patient than individual holders; they look for company competitiveness and clamor for change at the top when firms fall short' (Useem 1998: 45).

While there might be some impediments to using this power and some institutional investors could have longer time-horizons, there is clear evidence to suggest that because of competition between funds, a significant proportion of institutional owners favour investing in shares that deliver short-term earnings, even at the expense of long-term firm performance (Bushee 2001). The increasing dominance of the shareholder value discourse, which draws on agency theory, appears to be closely associated with this underlying shift in the power of shareholders vis-à-vis managers.

This is not to argue that managers are merely the victims of this shift in power or are unwilling participants in the deployment of the shareholder value discourse. Useem (1998) further demonstrates that despite increased institutional shareholding, corporate managers still retain considerable control over their organisations and use shareholder value to further their own interests. Nevertheless, there has been a significant reorientation of the strategic direction of US corporations during the 1980s and 1990s, and managers have willingly adopted policies that tend to maximise share prices in the short term (Lazonick & O'Sullivan 2000). These authors observe that during the 1990s there have been significant increases in dividend payout ratios and the use of retained earnings to fund share buybacks. There has also been a dramatic increase in the use of organisational downsizing, which has had the effect of improving some financial ratios (see Froud et al. 2000).

Lazonick & O'Sullivan (2000) trace the willingness of managers to adopt these practices, which they believe contain negative consequences for the long-term performance of the firm, to the growing proportion of executive remuneration that is either connected to share price or taken as equity. They argue that these structural changes in the composition of executive pay make managers directly interested in short-term organisational performance even at the expense of longer-term outcomes. Shareholder wealth maximisation, which promoted the interests of the owners of the firm above all others, helped to justify and reinforce this development. To this extent, strengthening the shareholder value discourse can be regarded as a consequence of a new political alignment between shareholders and managers.

Consistent with the view that particular discourses do not emerge or develop in isolation, we believe that CSR needs to be considered in light of this understanding of how the shareholder value discourse developed. In particular, we regard CSR as largely subordinate to shareholder wealth and, in effect, as representing an attempt to accommodate organisational concerns with social and ethical issues in a manner consistent with shareholder value. This can be illustrated in a number of ways. As many writers have noted, concerns about social and ethical responsibilities are not new and 'corporate social responsibility' is the latest, and arguably the most pervasive, discourse in a long line of arguments that make the case for business to behave in an ethical manner. In comparison with some other ethical theories of business, however, CSR makes modest claims about the obligations of corporations to society and, in its 'instrumental' form, sees societal benefits as a by-product of good business rather than treating it as a central objective.

Associated with the macro-level discourse of CSR has been that of 'stakeholders'. In other words, CSR is often taken to mean the non-legal obligations that firms have to relevant stakeholders in the organisation, other than shareholders. Freeman (1984: 46) was one of the first commentators to use the term 'stakeholder' in the management of organisations. He described a stakeholder as 'any group or individual who can affect or is affected by the achievement of the organisation's objectives'. This is a very broad definition because it can include virtually anyone. Freeman noted that the process (input into decision-making) as well as the outcomes (the distribution of benefits) is important in the stakeholder approach. This does not mean that all stakeholders are treated equally; rather, it means that 'benefits are distributed based on relative contribution to the organisation' (Phillips et al. 2003: 488). Here, contribution might refer to such factors as cost and risk.

Therefore, stakeholder management 'tries to integrate groups with a stake in the firm into managerial decision-making' (Garriga & Mele 2004: 59). But the reason why different stakeholders need to be considered can vary. For instance, their inclusion may be based on ethical grounds alone. Donaldson & Preston (1995) argue that first, stakeholders have legitimate interests in organisational activity even if this is not reciprocated by the firm and, second, that these stakeholder interests have intrinsic value for their own sake. Another reason why different stakeholders should be considered in corporate decision-making is because it is economically beneficial to do so. Organisations that act in a socially responsible way, for example, might enhance their image and reputation among their principal stakeholders in the marketplace, thereby improving financial returns.

On this last point, there is a growing body of evidence which suggests that CSR is associated with improved financial performance. In a comprehensive meta-analysis of studies that have explored the association between CSR and performance, Orlitzky and colleagues (2003) confirmed that CSR is financially beneficial. It is also the case that a pattern of strong financial performance might better enable organisations to act in a socially responsible manner (McGuire et al. 1988; Waddock & Graves 1997). If meeting an organisation's social obligations attracts any cost, those already profitable firms might be more willing to absorb this if they have available resources. The evidence therefore points to the existence of a 'virtuous circle' in that CSR is both a predictor and a consequence of an organisation's financial performance (Waddock & Graves 1997).

What this suggests for managers is that there is no detrimental impact or penalty from allocating some organisational resources towards improving a firm's social responsibility and performance. In fact doing so could enhance the organisation's financial position (Orlitzky et al. 2003). This is the case particularly where resources are used to develop relations with primary stakeholders like employees, customers, suppliers and communities (Hillman & Keim 2001). If acting in a socially responsible manner is positive or at least neutral for firms and for increased shareholder value (also see McWilliams & Siegel 2000; Margolis & Walsh 2003), the question remains why more organisations do not see this as an integral – rather than ancillary or periodically 'extra' – way of doing business. Consistent with our general argument, we believe the answer to this question lies in how the two meta-discourses have evolved.

We certainly need to be careful in thinking that any reference to stakeholder management or 'analysis' provides some kind of methodological direction to managers in terms of how to take the interests of others into account (Grace & Cohen 2005: 54). What the social obligations of organisations actually entail is not always apparent. For example, which other interest groups or stakeholders need to be accommodated? What are the most important preferences of each of these groups? How does the organisation reconcile competing preferences among different stakeholder groups? If one were to adopt a view of CSR that seeks to balance stakeholder interests – including those of shareholders – then in some cases the interests of shareholders might be considered secondary to other groups (Smith 2003). This argument is unlikely to be embraced by those who favour shareholder value (see Marcoux 2003). Answers to such questions as these therefore remain vague. When seen as synonymous with the stakeholder approach, it is very difficult either to reach a consensus as to what constitutes CSR, or to define it in terms of specific actions (Jones 1980: 65; Phillips et al. 2003: 485). As a result, the ability of the CSR discourse to 'take hold' in business organisations is weakened.

This is not the only way, however, to explain why CSR has not yet dislodged the pursuit of shareholder wealth. We see evidence that shareholder value has also tried to appropriate CSR within its own agenda. One illustration of the extent to which CSR has been subordinated and defined in terms of shareholder value is the emergence of so-called 'ethical or socially responsible investment'. In recent years, there has been a significant increase in investment funds that are specifically marketed as ethical or socially responsible. In 2001, it was estimated that one in every eight dollars invested in the USA was committed to an ethical fund (Social Investment Forum 2001). While not yet as large in Australia and other countries, this is a rapidly increasing sector of the financial market. The main feature of socially responsible investment is that companies are screened to ensure that, in addition to acceptable financial performance, they also meet some ethical standard. This can include screening companies to ensure that they do not engage in unethical practices (negative screening) or identifying those that clearly meet some predetermined ethical or social criteria (positive screening) (see Michelson et al. 2004).

It has been claimed that the growth of ethical investment has important implications for how companies will approach issues like CSR. Sparkes & Cowton (2004), for example, argue that the growth and subsequent maturity of this type of investment, and its movement from 'the margin to the mainstream', will produce increased levels of CSR. They note that the screening practices associated with ethical investment are increasingly being adopted by institutional investors and that 'it is institutional investors, which are both becoming more active as shareholders . . . and now taking into account (ethical) concerns, that are most likely to provide leverage on companies to improve their performance with respect to CSR' (Sparkes & Cowton 2004: 54).

While there are some grounds for optimism with respect to ethical or socially responsible investment impacting on corporate behaviour, there are also some limitations associated with this approach. Because of the diversity of ethical investment products and the different screening approaches adopted, there is a great deal of uncertainty about what constitutes an ethical investment. A survey of ethical investment products in Australia in 2002 revealed that only three of the top 200 companies were not included in the portfolios of at least one of the 12 Australian ethical funds. Those that were held included companies involved in gambling (Tabcorp), uranium mining (Rio Tinto) and asbestos (James Hardie). Given this variety, it can be argued that almost any publicly listed organisation could be regarded as 'ethical' for investment purposes (Frost et al. 2004: 5–6). As a result, while the increasing size of ethically screened funds might motivate firms to devote more resources to communicating their social and ethical activities, there is no *a priori* reason to suggest that it will force firms to actually act in a more socially responsible manner. Recently, there has been a shift in focus towards a broader set of 'engagement' strategies that include dialogue and investor activism at shareholder meetings; such approaches may enhance CSR (Guay et al. 2004).

It is worth noting that much of the debate about ethical investment has focused on whether it can match the financial performance of more conventional investment products. As Haigh & Hazelton (2004) observe, there are two sets of claims associated with ethical investment products: first, that they can influence companies to change their operations, and second, that the financial returns are no worse in the short term and are likely to be superior over the long term. This can be seen as an extension of the 'instrumental' view of CSR – that being socially responsible is good for business. Haigh & Hazelton (2004) question the extent to which financial markets can act as a tool for social responsibility. They demonstrate that the assumption that the existence of a pool of ethical funds will lower the costs of capital for screened companies is flawed because of the relatively low percentage of funds under management in this category and its failure to take into account the opportunities for arbitrage created by the existence of different classes of investment. Second, because there is little difference between what are marketed as ethical funds and other types of investment products, it is unlikely that ethical investment products will outperform other market indicators.

Because of such factors, we argue that ethical or socially responsible investment does not jeopardise the idea of shareholder value. While this form of investment draws attention to social returns as well as economic returns, the financial performance of ethical investments remains a central concern and cannot be neglected. Therefore, the discursive deployment of ethical or socially responsible investment as one form of CSR has not displaced the primacy of shareholder value. It simply turns questions about the extent to which CSR represents a threat to the interests of shareholders around to the advantage of these shareholders.

BOUNDED RATIONALITY AND THE DISCOURSE OF SHAREHOLDER VALUE

An understanding of the meta-discourses of shareholder value and CSR and the relationship between them makes it possible to explain why evidence that CSR does not necessarily harm firm performance is not enough to encourage managers to adopt socially responsible strategies. Furthermore, by focusing on the connections between the concept of bounded rationality and these meta-discourses, one does not have to go too far beyond mainstream management to show the potential contribution of meta-discourses in shaping decision-making processes.

As was asserted earlier, some writers assume that as corporate managers come to see that CSR can be good for business they will increasingly evaluate strategies against standards of social responsibility. Indeed, it is possible to think of a number of ways in which behaving in a socially responsible manner may enhance a firm's competitiveness and thus provide superior returns. For instance, social responsibility may be an important source of differentiation; it may help firms command a premium price and enhance their competitiveness through reputational effects. If firms gain competitive advantages from acting in an ethical or socially responsible manner, then it would be reasonable to expect such practices to diffuse across different industry sectors. An important corollary of this argument is that market competition itself will encourage CSR and that there is no need for regulation and laws that require firms to behave in a socially responsible manner. Rather, the main driver of an increase in CSR will be giving managers enough information to allow them to realise its organisational benefits.

While it is possible to identify a number of flaws in this argument, one major weakness is that it is based on the assumption that managers make strategic decisions in a rational fashion. It suggests that given the 'right' information managers will be able to identify the best response to the challenges facing their firms. As Whittington (1991) notes, the assumption that managers are perfectly rational is largely derived from classical economics and for a number of decades has been criticised as providing an unrealistic depiction of management decision-making. Indeed, in an argument that is consistent with the analytical approach adopted in the previous section, Whittington (1991: 34–7) suggests that the depiction of management as perfectly rational was part of an attempt to legitimate increasing managerial control of business firms in the first half of the 20th century.

The more widely accepted view is that managers' rationality is 'bounded'. This concept derives from the work of Simon, who in a series of papers written in the 1950s (for example 1955, 1956) argued that there are cognitive limitations on rational decision-making that lead individuals to deal selectively with aspects of their environments. Bounded rationality means that there is an inability to consider all possible alternatives at the same time, a tendency to be biased in perceptions of data (that is, subjectivities among different individuals will emerge), and a likelihood that individuals will settle on decisions that are 'good enough' or satisfactory, rather than reaching decisions that are based on optimal or maximum outcomes. On the basis of this view of the cognitive processes that affect decision-making, Simon, along with his colleagues (Cyert & March), explored the implications for understanding organisations and strategy.

The concept of bounded rationality has been influential in the management literature. For example, it underpins Mintzberg's famous distinction between intended strategy and realised strategy. Similarly, the idea that there are limits on management rationality also informs Quinn's (1980) view that successful strategies are developed through a process of 'logical incrementalism'. Bounded rationality has given rise to many studies about the internal politics of organisations and how this shapes the formation of decisions.

Put simply, the concept of bounded rationality suggests that managers' decisions are not merely a function of the information they have acquired. Decisions are also shaped by the source of that information and the context within which it is used. Thus while it might be possible to communicate to all managers that there are financial benefits associated with adopting socially responsible policies, not all managers will respond to this information in the same way. To take one hypothetical example: information that consumers are prepared to pay a premium for products that are manufactured in an environmentally sustainable fashion may not engender the same decision from all managers. We might expect, for example, that a manager with a marketing background, which makes them interested in what consumers think, would respond much more favourably to this information than, say, an accountant, who is likely to be more concerned with the costs of production. In this case we might contend that professional background has placed different bounds on the managers' understanding of the situation.

In a recent article, Foss (2003) contends that the notion of bounded rationality is often cited but little used and believes that there is considerable scope for its further theoretical development. For present purposes, we would argue that there is just as much scope in examining the role that different meta-discourses about the objective of business play in shaping managerial decisions as looking at a person's professional background. Indeed, it is possible to argue that professional identity itself is discursively constructed (Carter & Mueller 2002).

253

Therefore, in a situation in which the dominant discourse about what managers should do is one which privileges decisions that are seen to bolster short-term earnings, and which discounts any potential long-term consequences of these actions, managers are more likely to discount information that links CSR to long-term business performance. To the extent that the shareholder value discourse plays an important role in bounding the rationality of managers, it is unlikely that CSR will make much headway in organisations.

SHAREHOLDER VALUE DISCOURSE: THE CASE OF ENRON

So far we have presented evidence that CSR is not necessarily detrimental to the firm, although this will not automatically translate into organisational strategies that are more socially responsible. It has also been suggested that focusing on shareholder value may not be in the best interest of the firm because of the bounds on management rationality and the role that discourses play in shaping this rationality. In this section we briefly demonstrate this argument by focusing on the case of Enron. The widely publicised collapse of this organisation, seen to be a leading example of a firm run on shareholder value, has apparently not yet led corporate managers elsewhere to question the wisdom of shareholder value.

Enron is an interesting case because it was regarded by many as the paragon of a shareholder value-managed company and during the late 1990s enjoyed a period of unprecedented support from academics, media commentators and investors. Enron's filing for bankruptcy in late 2001 represented one of the biggest corporate collapses in US history, leaving shareholders with a fraction of their initial investment and thousands of employees without jobs or pensions. While this collapse had the potential to bring about significant questioning of the benefits of short-term concentration on shareholder wealth, the management and policy response merely stressed the failure of corporate governance.

Enron was formed in the mid-1980s by the merger of two energy companies: Houston Natural Gas and InterNorth. By the late 1990s, Enron appeared to have reinvented itself. It took advantage of the deregulation of US energy markets to diversify into energy trading, developing complicated financial instruments such as derivatives and futures. The head of trading at Enron, Jeffrey Skilling, argued that this strategy was 'asset lite', and in his book *Leading the Revolution*, management guru Gary Hamel held Enron up as the exemplar of corporate reinvention. With the launch of EnronOnline in 1999, the organisation was poised to become a new type of risk-management company that traded everything from energy and weather futures to fibre-optic bandwidth.

The optimism about Enron's 'asset lite' business model was reflected in its share price. Until 1997, Enron's share price remained relatively stable and its P/E Ratio (the ratio of share price to company earnings) was roughly in line with other Wall Street companies. From 1998, however, its share price skyrocketed. By 2000, shares were valued at $90 each and the company had a P/E ratio of 78:1 (four times greater than the market average and similar to those of highly successful dot.com companies at the same time). While Enron management stated that they were 'laser focused on earnings per share', the most significant increase was its sales revenue. Between 1995 and 1998 sales revenue tripled, and it tripled again between 1998 and 2001.

Despite the increases in its share price and sales growth, however, Enron was not performing particularly well. In an effort to improve its reported financial performance, Enron management had made aggressive use of a number of questionable accounting practices, including the creation of 'special purpose entities'. These were off balance sheet holding companies which allowed Enron management to make its earnings growth look more impressive than it was. By 2001, these accounting practices began to unravel and Enron eventually filed for bankruptcy (for a detailed analysis of Enron's financial performance, see Froud et al. 2004).

Given the extent to which Enron was seen as an archetypal company managed for shareholder value, its collapse had the potential to 'resonate . . . with widely expressed concerns about the effects of the dominance of the "shareholder value" norm in Anglo-American corporate governance' (Deakin & Konzelmann 2004: 135). While there were certainly elements of fraud underpinning the company's collapse, much of the explanation for its failure can be attributed to ensuring that Enron's performance matched the expectations of investors and analysts, and was consistent with the claims of the 'asset lite' business model. As Froud and her colleagues note:

> The fact that, to date, only two Enron executives . . . have been indicted for fraud suggests that only a few executives directed and personally gained from blatantly illegal accounting practices. But a much greater number were involved in aggressive accounting practice which kept

things going by delivering earnings and turnover increases that sustained the narrative of successful reinvention; and a much larger personal reward was legally claimed by the large number of managers with stock options. (Froud et al. 2004: 896)

Blair (2003) contends that the collapse of Enron throws the whole shareholder value model into question. For her it illustrates that current share price is not necessarily an indicator of value of the firm and that notions of shareholder value can easily be manipulated. Consequently, she has called for substantial changes in directors' duties and a rejection of the concept of shareholder primacy. Others have expressed a similar need for change (for example Watkins 2003).

While Enron's fall has certainly raised questions about the wisdom of shareholder value, the dominant policy response to this collapse in the USA and elsewhere has been to focus on corporate governance issues. For example, Deakin & Konzelmann (2004) believe that the resulting *Sarbanes-Oxley Act 2002* in the USA and the Higgs Review of Non Executive Directors in the UK are both based on the assumption that the collapse of Enron was brought about by a lack of oversight from its board and advisers, as well as conflicts of interest on the part of its senior managers. But these writers note that there is nothing in the *Sarbanes-Oxley Act* that would have prevented the Enron collapse.

Craig & Amernic (2004) have employed discourse analysis to explain why regulators appear to have learned the wrong lesson from Enron, and in doing so illustrate further the benefits of a discourse approach to studying issues like shareholder value and CSR. They argue that while Enron's collapse had the potential to disrupt the logic of shareholder value, a study of language used by key individuals in the series of events before and after the collapse reveals that discursive practices played an important part in preventing this from happening. The first text they focus on is a letter sent to shareholders by the chief executive officer and chairman of the board in 2000, before Enron's problems ostensibly began. They argue that a close analysis of the language in that letter reveals reference to terminology more commonly used in contexts of war, sport and extremism. This letter included the corporate expression, 'laser focused on earnings per share'. As Craig & Amernic (2004: 823) note, this phrase is particularly troubling because it 'suggests that earnings per share are a target to be conquered or destroyed'. This is a curious choice for a target because earnings per share are easily manipulated by decisions about how to allocate revenues and expenses.

The letter also contained ample evidence of the use of hyperbole – portraying the organisation as perfect in every way, capable of achieving almost anything. In the aftermath of Enron's collapse this letter is ironic, but it also stands as a summary of the beliefs and state of mind of the senior management team of the company. It seems to underline the extent to which the rationality of Enron management was bounded by a shareholder value discourse and the extent to which this shaped their actions (including their fraudulent ones).

The second text that Craig & Amernic (2004) analysed was the written evidence given by the chief executive officer of Andersen (Enron's auditor) to a hearing of the US Congress Finance Services Committee immediately after the collapse of Enron. This text was intended both to minimise the blame attributed to Andersen and to present the Enron collapse, not as a consequence of attempts to maximise short-term shareholder value at all costs and therefore systemic, but rather as the outcome of a series of unfortunate and complex events. This, it was argued, helped to construct a pervasive post-Enron discourse: the notion that the collapse was the result of a series of 'special' or 'unusual' circumstances which contained no wider implications for an ideology that privileges the pursuit by organisations of shareholder value over the short term. Any suggestion that this highly publicised collapse might offer some opportunity for the CSR discourse to become more established in business organisations was not considered. The post-Enron discourse informed the public policy response to the largest corporate collapse in US history which meant, in effect, that regulators took the wrong lesson away from Enron.

But this is not to deny the interest generated by the collapse of Enron in the broader discursive context. This event has been the catalyst for numerous books, conferences, speeches and academic commentaries (for example Watkins 2003; Coffee 2004). It is conceivable that these texts could begin to reconstruct the bounds of rationality among managers over time so that they might reappraise CSR and corporate conduct more generally. Nevertheless, at the present juncture the discourse of shareholder value is still paramount in shaping management attitudes and behaviour.

CONCLUSION

This chapter has sought to illustrate the potential benefits of a discourse-analytical approach to the study of how different ideas influence corporate thinking, purpose and behaviour. In particular, we used discourse analysis to show that corporate social responsibility has so far failed to take hold within organisations even as firms realise the financial benefits of doing so. This was attributed to an alternative orientation of organisations, that of maximising wealth for shareholders. The origins of the current shareholder value discourse were traced to a shift in the power relations within firms which began in the late 1970s. We argued that CSR, in its 'instrumental' form at least, is an attempt to present ethical and social claims about the role of organisations as being consistent with (rather than usurping) shareholder value. Even the emergence of the 'stakeholder' discourse and, more recently, the discourse of ethical or socially responsible investment, are examples of how, in spite of the 'struggle' to increase the role for CSR in firms, shareholder value remains dominant in organisational decision-making processes. While CSR is certainly important, it has not yet displaced the centrality of financial criteria in firms and therefore remains subordinate to shareholder value.

We further demonstrated that to the extent that the shareholder value discourse bounds the rationality of managers, then the claim that CSR is financially beneficial to the firm is not by itself sufficient to produce an increase in ethical or social behaviours. One implication of this is that an increased level of social responsibility on the part of organisations is unlikely to emerge by itself. Rather, the most appropriate way might be to regulate firms through legislation, thereby requiring firms to increase their commitment to social responsibility.

Discourse analysis was also used to explain why the recent collapse of Enron, a company which appeared to be an exemplar of the shareholder value-focused firm, has not produced a widespread and fundamental rethinking of the benefits of maximising shareholder value in the short term. The implication of this analysis is that as long as the shareholder value discourse remains dominant and legitimises organisational decisions and action, we could anticipate more high-profile corporate collapses as managers do 'whatever it takes' to maximise wealth for shareholders.

While some might contend that we have presented a fairly pessimistic assessment of CSR, one of the important insights to be gained from discourse analysis is that there is an ongoing discursive contest and that meaning is not fixed. To be fair, discourses of social responsibility (however expressed) are becoming increasingly common in corporations. Part of this discursive activity has been the significant growth in the number of large companies issuing environmental, social and sustainability reports in recent years (KPMG 2002). Although in its current form the discourse of CSR is subordinate to and appropriated by shareholder value, we also acknowledge the enduring 'struggle' over meaning and that over time the relationship between these two meta-discourses, and the meanings they produce, could change. For this reason, future studies which focus on the interplay between various texts that companies issue for different purposes – annual reports to shareholders and social and environmental reports to different investors and government agencies – could provide a lens into the dynamics of these power relations inside organisations.

References

Alvesson, M. & Karreman, D. 2000, 'Varieties of discourse: on the study of organisations through discourse analysis', *Human Relations* 53(9): 1125–49.

Anon, 2005, 'Leaders: the good company', *The Economist* 374(8410) 22 January: 11.

Blair, M.M. 2003, 'Directors' duties in a post-Enron world: why language matters', *Wake Forest Law Review* 38(3): 885–910.

Bushee, B. 2001, 'Do institutional investors prefer near term earnings over long run value?' *Contemporary Accounting Research* 18(2): 207–48.

Byrne, J. 2002, 'After Enron: the ideal corporation', *Business Week*, 19–26 August, pp. 68–72.

Carter, C. & Mueller, F. 2002, 'The long march of the management modernizers: ritual, rhetoric and rationality', *Human Relations* 55(11): 1325–55.

Coffee, J.C. 2004, 'What caused Enron? A capsule social and economic history of the 1990s', *Cornell Law Review* 89(2): 269–309.

Craig, R.J. & Amernic, J.H. 2004, 'Enron discourse: the rhetoric of a resilient capitalism', *Critical Perspectives on Accounting* 15(6/7): 813–51.

Crook, C. 2005, 'The good company', *The Economist* 384(8410) 22 January: 3–5.

de Graaf, G. 2001, 'Discourse theory and business ethics: the case of bankers' conceptualizations of customers', *Journal of Business Ethics* 31(4): 299–319.

Deakin, S. & Konzelmann, S. 2004, 'Learning from Enron', *Corporate Governance: An International Review* 12(2): 134–42.

Donaldson, T. & Preston, L.E. 1995, 'The stakeholder theory of the corporation: concepts, evidence, and implications', *Academy of Management Review* 20(1): 65–91.

Edwards, T. 2004, 'Corporate governance, industrial relations and trends in company level restructuring in Europe: convergence towards the Anglo-American model?', *Industrial Relations Journal* 35(6): 518–35.

Eisenhardt, K.M. 1989, 'Agency theory: an assessment and review', *Academy of Management Review* 14(1): 57–74.

Engelen, E. 2002, 'Corporate governance, property and democracy: a conceptual critique of shareholder ideology', *Economy and Society* 31(3): 391–413.

Fairclough, N. 1992, *Discourse and Social Change*, Cambridge: Polity Press.

Fairclough, N. 1995, *Critical Discourse Analysis: The Critical Study of Language*, London: Longman.

Foss, N.J. 2003, 'Bounded rationality in the economics of organisation: "much cited and little used"', *Journal of Economic Psychology* 24(2): 245–64.

Freeman, R.E. 1984, *Strategic Management: A Stakeholder Approach*, Boston: Pitman.

Friedman, M. 1970, 'The social responsibility of business is to increase its profits', *New York Times Magazine*, 13 September.

Frost, G., Michelson, G., Van Der Laan, S. & Wailes, N. 2004, 'Bringing ethical investment to account', *Australian Accounting Review* 14(3): 3–9.

Froud, J., Haslam, C., Johal, S. & Williams, K. 2000, 'Shareholder value and financialization: consultancy promises, management moves', *Economy and Society* 29(1): 80–110.

Froud, J., Johal, S., Papazian, V. & Williams, K. 2004, 'The temptation of Houston: a case study of financialisation', *Critical Perspectives on Accounting* 15(6/7): 885–909.

Garriga, E. & Mele, D. 2004, 'Corporate social responsibility theories: mapping the territory', *Journal of Business Ethics* 53(1/2): 51–71.

Grace, D. & Cohen, S. 2005, *Business Ethics: Problems and Cases*, 3rd edn, Melbourne: Oxford University Press.

Grant, D. & Hardy, C. 2003, 'Introduction: struggles with organisational discourse', *Organization Studies* 25(1): 5–13.

Grant, D., Hardy, C., Oswick, C. & Putnam, L. 2004, *The Handbook of Organisational Discourse*, London: Sage.

Guay, T., Doh, J.P. & Sinclair, G. 2004, 'Non-governmental organisations, shareholder activism, and socially responsible investments: ethical, strategic and governance implications', *Journal of Business Ethics* 52(1): 125–39.

Haigh, M. & Hazelton, J. 2004, 'Financial markets: a tool for social responsibility?', *Journal of Business Ethics* 52(1): 59–71.

Hansmann, H. & Kraakman, R. 2001, 'The end of history for corporate law', *Georgetown Law Journal* 89(2): 439–68.

Hardy, C. 2001, 'Researching organisational discourse', *International Studies of Management and Organization* 31(3): 25–47.

Hardy, C., Palmer, I. & Phillips, N. 2000, 'Discourse as a strategic resource', *Human Relations* 53(9): 1227–48.

Hillman, A.J. & Keim, G.D. 2001, 'Shareholder value, stakeholder management, and social issues: what's the bottom line?', *Strategic Management Journal* 22(2): 125–39.

Jacoby, S. 1997, *Modern Manors: Welfare Capitalism since the New Deal*, Princeton University Press.

Jones, T.M. 1980, 'Corporate social responsibility revisited, redefined', *California Management Review* 22(3): 59–67.

Jones, T.M. 1995, 'Instrumental stakeholder theory: a synthesis of ethics and economics', *Academy of Management Review* 20(2): 404–37.

Koslowski, P. 2000, 'The limits of shareholder value', *Journal of Business Ethics* 27(1/2): 137–48.

KPMG 2002, *International Survey of Corporate Sustainability Reporting*, De Meern, Netherlands: KPMG Global Sustainability Services.

Lazonick, W. & O'Sullivan, M. 2000, 'Maximizing shareholder value: a new ideology for corporate governance', *Economy and Society* 29(1): 13–35.

Marcoux, A.M. 2003, 'A fiduciary argument against stakeholder theory', *Business Ethics Quarterly* 13(1): 1–24.

Margolis, J.D. & Walsh, J.P. 2003, 'Misery loves companies: rethinking social initiatives by business', *Administrative Science Quarterly* 48(2): 268–305.

McGuire, J.B., Sundgren, A. & Schneeweis, T. 1988, 'Corporate social responsibility and firm financial performance', *Academy of Management Journal* 31(4): 854–72.

McWilliams, A. & Siegel, D. 2000, 'Corporate social responsibility and financial performance: correlation or misspecification?' *Strategic Management Journal* 21(5): 603–9.

Michelson, G., Wailes, N., van der Laan, S. & Frost, G. 2004, 'Ethical investment processes and outcomes', *Journal of Business Ethics* 52(1): 1–10.

Orlitzky, M., Schmidt, F.L. & Rynes, S.L. 2003, 'Corporate social and financial performance: a meta-analysis', *Organization Studies* 24(3): 403–41.

O'Sullivan, M. 2003, 'The political economy of comparative corporate governance', *Review of International Political Economy* 10(1): 23–72.

Phillips, R., Freeman, R.E. & Wicks, A.C. 2003, 'What stakeholder theory is not', *Business Ethics Quarterly* 13(4): 479–502.

Pollach, I. 2003, 'Communicating corporate ethics on the world wide web: a discourse analysis of selected company web sites', *Business and Society* 42(2): 277–87.

Quinn, J. 1980, *Strategies for Change: Logical Incrementalism*, Homewood, Ill.: Irwin.

Rappaport, A. 1986, *Creating Shareholder Value: The New Standard for Business Performance*, New York: Free Press.

Simon, H.A. 1955, 'A behavioral model of rational choice', *Quarterly Journal of Economics* 69(1): 99–118.

Simon, H.A. 1956, 'Rational choice and the structure of the environment', *Psychological Review* 63: 129–38.

Smith, N.C. 2003, 'Corporate social responsibility: whether or how?' *California Management Review* 45(4): 52–76.

Social Investment Forum 2001, *Report on Socially Responsible Investing Trends in the USA* (available at: www.socialinvest.org)

Sparkes, R. & Cowton, C.J. 2004, 'The maturing of socially responsible investment: a review of the developing link with corporate social responsibility', *Journal of Business Ethics* 52(1): 45–57.

Useem, M. 1998, 'Corporate leadership in a globalizing equity market', *Academy of Management Executive* 12(4): 43–59.

Waddock, S.A. & Graves, S.B. 1997, 'The corporate social performance–financial performance link', *Strategic Management Journal* 18(4): 303–19.

Watkins, S.S. 2003, 'Ethical conflicts at Enron: moral responsibility in corporate capitalism', *California Management Review* 45(4): 6–19.

Whittington, R. 1991, *What is Strategy and Does it Matter?* London: Routledge.

CHAPTER THIRTEEN

RETHINKING HRM

Contemporary Practitioner Discourse and the Tensions between Ethics and Business Partnership

Susan Ainsworth and Richard Hall

As a field of scholarship and practice, human resource management or HRM appears to be almost constantly in a state of crisis, tension and anxiety. This may reflect both the uncertainty and relative immaturity of HRM as a distinct area of academic research and theory, as well as its practical concern with a site of significant change and volatility in recent decades – the management of work and workers in the contemporary organisation. For some time a fundamental tension has been recognised between HRM's traditional concern with employee welfare and advocacy and its more recent concern with being an effective 'business partner' (Beer 1997; Storey 2001). In academic work this is evident in longstanding debates around 'soft' and 'hard' versions of HRM (Legge 1995a) and in the recent interest in the ethical and moral dilemmas confronted by human resources managers asked to manage the consequences of downsizing, delayering, work intensification and workplace change in organisations that purport to be high-performance workplaces (Sisson 1994). Recent academic research has suggested ways of reconciling or at least managing these tensions. To a greater or lesser extent these contributions have called for HRM to recover its lost tradition of concern for employee advocacy by paying renewed attention to ethics, values and the rights and entitlements of employees.

As a way of rethinking HRM, the renewed contemporary academic interest in ethics is reconsidered in this chapter in the context of the tension between the business partnership and employee advocacy roles implicit in strategic HRM theory and practice. First, we briefly review the historical emergence of this central tension and consider some of the responses and correctives proposed by academic commentators and researchers. Second, we compare these academic responses with practitioner understandings of these tensions and their implications for the role and identity of human resource professionals (whom we refer to as 'HR'). Third, we explain the approach we adopted to exploring the representations of these tensions (discourse analysis) in practitioner discourse and present our results. Following discussion of these results we conclude with some reflections on the character of that discourse, and the functions of these representations in the context of the relationship between the producers and consumers of practitioner-targeted texts.

STRATEGIC HRM: THE TENSION BETWEEN BUSINESS PARTNERSHIP AND EMPLOYEE ADVOCACY

The current predicament of HRM can be understood, in part, as the result of its history whereby the HR function has responded to a series of imperatives set for it by organisations. In Australia, as in the UK and the USA, HRM can be traced back to welfare officers employed in large organisations to provide advice, assistance, counselling and services to workers. This function responded to the practical need of organisations to attend to the welfare, safety and basic well-being of workers, ensuring their basic capacity to perform their work. As the regulation of employment became more elaborate after 1945, the administrative role of managing employment became more pronounced. By the early 1970s, personnel departments were playing a more explicit organisational service and support function, using HR planning techniques to achieve efficiency in staffing and compensation and to administer benefits and training. HRM emerged in the 1980s as a way of more closely integrating personnel functions with the broader strategic goals of the business. The more recent imperative of strategic HRM draws on personnel's traditional administrative and processing expertise, the data management and analytical possibilities afforded by information and communications technology, the intense interest of organisations in process efficiency, the outsourcing of non-core functions and, most importantly, the contested proposition that human resources are a crucial source of competitive advantage.

Strategic HRM presents both threats and opportunities for the HR function. It threatens the traditional administrative and relatively routine service and support functions of HR as these can fairly easily be outsourced, partly automated, devolved to the line, and/or relegated to the 'corporate services' margins of the contemporary business. On the other hand, if competitive advantage in the 'new' business environment includes recruiting, retaining, developing and empowering the best, then HR might be seen as crucial to business.

The academic and business literature on strategic HRM reflects both these inherent threats and opportunities. One influential US business commentator, after reflecting on the marginal contribution of most HR departments, exhorted senior managers to take drastic action on their HR departments: 'Why not blow it up?' (Stewart 1996 quoted in Wright et al. 2001: 111). HR has been repeatedly urged to adopt a business partner role, demonstrating to senior management its unique capacity to add value to the bottom line through its contribution to strategy formulation and implementation, measuring and stimulating improved employee performance, and the management of organisational development and change. Beer (1997) calls for the transformation of the HR function by shedding its traditional administrative concerns and concentrating on a 'new strategic role concerned with developing the organisation and the capabilities of its managers' (1997: 51). Beatty & Schneider (1997) argue that HR in fact needs to move beyond simply being a business partner to being a business 'player', actually delivering 'economic value to the organisation's external customers and investors' as well as adding value for internal clients.

Multi-functional HRM

Ulrich (1996, 1997, 1998) has been perhaps the most influential in contending that HR can transform itself into a business partner by focusing on what it delivers (outcomes) rather than on what it does (processes) while still retaining its full suite of traditional functions. He outlines four imperatives for the HR role: as partner in strategy execution, administrative expert, employee champion and change agent. While the role of 'employee champion' recalls HR's historic brief as an advocate of worker welfare, Ulrich (1998: 130) sees the contemporary manifestation as based on ensuring employee engagement, primarily through training line managers in how to improve employee morale and commitment as well as being an advocate for employee interests and providing opportunities for employee development. The rationale for this function, however, rests mainly with improving organisational performance rather than with any welfare or rights-based argument.

In his specification of four key imperatives for the new HR, Ulrich suggests that HR can successfully hold in balance the tension between the business partnership and more traditional roles identified by those such as Beer. According to Ulrich, HR can only achieve this by simultaneously pursuing excellence in all the above four functions, and in addition by their cultivation and demonstration of the key HR competencies of business understanding, HR practice knowledge, ability to manage culture, ability to manage change, and personal credibility (MacLachlan 1998).

HRM and the ethical imperative

Other academic researchers have called for a revitalisation of HR on the basis that it needs to rediscover and reassert its traditional employee advocacy role through the recognition and promotion of the crucial role of ethics in contemporary business. Implicit in contemporary HR is a tension between the values of 'economic rationality' and 'social responsibility', yet HR must retain values of 'care' and 'justice' inherent in the latter alongside the more commonly referenced values of 'efficiency' and 'competitiveness' central to the former (Carey 1999: 54–5). For Carey, the new imperative for HR is to balance these competing concerns and build consensus for this balance within the organisation. She recognises the difficulties in this project for HR professionals, but argues, quoting Newton (1983), that the capacity to hold conflicting values in tension is one of the hallmarks of a profession. The way forward is for HR managers to recognise the key ethical issues of the profession: how to balance the dual loyalties to management and employees, to see ethics as more than just 'legal compliance' and to recognise that HR professionals bear an 'agent and role moral responsibility within a strategic HRM paradigm' (Carey 1999: 58). Carey makes two concrete suggestions. First HR managers need to recognise the duty they owe to multiple stakeholders. Revised professional standards and codes of conduct should specify a clear priority in HR's loyalties: the public (including present and future employees); the profession; the employing enterprise; and the individual professional (Carey 1999: 66). Public and professional obligations are thus explicitly placed before business obligations. Second, HR needs to develop an 'integrity-based' partnership with the business, moving beyond seeing ethics as simply monitoring for legal compliance, to educating about ethics and questioning the ethical basis of management decisions (Carey 1999: 61). In a similar vein, in the UK Winstanley & Woodall (2000) lament the reduction of contemporary corporate ethics to 'corporate social responsibility' programs and call for an 'ethical rearmament' of HR. This would involve HR becoming a 'champion, architect and steward of the ethical management of people' by raising awareness of ethical issues, promoting ethical values, and educating line managers in the ethical management of employees.

HRM and the pluralist imperative

Other academic commentators have called for a return to pluralism to counter the unitarism implicit in HRM and, in particular, strategic HRM (Legge 1995b): in its enthusiasm to be seen as a valued business partner, HR has too thoroughly embraced managerialism, marginalised any concern for ethics and forgotten its role in promoting values. Ultimately, this is threatening the status and meaning of the HRM function (Chater 1993). Foote & Robinson's (1999) survey found that despite widespread recognition among HR professionals that contemporary workplace policies and practices were being driven by a managerialist agenda with adverse consequences for employees, that there was little recognition of the importance of ethics and little indication that HR professionals were effective in promoting ethics. They suggest that HR's role should ensure a balance of power between management and workers, and given the relative strength of management, HR should align itself more strongly with the promotion of the interests of workers. Failure to do so will likely see HR relegated to 'routine administrative duties'.

Kochan has argued that HR's conversion to business partner has been so complete that it now threatens its identity and distinctiveness as a profession. He argues that by the end of the 1990s, in the USA at least, 'HR professionals lost any semblance of credibility as a steward of the social contract because most HR professionals had lost their ability to seriously challenge or offer an independent perspective on the policies and practices of the firm' (Kochan 2004: 134). With the gulf between the needs and interests of the firm and employees in America arguably at its greatest at any time since the depression, HR must find and promote a 'workable balance' or lose its status and legitimacy. Kochan's proposals are again distinctly pluralist. Specifically, he calls for HR to look 'outwards' instead of 'inwards' and build links with a broader range of stakeholders beyond the firm in activities such as skills development that benefit workers as well as firms, forms of work organisation that promote better work–life balance, and a greater voice for workers.

Thus, since the mid to late 1990s, the academic and business literature has offered various perspectives on the current crisis allegedly confronting HR. Each of these perspectives contends that the legitimacy and distinctiveness of HR is at stake and each offers practical recommendations for its future. Authors such as Ulrich suggest that HR can pursue its business partnership imperative while sustaining its other goals through a multifunctional approach based on excellence in strategy formulation and implementation, personnel administration, employee advocacy, and development and change. Others such as Carey and Winstanley & Woodall see a future in HR adopting a more aggressive promotion of corporate and workplace ethics. Revising professional standards and codes of conduct, promoting ethics and educating colleagues about the ethical implications of decisions, and raising ethical issues with management are all suggested by this approach. Yet others such as Kochan adopt a more avowedly pluralist position in seeing HR's vital imperative as being the advocacy of worker interests, not for moral reasons but to ensure a healthy and sustainable power balance in contemporary organisations.

All of these academic researchers recognise significant challenges, if not crises, confronting HR. While their diagnoses and prescriptions differ, threats to the legitimacy and distinctiveness of HRM represent common themes. This in turn relates to the status and identity of HRM as a profession. The HR academics reviewed above have some concrete suggestions for renewing the profession through strategies that might help HR professionals hold in tension the potentially conflicting values inherent in contemporary strategic HRM. But it is unclear to what extent these debates are impacting on practitioner discourse. Accordingly, we attempt to investigate whether similar tensions are present and how the HR role is represented and reflected in practitioner literature. In the next section we explain the approach we adopted to explore these issues.

METHODS: CRITICAL DISCOURSE ANALYSIS

Our dataset comprised an illustrative sample of articles from the practitioner-targeted publication (*HR Monthly*) produced by the Australian professional body for human resource professionals, the Australian Human Resources Institute (AHRI). We selected articles

Table 13.1 *List of HR texts*

Article	Title	HR Monthly	Section	Author
1	'The Human Resource Management (HRM) Professional (to the tune of Gilbert & Sullivan's 'Modern Major General')	October 1998, p. 14	Humour	Brett Foster, HR manager
2	'Ethics: the core of good business'	June 1999, pp. 16–19	Cover Feature	Helen Vines, freelance writer
3	'Selling the concept of strategic HR'	July 1999, pp. 16–20	Cover Feature	Cyndi Tebbel, freelance writer
4	'HR just makes the grade'	February 2000, pp. 16–21	Cover Story	Cyndi Tebbel, freelance writer
5	'Another day, another crisis'	May 2001, pp. 21–26	Cover Story	Danielle Townsend, freelance writer
6	'Sacred cows: workers and employers lock horns over entitlements'	October 2001, pp. 20–28	Cover Story	Janine Ogier, freelance writer
7	'Moving targets'	February 2002, pp. 18–23	Cover Story	Janine Ogier, freelance writer
8	'Advancing the profession'	February 2003, pp. 30–32	Not specified	Janine Ogier, freelance writer

over a five-year period (1998–2003) that explicitly commented on the role of human resource management. Full details of these articles are included in Table 13.1. Our approach can be characterised as critical discourse analysis (van Dijk 1993a, 1993b; Fairclough 1995; Fairclough & Wodak 1997) in that we are interested in how 'power relations are reproduced and exercised in discourse' (Fairclough & Wodak 1997: 272). Consistent with this tradition, we assume that, being mutually constitutive, discourse has a dialectical relationship with society and culture (van Dijk 1993b; Phillips & Hardy 1997): 'every instance of language use makes its own small contribution to reproducing and/or transforming society and culture, including power relations. That is the power of discourse; that is why it is worth struggling over' (Fairclough & Wodak 1997: 273).

More specifically, discourse constructs versions of social reality and represents individuals, groups, social relations and arrangements in particular ways. We can explore these constructions and their affects through textual analysis. Discourse is not accessible in its entirety but traces of it are found in texts (Parker 1992; Burman & Parker 1993), which give cues to discourse and broader societal contexts. While discourses are realised through texts, they are much broader than texts and include the social and cultural structure and practices that surround and inform the production and consumption of texts (Fairclough 1992; Phillips & Hardy 1997). Texts can be viewed as multifunctional: they have an 'ideational' function in that they constitute forms of knowledge and beliefs; they have an interpersonal function in that they help to construct certain forms of self or social identities; and they contribute to social relations between different subjects or actors. These interpersonal and social functions of language constitute it as a form of social practice and action (Halliday 1994; Fairclough 1995).

Critical discourse analysis is a broad perspective towards discourse studies, rather than a specific method, and the scholars who use it employ a variety of discourse-analytic techniques (van Dijk 1993a, 1997; Fairclough 1995; Wodak & Meyer 2001). We approached our analysis at a variety of levels from the micro-level of word choice to more macro consideration of the context of the text's production and consumption.

At the micro-level, we explored the associations and connotations of employing particular vocabularies. Word choice is relevant because it gives cues to the use of broader discourses that may be being used for strategic effect, such as in the use of marketing and promotional discourse to represent the activities of universities (Fairclough 1993) as part of attempts to 'reform' this sector.

Our analysis also included sentence-level and clause-level techniques. We examined sentence topics and sentence structure (through combinations of clauses) as well as transitivity, mood and modality. Transitivity includes the representation of processes, their meanings, participants and circumstances (Halliday 1994; Paltridge 2000). It is central to understanding constructions of agency and relationships between actors or 'who is doing what to whom?' Mood reflects the relationship between the writer and reader as well as the writer's attitude towards the subject. This is also captured in modality, which includes indicators of relative certainty, for example through the use of words such as 'probably', 'sometimes', or 'usually' and through the type of sentences (declarative, interrogative or imperative) (Paltridge 2000; Fairclough 2001).

At the 'whole-text' level, we examined how the text was structured and whether it drew on, or conformed to, a particular genre or 'text type' (Dudley Evans & St John 1989) such as news story, dialogue, narrative. We also noted the sequence of ideas, and links or connections (implicit and/or explicit) between paragraphs as well as material given informational prominence in the texts (for example through initial placement). In addition we examined the perspective adopted by the writer (*framing*), the concepts featured in the texts (*foregrounding*) as opposed to those that were marginal or absent (*backgrounding*) and how texts constructed the reader in terms of assumed background knowledge, shared values and so on (*presupposition*) (Huckin 1997).

Finally, as discourse is a situated form of social action (Fairclough & Wodak 1997), we considered how these texts related to, and functioned within, specific contexts. At this level we explored the circumstances of the texts' production and consumption including connections between textual representations and the context in which the texts appeared. Fairclough (2001: 238) describes this type of analysis as asking the question: 'does the social order need' certain constructions of reality, identities and relationships?

REPRESENTATIONS OF HRM IN PRACTITIONER DISCOURSE

The results of our analysis of the eight illustrative texts are summarised in Table 13.2. In the following section, we outline how the employee advocacy and welfare role as well as the business partner and strategy role were represented in the practitioner literature. We also explore how ethics and employees are constructed in these texts and comment on patterns in the constructions of crises, tensions and contradictions in HRM. While each text was analysed separately, we also include some comparative analysis, for example in the degree of presence or absence of different roles and issues (Table 13.2). Where an issue or role is referred to as 'absent', this means it did not appear at all in the text. 'Marginal' indicates that the issue or role was present, but was

Table 13.2 *Incidence in HR texts*

Article	Employee advocacy/ welfare role	Business partner/ strategy role	Ethics	Employees
1	Absent	Present	Present	Absent
2	Marginal	Present	Featured	Featured
3	Absent	Featured	Marginal	Marginal
4	Marginal	Featured	Absent	Marginal
5	Featured	Present	Marginal	Present
6	Marginal	Marginal	Present	Featured
7	Present	Marginal	Present	Featured
8	Marginal	Featured	Absent	Present

Absent: does not appear at all; Marginal: present but is mentioned twice or less; Present: present and mentioned more than twice, but not central to the article; Featured: present and central to the article.

mentioned twice or less in the text. Degrees of presence of an issue or role are indicated by 'marginal' (mentioned twice or less in the text), 'present' (mentioned more than twice but not central to the article) and 'featured' (central to the article).

The employee advocacy/welfare role

As can be seen in Table 13.2, the employee advocacy and welfare role was present in six of the eight articles, but in four of these it had only a marginal presence. For example, in article 4, the employee advocate role appeared in the first paragraph in a subordinate clause but was not mentioned again. In other articles, it was represented in instrumental terms, that is, as a means to an end: developing a 'high-performance culture' (article 2), avoiding industrial action (article 6) and complying with legislative requirements relating to redundancy (article 7). Further, in article 2, it is external consultants rather than internal HR practitioners who adopt this role, listening to employees and articulating their concerns to management. But this is then used by management to institute greater control in the form of values statements and behavioural indicators to clarify the expectations they have of employees.

In accounts of HRM's development, there are repeated attempts to consign the employee advocacy/welfare role to history, for example 'gone are the days when HR people were purely staff advocates' (article 5, see also article 8). Such historical accounts convey an implicit valuation of HR roles, connoted by use of the word 'evolution' – not only does this role belong to an earlier period but it was an inferior and less sophisticated stage in HRM's development. This construction is featured in the short abstract (in larger bold type) that appears between the title of the article and the text in article 8: 'Over the course of 60 years, AHRI's members have gone from being workplace welfare officers, to administrators, to valued business partners. We look at the evolution of both the industry and the institute in this, the first of a series of articles marking AHRI's anniversary.'

Despite these attempts to consign the employee advocacy/welfare role to history, it is not completely absent from current practitioner discourse. It continues to be reasserted (albeit in marginal and sometimes contradictory ways) as relevant to contemporary HRM practice. Some external experts urge HR staff to retain this role: 'HR professionals should attempt to act in the interests of both staff and employers' (article 6) and HR staff are advised to 'be honest and to find out what employees are thinking' (article 7). But there are also contradictions in the representations of this role. For example, while in article 5 the employee advocacy/welfare role is consigned to history, much of the article focuses on this role in relation to HR staff responsible for implementing redundancies, using advice from organisational psychologists about how to 'care for' HR staff who suffer anxiety, stress and pain from having to face 'hostile employees' and break bad news.

The business partner/strategy role

The business partnership/strategy role is clearly the preferred role for HRM, but it is represented as problematic, mainly because of a lack of progress in implementation (articles 2, 3, 4, 5, 8). Both the explanations for this problem and the remedies reveal a deeper ambivalence about this role.

First, HR finds it hard to convince senior management of the value of its 'business partner' role (article 8), but blame rests on HR staff (rather than senior management) and remedies largely relate to initiatives within the HR department itself, rather than the wider organisation. For example, in article 4, 'HR for HR' is recommended and in article 3, HR managers are urged to demonstrate their business credibility by managing their own departments like businesses.

Moreover, this role is represented as having negative effects on HR staff. While they are involved only at a 'tactical' rather than strategic level (article 1), they suffer stress and pain (article 5) from playing 'the bad guy' in implementing strategic decisions (articles 5 and 7). Trying to do the 'right thing' by employees brings them into conflict with management (article 7). Management do not give clear instructions and are perennially dissatisfied with the outcomes (article 1), and HR is used by management in an opportunistic way (article 5). In article 8, which recounts the history of Australian HRM and its professional body, the business partner/strategy role is represented as the pinnacle of HRM's development and its certain future. At a textual level, however, there are contrary indicators: the problematic nature of the business partner/strategy role is evident in the sequence of events in the story, represented through the ordering of paragraphs. In this case, the shift to the strategy role immediately precedes a crisis in the professional body (when it went into voluntary administration in 1999). This illustrates the importance of examining not only patterns in the content of texts, but also the ways in which texts are constructed.

When we compared patterns across our sample of texts we found key differences in the appearance of the employee advocacy/welfare role and the business partner/strategy role. Where the business partner/strategy role was featured, the employee advocacy/welfare role was either marginal or absent (articles 3, 4, 8). Conversely, the employee advocacy/welfare role only featured in one article (5) where the strategy role was also present. However, this article focused almost exclusively on the welfare of HR staff suffering as a result of the business partnership/strategy role (in having to implement redundancies). Thus the roles were represented as mutually exclusive rather than held in balance as advocated by Carey (1999).

Ethics

Ethics is absent in two articles and where it does appear, it is represented in a limited and instrumental way. It appears in association with legislative compliance (articles 1 and 6), in fairness and equity (article 5), in honesty in dealings with employees in industrial negotiations (article 2) and in retrenchments (article 7). Ethics is represented as a means to an end; for example, the organisation is urged to take care of employees in order to elicit high performance from them and to avoid negative media coverage (articles 6 and 7): 'The difficulty for governments and business is that while the problem may be statistically insignificant, the consequence of employees losing their entitlements in a corporate collapse is days of sensational media coverage' (article 6). Article 2 also features this instrumental view with its hierarchy of reasons for business ethics:

> Ensuring ethical behaviour is seen by some as a way of improving the bottom line and of winning the approval of shareholders. For other organisations it may be customer driven. And then there is the handful of companies that promote ethical behaviour because they believe it's simply the right thing to do.

The first two instrumental reasons are discussed but the third – a normative view of ethics – is not mentioned again.

Ethics is not represented as integral to HRM. In two articles, it is represented as an 'add-on' to HR's role. In article 1, ethics is constructed as an additional burden that precipitates a crisis for the model HRM professional. Essentially cast as an example of work intensification for HRM, business ethics and corporate social responsibility contribute to the crisis in stanza 7, where cumulative clauses 'pile up' additional responsibilities:

> In matters of community and issues Aboriginal/Of heritage and equity and other issues cultural/When safety's a priority yet bottom lines are critical/Consulting with environmental groups about the EIS/And chasing down the subsidies supposed to flow from CES/Wondering while poring over papers actuarial/How long before this crazy life delivers me to burial.

In article 3, ethics is an afterthought for HRM. It is not mentioned until the very last sentence: 'Basically, HR should act as the conscience of the organisation.' Rather than summarising or commenting on the preceding discussion, as might be expected, this final sentence bears no relation to the rest of the article. This contributes to the impression of ethics as an 'add-on' to HRM.

In article 2, HR is represented as playing a part in discouraging unethical behaviour in organisations. After touching on the role of senior management (in acting as role models for employees), it moves to discussing how HR can help the organisation influence employee behaviour, specifically how it can defend and protect the organisation from unethical employees. In this context, ethics is interpreted as synonymous with organisational interests. The threat of unethical behaviour from employees elicits an essentially bureaucratic response:

the remedies all involve written statements and codifications that attempt to specify what is expected of employees (in the form of job descriptions, codes of conduct, values statements, rules and policies etc.). There is no consideration of alternatives such as HR playing a questioning and educating role (see Carey 1999) for both employees and managers, or of developing the ethical awareness, decision-making and moral reasoning abilities of employees (see Kjonstad & Willmott 1995).

Employees

Employees were represented as part of the background of HRM; for example, near the beginning of articles they are mentioned in relation to workforce trends. In articles where constructions of employees were more central, they were largely negative and featured in three of the articles (2, 6 and 7). The only positive constructions of employees referred to HRM staff (for example articles 4 and 5).

In article 2, the negative construction of employees focused on unethical behaviour. Rather than dwell on criticisms of senior management, the discussion quickly shifts to unethical employees. Here employees are represented as fraudulent, acting improperly, cheating the organisation (and customers) and being manipulative (for example manipulating rules and codes of conduct). HR's role in relation to this construction is to protect the organisation from potentially unethical employees: 'HR professionals are the first line of defence in the company battle against bringing in people who are willing to commit fraud.'

Employees are also constructed as a threat to the organisation and to HR in other ways; for example, in articles 6 and 7 they are represented as militant and as initiating problems. Article 6 features a classic construction of industrial conflict as originating with employees and unions. Ostensibly about the protection of worker entitlements, it begins by talking about 'frustration from employees, and industrial action by unions whose members have lost entitlements when a company has collapsed'. Prominence is given to employee and union actions and reactions as the cause of the problem, rather than alternatives such as the loss of entitlements in itself or in organisations' actions. In article 7, which deals with employee retrenchments, the employee threat is conveyed visually: accompanying the text are two photos of groups of employees marching with placards. Employee militancy is also conveyed through the use of military discourse. Besides the word 'strategy' there are many other military references across the eight articles: 'tactics', 'defence', 'battle', 'locking horns', 'hostile environment', 'fighting', as well as the HRM professional as 'Modern Major General' in article 1. Using this terminology, HR is constructed either as a victim of a battle between employees and employers (as in article 7) or as defending the organisation from its employees.

Employees are also constructed as emotional rather than rational beings. In article 7, they are 'anxious', 'shamed', 'resentful', 'angry', 'defensive', 'grieving', and 'making up rumours'. In article 5 they are 'hostile', 'angry', 'demanding', 'preoccupied', 'unsettled', 'making up rumours' and 'anguished'. Importantly, employees are associated with mainly negative and hostile emotions. Emotional words are also used to represent HR staff, but their construction is more sympathetic (in article 5). The hostility and anger of employees causes HR staff to be 'frightened', 'incredibly anxious, incredibly stressed', 'feel undervalued', 'under strain', 'hurting'. Here HR staff are portrayed as the victims of employees' more negative emotional reactions to the news of their redundancies.

Contradictions, tensions and crises in HR's role

Finally, in our examination of practitioner discourse, we focused on the construction of contradictions, tensions, crises and confusion in HR's role. From our analysis of this sample of articles, we found they were recurrent and central to representations of HRM.

A sense of crisis and conflict was represented using words that connoted broader discourses of war and death. In addition to military discourse (previously discussed), a discourse of death featured strongly; for example, HR was urged to 'execute or be executed' (article 4), and a 'death knell' was sounding for HR (article 3). A discourse of death was also used to represent contradictions in HR's role. Article 1 relied on 'gallows humour' to depict the HR professional's experience and awareness of these contradictions. Contradictions are introduced progressively throughout the text until the song reaches a crisis in stanza 7 where their cumulative effects precipitate the HR professional's (imagined) death. In this context, death appeared to be the only conceivable way out of such endemic contradictions.

Contradiction and confusion feature prominently in other texts. While HR is urged to make a forced choice between old and new world HRM in article 3, in article 5 this tension is represented in terms of HR

caught in a 'tug of war' by management and employees pulling in oppo-
site directions. Similarly, in article 6, HR is depicted as the 'meat in the
sandwich' between employers and employees. Confusion is apparent in
assertions of the importance and relevance of HRM. For example, in the
preface to article 6, HRM is central: 'The stand-off between employer
groups and unions over the protection of worker entitlements puts HR
departments in a delicate position. But some argue that it is the perfect
opportunity for HR to demonstrate its value as the conduit between
management and employees.' However, HR is largely absent from the
rest of the article, an indication of its limited usefulness – the main
protagonists in this case are legal experts, unions and government.

Contradictory assessments of problems, advice and solutions are also
apparent. For example, HR staff are urged to be proactive and to take
the initiative but they also have to 'wait to be invited' to participate in
strategy by CEOs (article 3). Similarly in article 8, while AHRI members are instructed to take a proactive role in reinvigorating the profession and focusing on becoming better business people, the history of the
profession is told in terms of its reactions and responses to other actors
and events in the environment. HR staff are also criticised for being
'all talk and no action', but in the same article they are advised that the
remedy is 'about discussing the issues' (article 4). There are repeated
calls for HR to be more outward-looking and business-focused, yet these
occur alongside remedies that are self-referential, inward-looking initiatives aimed at HR departments (articles 3 and 4). According to one HR
expert quoted, the best advice for HR professionals is 'Physician Heal
Thyself' (article 4).

DISCUSSION: ROLE AMBIVALENCE AND THE REPRODUCTION
OF CRISIS AND CONTRADICTION

Our analysis of the texts suggests an HR practitioner discourse which,
while highly sympathetic to the plight and predicament of contemporary HR managers and officers, ultimately offers little practical assistance to HR professionals seeking to reconcile or manage the tensions
that are central to their role. Far from furthering a greater focus on
'the business', the prescriptions that are offered are distinctly inward-
looking, even introspective. HR professionals are routinely exhorted
to consider their own failings: the failure to promote adequately the
value-adding potential of the HR function; the failure to manage their
own teams and departments with the same business discipline expected

of operational departments; the failure of HR to truly earn its place at the 'top table' of senior management decision-making. The discourse thereby succeeds in sustaining the impression of HR in crisis without ever offering a compelling or clear set of strategies for redemption and renewal beyond a good dose of critical self-reflection and a new determination to 'do better' (article 4).

The discourse analysis investigated, in some detail, the construction of the employee advocacy and business partnership tendencies that are taken to constitute the elements of the central tension inherent in contemporary HRM. Employee advocacy and a concern with the welfare of workers is recognised as part of the HRM mandate, but in these texts it tends to be consistently backgrounded after being initially recognised. On deeper analysis it became apparent that the employee advocacy role was typically dealt with in one of three ways: it was dismissed as an historical legacy, an anachronism belonging to a bygone era of HRM from which the profession has now evolved; it was reduced to a particular operational consideration, for example in the context of discussing redundancy; or it was cast in largely instrumental terms – HRM needs to be concerned with the welfare and attitudes of employees in order to lessen the likelihood of industrial action and facilitate a high-performance culture. In other words, there was typically little credence given to the idea that employee welfare might be a key HRM value in its own right. Certainly there was no suggestion that the more committed promotion of the interests and welfare of employees might be central to a renewal of the credibility of HRM.

The business partnership role, central to the contemporary rhetoric surrounding strategic HRM, generally received much greater attention in the texts we studied. The need for HR to become 'more strategic' was, of course, an oft-repeated refrain, although the precise substance of what this more strategic orientation might actually look like was rarely indicated. Our deeper analysis suggests that beneath this superficial promotion of strategic HRM and the need for HR 'executives' (rather than 'professionals') to promote the business credentials of HR, lies a profound ambivalence and uncertainty. Strategic HRM is portrayed as an inevitable, if somewhat lamentable (and potentially dangerous), reality of modern corporate life. The ambivalence about HR's business partnership role is likely to be based on a combination of both unease and insecurity – unease with the prospect of HR being seen to be part of management, which might threaten its distinctive professional character; and, insecurity as to whether HRM, as an essentially ancillary function, really deserves its place in (strategic) management. This impression is reinforced by the sheer regularity with which consumers of the discourse are reminded that 'HR has become more strategic', or 'HR needs to demonstrate that it is more strategic' or that 'good organisations realise that HR is a valued business partner'. This constant reiteration of HR's strategic character belies a deeper insecurity and self-doubt. Curiously, however, despite the implicit recognition that strategic HRM might not actually work (for HR or for employees) and that being too closely identified with management might be dangerous for HR, there is rarely any serious criticism of senior management in this discourse. The CEO and the overall strategic direction of the organisation is generally regarded as inviolate – senior management are not criticised for failing to invite HR to the 'top table', for presiding over cutbacks that threaten the performance of HR, or for pursuing policies of work intensification, labour flexibility and asset sweating that are often deleterious to employees.

Despite the ambivalence towards the business partnership role that our discourse analysis reveals, the practitioner discourse fails to offer any clear alternatives. Despite the dangers for HR professionals inherent in strategic HRM, the texts consistently imply that there is simply no realistic alternative. To countenance a stronger employee champion role (other than rhetorically) would be to risk consigning HRM to the irrelevancy of the past. Another potential alternative, raised in the academic literature, is for HR professionals to seek renewal by embracing a more pronounced role for ethics and ethical decision-making in the organisation, especially with respect to the management of people. In our analysis, however, this alternative was not represented as significant for HRM, or a potential source of greater legitimacy and status for the HR function. Both business ethics more generally and ethics in employment in particular are represented in instrumental terms and HR's role is confined to the development of codes and policies that function as mechanisms of management control. There is no reflection in this discourse of the stronger role for HRM in educating employees about ethical principles and introducing ethical considerations into management decision-making as implied in the academic literature.

In contrast to the calls for greater pluralism in the academic literature, employees were strangely absent in much of the practitioner discourse. Employees populate the general context of the organisation and of HR's work, of course, but their lack of personality or real-life character tends to mirror strategic HRM's overriding image of employees as 'resources'. Where employees are more clearly recognised as actually present, their treatment is often negative. It is striking that the sympathy afforded HR professionals in the discourse is not matched by any equivalent expressions of sympathy for employees working in contemporary organisations. To the extent that employees are seen as something more than resources, they tend to be constructed as emotional, potentially fraudulent or prone to industrial militancy. In general the discourse constructs employees as a source of difficulty and disruption for strategic HR executives. Far from being the focus for HR professionals (as might be expected from the academic literature), employees emerge as a prime source of frustration. This construction is, of course, entirely consistent with the implicit endorsement of the business partnership model where HR's prime responsibility is to ensure the alignment of (potentially difficult) human resources with corporate objectives.

Crisis and contradiction were both recurrent and central to constructions of HRM in practitioner discourse. We were able to show how this was discursively accomplished in different ways, for example through vocabularies associated with military conflict and death, and through constructions of HR in terms of their problematic position between employers and employees, whether that be HR as the 'meat in the sandwich' or the fraying rope in a 'tug of war'. While featured in the articles, there was no resolution to these crises and contradictions. The most that was offered were suggestions to help HR staff cope with the crises, tensions, confusion and contradiction that appeared fundamental to their role.

IMPLICATIONS: TEXTS IN CONTEXT

In this final section, we reflect on our analysis of these texts in terms of the context of their production and consumption. The analysis presented in this chapter suggests that the HR practitioner discourse surrounding the vexed question of HR identity in the era of strategic HRM is functional for the producers of that discourse (in this case the writers, editors and publishers of *HR Monthly*) and its direct consumers (HR professionals) and indirect consumers (managers more generally).

The sympathetic treatment of the predicament of HR professionals disclosed by the practitioner discourse can easily be seen to be functional for the producers of the discourse. By offering its professional readers sympathy, reassurance and even an element of therapy, *HR*

Monthly serves to build the identification of HR professionals with the magazine, and through it, with their professional association. But this function may well go beyond simply building identification with the readership. One of the central arguments in this analysis has been that the discourse is fundamentally unable to offer any clear resolution of the central tension confronted by contemporary HR professionals. This appears to foreclose one key potential means of securing a stronger professional identity for HR (Newton 1983). In the absence of that possibility it is plausible that the sympathetic tone of the discourse is actually acting as a substitute foundation for professional identity. The discourse, in recognising but not resolving the central tension, under-lines the unique and distinctive nature of the challenges faced by HR practitioners. It implies that only they are caught in the uniquely 'hard place' in modern organisations, unable to escape their historical respon-sibility for employee welfare and advocacy and yet forced to respond to the increasingly intense demands of senior management for high perfor-mance, efficiency and value-adding HR. The discourse uses this point of differentiation characteristic of HR work as a foundation for building identity in the absence of other, more traditional sources of professional identity.

The discourse is also functional for its producers in another, more insidious way. Consumers of the discourse are, in the individual texts, often promised some resolution of their anxieties relating to their pro-fessional role. However, as argued in the analysis above, the texts typi-cally fail to provide such resolution. As a result, consumers tend to be left unsatisfied, and, as a consequence, the crisis continues unabated. This might well be functional to the extent that the producers are con-cerned to ensure that their audience remains, in a sense, captive to the future prospect and promise of resolution and ultimate satisfaction.

The practitioner discourse might also be functional for its direct consumers, HR professionals. Perversely, the implicit conclusion that the central tension cannot actually be resolved might serve to com-fort HR professionals struggling to manage these tensions in their own work context. Further, the declarative and imperative character of the central messages that business partnership is ultimately the only legit-imate role for HR, and that strategic HRM is inevitable, might also serve to absolve HR practitioners from any residual guilt they may feel for the current state of affairs. This is one way of understanding the military theme in texts such as 'The HRM Professional' – the HR professional is not really to blame for the 'atrocities of war', because he or she is ultimately just following someone else's (the CEO's) orders.

Finally, the discourse can also be seen to be functional for its indirect consumers, senior managers. The practitioner discourse is 'safe' for senior management in the sense that it does not challenge their power and authority. As argued above, the discourse typically constructs senior management as inviolate, as beyond reproach for organisational problems. The discourse, in its recognition but not resolution of the central tension, might also serve to allow senior managers to rationalise away problems with the performance or management of its human resources – senior management need not be overly concerned with employee welfare, because it remains a problem, albeit an unresolved problem, for their HR managers and officers alone.

References

Beatty, R.W. & Schneider, C.E. 1997, 'New HR roles to impact organizational performance: from "partners" to "players"', *Human Resource Management* 36(1): 29–37.

Beer, M. 1997, 'The transformation of the human resource function: resolving the tension between a traditional administrative and a new strategic role', *Human Resource Management* 36(1): 49–56.

Burman, E. & Parker, I. 1993, 'Against discursive imperialism, empiricism and constructionism: thirty-two problems with discourse analysis', in E. Burman & I. Parker (eds) *Discourse Analytic Research: Repertoires and Readings of Texts in Action*, London: Routledge, pp. 155–72.

Carey, L. 1999, 'Ethical dimensions of a strategic approach to HRM: an Australian perspective', *Asia-Pacific Journal of Human Resources* 37(3): 53–68.

Chater, R. 1993, 'Death of a profession', *Personnel Today* 14(9): 21.

Dudley-Evans, T. & St John, M.J. 1989, *Developments in English for Specific Purposes: A Multi-disciplinary Approach*, Cambridge University Press.

Fairclough, N. 1992, *Discourse and Social Change*, Cambridge: Polity Press.

Fairclough, N. 1993, 'Critical discourse analysis and the marketization of public discourse: the universities', *Discourse & Society* 4(2): 33–68.

Fairclough, N. 1995, *Critical Discourse Analysis: The Critical Study of Language*, London: Longman.

Fairclough, N. 2001, 'The discourse of New Labour: critical discourse analysis', in M. Wetherell, S. Taylor & S.J. Yates (eds) *Discourse as Data: A Guide for Analysis*. London: Sage, pp. 229–66.

Fairclough, N. & Wodak, R. 1997, 'Critical discourse analysis', in T.A. van Dijk (ed.) *Discourse as Social Interaction*, London: Sage, pp. 258–84.

Foote, D. & Robinson, I. 1999, 'The role of the human resources manager: strategist or conscience of the organisation?', *Business Ethics: A European Review* 8(2): 88–98.

Halliday, M.A.K. 1994, *An Introduction to Functional Grammar*, 2nd edn, London: Edward Arnold.

Huckin, T. 1997, 'Critical discourse analysis', in T. Miller (ed.) *Functional Approaches to Written Text: Classroom Applications*, Washington: US Information Agency.

Kjonstad, B. & Willmott, H. 1995, 'Business ethics: restrictive or empowering?' *Journal of Business Ethics* 14(6): 445–64.

Kochan, T.A. 2004, 'Restoring trust in the human resource management profession', *Asia-Pacific Journal of Human Resources* 42(2): 132–46.

Legge, K. 1995a, 'HRM: rhetoric, reality and hidden agendas', in J. Storey (ed.) *Human Resource Management: A Critical Text*, London: Routledge, pp. 33–59.

Legge, K. 1995b, *Human Resource Management: Rhetoric and Realities*, Basingstoke: Macmillan.

MacLachlan, R. 1998, 'HR with attitude', *People Management* 4(16): 36–9.

Newton, L.H. 1983, 'Professionalisation: the intractable plurality of values', in P. Windt, P. Appleby, M. Battin, L. Francis & B. Landesman (eds) *Ethical Issues in the Professions*. Englewood Cliffs, NJ: Prentice Hall.

Paltridge, B. 2000, *Making Sense of Discourse Analysis*, Gold Coast, Qld: Antipodean Educational Enterprises.

Parker, I. 1992, *Discourse Dynamics*, London: Routledge.

Phillips, N. & Hardy, C. 1997, 'Managing multiple identities: discourse, legitimacy and resources in the UK refugee system', *Organization* 4(2): 159–85.

Storey, J. 2001, 'Human resource management today: an assessment', in J. Storey (ed.) *Human Resource Management: A Critical Text*, London: International Thomson Business Press, pp. 2–30.

Ulrich, D. 1996, *Human Resource Champions: The Next Agenda for Adding Value and Delivering Results*, Boston: Harvard Business School Press.

Ulrich, D. 1997, 'Measuring human resources: an overview of practice and a prescription for results', *Human Resource Management* 36(3): 303–20.

Ulrich, D. 1998, 'A new mandate for human resources', *Harvard Business Review* Jan.–Feb.: 124–34.

Van Dijk, T.A. 1993a, 'Editor's foreword to critical discourse analysis', *Discourse and Society* 4(2): 131–2.

Van Dijk, T.A. 1993b, 'Principles of critical discourse analysis', *Discourse and Society* 4(2): 249–84.

Van Dijk, T.A. 1997, 'The study of discourse', in T.A. van Dijk (ed.) *Discourse as Social Structure*, London: Sage, pp. 1–34.

Winstanley, D. & Woodall, J. 2000, 'The ethical dimension of human resource management', *Human Resource Management Journal* 10(2): 5–20.

Wodak, R. & Meyer, M. (eds) 2001, *Methods of Critical Discourse Analysis*, London: Sage.

Wright, P., McMahan, G., Snell, S. & Gerhart, B. 2001, 'Comparing line and HR executives' perceptions of HR effectiveness: services, roles, and contributions', *Human Resource Management* 40(2): 111–123.

CHAPTER FOURTEEN

IDENTIFYING THE SUBJECT
Worker Identity as Discursively Constructed Terrain

David Grant and John Shields

For all their centrality to the employment relationship, far too much has been assumed and far too little asked about how workers see themselves and their role in this 'exchange'. As this chapter seeks to demonstrate, those management thinkers who write about human resource management base their understandings of what it is that employees themselves 'really' want from the employment relationship on *a priori* and essentialist assumptions about worker identity. Yet to dismiss these depictions of the worker as simply 'flawed' or 'wrong' would be to overlook important aspects of the nature and purpose of HRM – and, indeed, of all 'modern' labour management thought, talk and text. Whether formulated by academics or practitioners, the HRM literature is, we suggest, best understood not as a series of disinterested attempts to 'understand' the worker but rather as a sequence of normative interventions intended to objectify the worker and to shape the employment relationship and the identities of workers and managers alike within that relationship. As Jacques (1996: 69) observes, management texts are written *for* managers but *about* employees, 'who are the object of research and theorising'. While this may no longer be a particularly novel insight, it does highlight the modern managerialist imperative to reduce worker identities to manageable proportions. More controversially, we suggest that a comparable process of worker objectification and essentialisation is evident in much of the literature in the *critical* management genre. We suggest that this applies not only to those post-structuralist critics who depict workers as self-subjugating victims of HRM but also to their neo-Marxist adversaries who prefer to see workers as natural if not habitual recalcitrants.

In this chapter we examine competing accounts, 'narratives' or 'discourses' about the essence of worker selfhood and identity. As several commentators have noted, identities are often constituted in the form of narratives – that is, written or verbal accounts with a focus on common themes or issues and that link a set of ideas or a series of events (Czarniawska-Joerges 1994; Czarniawska 1998; Alvesson 2000; Boje 2001; Gabriel 2004). Such narratives are disseminated in the form of social or organisational discourses. Discourses comprise interrelated sets of spoken or written texts, and the practices of their production, dissemination and reception bring various social phenomena (objects) into being (Fairclough 1992; Oswick et al. 2000; Hall 2001; Phillips & Hardy 2002; Grant et al. 2004). Here we argue that where applied to worker identity, narratives or discourses of HRM have assumed 'meta-like' attributes and in so doing they have influenced conventional understandings of workers' inherent needs, motives and self-image. We argue that whether managerialist or anti-managerial in nature, such narratives amount to normative and selective constructions of worker identity.

To elaborate these arguments, we use a discourse-analytic method to explore the nature and significance of these competing and changing constructions of HRM since its advent in the early 1980s. Using a framework of analysis that distinguishes between discursive concepts, objects and subjects, we explore the normative assumptions underpinning the various discourses that have been used to describe, analyse and theorise HRM, as well as those that critique it. Our analysis enables us to examine their impact on conventional thinking about workers' identity where it is framed in terms of, for example, worker expectations, needs and motives. Moreover, it enables us to examine the ways in which these assumptions lock their proponents into essentialist positions about the nature of the 'human resource'; about the 'object' of people management. In taking this approach we argue that each represents an attempt to project an idealised conception of worker identity and subjectivity. In essence, we contend that *all* HRM-related discourses as well as those that critique HRM are concerned to *identify* the subject.

The chapter is divided into four sections. The first considers recent insights on the relationship between discourse and work identity, arguing that discourses play a central role in the shaping and reshaping of work identity in particular social contexts. We outline a conceptual framework that draws on a discourse-analytic approach and

286

distinguishes between discursive concepts, discursive objects, and discursive subjects. We go on to explain the value of this framework and discuss its relevance to our argument. Section two applies the framework of analysis to key bodies of HRM thought and writing. We show how each approach can be seen as promulgating its own distinct concept of worker identity. In line with Potter & Wetherell's (1987: 6) observation that discourses 'do not just describe things; they do things', we also show how the authors of these texts have *sought* to influence worker identity and behaviour through a process of objectification. Section three applies the same mode of analysis to the work of critical management writers where they have sought to critique HRM and its associated practices from either a post-structuralist or a neo-Marxist perspective. In doing so, we identify processes of objectification paralleling that evident in mainstream management texts. The fourth and concluding section summarises the argument and considers the wider implications of our discursive study. It suggests that an approach combining identity theory with discourse analysis provides the best means of understanding worker identity as a primary site of discursive and material contestation within the modern employment relationship.

DISCOURSE AND IDENTITY AT WORK: CONCEPTS, OBJECTS AND SUBJECTS

Work identity and how it is constructed have now become issues of major interest and controversy in both mainstream management and critical management thought and writing. Worker identity is undoubtedly the new 'contested terrain', both within the workplace and in the academy. We would stress, however, that worker identity has been an abiding concern of those studying management since the advent of 'modern' labour management thought over a century ago. What have changed are the concepts and norms associated with management's preferred/ideal worker identity and how (and how successfully) these have been applied – and opposed. For example, it is noticeable that in much contemporary HRM thinking, the 'development' of the employee's 'inner self' (that is, their identity, values, beliefs, emotions, self-concept, personality, and even spirituality) has replaced external rewards and extrinsic motivation as the perceived key to performance enhancement. Likewise, in much of the critical management writing the emphasis has shifted from the structure-control-resistance framework that dominated 'labour process theory' in the 1980s to a concern with the interplay of discourse, context and subjectivity in the shaping of work identity and the meanings ascribed to work. Whether the preferred critical framework happens to be post-structuralist or neo-Marxist, the issues of worker subjectivity and identity now occupy centre-stage in the polemical and often acrimonious debates (for example Thompson & Ackroyd 1995; O'Doherty &Willmott 2001; Friedman 2004) between anti-management critics themselves.

There is a growing interest among organisational researchers in examining the discourses – that is, the normative assumptions, talk and texts – that may be used in order to understand more accurately the processes and practices that contribute to the construction of identity in organisational contexts. Discourse analysis is multi-disciplinary in origin, being informed by a variety of sociological, socio-psychological, anthropological, linguistic, philosophical, communications and literary-based studies and approaches (Grant et al. 2004). To date, discourse analysts have used these approaches to study a variety of identity-related issues in organisations at the individual, group and organisational levels (Grant et al. 2004). These include, for example, professional identity (Bruni & Gherardi 2002), individual identity (Karreman & Alvesson 2001), gender and identity (Cameron 1996), identity and loyalty in knowledge-intensive firms (Alvesson 2000), identity regulation and workplace control (Doolin 2002), managerial identity (Sveningsson & Alvesson 2003) and collective identity (Czarniawska-Joerges 1994). We see no reason why further research should not build on the insights offered by these studies in order to provide a more accurate and meaningful understanding of the context-specific processes and tensions associated with the construction of worker identity and hence the shaping of worker subjectivity (that is, self-concept, beliefs, values, attitudes and behaviour). We also believe that discourse analysis offers a powerful means of furthering the critical management project; that is, of contributing to a sustained critique of mainstream managerialist thought and practices.

An acceptance of the role of discourse in constituting social phenomena such as worker identity leads on to an important question: how does this actually occur? Identity is based on a set of understandings of 'what is appropriate and natural' (Alvesson 2000: 1105). By implication, this understanding of who a person is leads on to the issue of how they are *expected* to think and behave. In discursively creating a worker identity it becomes (theoretically) incumbent on the worker to think and act in ways that are consistent with this idealised identity. But how and to what extent does this internalisation of discursively projected identity really happen? How is the 'identity' concept transmitted, received and acted upon? To address these crucial questions, we use a conceptual framework that identifies and differentiates between three kinds of discursive entity: concepts, objects and subjects (Fairclough 1992; Phillips & Hardy 1997; Oswick et al. 2000; Grant & Shields 2002; Grant et al. 2003). In this chapter we analyse each of these entities in relation to discourses of worker identity that appear within the HRM literature. This enables us to generate a range of insights into the meanings and impact both of these discourses and of the various counter-discourses espoused by those critical of HRM.

Discursive concepts

Discursive concepts are the ideas, notions and thoughts 'through which we understand the world and relate to one another' (Phillips & Hardy 1997: 167). Participation in the formulation of concepts via discourse is in itself a political act since the concept may well redefine and transform the world to which it is applied. Proponents of a concept will believe that it is morally correct and valid and will seek to use it to change social structures and relationships. At the same time, they may encounter resistance to its accomplishment from those whose evaluation of the concept is unfavourable.

The notions of 'the worker' and 'worker identity' are examples of discursive concepts. As Alvesson & Deetz (1999: 201) have observed, what constitutes 'a worker' is not the bodily object but rather the language and practices that differentiate socially between those categorised as 'worker' and those classified otherwise. These constellations of talk, text and practice incorporate and project sets of assumptions and understandings about who workers are, what they think, what they want, and how they can be expected to behave. Central to the concept of worker identity are their expectations of the employment relationship and what it is they want out of it. The basic managerial assumption is that they have a set of 'needs' and 'wants' and thus will act in particular ways in order to 'satisfy' these; that is, the worker is essentially a needful resource. This broad conception of worker identity is easy to recognise. Since the early 20th century, however, there have been several variants on this general theme, notably Taylorism, human relations, neo-human relations and HRM. While this chapter focuses only on the last of these, each variant has led its proponents to draw markedly differing conclusions as to the basis of workers' needs and identity and thus how these can best be managed. In short, as a discursive concept, worker identity has been subjected to a variety of sometimes complementary, sometimes conflicting conceptualisations.

Discursive objects

While discursive objects are closely related to discursive concepts, there is a key difference. Unlike concepts, which exist only in the realm of ideas, objects can exist in a physical sense and have an ontological reality. However, the social accomplishment of a concept requires that it be applied to, or become, an object. Changing the concept stands to change the way in which the object itself is socially accomplished, acknowledged and related to (Phillips & Hardy 1997: 168).

Our framework assumes that if the idea of what constitutes worker identity changes, then so too does the discursive 'object' onto which these concepts are projected, namely 'the worker'. Accordingly, an understanding of worker identity requires that we pay close attention to how particular conceptual variants of it perceive, 'imagine' or objectify the employee, since this is the target towards which particular management and organisational policies and practices will be directed. Moreover, it is these policies and practices that determine how the worker is treated. In other words, for workers, the concept becomes a lived reality (though not necessarily in the way that either they or managers might like). In this sense, the process of discursive objectification is profoundly political in nature, since it stands to empower the perpetrator (for example the manager) while simultaneously disempowering the objectified (for example the employee).

Discursive subjects

Whether a discursively constructed concept 'works' once it becomes an ontological reality – an object of practice – can only be assessed by paying particular attention to the relevant discursive subjects. Individuals who are the subject of a particular discourse are not simply passive receptacles for that discourse; rather, they are active organisational agents with their own interests and subjectivities who are seeking to establish their own social and power relations (Phillips & Hardy 1997: 170). Thus it becomes important to know how discursive subjects react to a particular discourse. We need to know, for example, whether the actual subjects of a particular discourse of HRM (workers) respond to the particular identity being projected upon them. Do they identify with it or do they resist it in various ways? Might they create counter identities? Might they enact multiple identities, only invoking a projected identity concept when they believe that it is in their interests to do so – and then only as a form of calculative role- or game-playing, or perhaps as a form of subtle subversion (Fleming & Sewell 2002)? In sum, an accurate evaluation of the discursive concept of worker identity only becomes possible via rigorous analysis of the primary discursive object (workers) as discursive subjects.

With these points in mind, we now turn to consider how, since the late 1980s, HRM thinkers and their critics have approached the phenomenon of worker identity. In doing so, we use our discursive framework of analysis to examine the way in which each of these texts constructs worker identity as concept and object, as well as exploring what the key texts in each stream reveal about their authors' attitudes to employees as subjects. Our purpose here is not to explore empirically how workers as discursive subjects do respond to HRM discourse in specific contests; rather, our aim is to expose the nature of the discursive concepts of worker identity evident both in mainstream HRM texts *and* in the critical management literature itself.

WORKER IDENTITY IN CONTEMPORARY HRM TEXTS

'Human resource management' emerged in the USA in the early 1980s as a response to the perceived inadequacies of existing labour management practices in US firms, particularly the top-down, bureaucratic practices characteristic of 'personnel management' of the 1950s, 1960s and 1970s. As with its human relations and neo-human relations antecedents, HRM discourse is essentially the work of American and British academic writers, although its dissemination owes much to the presence of a relatively new group of discursive agents, namely management consultants and 'pop' management writers (see, for example, Huczynski 1993; Micklethwait & Wooldridge 1996).

While the concept of HRM involves some broad and commonly applied elements – perhaps most importantly the proposition that 'human resources' are the crucial ingredients for organisational effectiveness – there are also a host of variants. The discursive concept of HRM might be best thought of as a terrain comprising a number of competing and coexisting ideas and perspectives, of which the 'hard'/'soft' dichotomy is perhaps the most commonly used and understood. In each case, the discursive concept of the employee is cast very differently. In the 'soft' or 'developmental humanist' conception of HRM (Legge 1995), employees are presented as valued resources, or even as resourceful humans, warranting significant 'development' and 'involvement'; in the 'hard' conception, the employee is presented as a strategic resource object 'to be used dispassionately and in a formally rational manner' (Storey 1992: 26). Whereas contributors to the 'hard' version, including writers from the 'Michigan School' (for example Fombrun et al. 1984; Schuler & Jackson 1987) tend to view employee identity per se as both unimportant and unproblematic, those associated with the 'soft' or 'Harvard School' version regard identity-shaping as *the* pivotal task in the HRM project. In essence, the goal is to *reconstitute* the employee-subject, including their values, needs and identity, in the image of an idealised resource-object. Far from being acknowledged as an end in itself, employee subjectivity is viewed as the means to achieving a high-performance end.

Given the emphasis of the 'soft' HRM stream on identity-shaping or 'changing the subject', the remainder of this section focuses selectively on three of its iterations: culture management, high-commitment management, and trust management. While there has been an apparent widening of the degree of recognition accorded to the employee as a discursive subject in texts associated with these iterations, the underlying discursive intent remains one of objectification.

The encultured resource

Largely a product of the successful Japanese assault on US multinational dominance in global markets for manufactured goods in the 1970s, the 'excellence' and culture management literatures of the early 1980s, most notably the work of Deal & Kennedy (1982) and Peters & Waterman (1982) made the *transformation* of worker identity a central issue in Western management thinking and action. A homogeneous corporate culture based on espoused 'core values' (the corporate 'mission, vision and values') was to be the normative 'glue' binding the organisation together. Worker values, beliefs, self-concept and self-worth were to be reshaped by the embrace of corporate values – the human resource was to be encultured. We shall turn to the criticisms of this highly unitarist discourse in the next section. For now, we simply note the unambiguously discursive intent of the culture management literature and its thoroughly instrumental conception of worker identity.

The committed resource

As Guest (1987), Legge (1995: 174–5) and others have observed, 'commitment' is one of the defining norms of (soft) HRM. While the ideal resonates through the culture management literature, it was Harvard's Richard Walton who first asserted its centrality to effective HRM. Building on McGregor's Theory X/Theory X model, Walton (1985: 77) posited a moral dualism between 'control' and 'commitment': 'workers respond best – and most creatively – not when they are tightly controlled by management, placed in narrowly defined jobs, and treated like an unwelcome necessity, but, instead, when they are given broader responsibilities, encouraged to contribute, and helped to take satisfaction in their work.' Advocates of the high-commitment model contend that the purpose of HRM practice should be to 'shape desired employee behaviour and attitudes by forging psychological links between organizational and employee goals' (Arthur 1994: 672). In essence, this logic constitutes the core of all 'high-performance' and 'high-involvement' models of HRM (for example Lawler 1992; Huselid 1995; Meyer & Allen 1997; Pfeffer 1998). Involving and engaging employees in their work stands to elicit stronger task motivation and a greater degree of 'extra-role' or 'organisational citizenship' behaviour (for example Moorman et al. 1993; Motowidlo 2000; Podsakoff et al. 2000). As such, the discursive centrepieces of the high-commitment model are the 'self-managing' worker and the good 'organisational citizen'.

However, as with the culture management texts, in the commitment literature the worker remains a 'resource' object, albeit of a selectively developed and empowered kind, while the identity-selecting/shaping intent remains equally clear. This is attested by Lawler's remarkably candid assertions (1992: 107) regarding the type of employee ideally suited to a high-involvement approach, which, he suggests, requires

> individuals who value internal rewards and the kind of satisfaction that comes from doing challenging work well. Not all people in the work force have these characteristics, and even those who do may not look to the workplace for their intrinsic satisfactions and sense of accomplishment . . . Those individuals who do not look to their work for this kind of satisfaction simply cannot be tolerated in an organization that designs work to involve employees. They are in a very real sense uncontrollable because they do not respond to the rewards that are counted on to create a motivating work situation for most individuals.

Here the discourse reveals a sharp moral dualism: between the fully committed, intrinsically motivated organisational citizen and the instrumentally motivated time-server. Such a position also leads inexorably to the systematic use of personality assessment and the application of deep 'competencies' criteria to staff selection, development and reward practices which are but the most recent instances of the longstanding managerialist impetus to measure, classify, essentialise and psychologise the worker. Yet there is also a certain irony here since one could reasonably expect that a perspective of HRM that is so clearly focused on eliciting higher levels of commitment and motivation would lead to studies that go beyond simply seeing the employee as a high-performance object and seek to recognise their presence as subjects. Yet, with few notable exceptions (for example Guest 1999, 2002; Applebaum et al. 2000; Ramsay et al. 2000), most empirical studies linking commitment-based HRM to organisational performance (for example Arthur 1994; Gratton 1995; Huselid 1995; Capelli & Neumark 2001) rarely go beyond considering workers (discursively) as resource-objects. In this conception, worker identity remains primarily the repository of job satisfaction and organisational commitment.

The trusting resource

Two more recent bodies of academic writing in the high-commitment management genre draw on rather more subtle sets of assumptions about the nature of employee expectations and identity. One is concerned with the nature, determinants and consequences of the 'psychological contract'; the other has to do with 'organisational justice' cognitions and behaviour.

A number of academic commentators (for example Argyris 1960; Hiltrop 1995; Rousseau 1995, 1998; Kessler & Undy 1996; Robinson 1996; Guest 1998a; Coyle-Shapiro & Kessler 2002) have suggested that the 'psychological contract' is the key determinant of employee work attitudes and behaviour and that these cognitive contracts are, in turn, shaped by socialised values, expectations and self-concept and also by current HRM practices. Where employee expectations are met and promises and obligations are fulfilled, the behavioural consequences are likely to be positive. Conversely, where expectations or promises and obligations are not met, then in the context of a broken psychological contract, workers are likely to react negatively. To be sure, as with all iterations of soft HRM, the concept acknowledges workers' subjectivity. However, it does so for quite instrumental reasons. According to Guest (1998a), the core cognitions of the psychological contract are those of generalised trust, felt-fairness and honouring the promised deal. What this does is to cast the worker as a trust-seeking resource – but a malleable resource nonetheless. Trust is transformed from an ethical end into an emotional tool. The proposition that employee expectations and the basis of the employment 'contract' itself are both open to deep psychological manipulation stands to empower those who manage rather than those who are managed. It is therefore unsurprising that the concept of the psychological contract is now beginning to be taken up in the mainstream practitioner literature (see Armstrong & Stephens 2005: 85–8).

Like other iterations of soft HRM, the organisational justice literature (Greenberg 1990, 1996; Folger & Cropanzano 1998; Konovsky 2000; Greenberg & Colquill 2005) also psychologises the worker. Employees are portrayed as seekers of trust through fair treatment, which, in turn, elicits high commitment and high performance, so HRM practices aimed at nurturing trust and felt-fairness are predicted to deliver desired behavioural outcomes. In this way, employee self-concept and identity are again reduced to a manipulable cognitive essence. As Greenberg (1990) has all but conceded, managing 'felt-fairness' is essentially the art of 'impression management' in the cause of performance enhancement.

In sum, we suggest that even those iterations of soft HRM which appear to be most academically detached and cognisant of workers as organisational subjects still essentialise and objectify worker expectations and identity – and do so for quite instrumental reasons. Understanding the wellsprings of employee commitment (expectations, values, beliefs, emotions) appears not as an end in itself but rather as the means to a managerial end. The worker remains (discursively) a resource-object; a sentient but impressionable medium for the accomplishment of predetermined goals and objectives.

WORKER IDENTITY IN CRITICAL MANAGEMENT TEXTS

Exposing and assailing the normative assumptions and implications of soft HRM is without doubt the defining feature of the critical management stream. Virtually all writers in this stream 'focus on the repressive side of power and how it is used in hidden ways by dominant groups to maintain the status quo, leaving other groups at a constant disadvantage since these invisible aspects are difficult to resist' (Palmer & Hardy 2000: 79). Critical writers are also in broad agreement with the central tenets of labour process theory. Thus they see the soft/high-commitment HRM texts discussed above, including those authored by fellow academics, as being managerialist in nature: viewing the worker purely as a resource or commodity that is to be exploited for the benefit of the organisation. Accordingly, they see the conceptualisations of worker identity in these texts largely as the most recent ideological formulations in the longstanding managerial pursuit of greater control over, and therefore greater efficiency from, employees. A further defining feature of the critical stream is a focus on the nature and implications of worker subjectivity.

However, the critical stream is itself rent by deep conceptual divisions over the issues of worker identity and subjectivity. On the one hand there are the critical post-structuralist commentators (for example Knights & Willmott 1989; Knights & Morgan 1991; Keenoy & Anthony 1992; Willmott 1993, 2003; Townley 1994; Alvesson & Deetz 1999); on the other, there are those who adopt either a neo-Marxist stance (for example Thompson & Ackroyd 1995; Friedman 2004) or a critical-pluralist position (Scott 1994). These divisions are at once a source of weakness in the critical stream and, we argue, a source of potential analytical strength. What is most germane to our purpose here is the markedly different representation of worker identity and subjectivity between the post-structuralists and the neo-Marxists, and it is to this that we now turn.

The subjugated subject

Critical writers have traditionally focused on explicit attempts by management to deskill workers (for example Braverman 1974) and to authorise and enforce rules and procedures to control employees (for example Edwards 1979). However, since the advent of culture management and high-commitment management discourses and practices in the 1980s, and the accompanying turn to post-structuralist theory and interpretation in the academy, many critical management writers have been vociferous in their condemnation of these supposedly more subtle and sophisticated means of controlling work behaviour and effort. The conceptualisations of worker needs and identity that underpin soft HRM are seen as devices for subordination and exploitation, operating to objectify (determine) the worker as a person, and typically constraining, subverting and subordinating the person's fuller social being. Drawing on Foucault's (1980) contention that human subjectivity is not volitional but rather 'the constitutive product of a plurality of disciplinary mechanisms' (Knights & Willmott 1989: 549), post-structuralist management critics contend that the discursive concepts and practices associated with high-commitment management are directed at value internalisation; at 'determining how employees should *think* and *feel* about what they produce' (Willmott 1993: 522); at the 'redesign [of] human understanding to fit the organization's purpose' (Keenoy & Anthony 1992: 239).

Accordingly, post-structuralist critics have attacked soft HRM discourse and practice as incorporating 'insidious controls' that are designed to secure worker compliance by a process of value internalisation (for example Knights & Willmott 1989; Keenoy & Anthony 1992; Willmott 1993, 2003; Townley 1994). In the process, workers' subjectivity turns in on itself, becoming not the means to emancipation but rather the instrument of subjugation. According to Willmott (1993), professing to provide employees with greater freedom and decision-making autonomy leads to what is tantamount to their self-incarceration in a psychic prison. While Willmott's position seems to have shifted somewhat in recent times (see O'Doherty & Willmott 2001; Willmott 2003), and while he has certainly acknowledged the possibility of 'micro-emancipatory' outcomes under high-involvement management (for example Alvesson & Willmott 1992), on our reading, Willmott's underlying position still appears to be that of Foucaldian pessimism; namely that in the presence of the managerialist mantra of self-management, empowerment and autonomy, worker subjectivity remains essentially self-entrancing and self-defeating (for example O'Doherty & Willmott 2001: 469, 471).

While these criticisms are important in that they compel us to consider and debate the conceptualisations of employee identity that exist in the more managerialist realms of literature on work and organisation, they themselves are also conceptually problematic. Like the HRM writers that they condemn, the post-structuralist critics have themselves tended to offer totalising portrayals of HRM practices and unflattering images of employees as 'supine, docile and biddable' (Fleming & Sewell 2002: 859); as credulous receptacles for management ideas. Just as in the mainsteam HRM texts, the post-structuralist critique tends to get no further than considering workers as organisational objects. In this sense, the accusers may be just as guilty as the accused of objectifying and essentialising the subject. As Tinker (2002: 267), for instance, remarks: 'post-structural labour process theorists posit the existence of a repressed (and unexplained) human essence that is imprisoned by the cage of modern civility . . . These are the self-same post-structuralists who previously condemned earlier work for essentialist precepts.'

The recalcitrant subject

The post-structuralist position has called forth what can only be described as a polemical counter-offensive by critics of a neo-Marxist bent (for example Thompson & Ackroyd 1995; Ackroyd & Thompson 1999; Tinker 2002; Friedman 2004). The basic position here is that HRM has not 'worked', that employee performance has not been significantly enhanced, and that workers and management remain locked into their conflictual positions. The implication is that while workers may appear compliant and accommodating under these approaches, this should not detract from the fact that they are still capable of – and are, indeed, practising – resistance. Neo-Marxist writers insist that the post-structuralists overstate the extent and effectiveness of HRM practices and ignore the potential for worker recalcitrance or resistance. With more than a hint of sarcasm, Thompson & Ackroyd (1995: 14) observe: 'Even when employees are not entirely subjugated, seduced or self-disciplined, they are [still seen as] prisoners of their own identity projects.'

While the neo-Marxist counter-critique offers a potentially valuable corrective to the shortcomings of the post-structuralist position, it also suffers from a tendency to reify the *recalcitrant* worker. In the neo-Marxist schema, the concept of the self-subjugated worker is supplanted by that of the habitual dissenter (for example Ackroyd & Thompson 1999; Friedman 2002). Indeed, the quest to establish the validity of the neo-Marxist position – and the omnipresence of worker resistance, in particular – has produced a number of examples of quite novel argument by analogy and extension. For instance, in arguing the case for recognition of 'the more inconspicuous, subjective, subtle and unorganised' modes of resistance, Fleming & Sewell (2002: 859) invoke not a solid body of temporally or organisationally relevant empirical evidence but rather historical novelist Jaroslav Hašek's portrayal of 'disengagement' – or '*Švejkism*' – in a First World War military context. On this basis, virtually all worker behaviour, including 'exaggerated' displays of 'deference, enthusiasm, or conformity' (Fleming & Sewell 2002:

866), would seem to amount to calculated acts of defiance. Resistance, it seems, is everywhere and everything. Such a position is no less totalising and objectifying than its post-structuralist antithesis. Albeit on the basis of very different premises, both positions seem to us to overstate the constancy of worker identity and consequently the cognitive and behavioural consistency of worker subjectivity. Like managerialist discourse itself, these competing critical perspectives seem all too willing to impose their own preferred organisational script on worker identity and subjectivity.

Saving the subject

For all of their mutual antipathy, and notwithstanding their professed concern at the plight of ordinary workers, the fact is that neither of the warring critical camps have made much effort to engage with employees as diverse discursive subjects, let alone to understand them on their own terms. For this reason, we never find out whether the critics' assertions about those managerialist HRM projects that they seek to undermine are correct because, as Guest (1999) and Clark and colleagues (1998) have pointed out, few of them have bothered to document *real* employees' reactions to such projects. This shortcoming has not been lost on some of the critical commentators themselves. For example, Legge (1998) concedes that there are few solid case studies or surveys that seek to assess whether the critical perspective has empirical merit. Instead, the critical stream of literature seems to remain obstinately wedded to the notion of the employee as a discursive object and avoids any serious examination of them as discursive subjects. Worse still, where workers are allowed a voice, it is only by proxy. All too often the job of the critical analyst becomes one of projecting their own opinion onto workers as objects. We are therefore only told what workers would say about the way they are managed and organised and what it is that they would want *if* they were treated as subjects and not because critical studies of work and organisation *do* treat them as subjects. Furthermore, and as Legge (1998) has reflected, where presented with evidence of workers as subjects reacting positively to managerial initiatives such as HRM, there is a propensity for critical writers of both persuasions to run for cover behind the 'false consciousness' argument. This is a risky position to take in that it leaves those who adopt the critical perspective open to accusations of offering no real evidence in support of their position and of practising what Guest (1999: 8) has termed 'the superior insight of the analyst'. Moreover, and as Legge (2000: 22) has conceded, it means that the critical post-structuralist tendency to treat workers as cultural dupes can be construed as being equally condescending. We would argue that the neo-Marxist insistence on the omnipresence of resistance is no less culpable.

While the critical stream antagonists stand accused of propounding essentialist understandings of worker identity and of largely ignoring employees as subjects, several critical writers have, thankfully, gone some way to remedying this position. Townley (1994), for example, has noted how HRM practices such as performance appraisal by their very nature and purpose require us to consider employees as more than 'objects' and, in so doing, to examine their response to these practices *as subjects*. How else, she asks, would one want to study HRM given its emphasis on the individual and on the 'importance of recognizing the inherent needs and attitudes' of those 'that have to be managed for the effective organization of work' (Townley 1994: 109)? The importance of 'saving the subject' (Steyaert & Janssens 1999) in critical writings has not been lost on those such as du Gay (1991) and, more recently at least, Willmott (2003). Both recognise that culture change initiatives designed to win the hearts and minds of workers, and which involve an internalisation of managerial values to the extent that they become 'self-managing', can only be studied via an appreciation of worker perspectives and responses to such initiatives.

None of these authors has gone so far as to produce major studies in which worker views and perspectives are documented, and talk of 'saving the subject' is itself more than a little patronising. But what is particularly significant about their work is that underlying the emphasis on the importance of studying the worker as a subject is a call to understand employee identity and how it is constituted. For example, Townley (1994: 107) places considerable emphasis on the construction of worker identity under HRM, noting that 'workers are not simply passive receptacles of a management constituted identity and that the process of identity construction also involves how the individual sees him or herself; that is how they view themselves as subjects'. Similarly, du Gay (1991: 54) has homed in on the central importance of identity construction in order to examine culture change initiatives.

The agenda here is, of course, to further the critical project. Nevertheless, these writers make an important point: in order to be able to critique more effectively the HRM literature on employee wants, needs, and work attitudes and behaviour, a better understanding is needed of the complex set of social factors that determine worker identity, thereby making its construction 'open and contingent' and not simply or solely a register of the structures of subordination in the workplace (Willmott 2003: 85). Here, then – and as Thompson & McHugh (1995: 225, 358) have at least implied – there would seem to be considerable scope for accommodation between the critical post-structuralist and neo-Marxist positions on worker subjectivity and identity.

In sum, the existing critical literature fails adequately to address workers as subjects and presents largely untested and contradictory conceptions of worker identity and subjectivity. Nonetheless, there is now a flow of critical work which recognises the importance of (a) studying workers as subjects; (b) securing a better understanding of worker identity and how it is constituted; and (c) investigating (rather than *presuming*) worker responses to managerialist discourse and practice, and how these are shaped by, and in turn reshape, both workers' worldview and their self-concept. We concur with these objectives, but are troubled by the failure of the critical stream to go about achieving them. Nevertheless, we see discourse-analytic approaches such as that outlined in this chapter as offering a promising way forward for the critical project.

CONCLUSION: CENTRING THE SUBJECT

Worker identity is now a central concern in both the mainstream management literature and in critical management texts. A major weakness in all the bodies of literature we have examined is a failure to interrogate adequately what we refer to as the discursive subject and thus to produce a genuinely *employee-centred* understanding of worker identity. Academic researchers and writers figure centrally as active agents in the production and dissemination of managerial and anti-managerial discourse. Significantly, however, and as our examination of HRM discourses shows, the dominant tendency among both managerialist and anti-managerialist academics has been to objectify the worker-subject and to essentialise worker identity for instrumental and/or ideological purposes. With this in mind, we have proposed an alternative approach that we believe offers a meaningful way forward.

In line with Ainsworth & Hardy's (2004: 153) observation that 'discourse analysis can help us understand the construction of identities in organizational settings', we have examined the changing conceptions and interpretations of worker identity in these texts using a

301

discourse-analytic framework which distinguishes between discursive concepts, objects and subjects. In taking this approach we have suggested that a comprehensive evaluation of the discursive concept of 'worker' only becomes possible where analysis moves beyond discussion and analysis of workers as objects and on to workers as discursive subjects. More specifically, we have advanced two main contentions concerning worker identity and HRM discourse.

First, we suggest that worker identity under HRM is best understood neither as being objectively 'real' or 'true' (à la managerialist positivism), nor as a psychic prison (à la post-structuralism), nor as an oppositional reflex of structural inequality and exploitation (à la neo-Marxism). Rather, we suggest, it is best understood as a discursive construct in particular temporal and spatial contexts. Worker cognitions and identity are not objectively fixed or real but constituted and reconstituted by discursive means continuously and interactively. On the basis of our discourse-analytic approach, we argue that worker identity is a socially constructed reality in which workers, managers and a range of other discursive subjects are actively implicated. It follows that worker identity has to do with negotiated meaning around competing discourses in particular contexts. Worker identity is also an intertextual phenomenon involving a complex interplay of texts that is continuous, iterative and recursive. For these reasons, we suggest that identity-making is best regarded as a multifaceted work in progress.

Second, we contend that the impact of management discourse on worker identity cannot be assumed – or, for that matter, assumed away. It is not a matter of ascertaining whether any particular discursive concept 'works' or fails; rather, as the small but growing body of mainstream employee-centred empirical research on HRM impact (for example Guest 1999) indicates, the challenge is to establish how, to what extent and under what circumstances management discourse and practice influence employee values, attitudes, self-concept and behaviour. As we argue, this should preferably be undertaken by means of empirically specific discourse analysis which is contextually (that is, temporally and spatially) anchored. Resort to polemic and meta-narrative will no longer suffice. For academic commentators, the key challenge will be to transcend the longstanding habit of perceiving workers as research objects and to recognise and respect them as whole subjects more than capable of 'saving' themselves – on their own terms.

References

Ackroyd, S. & Thompson, P. 1999, *Organizational Misbehaviour*, London: Sage.

Ainsworth, S. & Hardy, C. 2004, 'Discourse and identities', in D. Grant, C. Hardy, C. Oswick & L. Putnam (eds) *The Handbook of Organizational Discourse*, London: Sage, pp. 61–78.

Alvesson, M. 2000, 'Social identity and the problem of loyalty in knowledge-intensive companies', *Journal of Management Studies* 37(8): 1101–25.

Alvesson, M. & Deetz, S. 1999, 'Critical theory and post-structuralism: approaches to organizational studies', in S.R. Clegg & C. Hardy (eds) *Studying Organization: Theory and Method*, London: Sage, pp. 184–211.

Alvesson, M. & Willmott, H. 1992, 'On the idea of emancipation in management and organization studies', *Academy of Management Review* 17(3): 432–64.

Applebaum, E., Bailey, T., Berg, P., & Kalleberg, A. 2000, *Manufacturing Advantage*, Ithaca, N.Y.: Cornell University Press.

Argyris, C. 1960, *Understanding Organizational Behaviour*, Homewood, Ill.: Dorsey Press.

Armstrong, M. & Stephens, T. 2005, *A Handbook of Employee Reward Management and Practice*, London: Kogan Page.

Arthur, J. 1994, 'Effects of human resource systems on manufacturing performance and turnover', *Academy of Management Journal* 37(3): 670–87.

Bakhtin, M. 1986, *Speech Genres and Other Late Essays* (edited and translated by C. Emerson and M. Holquist), Austin, Texas: University of Texas Press.

Bernoux, P. 1998, 'Herzberg, Frederick (1923–)', in M. Warner (ed.) *The Handbook of Management Thinking*, London: International Thomson Business Press, pp. 294–300.

Boje, D. 2001, *Narrative Methods for Organizational and Communications Research*, Sage: London.

Braverman, H. 1974, *Labour and Monopoly Capital. The Degradation of Work in the Twentieth Century*, New York: Monthly Review Press.

Bruni, A. & Gherardi, S. 2002, 'Omega's story: the heterogenous engineering of a gendered professional self', in M. Dent and S. Whitehead (eds) *Managing Professional Identities: Knowledge, Performativity and the 'New' Professional*, London: Routledge, pp. 87–110.

Cameron, D. 1996, 'The language–gender interface: challenging co-optation', in V. Bergvall, J. Bing & A.F. Freed (eds) *Rethinking Language and Gender Research: Theory and Practice*, London and New York: Longman, pp. 31–53.

Capelli, P. & Neumark, D. 2001, 'Do "high-performance" work practices improve establishment-level outcomes?' *Industrial and Labor Relations Review* 54(4): 737–59.

Clark, T., Mabey, C. & Skinner, D. 1998, 'Experiencing HRM: the importance of the inside story', in C. Mabey, D. Skinner & T. Clark (eds) *Experiencing Human Resource Management*, London: Sage, pp. 4–16.

Coyle-Shapiro, J. & Kessler, I. 2002, 'Exploring reciprocity throught the lens of the psychological contract: employee and employer perspectives', *European Journal of Work and Organizational Psychology* 11(1): 69–86.

Czarniawska, B. 1998, *A Narrative Approach to Organization Studies*, Newbury Park, Calif.: Sage.

Czarniawska-Joerges, B. 1994, 'Narratives of individual and organizational identities', in S. Deetz (ed.) *Communication Yearbook* 17, Newbury Park, Calif.: Sage.

Deal, T. & Kennedy, A. 1982, *Corporate Cultures: The Rites and Rituals of Corporate Life*, Harmondsworth: Penguin.

Doolin, B. 2002, 'Enterprise discourse, professional identity and the organizational control of hospital clinicians', *Organization Studies* 23(3): 369–90.

du Gay, P. 1991, 'Enterprise culture and the ideology of excellence', *New Formations* 13: 45–61.

Edwards, R. 1979, *Contested Terrain. The Transformation of the Workplace in the Twentieth Century*, New York: Basic Books.

Fairclough, N. 1992, *Discourse and Social Change*, Cambridge: Polity Press.

Fleming, P. & Sewell, G. 2002, 'Looking for the good soldier, Švejk: alternative modalities of resistance in the contemporary workplace', *Sociology* 36(4): 857–73.

Folger, R. & Cropanzano, R. 1998, *Organizational Justice and Human Resource Management*, London: Sage.

Fombrun, C., Tichy, N. & Devanna, M. 1984, *Strategic Human Resource Management*, New York: Wiley.

Foucault, M. 1980, *Power/Knowledge*, New York: Pantheon.

Friedman, A. 2004, 'Strawmanning and labour process analysis', *Sociology* 38(3): 573–91.

Gabriel, Y. 2004, 'Narratives, stories and texts', in D. Grant, C. Hardy, C. Oswick & L. Putnam (eds) *The Handbook of Organizational Discourse*, London: Sage, pp. 61–78.

Grant, D. & Shields, J. 2002, 'In search of the subject: researching employee reactions to HRM', *Journal of Industrial Relations* 44(3): 313–34.

Grant, D., Hardy, C., Oswick, C. & Putnam, L. 2004, 'Introduction – organizational discourse: exploring the field', in D. Grant, C. Hardy, C. Oswick & L. Putnam (eds) *The Handbook of Organizational Discourse*, London: Sage, pp. 1–36.

Grant, D., O'Donnell, M. & Shields, J. 2003, 'The new performance paradigm in the Australian public service: a discursive analysis', in T. Duvillier (ed.), *La Motivation Au Travail Dans Le Secteur Public* (The Motivation of Work in the Public Sector), Paris: Harmattan Publishers, pp. 165–80.

Gratton, L. 1995, 'The art of managing people', *Financial Times*, Mastering Management Series, November.

Greenberg, J. 1990, 'Looking fair vs. being fair: managing impressions of organizational justice', *Research in Organizational Behavior* 12: 111–57.

Greenberg, J. 1996, *The Quest for Justice on the Job: Essays and Experiments*, Thousand Oaks, Calif.: Sage.

Greenberg, J. & Colquill, J.A. (eds) 2005, *Handbook of Organizational Justice*, Mahwah, N.Y.: Lawrence Erlbaum.

Guest, D. 1987, 'Human resource management and industrial relations', *Journal of Management Studies* 24(5): 503–21.

Guest, D. 1998a, 'Is the psychological contract worth taking seriously?', *Journal of Organizational Behavior* 19: 649–64.

Guest, D. 1998b, 'On meaning, metaphor and the psychological contract: a response to Rousseau (1998)', *Journal of Organizational Behavior* 19: 673–7.

Guest, D. 1999, 'Human resource management: the workers' verdict', *Human Resource Management Journal* 9(3): 5–25.

Guest, D. 2002, 'Human resource management, corporate performance and employee wellbeing: building the worker into HRM', *Journal of Industrial Relations* 44(3): 335–58.

Hall, S. 2001, 'Foucault: power, knowledge and discourse', in M. Wetherell, S. Taylor & S. Yates (eds) *Discourse Theory and Practice: A Reader*, London: Sage, pp. 72–81.

Hiltrop, J.-M. 1995, 'The changing psychological contract: the human resource challenge of the 1990s', *European Management Journal* 13(3): 286–94.

Huczynski, A. 1993, *Management Gurus: What Makes Them and How to Become One*, London: Routledge.

Huselid, M.A. 1995, 'The impact of human resource management practices on turnover, productivity, and corporate financial performance', *Academy of Management Journal* 38(3): 635–72.

Jacques, R. 1996, *Manufacturing the Employee: Management Knowledge from the 19th to the 21st Centuries*, London: Sage.

Kärreman, D. & Alvesson, M. 2001, 'Making newsmakers: conversational identities at work', *Organization Studies* 22(1): 59–90.

Keenoy, T. & Anthony, P. 1992, 'HRM: metaphor, meaning and morality', in P. Blyton & P. Turnbull (eds) *Reassessing Human Resource Management*, London: Sage, pp. 233–52.

Kessler, I. & Undy, R. 1996, *The New Employment Relationship: Examining the Psychological Contract*, London: Institute of Personnel and Development.

Knights, D. & Morgan, G. 1991, 'Strategic discourses and subjectivity: towards a critical analysis of corporate strategy in organizations', *Organization Studies* 12(3): 251–73.

Knights, D. & Willmott, H. 1989, 'Power and subjectivity at work', *Sociology*, 23(4): 535–58.

Konovsky, M. 2000, 'Understanding procedural justice and its impact on business organizations', *Journal of Management* 26(3): 489–511.

Lawler, E.E. 1992, *The Ultimate Advantage: Creating the High-Involvement Organization*, San Francisco: Jossey-Bass.

Legge, K. 1995, *Human Resource Management: Rhetorics and Realities*, London: Macmillan.

Legge, K. 1998, 'The morality of HRM', in C. Mabey, D. Skinner & T. Clark (eds) *Experiencing Human Resource Management*, London: Sage, pp. 112–45.

Legge, K. 2000, 'Silver bullet or spent round? Assessing the meaning of the 'high commitment management'/performance relationship', in J. Storey (ed.) *Human Resource Management: A Critical Text*, 2nd edn, London: Thomson Learning, pp. 21–36.

Meyer, J.P. & Allen, N.J. 1997, *Commitment in the Workplace*, Thousand Oaks, Calif.: Sage.

Micklethwait, J. & Wooldridge, A. 1996, *The Witch Doctors: What the Management Gurus are Saying, Why It Matters and How to Make Sense of It*, New York: Heinemann.

Moorman, R.H., Niehoff, B.P. & Organ, D.W. 1993, 'Treating employees fairly and organizational citizenship behavior: sorting the effects of job satisfaction, organizational commitment, and procedural justice', *Employee Responsibilities and Rights Journal* 6(3): 209–25.

O'Doherty, D. & Willmott, H. 2001, 'Debating labour process theory: the issue of subjectivity and the relevance of poststructuralism', *Sociology* 35(2): 457–76.

Oswick, C., Keenoy, T. & Grant, D. 2000, 'Discourse, organizations and organizing: concepts, objects and subjects', *Human Relations* 52(9): 1115–24.

Palmer, I. & Hardy, C. 2000, *Thinking about Management*, London: Sage.

Peters, T. & Waterman, R. 1982, *In Search of Excellence*, New York: Harper & Row.

Pfeffer, J. 1998, *The Human Equation*. Boston, Mass.: Harvard Business School Press.

Phillips, N. & Hardy, C. 1997, 'Managing multiple identities: discourse legitimacy and resources in the UK refugee system', *Organization* 4(2): 159–85.

Phillips, N. & Hardy, C. 2002, *Discourse Analysis: Investigating Processes of Social Construction*, Thousand Oaks, Calif: Sage.

Podsakoff, P.M., MacKenzie, S.B, Paine, J.B & Bachrach, D.G. 2000, 'Organizational citizenship behaviors: a critical review of the theoretical and empirical literature and suggestions for future research', *Journal of Management* 26: 513–63.

Potter, J. & Wetherell, M. 1987, *Discourse and Social Psychology*, London: Sage.

Ramsay, H., Scholarios, D. & Harley, B. 2000, 'Employees and high-performance work systems: testing inside the black box', *British Journal of Industrial Relations* 38(4): 501–31.

Robinson, S.L, 1996, 'Trust and breach of the psychological contract', *Administrative Science Quarterly* 41(4): 574–99.

Rousseau, D.M. 1990, 'New hire perceptions of their own and their employer's obligations', *Journal of Organizational Behavior* 11: pp. 89–400.

Rousseau, D.M. 1995, *Psychological Contracts in Organizations: Understanding Written and Unwritten Agreements*, London: Sage.

Rousseau, D.M. 1998, 'The "problem" of the psychological contract considered', *Journal of Organizational Behavior* 19: 665–71.

Schuler, R.S. 1992, 'Strategic human resource management: linking the people with the strategic needs of the business', *Organizational Dynamics* 21(3): 18–32.

Schuler, R.S. & Jackson, S. 1987, 'Linking competitive strategies with human resource management practices', *Academy of Management Executive* 1(3): 209–213.

Scott, A. 1994, *Willing Slaves? British Workers Under Human Resource Management*, Cambridge University Press.

Steyaert, C. & Janssens, M. 1999, 'Human and inhuman resource management: saving the subject', *Organization* 6(2), 181–98.

Storey, J. 1992, *Developments in the Management of Human Resources*, Oxford: Basil Blackwell.

Sveningsson, S. & Alvesson, M. 2003, 'Managing managerial identities: organizational fragmentation, discourse and identity struggle', *Human Relations* 56(10): 1163–93.

Thompson, P. & Ackroyd, S. 1995, 'All quiet on the workplace front? A critique of recent trends in British industrial sociology', *Sociology* 29(4): 615–33.

Thompson, P. & McHugh, D. 1995, *Work Organisations: A Critical Introduction*, 2nd edn, London: Macmillan.

Tichy, N., Fombrum, C. & Devanna, M.A. 1982, 'Strategic human resource management', *Sloan Management Review* 23(2): 98–113.

Tinker, T. 2002, 'Spectres of Marx and Braverman in the twilight of post-structuralist labour process research', *Work, Employment and Society* 16(2): 251–81.

Townley, B. 1994, *Reframing Human Resource Management: Power, Ethics and the Subject at Work*, London: Sage.

Walton, R. 1985, 'From control to commitment in the workplace', *Harvard Business Review* 64(5): 12–16.

Willmott, H. 1993, 'Strength is ignorance; slavery is freedom: managing culture in modern organizations', *Journal of Management Studies* 30(4): 515–52.

Willmott, H. 2003, 'Renewing strength: corporate culture revisited', *M@n@gement* 6(3): 73–87.

CHAPTER FIFTEEN

CONSTRUCTING OLDER WORKERS
Cultural Meanings of Age and Work

Susan Ainsworth

Older workers have been attracting increasing public, government, academic and organisational interest over the last two decades. Demographic projections are often cited to emphasise the importance of the issue, for example the International Labour Organisation has estimated that by 2025, 32 per cent of the population in Europe will be over 55 years compared to 30 per cent in North America, 21 per cent in Asia, and 17 per cent in Latin America (Ilmarinen 2001). In the year 2000, the median age of a worker in the USA was 40 years, the age at which they are considered to be an 'older worker' under the *Age Discrimination and Employment Act* (McMahan & Phillips 2000). More broadly, the consequences of population ageing constitute a central concern for advanced industrialised countries; for example, the proportion of the Japanese population over 65 years is currently 20 per cent and by 2025 it is expected to increase to 29 per cent, and 36 per cent by 2050 (Pearson 2003), while in Australia, forecasts project that by 2021 more than 20 per cent of the population will be over 65 years (Encel 2003). As a result, governments and organisations in many countries are concerned with the implications of an older workforce and its potential impact on economic growth, productivity, labour and skill shortages. It is, however, arguably the economic effects of supporting ageing populations that preoccupies governments.

This chapter begins by reviewing reasons for current interest in older workers and reflects on the assumptions underpinning such interest. On the basis of this review, I argue that if we are to better understand the persistence of negative attitudes about older workers, more attention needs to be paid to the cultural meanings of age and work. Accordingly, in the second part of the chapter, I advocate an approach to the study of older workers that draws on insights from cultural studies and age theory. From this perspective, the meanings of age and work can be understood as socially constructed, variable and contingent on particular circumstances. By itself, however, it is insufficient because we need to understand *how* such meanings are constructed, and thus how they are reproduced and maintained. In this context, discourse analysis offers methods of exploring processes of social construction as well as providing an established body of work examining how prejudice about different social groups is perpetuated in discourse. Together, social construction and discourse analysis give a way of 'rethinking' the study of older workers that enables exploration of the cultural meanings of age and work and how negative stereotypes about older workers are able to persist.

INTEREST IN 'OLDER WORKERS'

Alarmed by the prospect of labour shortages and growing burdens on state budgets, governments have responded to the 'problem' of ageing populations by developing policies and programs designed to encourage older people to remain in the workforce for as long as possible and to retrain (Encel 2003; and see Uren 2004). Yet despite such measures, many countries encounter declining labour force participation rates (for older men), and early exit from the workforce (Duncan 2003), and once unemployed, older workers face difficulties in regaining employment, experiencing longer periods of unemployment than younger workers (Redman & Snape 2002).

In this context, research, media and policy discussion of older workers exhibits some recurring themes: the consequences of population ageing; shifts in state support for older people; the declining labour force participation of older men; social equity concerns about older workers as a disadvantaged group; and the changing nature of work and retirement.

Population ageing

The ageing of populations in developed economies has been a key factor in the interest in older workers. It has become a convention for researchers to cite a variety of demographic forecasts to underscore the importance of their project, often accompanied by two key assumptions. The first is that the demographic projections of population ageing construct a social and economic problem about which something needs to be done – 'a looming old age crisis' in the language of the World Bank (Saunders 1996), a view described as 'apocalyptic demography' by Clark (1993) and symptomatic of a 'new ageism' (Butler 1989). Second, if older people are experiencing problems remaining in, or re-entering, the labour market, a substantial future increase in this segment of the population will exacerbate this situation. It is arguably the first issue that has received the most interest. Attention has focused mainly on the budgetary and economic consequences of population ageing, that is, whether a society can afford its ageing population (Saunders 1996; see, for example, Commonwealth of Australia 2002 and Productivity Commission 2005), rather than on the wider social implications of population ageing. This has important implications for the way the issue is framed in the public domain: rather than seeing increasing longevity as a social achievement (Butler 1989), older people risk being constructed as an economic burden on the rest of society.

The changing role of state support

Public policy interest in the subject of older workers has a similar underlying concern with the costs of an economically dependent ageing population. Indeed Saunders (1996) argues that while the issue has been presented as a 'crisis of ageing', it more accurately reflects a political crisis as governments struggle to respond to changing structures and composition of society. Considerable debate over the future viability of the welfare state is one expression of this crisis and, in the UK and the USA, has taken the form of intergenerational conflict over resources where an economically dependent older population is seen as a burden on the younger productive members of society (Butler 1989; Laczko & Phillipson 1991; Ginn & Arber 1995; Saunders 1996).

In Australia employment has been a more recent addition to an ageing policy agenda traditionally dominated by health and social security. This reflects a broadening view of the older population to include productive older people rather than just the frail and dependent aged, as well as a key shift in ideology regarding the role of the state. The focus on assisting older people to remain employed is an expression of an ideology of financial self-reliance as against one of collective or state support through mechanisms such as social security and the state-funded pension. This link was demonstrated by the release of two 'companion' discussion papers in 1999 (the International Year of Older Persons) by the then Minister for Aged Care, Senator Bronwyn Bishop, one on employment for mature workers (Commonwealth of Australia 1999a) and the other entitled *Independence and Self Provision* (Commonwealth of Australia 1999b). This illustrates that the policy focus on older workers at least partly stems from an underlying concern over the costs of supporting an ageing population who have become, in many cases, detached from the labour force and reliant on state support.

Declining labour force participation rate of older men

The declining labour force participation rate of older men is closely linked to the current concern over the economic implications of population ageing. At a time when people are living longer, the proportion of older men remaining in the workforce has decreased, relative to other age groups (Laczko & Phillipson 1991). Thus the concern over the budgetary consequences of an ageing population is also partly about the costs of supporting a growing number of older people (particularly men) no longer in full-time work (Johnson & Zimmerman 1993; Saunders 1996). In the 1980s and 1990s, older men left the workforce at earlier ages than in previous periods due to redundancy and early retirement programs used to reduce the size of the workforce, in response to economic recession and industry restructuring, and created large groups of displaced workers (Sum & Fogg 1990a,b). Evidence also suggests that much of the early exit was involuntary – significant numbers of older workers wanted to continue working according to surveys in the USA and Australia (White Riley & Riley Jr 1989; Bennington & Tharenou 1996; Encel & Studencki 1996) – and these people subsequently faced substantial barriers to re-employment (Laczko & Phillipson 1991). While the rapid decline of participation in the labour force among older men might initially have been the result of organisational responses to economic recession, this decline did not reverse with improved economic conditions, although there is some evidence to suggest that it has stabilised more recently (Encel 2003). However, Johnson & Zimmerman (1993) have argued that significant intervention would be required to halt or reverse the trend to early retirement.

Thus the growing number of older men no longer in full-time work appears to be central to concerns over public expenditure on the aged.

Social equity

Older workers have also attracted interest from researchers, the media and policy-makers because of their burgeoning status as a disadvantaged group in the community. Their potential economic and social vulnerability is in part due to their marginal attachment to the workforce and lack of access to income. For example, once unemployed, older people experience much longer average rates of joblessness than other groups (Council on the Ageing 1999; VandenHeuvel 1999; Redman & Snape 2002): the average duration of unemployment for people over 55 was 104 weeks for males and 107 weeks for females in 1998 compared to an average duration of all males of 70 weeks and 52 weeks for females (VandenHeuvel 1999). There are also definable subgroups of the older population who are both 'at risk' and likely to experience future growth such as older single women, who exhibit a marginal attachment to the labour force (Ginn & Arber 1995), and some ethnic groups who may have had fewer opportunities to accumulate social and economic capital in the form of skills, education and continuous work histories. Such subgroups may attract particular social policy and research attention due to their extreme economic and social disadvantage.

In addition, social equity concerns have focused on age discrimination in employment. Age discrimination persists despite a body of research debunking many of the widely held prejudices and stereotypes about older workers (Levine 1988; White Riley & Riley Jr 1989; Laczko & Phillipson 1991; Chapman 1993; Johnson & Zimmerman 1993; Warr 1994; Bennington & Tharenou 1996; Lim 2003). For example, studies have explored stereotypes about inevitable age-related intellectual decline and found that few generalisations can be made about differences in learning ability and memory between younger and older adults and that intelligence in older adults is marked by both growth and decline (Levine 1988; Staudinger et al. 1989; Cremer 1994; Warr 1994; Agarwal & deGroote 1998). Such stereotypes have been found to influence employment-related decisions in areas such as recruitment, training and development, performance appraisal and redundancy (Rosen & Jerdee 1976; Cleveland & Landy 1983; Ferris et al. 1985; Avolio & Barrett 1987; Finkelstein et al. 1995).

Many of the widely held stereotypes about older workers are negative, for example that older workers are less motivated, less able to learn, possess fewer physical abilities and are more resistant to change than younger workers (Cleveland & Landy 1983). However, even the positive qualities of older workers identified in qualitative research on employers' perceptions, such as reliability, personal maturity, stability and punctuality (Finkelstein et al. 1995; Oswick 1998) are 'negative' in that they stand in opposition to the mercurial qualities valued in current business environments, such as flexibility and dynamism (Encel 1999).

Change in key social institutions

Interest in older workers has also arisen because of major changes in key institutions (such as stable full-time work and secure retirement) and in the social roles available to older people. Such changes have prompted researchers to explore these social trends in ageing. For example, within the space of a decade, the meaning of retirement fundamentally altered: in the 1980s retirement was seen as the permanent withdrawal from the labour force at a specific age, for example 62 or 65 (Doeringer 1990; Mitchell 1993), whereas from the 1990s it signified a much more uncertain and diverse process. From then on it included time spent in transition or 'bridge' jobs perhaps unrelated to previous occupation (Doeringer 1990), periods of unemployment following early exit from work, becoming a 'discouraged job-seeker', being eligible for state support under the category of long-term disability, or partial withdrawal from the workforce and working in part-time or casual jobs (Laczko & Phillipson 1991).

Overall, pathways from work to retirement have become more complex and heterogeneous because of labour market changes, such as the move to more flexible forms of employment and legislative changes ending compulsory or mandatory retirement in countries such as the USA and Australia. At a more fundamental level, the fragmentation of secure retirement, changes in the welfare state and the goal of full employment have led to ambiguity in the identity and social status of older people (Phillipson 1998), leading to a 'crisis in the identity of ageing' (Laczko & Phillipson 1991; Phillipson 1998). Old age now appears as a 'roleless role' due to a 'structural lag' or mismatch between the roles available to older people and their strengths, capacities, skills and abilities (White Riley & Riley Jr 1989; Taylor & Walker 1998). To compensate, some have envisaged that older people should occupy roles as consumers or sustainers of communities and culture in their later years, sometimes referred to as the 'Third Age' (Laslett 1987; Manheimer 1998; Curran & Blackburn 2001). But this is problematic because it assumes that older people have access to resources while, for many people in their fifties, retirement income is inadequate and there are substantial barriers in returning to paid work roles (Ginn & Arber 1995; Elder 1997).

While there are a number of reasons for the increasing attention older workers have received from government, researchers and the media, one prominent theme is the underlying concern about the economic consequences of population ageing and public expenditure on older people. As a result, population ageing and older workers have been constructed as problems or crises that warrant government and public action. But not all research shares this perspective; some focuses more on understanding and exploring the broader implications of these social trends (Ginn & Arber 1995; Saunders 1996). The differences between these approaches reflect a more fundamental diversity in the ideological assessment of older people and their role in society: the interest in older people as workers is underpinned by cultural values towards older people, yet these have rarely been the subject of explicit discussion. This constitutes an important gap, particularly given the persistence of age-based stereotypes despite research disproving their accuracy and the lack of impact such research has had on business and organisational practices in relation to older workers (Encel 1999). In order to investigate these cultural meanings of age and work, it is necessary to go beyond the traditional fields associated with research on older workers (such as economics, industrial relations and psychology [see Ainsworth & Hardy 2004]), and draw on insights from cultural studies, age theory and discourse analysis.

AGE AS A CULTURAL CONSTRUCTION

Research and theory on ageing within cultural studies explicitly focus on the meaning of ageing (for example Atchley 1993; Friedan 1994; Hazan 1994; Gullette 1997; Warren 1998; Andrews 1999; Tulle-Winton 1999) and challenge biologically determinist views of age. Such a perspective does not suggest there is no biological change with ageing but that the meaning of these changes is culturally and socially constructed (Gullette 1997) and contingent on context. Work in cultural studies offers a number of important insights relevant to understanding older workers and their labour market experiences. First, it provides a basis for exploring the contingent nature of the older worker category: in research and policy discussion, the category of 'older worker' is often unclear in meaning; for example, threshold chronological ages for inclusion range from 40 to 65, with a trend for the lower age limit to be set at progressively younger ages. Moreover, individuals are considered 'older workers' at different ages depending on their gender, occupation and industry. Women are reported to experience age discrimination at earlier ages than men (Bernard et al. 1995; Ginn & Arber 1995; McMullin 1995; Encel & Studencki 1997) and there are age associations with certain jobs and industries that reflect collective cultural beliefs (and stereotypes) about ageing: older age may be acceptable in professions such as law but not in 'new economy' sectors such as information technology. Drawing on insights from cultural studies and approaching older workers as a culturally constructed category provide a way of exploring this fluidity and contingency and understanding negative collective beliefs about older workers.

Second, they provide a way of conceptualising negative beliefs about older workers and their persistence in the face of 'rational' evidence to the contrary. It has become well accepted that gender and ethnicity are socially constructed categories (Fulcher & Scott 1999), and age can also be understood as a body-based system of social categorisation, rather than an objective phenomenon. Older age is not the only stage of the lifecycle that is socially and culturally constructed, but it is the target of particular cultural ambivalence and hostility. This is evident in the tendency towards denying the category altogether, as a way of dealing with the issue of older age:

> there is not much serious discussion about eliminating infancy, adolescence or adulthood from the developmental landscape. It is only old age which comes under the scalpel. Why? Why is this such an appealing strategy to so many? . . . We do not fight sexism or racism solely by challenging the existence of the categories of sex and race (though these, too, are social constructs, and as such remain contested territory). (Andrews 1999: 302)

While there are clear parallels between age and other body-based systems of social categorisation, such as gender or ethnicity, one feature that distinguishes ageism from sexism or racism is its element of self-hatred. Ageism directed against the old is hostility towards a future self, not a clearly differentiated 'other':

> Ageism is unique in that those who practise it will one day join the group they presently discriminate against, if longevity is granted them . . . The key lies in the ability of people to see old people not as an extension of their future (or even present) selves, but rather as totally apart from themselves. (Andrews 1999: 303)

While many people may be able to maintain a perception of older people as totally separate from themselves, the point at which people identify with the category of older age and the 'mid-life' has been described as a process of 'self-labelling'. The entrance to older age is created and signified by language use, according to Gullette (1997). For example, when an individual notices biological or physical change and attributes it to, or describes it as, age-related decline, they are reproducing or sustaining the 'master cultural narrative' of ageing as inevitable decline.

Moreover, ageing can be seen as an embodied process, that is, a gendered and biomedicalised body is the site of ageing (Warren 1998; Tulle-Winton 1999). The cultural meanings of physical change associated with ageing lead to social, cultural and economic change for older people – a shift in their position in society. According to Warren (1998), Western societies have a long history of cultural ambivalence towards ageing, seeing it as a form of 'bodily betrayal'. The ageing body is a 'cultural icon of decline and helplessness' (Tulle-Winton 1999: 297) and represents the key link between the processes of ageing and the social status and identity of older people. While cultural studies generally has been criticised for neglecting 'the economic' and issues of work and employment (Morris 1988; du Gay 1996, 1997), a connection can be made between the commodification of the body and its relationship to the removal of older people from the workforce: the cultural construction of physical decline beginning in the 'mid-life' period is underpinned by the increasing economic insecurity among that group expressed through early retirement, increased competition for jobs, unemployment or decline in status and earnings in flexible employment (Gullette 1997).

While being perceived as 'older' represents a barrier to gaining or retaining employment, the ageing process and its techniques of minimisation are providing growing employment opportunities. Substantial growth has occurred in industries concerned with combating or disguising the signs of physical ageing, or 'anti-ageing' (as it is commonly promoted in popular culture and the health, beauty and self-help industries), and 'successful ageing', which involves adapting to the changes of old age and loss and the use of 'lifestyle choices' to fulfil the health and welfare needs of individuals (Tulle-Winton 1999). However, the economic resources required to participate in the techniques of successful ageing are less secure. Thus there is a simultaneous commodification of the body through the growing commercial activity associated with 'successful ageing' and a 'decommodification' of older people as they are forced out of the labour market.

While less focused on influencing organisations and government than some other disciplinary fields (such as labour market research, economics or psychology), cultural studies research on ageing could enable the radical 'rethinking' of policies and practices related to older workers. A constructionist approach to age identity asserts that any meaning of older age is contingent on social and historical context, and reflects the meaning-making of a given community. Thus the common understanding of an object or situation is not 'inevitable' because it can be shown to have developed in relation to particular circumstances (Hacking 2000). Such contingency has a radical potential by demonstrating that certain situations or versions of reality that are 'taken for granted' are not 'natural': in Hacking's (2000: 49) terms the central project of social constructionism is to show that 'things are not what they seem' and 'social constructionists teach that items we had thought were inevitable are social products' (2000: 47). It follows therefore that these socially constructed meanings do not have to remain the way they are, and as such are open to the possibility of change.

But the radical potential of social constructionism has been 'blunted' by its indiscriminate use in research. The term has become so widely used that it risks becoming 'meaningless' and stale: 'the metaphor of social construction once had excellent shock value, but now it has become tired' (Hacking 2000: 35). As social construction has itself become commonplace, fashionable and another 'dominant paradigm', it has become a 'dead' rather than a living metaphor in the sense that it is used so often people are no longer aware it is a metaphor (Fowler 1926 in Hacking 2000: 49). Hacking (2000: 49) argues that one way of rescuing social construction from such 'fatigue' is to return to the original metaphor of constructing, that is, building or assembling from parts:

> Construction has become stale. It can be freshened up if we insist that the metaphor retain one element of its literal meaning, that of building, or assembling from parts . . . If we are to return 'construction' to life, we should attend to its ordinary meanings, as in constructing a five-string banjo. The core idea, from Latin to now, is that of building, of putting together.

DISCOURSE ANALYSIS: EXPLORING THE PROCESSES OF CONSTRUCTION

It is in the context of these comments that the value of discourse analysis becomes evident. Combined with a social constructionist epistemology, discourse analysis can be used to study the products and the processes of social construction, in other words, how meanings of objects and situations are 'put together'. Within discourse analysis, language is not seen as a 'transparent' medium used to represent an objective reality, but as a shared social resource and a key means of actively constructing the meaning of reality and objects within it. Language, and discourse more broadly (the latter encompassing non-linguistic semiotic modes), creates 'the social world in a continuous, ongoing way; it does not simply reflect what is assumed to be already there' (Wood & Kroger 2000: 4). Discourse has been variously defined as a 'recognizable collection of statements which cohere together' (Wetherell 2001: 194), the 'institutionalized use of language and language-like sign systems' (Davies & Harré 1990: 47), the 'set of social practices which "make meaning"' (Jaworski & Coupland 1999: 7) or as du Gay (1996: 43) has expressed it,

> a group of statements which provide a language for talking about a topic and a way of producing a particular kind of knowledge about a topic. Thus the term refers both to the production of knowledge through language and representations and the way that knowledge is institutionalized, shaping social practices and setting new practices into play.

Studying discourse thus means more than examining language use. It entails studying language use (and other systems of meaning) as a form of social practice (Fairclough 1992; Candlin 1997), as a way of reflecting and shaping society (Jaworski & Coupland 1999) by constructing versions of the social order.

Discourse analysis has the potential to rescue constructionism from its 'fatigued' state by providing multiple approaches and methods that enable exploration of the processes of social construction. For example, approaches differ in their level of analysis: some focus on the micro-level of language use whereas others discuss discourse as a much broader phenomenon as a way of communicating about a particular topic – as in the 'discourse of enterprise' (for example Burchell 1993; du Gay 1996, 2004). There are studies that focus on the structure of 'text and talk' while others discuss discourse in more abstract and philosophical terms. Other distinctions can be drawn between studies that are descriptive and attend to local language use and those that are critical and focus on the relationship between discourse and broader social and political contexts (van Dijk 1997a; Jaworski & Coupland 1999; Alvesson & Karreman 2000). But discourse analysis also provides ways of connecting different dimensions, for example of showing how local features of communication are linked to broader social characteristics: 'It can let us see how macro-structures are carried through micro-structures' (Jaworski & Coupland 1999: 13).

While newcomers to discourse analysis may find the range of methods and approaches 'bewildering' (Burman & Parker 1993), it is this variety that can potentially revitalise social constructionism. By providing different ways of exploring how objects are constructed, construction can be 'brought back to life'. Moreover, different approaches to discourse analysis can provide insights into processes of construction at different levels of analysis and provide ways of connecting these levels, showing, for example, how language use shapes, and is shaped by, broader society.

'Discourses of difference'

In addition to this methodological contribution, there is an established body of discursive research exploring the contingent nature of identity and how collective beliefs and prejudice about social groups are maintained and reproduced in discourse. Social categorisation is central to constructions of social groups – through discourse, various classifications or 'concepts' of people are 'brought into being' that have important practical effects for those targeted by these categories and those involved in their construction. Discourse constructs social or collective identity (Mumby & Clair 1997; Hardy et al. 2000) by defining groups, groups' interests, their position within society and their relationship to other groups (van Dijk 1997b), acting as an interpretive frame for action (du Gay 1996). It indicates to people what they should think about a particular issue or group of people and, in doing so, functions as a mechanism through which collective group interests are played out in the social practices of individuals (van Dijk 1997b). Language users engage in text and talk not just as individuals but also as members of multiple social categories, and they construct and display these social identities in discourse. The power of such views is not derived from their 'truth', accuracy or logical consistency, but from their social effectiveness in assisting groups to maintain their power and further their interests (van Dijk 1997b). This suggests how prejudice and negative stereotypes are able to be sustained and do not 'collapse' by revealing their inaccuracy or logical contradictions – they do not operate as logical, rational discourse (van Dijk 1984; du Gay 1996; de Cilia et al. 1999).

While such categories or social identities may seem natural and obvious, discursive research has been particularly important in showing how they are contingent, unstable and the product of particular historical circumstances (Hall 1996). Identity's relational nature contributes to its contingency and instability: it is achieved by differentiating and excluding that which is 'other', though such exclusion is conditional and apparent (Laclau 1990). Such definition and differentiation always occur within discourse and representation, not outside it (Hall 1996). Yet such definitions are never fixed or stable as they are the outcome of a complex and contradictory interplay of discourses (Garsten & Grey 1997; Hardy et al. 2000). Thus social identity may be fragmented, ambiguous and subject to continuous reproduction through political, social and discursive processes (Hardy et al. 2000).

The construction of social identity has been the focus of a number of studies collectively termed 'discourses of difference' (Wodak 1996) or the discursive 'politics of representation' (Hall 1997; Pickering 2001). Such research explores the discursive construction of identity of marginalised groups, most often relating to gender and ethnic or racial identities. For example, discursive studies of gender have explored how talk and behaviour constructs, reproduces and resists masculine and feminine identities (Tannen 1994; Nilan 1995; Cameron 1997; Edley & Wetherell 1997; Mumby & Clair 1997; West et al. 1997; Alvesson 1998; Stokoe 1998). Other discursive research has focused on the construction of racial and ethnic identities; for example, exploring how dominant racist stereotypes are reinforced by the media using frames (rhetorical devices that define or assign interpretation to the social event [Clair 1993: in Mumby & Clair 1997]) which influence how people come to understand a topic (van Dijk 1996; Mumby & Clair 1997). Other research has looked at how racism is enacted and perpetuated in talk about minority groups in terms both of the content of talk and the language used (Wodak & Matouschek 1993; Bigler 1996; van Dijk 1997c; van Dijk et al. 1997; Wodak 1997; Kleiner 1998; de Cilia et al. 1999).

In contrast, the discursive construction of age identity has been less frequently studied. Some research has focused on 'youth' identities (Williams et al. 1997; Tannock 1999). Other research has explored the discursive construction of older age identities in relation to health and aged care services (Coupland et al. 1991; Stephenson et al. 1999; Ylanne-McEwen 2000), intergenerational relations and constructions of age across the life-course (Coupland et al. 1991; Coupland & Nussbaum 1993). But few discursive studies have focused specifically on the intersection of age and work identities. One exception is Tretheway's (2001) exploratory study on mid-life professional women and their reproduction of, and resistance to, the 'master narrative' of 'ageing-as-decline' (Gullette 1997: 160–1). Tretheway concludes that the 'enterprise ideal' promoted by contemporary work organisations disadvantages 'middle-aged' women as it makes them individually responsible for managing their 'aged' selves through strategies of consumption and self-presentation. Tretheway draws on both feminist literature and cultural and political frameworks influenced by Foucault (Miller & Rose 1990; du Gay 1996) to critique the emphasis within liberal feminism and enterprise discourse on self-interest and individual self-reliance which, she argues, undermines the 'collective critical consciousness' (Mumby 1997: 371 in Tretheway 2001) needed to transform organisations and age-based identities.

Thus while the topic of older workers has been of marginal interest to discourse scholars to date, discourse analysis provides an established basis for exploring both the contingent nature of age and work identity and its relationship to context, as well as how ageism and negative stereotypes are reproduced and maintained in discourse. By showing how ageism operates in discourse, such an approach can also identify possibilities for resistance and change: if the meaning of 'older workers' can be shown to be a cultural construction, the product of particular circumstances, and the outcome of identifiable discursive mechanisms, then the 'rethinking' of older workers becomes more realisable.

CONCLUSION

Older workers have been the subject of an increasingly prominent focus in academic research and policy debates. But much of this work takes the 'older worker' category for granted. In this chapter I have argued for the rethinking of this category as a way of unpacking assumptions, including those based on views of older people as 'problematic' and a potential economic and social burden. Such rethinking can be facilitated by drawing on other disciplines of enquiry and I have explored how cultural studies, social constructionism and discourse analysis could add to our understanding of older workers. Such an approach provides a basis for examining some of the recurring features and underlying assumptions of public and academic commentary on older workers. Specifically, it enables investigation of the cultural meanings of age and work, how those meanings are constructed and perpetuated in discourse, and thus how negative prejudice and stereotypes about older workers are able to be maintained, despite 'objective' research to the contrary.

Such an approach could also start to examine one of the key problems for academic research on older workers – its lack of impact on organisational policies and practices (Encel 1999). A constructive and discursive approach to studying older workers could further explore the connections between commonly held views of older workers and organisational and policy outcomes. This could include examining how certain constructions of older workers are reflected in recruitment, redundancy programs, and training and development practices, as well as legislation and government policy. While the epistemological framework of such an approach precludes demonstrating cause-and-effect relationships, such research would further our understanding of the connections between discourse and material outcomes. It could show how constructing older workers in a certain way, and using particular discursive resources and processes, is reflected in employment practices within organisations as well as in broader economic and social trends. While cultural and discourse studies have been slow to engage with topics such as older workers, they provide potential avenues for reconceptualising and revitalising academic research, and the potential to move policy debates and public commentary beyond 'apocalyptic demography' (Clark 1993).

References

Agarwal, N.C. & deGroote, M.G. 1998, 'Retirement of older workers: issues and policies', *Human Resource Planning* 23(1): 14–25.

Ainsworth, S. & Hardy, C. 2004, 'Critical discourse analysis and identity? Why bother?' *Critical Discourse Studies* 1(2): 225–59.

Alvesson, M. 1998, 'Gender relations and identity at work: a case study of masculinities and femininities in an advertising agency', *Human Relations* 51(8): 969–1005.

Alvesson, M. & Karreman, D. 2000, 'Varieties of discourse analysis: on the study of organizations through discourse analysis', *Human Relations* 53(9): 1125–50.

Andrews, M. 1999, 'The seductiveness of agelessness', *Ageing and Society* 19: 301–18.

Atchley, R.C. 1993, 'Continuity theory and the evolution of activity in later adulthood', in J.R. Kelly (ed.) *Activity and Aging: Staying Involved in Later Life*, London: Sage, pp. 5–16.

Avolio, B.J. & Barrett, G.V. 1987, 'Effects of age stereotyping in a simulated interview', *Psychology and Aging* 2(1): 56–63.

Bennington, L. & Tharenou, P. 1996, 'Older workers: myths, evidence and implications for Australian managers', *Asia Pacific Journal of Human Resources* 34(3) 63–76.

Bernard, M., Itzin, C., Phillipson, C. & Skucha, J. 1995, 'Gendered work, gendered retirement', in S. Arber & J. Ginn (eds) *Connecting Gender and Ageing: A Sociological Approach*, Buckingham: Open University Press, pp. 56–68.

Bigler, E. 1996, 'Telling stories: on ethnicity, exclusion and education in upstate New York', *Anthropology and Education Quarterly* 27(2): 186–203.

Burchell, G. 1993, 'Liberal government and techniques of the self', *Economy and Society* 22(3): 267–81.

Burman, E. & Parker, I. 1993, 'Against discursive imperialism, empiricism and constructionism: thirty-two problems with discourse analysis', in E. Burman and I. Parker (eds) *Discourse Analytic Research: Repertoires and Readings of Texts in Action*, London and New York: Routledge, pp. 155–72.

Butler, R.N. 1989, 'Dispelling ageism: the cross-cutting intervention', *Annals of the American Academy of Political and Social Science* 503: 138–47.

Cameron, D. 1997, 'Performing gender identity: young men's talk and the construction of heterosexual masculinity', in S. Johnson & U.H. Meinhof (eds) *Language and Masculinity*, Oxford: Blackwell, pp. 47–64.

Candlin, C.N. 1997, 'General editor's preface', in B.-L. Gunnarsson, P. Linell & B. Nordberg (eds) *The Construction of Professional Discourse*, London: Longman, pp. ix–xiv.

Chapman, P.G. 1993, 'Discussion' in P. Johnson & K.F. Zimmerman (eds) *Labour Markets in an Ageing Europe*, Cambridge University Press, pp. 146–50.

Clark, P.G. 1993, 'Public policy in the United States and Canada: individualism, familial obligation, and collective responsibility in the care of the elderly' in J. Hendricks and C.J. Rosenthal (eds) *The Remainder of their Days: Domestic Policy and Older Families in the United States and Canada*, New York: Garland Publishing, pp. 13–48.

Cleveland, J.N. and Landy, F.J. 1983, 'The effects of person and job stereotypes on two personnel decisions', *Journal of Applied Psychology* 68(4): 609–19.

Commonwealth of Australia 1999a, *The National Strategy for an Ageing Australia: Employment for Mature Age Workers Issues Paper*, November.

Commonwealth of Australia 1999b, *The National Strategy for an Ageing Australia: Independence and Self Provision Discussion Paper*, November.

Commonwealth of Australia 2002, *Intergenerational Report 2002–03*, 2002–03 Budget Paper no. 5, Canberra: Info Access.

Council on the Ageing 1999, 'Older Australians: working for the future', *Strategic Ageing: Australian Issues in Ageing* 9(19): 10–18.

Coupland, N., Coupland, J. & Giles, H. 1991, *Language, Society and the Elderly: Discourse, Identity and Ageing*, Oxford: Blackwell.

Coupland, N. & Nussbaum, J.F. (eds) 1993, *Discourse and Lifespan Identity*. Newbury Park, CA: Sage.

Cremer, R. 1994, 'Matching vocational training programmes to age-related mental change: a social policy objective', in J. Snel & R. Cremer (eds) *Work and Ageing: A European Perspective*, London: Taylor & Francis, pp. 273–82.

Curran, J. & Blackburn, R.A. 2001, 'Notes and issues: older people and the enterprise society: age and self-employment propensities', *Work, Employment and Society* 15(4): 889–902.

Davies, B. & Harré, R. 1990, 'Positioning: the discursive production of selves', *Journal of Theory of Social Behaviour* 20: 43–65.

De Cilia, R., Reisigl, M. & Wodak, R. 1999, 'The discursive construction of national identities', *Discourse & Society* 10(2): 149–73.

Doeringer, P.B. 1990, 'Economic security, labor market flexibility, and bridges to retirement', in P. Doeringer (ed.) *Bridges to Retirement: Older Workers in a Changing Labor Market*, Ithaca, NY: ILR Press, pp. 3–22.

du Gay, P. 1996, *Consumption and Identity at Work*, London: Sage.

du Gay, P. 1997, 'Introduction', in P. du Gay (ed.) *Production of Culture/Cultures of Production*, London: Sage, pp. 1–10.

du Gay, P. 2004, 'Against "Enterprise" (but not against "enterprise", for that would make no sense)', *Organization* 11(1): 37–57.

Duncan, C. 2003, 'Assessing anti-ageism routes to older worker re-engagement', *Work, Employment and Society* 17(1): 101–20.

Edley, N. & Wetherell, M. 1997, 'Jockeying for position: the construction of masculine identities', *Discourse & Society* 8(2): 203–17.

Elder, J. 1997, Untitled paper presented to Over Fifties Focus Workshop. *Making it Work*. A Collection of Papers Presented at Making it Work: A Major National Summit on the Future of Work in Australia, 23–24 May 1996, Melbourne: Brotherhood of St Laurence, pp. 89–93.

Encel, S. 1999, 'Productivity of mature age workers'. Paper presented to inaugural national Council on the Aging Congress: *Older Australians: a working future?* Adelaide, 7–9 November.

Encel, S. 2003, Age Can Work: The Case for Older Australians Staying in the Workforce. A Report to the Australian Council of Trade Unions and the Business Council of Australia, April.

Encel, S. & Studencki, H. 1996, *Retirement: A Survey*, Sydney: NSW Consultative Committee on Ageing.

Encel, S. & Studencki, H. 1997, *Gendered Ageism: Job Search Experiences of Older Women*, Sydney: NSW Committee on Ageing and the Department for Women.

Fairclough, N. 1992, *Discourse and Social Change*, Cambridge: Polity Press.

Ferris, G.R., Yates, V.L., Gilmore, D.C. & Rowland, K.M. 1985, 'The influence of subordinate age on performance ratings and causal attributions', *Personnel Psychology* 38: 545–57.

Finkelstein, L.M., Burke, M.J. & Raju, N.S. 1995, 'Age discrimination in simulated employment contexts: an integrative analysis', *Journal of Applied Psychology* 80(6): 652–63.

Friedan, B. 1994, *The Fountain of Age*, London: Vintage.

Fulcher, J. & Scott, J. 1999, *Sociology*, Oxford: Oxford University Press.

Garsten, C. & Grey, C. 1997, 'How to become oneself: discourses of subjectivity in post-bureaucratic organizations', *Discourse and Organization* 4(2): 211–28.

Ginn, J. & Arber, S. 1995, '"Only connect": gender relations and ageing', in S. Arber and J. Ginn (eds) *Connecting Gender and Ageing: A Sociological Approach*, Buckingham: Open University Press, pp. 1–14.

Gullette, M.M. 1997, *Declining to Decline: Cultural Combat and the Politics of the Midlife*, Charlottesville, Va: University of Virginia Press.

Hacking, I. 2000, *The Social Construction of What?* Cambridge Mass. and London: Harvard University Press.

Hall, S. 1996, 'Introduction: who needs identity?' in S. Hall & P. du Gay (eds) *Questions of Cultural Identity*, London: Sage, pp. 1–17.

Hall, S. 1997, 'The work of representation', in S. Hall (ed.) *Representation: Cultural Representations and Signifying Practices*, London: Sage in association with The Open University, pp. 15–64.

Hardy, C., Lawrence T.B. & Grant, D. 2000, 'In search of an identity: collective identities and interorganizational collaboration'. Paper presented to the Western Academy of Management Conference, Hawaii, 5–8 April.

Hazan, H. 1994, *Old Age: Constructions and Deconstructions*, Cambridge University Press.

Ilmarinen, J.E. 2001, 'Aging workers', *Occupational and Environmental Medicine* 58(8): 546–57.

Jaworski, A. & Coupland, N. 1999, 'Introduction: perspectives on discourse analysis' in A. Jaworski & N. Coupland (eds) *The Discourse Reader*, London and New York: Routledge, pp. 1–44.

Johnson, P. & Zimmerman, K.F. 1993, 'Ageing and the European labour market: public policy issues', in P. Johnson & K.F. Zimmerman (eds) *Labour Markets in an Ageing Europe*, Cambridge University Press, pp. 1–25.

Kleiner, B. 1998, 'The modern racist ideology and its reproduction in "pseudo-argument"', *Discourse & Society* 9(2): 187–215.

Laclau, E. 1990, *New Reflections on the Revolution of our Time*, London: Verso.

Laczko, F. & Phillipson, C. 1991, *Changing Work and Retirement: Social Policy and the Older Worker*. Buckingham: Open University Press.

Laslett, P. 1987, 'The emergence of the third age', *Ageing and Society* 7(2): 133–160.

Levine, M.L. 1988, *Age Discrimination and the Mandatory Retirement Controversy*, Baltimore: Johns Hopkins University Press.

Lim, V.K.G. 2003, 'An empirical study of older worker attitudes towards the retirement experience', *Employee Relations* 25(4): 330–46.

McMahan, S. & Phillips, K. 2000, 'Aging and employment: characteristics of those working and retired in California', *Journal of Education for Business* 76(1): 11–18.

McMullin, J. 1995, 'Theorizing age and gender relations', in S. Arber and J. Ginn (eds) *Connecting Gender and Ageing: A Sociological Approach*, Buckingham: Open University Press, pp. 30–41.

Manheimer, R.J. 1998, 'The promise and politics of older adult education', *Research on Aging* 20(4): 391–414.

Miller, P. & Rose, N. 1990, 'Governing economic life', *Economy and Society* 19(1): 1–31.

Mitchell, O.S. 1993, 'As the workforce ages' in O.S. Mitchell (ed.) *As the Workforce Ages: Costs, Benefits, and Policy Challenges*. 3–18. Ithaca NY: ILR Press.

Morris, M. 1988, 'Banality in cultural studies', *Discourse* X(2): 3–29.

Mumby, D.K. & Clair, R.P. 1997, 'Organizational discourse', in T.A. van Dijk (ed.) *Discourse as Social Interaction*, London: Sage, pp. 181–205.

Nilan, P. 1995, 'Negotiating gendered identity in classroom disputes and collaboration', *Discourse & Society* 6(1): 27–47.

Oswick, C. 1998, An analysis of age discrimination in employment. Unpublished PhD thesis, King's College, University of London.

Pearson, B. 2003, 'Japan battles an ageing nation', *Weekend Australian Financial Review*, 25–26 October: 10.

Phillipson, C. 1998, *Reconstructing Old Age: New Agendas in Social Theory and Practice*, London: Sage.

Pickering, M. 2001, *Stereotyping: The Politics of Representation*, Basingstoke: Palgrave.

Productivity Commission 2005, *Economic Implications of an Ageing Australia*, Research Report, Canberra.

Redman, T. & Snape, E. 2002, 'Ageism in teaching: stereotypical beliefs and discriminatory attitudes towards the over-50s', *Work, Employment and Society* 16(2): 355–71.

Rosen, B. & Jerdee, T.H. 1976, 'The nature of job-related age stereotypes', *Journal of Applied Psychology* 61(2): 180–3.

Saunders, P. 1996, *Dawning of a New Age? The Extent, Causes and Consequences of Ageing in Australia*, Social Policy Research Centre Discussion Paper no. 75. Sydney: University of New South Wales.

Staudinger, U.M., Cornelius, S.W. & Baltes, P.B. 1989, 'The aging of intelligence: potential and limits', *Annals of the American Academy of Political and Social Science* 503: 43–112.

Stephenson, P.H., Wolfe, N.K., Coughlan, R., & Koehn, S.D. 1999, 'A methodological discourse on gender, independence and frailty: applied dimensions of identity construction in old age', *Journal of Aging Studies* 13(4): 391–401.

Stokoe, E.H. 1998, 'Talking about gender: the conversational construction of gender categories in academic discourse', *Discourse & Society* 9(2): 217–140.

Sum, A.M. & Fogg, W.N. 1990a, 'Labor market and poverty problems of older workers and their families', in P. Doeringer (ed.) *Bridges to Retirement: Older Workers in a Changing Labor Market*, Ithaca, N.Y.: ILR Press, pp. 64–91.

Sum, A.M. & Fogg, W.N. 1990b, 'Profile of the labor market for older workers', in P. Doeringer (ed.) *Bridges to Retirement: Older Workers in a Changing Labor Market*, Cornell University, Ithaca, N.Y.: Industrial and Labor Relations Press, pp. 33–63.

Tannen, D. 1994, *Gender and Discourse*, New York: Oxford University Press.

Tannock, S. 1999, 'Working with insults: discourse and difference in an inner-city youth organization', *Discourse & Society* 10(3): 317–50.

Taylor, P. & Walker, A. 1998, 'Policies and practices towards older workers: a framework for comparative research', *Human Resource Management Journal* 8(3): 61–76.

Tretheway, A. 2001, 'Reproducing and resisting the master narrative of decline', *Management Communication Quarterly* 15(2): 183–226.

Tulle-Winton, E. 1999, 'Growing old and resistance: towards a new cultural economy of old age?' *Ageing and Society* 19: 281–99.

Uren, D. 2004, 'Get super while you work', *Australian*, 26 February, p. 1.

van Dijk, T.A. 1984, *Prejudice in Discourse: An Analysis of Ethnic Prejudice in Cognition and Conversation*, Amsterdam and Philadelphia: John Benjamins Publishing.

van Dijk, T.A. 1996, 'Discourse, power and access', in R. Caldas-Coulthard & M. Coulthard (eds) *Texts and Practices: Readings in Critical Discourse Analysis*, London: Routledge, pp. 84–106.

van Dijk, T. 1997a, 'The study of discourse', in T.A. van Dijk (ed.) *Discourse as Social Structure*, London: Sage, pp. 1–34.

van Dijk, T. 1997b, 'Discourse as interaction in society', in T.A. van Dijk (ed.) *Discourse as Social Interaction*, London: Sage, pp. 1–37.

van Dijk, T. 1997c, 'Political discourse and racism: describing others in Western parliaments' in S.H. Riggins (ed.) *The Language and Politics of Exclusion*, Thousand Oaks, Calif.: Sage, pp. 31–64.

van Dijk, T., Ting-Toomey, S., Smitherman, G. & Troutman D. 1997, 'Discourse, ethnicity, culture and racism', in T.A. van Dijk (ed.) *Discourse as Social Interaction*, London: Sage, pp. 144–80.

VandenHeuvel, A. 1999, 'Older workers: how do they fare in today's labour market'? Paper presented to inaugural national Council on the Ageing Congress, *Older Australians: a working future?* Adelaide, 7–9 November.

Warr, P. 1994, 'Age and job performance', in J. Snel & R. Cremer (eds) *Work and Aging: A European Perspective*, London: Taylor & Francis, pp. 309–22.

Warren, C.A.B. 1998, 'Aging and identity in premodern times', *Research on Aging* 20(1): 11–35.

West, C., Lazar, M.M. & Kramarae, C. 1997, 'Gender in discourse', in T.A. van Dijk (ed.) *Discourse as Social Interaction*, London: Sage, pp. 119–43.

Wetherell, M. 2001, 'Minds, selves and sense-making: editor's introduction', in M. Wetherell, S. Taylor and S.J. Yates (eds) *Discourse Theory and Practice: A Reader*, London: Sage, pp. 186–97.

White Riley, M. & Riley, J.W. Jr 1989, 'The lives of older people and changing social roles', *The Annals of the American Academy of Political and Social Science* 503: 14–28.

Williams, A., Coupland, J. Folwell, A. & Sparks, L. 1997 'Talking about Generation X: defining them as they define themselves', *Journal of Language and Social Psychology* 16(3): 251–77.

Wodak, R. 1996, 'The genesis of racist discourse in Austria since 1989', in C.R. Caldas-Coulthard and M. Coulthard (eds) *Texts and Practices: Readings in Critical Discourse Analysis*, London: Routledge, pp. 107–28.

Wodak, R. 1997, 'Das Ausland and anti-semitic discourse: the discursive construction of the other', in S.H. Riggins (ed.) *The Language and Politics of Exclusion*, Thousand Oaks, Calif.: Sage, pp. 65–87.

Wodak, R. & Matouschek, B. 1993, '"We are dealing with people whose origins one can clearly tell just by looking": critical discourse analysis and the study of neo-racism in contemporary Austria', *Discourse and Society* 4(2): 225–48.

Wood, L.A. & Kroger, R.O. 2000, *Doing Discourse Analysis*, Thousand Oaks, Calif.: Sage.

Ylanne-McEwen, V. 2000, 'Golden times for golden-agers: selling holidays as lifestyle for the over-50s', *Journal of Communication* 50(3): 83–99.

RETHINKING WORK: A REVIEW AND ASSESSMENT

Tim Morris

Time, space and discourse have become important themes in the arena of work and organisation theory in recent years. Time and discourse have each developed as distinctive areas of enquiry (for example Schor 1992; Ancona et al. 2001; Grant et al. 2001; Bluedorn 2002), while space has been a central concept in debates about the globalisation of production and consumption. But what do they tell us about how work is changing? In this concluding chapter, I will review what these themes contribute, first from a policy angle in relation to some of the major changes that are occurring within European economies at this time, and second from the point of view of theoretical development in relation to understanding the contours of work and how they are changing. I argue that thematic approaches, individually and in combination, are a useful way forward, not least because much existing theory does not engage centrally with the concept of work. Using the example of the value chain as it applies in one industry, I will also suggest that we need such thematic approaches to remind ourselves of the changing relationship between value generation and work. I conclude by suggesting some of the ways that research endeavours might proceed in the future.

POLICY IMPLICATIONS FROM A EUROPEAN PERSPECTIVE

From a European perspective, the book's themes link to some of the most important debates on social policy at this time. The context for these debates is residual high unemployment and relatively slug-gish growth in some parts of Europe. This situation reflects important differences within Europe, often characterised as a clash of principles and discourse between the social interventionist model of the continental economies and the more neo-liberal Anglo-American model. Certainly, compared to the Australian economic performance over the past 10 years, many Western European countries have underperformed: the most notable exception to this story of stagnation is Ireland, where GDP per capita is nearly at US levels. These debates have been highlighted by comparing the performance of the UK economy with the 'Eurozone'. The UK has clearly diverged from the dominant pattern, particularly since it left the European exchange rate mechanism in 1992, in growth, inflation and unemployment levels (see *Financial Times* 7 February 2005: 16). Throughout that period the UK has been pursuing policies that are in many respects closer to the US model and that emphasise labour market flexibility, the importance of small business formation, and human capital development as the sources of growth in employment and productivity. According to OECD data, the gap between US and European GDP per capita has widened since the mid-1990s partly because of productivity differences (that is, product per hour worked) but more because of labour resource utilisation, in other words differences in the time worked divided by population (see OECD 2005: chapter 1). Thus time has become a major policy issue in relation to employment.

In particular, the 35-hour working week, adopted in Europe's two largest economies, Germany and France, has come under criticism because it has failed to resolve rather high levels of unemployment: in 2005 France's unemployment rate was just under 10 per cent; Germany's was also around 10 per cent although re-calculations by the federal government put the real figure at 5.2 million unemployed or 12.6 per cent (Federal Labour Bureau 2005). Major employers have argued that the 35-hour week has further weakened the relative competitiveness of their production units. As a result, negotiations between certain key employers and unions in Germany have effectively started to unravel the 35-hour week agreements. Volkswagen has introduced new working arrangements in some plants which exceed 35 hours, and other firms, notably Bosch & Siemens, have negotiated reforms with unions under the tacit threat of moving work into Eastern Europe. In France, commitment to this principle was enshrined in law in 1998 and appears more deeply embedded, but recent statutory amendments have proposed the right for employers to negotiate collective agreements to allow longer hours, and deals to work outside the 35-hour principle are beginning to emerge. From another angle, assumptions about time are central to ongoing discussions across Europe about pension costs and retirement. With ageing populations and underfunded pension systems, governments face difficult and potentially unpopular policy problems which are likely to lead to relaxations in formal retirement ages and incentives to continue working.

In terms of the spatial distribution of work, one can observe major changes resulting from the widening of membership of the European Union with the accession of states in Eastern Europe. Labour markets have been affected by the supply into the economies of Western Europe of mobile workers from the former Eastern bloc. Many of these workers are filling relatively low-skilled jobs in agriculture, construction, services and manufacturing; others with high skill levels are filling jobs in technology and professional services. At the same time, investment in Eastern Europe means that manufacturing jobs are moving away from the higher-cost areas of Western Europe. The most extreme case is arguably the former East Germany, where after initial investment by the German federal government, capital investment dried up. Deep structural unemployment has developed as jobs have migrated either to the east or into the former West Germany. Estimates in 2005 put unemployment in the states of the former East Germany at around 25 per cent.

Thus debates around time and space are at the heart of macro-economic discussions on the future of European economic and social policy. But it is also worth noting that the arguments about radical changes in patterns of work often outrun the evidence of change thus far – the network economy is not the norm. Forecasters fall into either optimist or pessimist camps: changes to work will either destroy security and career opportunities or offer enormous scope for more creative employment with greater control over working processes (Nolan & Wood 2003). While over the last quarter of a century non-standard forms of employment (such as temporary work, part-time employment and self-employment) have grown, four out of five people still work in permanent employment and job tenure rates have remained almost constant (Dickens 2004). Indeed there is some evidence that, in the UK at least, the ratio of full-time permanent employees to others has grown in the last decade and the proportion of workers employed in one specific workplace increased marginally between 1990 and 2000 (Taylor 2002). Across Europe, patterns of change in work appear to be diverging, with some economies seeing growth in full-time employment

(Greece, Portugal and Denmark), others in temporary work (Spain) and others in part-time employment (Bosch 2004). Thus the thrust of the evidence is that while changes in employment are occurring, arguments suggesting the demise of traditional full-time work and lifetime careers (Castells 1996) are not (yet) borne out.

HOW DO THE THEMES OF TIME, SPACE AND DISCOURSE HELP US UNDERSTAND CHANGES TO WORK?

Notwithstanding the evidence of continuity, there is little doubt that in the last part of the 20th century and the early years of the 21st, changes to work, in terms of employment contracts, occupational developments and the substance of tasks and roles, do seem to be emerging. Kallinikos (2003) has referred to these changes as the destandardisation of labour (see also Beck 2000) through changes to work time, the dissolution of work from particular sites, and different forms of labour contract. Another way of expressing this is as the demise of Fordist models of production work, based on fixed schedules, strong time discipline at work and the concentration of production in relatively large-scale factory locations. Associated with this demise of Fordism is declining employment in traditional industries (mining, manufacturing, dock labour), which has affected occupational identities, forms of organisational commitment and notions of trust, career and community; in other words, the ties that bound workers to organisations for much of the 20th century (also see Kitay & Lansbury this volume).

Trends towards greater labour mobility, and towards flexibility in task and worker attitudes, appear to signal important changes in work relating to time, space and discourse. The notion of employment contracts being time-limited seems to be becoming a more accepted part of the discourse of work and careers (Peiperl et al. 2000), even though this form of employment still only predominates in certain project-based industries like information technology or entertainment. Work and consumption also appear to be becoming less concentrated around particular spaces as remote working, virtual linkages and tele-working develop. As service-based employment has expanded, the 'standard hours' model of employment is surely becoming less common both within 'unrationalised labour-intensive' work in industries like home care and security and 'high-skill autonomous' work systems such as professional work (Herzenberg et al. 1998). Linked to this is the important development of the disintegration of production systems commonly linked to lean production techniques, which means that work can be modularised and spatially distributed. The latest example of this trend is the growth of 'offshoring', or the outsourcing of modules of production to other countries, a phenomenon that affects high-value, core production activities in professional services as well as more routine service support activities. Thus work duration and location are components of more distributed and flexible employment models wherein the ability to adapt roles and attitudes is crucial.

In *Rethinking Work*, these themes offer us different types of purchase. Time and space both link to the conceptualisation of work that is usually, but not exclusively, linked to categories of *employment*: that is, full or part-time, temporary or permanent. In contrast, discourse analysis has not been so closely concerned with work *qua* employment; rather it has attempted to get at the meaning of work as it is perceived as a series of subjectively experienced *tasks, working relationships and forms of control* – the lived experience of work more in the tradition of Chicago sociologists or ethnographers such as Studs Terkel. Changes to work have clearly involved changes in both patterns of work time and the distribution of workplaces, but these changes also link to discourses about work. For example, the discourse of flexibility, often linked to the globalisation of production and consumption, is a common descriptor of the major changes in patterns of work and in turn is linked to widespread anxiety about the future prospects for work opportunities and requirements.

It is this difference in the way work is conceptualised through the central themes that, to me, is a strength of this book. For example, the sheer growth of service work and with it the emphasis on customer service, facilitated by technologies that permit constant communications, has clear implications for work/time pressures which are neatly discussed in relation to banking by Cutcher & van den Broek. Ainsworth takes an interesting cultural perspective on how older workers have been problematised in orthodox assumptions about work, productivity and careers (and society in general). By implication, as the workforce continues to 'age' this stigmatisation will have to change, but economic circumstances and labour market demand remain constrained by underlying beliefs. The chapter by Ainsworth & Hall on HRM and ethics demonstrates, for example, how by studying discourse we can understand the way in which the human resource function seeks to construct a role and identity that balance different ideologies and traditions. Michelson & Wailes perceptively link discourse, in this

Figure 16.1 *Representation of value chain in mobile telecoms*

case about ethics, with questions of interests, material strategies and power. Both of these latter chapters display the analytic power of discourse in offering powerful insight into material reality. Further, one can argue that there is an interplay between the discourse and material changes to work. Discourse clearly does more than reflect or make sense of change: by triggering new ways in which the world of work is rationalised, it becomes part of the process whereby institutional changes actually occur. For instance, as this book demonstrates, the discourse about employment flexibility is more than a descriptor of change; it also legitimates (or underpins resistance to) strategies of change to the spatial distribution of work.

One can demonstrate this by displaying and considering a representational form, or model, that is part of everyday discourse and analysis within management today – the value chain (see Figure 16.1). We have come to think of the world of work through such representations; they reveal a great deal while hiding much as well. For one thing, the value chain is a telling example of how business strategy has come to dominate management thinking across the world. Indeed, the resource-based view of the firm, which has been central to strategic theorising in recent years, is said to be a theory of value creation within the firm (Barney 1991). While focusing on distinctive resources and how they are combined as the source of the value-creating process, it says little about work or production as part of this process. In particular, it adopts a highly functional approach to knowledge and the deployment of workers. Yet, having been widely disseminated by business schools, media and publishing groups and consultants (Sahlin-Andersson & Engwall 2002), it is now part of an orthodox discourse about how to understand organisations and the systems in which they are embedded that reflects the hegemony of strategic management. Behind the spread of such ideas about strategic management are important themes concerning the legitimacy that strategic planning and analysis has attained in the discourse among those making key decisions and those advising them. It is, in short, a representational device that aids those with power and it emphasises the notions of value creation and appropriation.

Such models can also help us understand what has changed about work. It is worth remembering that this value chain is a representation of an industry which did not really exist 15 years ago but which is now of global proportions, so that it connects to the themes of changes in time and of space which have also been developed in this book. Thinking of mobile telecommunications as a *product*, it is clear that these devices have facilitated the changing distribution of work and the time in which it is accomplished. They have also had an important influence on forms of discourse through 'texting' and imaging as well as through telephony. It is also evident that such tools have done much to affect the work–life balance, or, more specifically, the relationship between work and non-work time and space for managers, technocrats and experts such that the boundary between these categories is increasingly blurred. With the 'Blackberry' device, is there ever a period when the user is beyond the call of duty?

Further, because it has changed rapidly through the application of – to use the conventional discourse – successive *generations* of technology (3G, 4G etc.), it calls into question what the nature of the product actually is, and therefore how we should understand it. Clearly, it is no longer adequate to define the industry as mobile telephony: it has developed into much more than telephony, and is progressively converging with the computing and media industries. The value chain emphasises the discourse of strategic management in focusing on value, but implicitly it is also a model of the division of production activities, which thereby links value to work. What, then, is a mobile telephone company and what does it do?

Asking this brings the analysis closer to some of the important questions about work itself. The value chain allows us to understand that a mobile telephone company typically does very little of the total production in constructing and delivering telephony – the industry is disintegrated. Mobile telecommunications companies typically coordinate the activities of other producers who make the handset, develop the 'content' and possibly own a communications network. Indeed, such a company may be little more than a brand with a distribution system (for coordinating and selling 'content') and a billing system.

Thus the discourse embedded in the concept of a value chain is paradoxical, revealing everything and nothing. It seems to disconnect the relationship between work and economic value by indicating very little about the nature of the tasks and activities, that is, the production processes and work activities which go to make up this product, or how these are changing. At another level, value chains can express many of the themes and ideas that have been discussed in this book: billing and fault-solving is based on call-centre work, some of which may be out-sourced or 'offshored'. Production of the hardware and software of this industry is globally distributed, involves a progressive shift from man-ufacturing to service-based activity, and facilitates the development of home or remote working and the use of information technologies to coordinate virtual teams in different countries and time zones. In short, the value chain represents a set of ideas and a discourse that has become extremely powerful over the last couple of decades in describing and helping to enact changes to work in terms of time and space.

EXISTING THEORY AND THE BENEFITS OF THEMATIC WORK

So far I have suggested that the themes of this book are relevant to pol-icy issues and help us demystify some of the major changes to work that are occurring. This is also important because they offer us a means of focusing on changes in work in ways that other disciplines or theories have not done or cannot do. Consider, for example, the discipline of industrial relations. Clearly, industrial relations research does have to connect to changes in work if it is to maintain its vitality and, from a European perspective, the decline of the importance of industrial rela-tions as a subject area is more marked than in Australia. Yet changes in work have not been adequately addressed by traditional industrial relations scholarship (Wood 2000). The notion that labour represented a core problem for advanced capitalism, as evidenced by strike pat-terns, fragmented or disorderly collective bargaining systems, low lev-els of worker commitment and challenges to managerial authority in the workplace, drove much of the interest in industrial relations as an academic discipline and as a policy problem, particularly in the UK up to the 1990s. Outside the specialist academic arena, the subsequent decline in interest in the subject reflected changes in the outcomes of industrial relations, such as strikes and labour productivity and changes in the institutions of industrial relations, notably the diminished power of trade unions. Moreover, the rise of HRM as a management func-tion may or may not reflect the demise of industrial relations, enacted through collective bargaining, but it surely reflects a growing confidence among managers in their authority and the belief that work does not inevitably involve conflicts of interest between workers and managers. Clearly, the discourse of HRM is more positive and ambitious in its emphasis on commitment, loyalty and high-performance work systems.

In terms of theory, one problem for industrial relations now is its appropriate scope: industrial relations has been traditionally concerned with the institutional actors in the 'system', essentially unions, managers and the state, and the conduct of their relations through collective bargaining. One consequence of the focus on actors and their relations is that it remains difficult to generate strong, comparative theory-driven analysis. With some honourable exceptions, the default model of textbooks that include cross-national analyses is to offer a series of discrete country-based studies or issue-based comparisons that lack a strong integrating framework. As the state has become less directly interventionist in industrial relations matters, important themes in industrial relations research work have focused on the effectiveness of union strategies to rebuild their power base, such as partnership arrangements in the UK, and the role of law as an agent of change. While broad theories of change in industrial relations are generally built upon some reference to the workplace and to aspects of work and occupations, be it to explain changes in union membership, attitudes to employment or declines in strike activity, the general scope of the subject has not broadened sufficiently to embrace studies of work itself.

It is when industrial relations is defined more broadly to include employment relations, HRM and labour process studies, as in this book, that studies of the process and substance of changes to work and authority relations can be more fruitfully explored. For example, one might argue that a traditional strength of labour process studies is the focus on work: their strength comes from the descriptive base derived from empirical studies, often of new or growing areas of work, such as in call centres, retailing and homeworking. Thus labour process research is often strongly placed to tease out the effects of work changes in terms of temporal, spatial and discursive dimensions. Their emphasis on the day-to-day forms of work organisation, and the material consequences of what are otherwise usually characterised in rather abstract terms as organisational strategies or systems, is also a strength. If there are weaknesses in these labour process studies, they often lie in the failure to link the close empirical analysis of workplace control to wider macro-level changes in occupations and employment.

In contrast, when one looks at the major theories in the field of organisation studies, particularly in North America, the concern with 'work' is notably absent. The academy in North America is clearly structured into a set of broad schools or 'churches', which Donaldson (1995) has criticised as being anti-management. One could also argue that they have been largely anti-work as well, or at least uninterested in work, either defined as employment or as task and collaborative relationships. Barley & Kunda's (2001) recent critique of this omission and call for work to be brought back into organisation studies expresses the theoretical deficit well. Indeed, one might argue that one influential theory that came to prominence in the 1990s, that of social networks or capital, ironically portrays a description of work with its images of the 'water cooler conversation' and 'elevator pitch' as the essence of social capital production where the most important activities of workers have precious little to do with actual work activities. A brief reference to two other major organisation theories will also demonstrate that their focus and main contributions say little about work and how it can be conceptualised. These theories are population ecology and neo-institutionalism. Both were first propounded nearly 30 years ago, in 1977.

Population ecology clearly draws on concepts from biology to explain the existence of diverse organisational forms and the likelihood of their survival. It is distinctive in operating at the level of populations of organisations and focuses on founding and failure. It has no theoretical interest in the activities of workers or of managers because it is focused above the level of the individual workplace or organisation. One of its distinctive arguments is that it is difficult for organisations to adapt to environmental shifts by changing organisational form due to what is termed structural inertia. This argument, that it is difficult to change, places population ecology in a tenuous position in contrast to other organisation theories, such as contingency theory, which have been predicated on the idea of adaptation to the environment. Thus a core assumption is that survival is predicated on much wider forces than the activities of individuals or groups within the workplace.

Neo-institutionalism has also grown to become a dominant theory in organisation studies and it, too, has little to say about work. Again, this reflects its primary focus at the level of the 'field', clusters of organisations and occupations that share common 'logics' (Scott 2001) and that are a long way from the workplace. The embeddedness of organisations within fields acts as a constraint on their actions, and organisation forms follow strongly prescribed templates which are taken for granted. Conformity provides legitimacy to actors, which enhances survival prospects so that organisations are not free-floating islands of rationality or units of political expediency (Greenwood & Hinings 1996). While recent work in institutionalism has concentrated on explaining field change and has placed more emphasis on actors as agents of change, this theory remains largely divorced from any real interest in work processes or in the changing content of work itself, precisely because the fundamental focal level of analysis is so far removed from day-to-day work activity, and the underlying assumption that the key problems to explain are not so much about material work activities as about the consequences of organisations being embedded within and shaped by wider systems and values. Thus the material world of work activities seems to be entirely outside the sphere of organisational studies. One could likewise point to other schools of thought that also focus on organisations but not work: network theory, for instance, or theories of change such as punctuated equilibrium. Ironically, in the field of strategy, the resource-based view of the firm is in some senses more focused on work within organisations through its concern with strategic assets and resources and even routines, but it does not place work, that is, a division of labour or, at a micro-level, a set of tasks and relationships between workers, at the centre of its focus.

MOVING FORWARD WITH THESE THEMES?

First, thinking about time and work, it seems to me that we need to take more account of two themes in work on time, both of which are presented well in chapters in this book. One is a longer time perspective on aspects of work and how it has evolved than is normally taken within organisation studies. The other is the multiple perceptions of time as it relates to work. As Patmore's chapter indicates, one problem of work analysis is the tendency to 'presentism', which needs correcting. For example, the lengthening of work time has occurred only after a long period in which the formal shortening of the working day occurred. Many manufacturing industries operated six- or five-and-a-half-day working weeks until the 1960s, and in the UK banking sector a long-running source of conflict concerned the ending of Saturday opening in the 1960s. Yet within 20 years, the banks had decided unilaterally to reintroduce this and to re-extend opening hours, while in retailing the adoption of seven-day opening on the High Street became the norm in the 1990s.

In other words we need longer-term, careful historical analyses of aspects of work and organisational life. Not least, such research needs to question carefully the rather extravagant claims of radical change that seem to predominate in much of the literature. If we define work in terms of task and work authority, as opposed to employment patterns, long-term studies tracking how the day-to-day work of particular occupations has changed, or not, would be appropriate. These might include occupations that have apparently been deeply affected by technological and organisational change, such as semi-skilled work in automobile manufacture, retail work, and craft work. Indeed, studies that combined the tracking of objective changes over time with an examination of the discourse of craft work – its ethic, values, notions of autonomy and distinctiveness from automated production and professional work – would provide a major insight into an area of work that seems to have been ignored in recent years. Other areas where such longer-term historical analysis would be illuminating are careers and labour mobility. The chapter by Groutsis is a useful contribution in this general area. I would also like to see the theme of time and time-based forms of control over work extended to different forms of service work. How, for example, do pressures on professionals to bill on the basis of time (Covaleski et al. 1998; Yakura 2001) relate to their perceptions of professional work, to the achievement of appropriate standards of expertise, or of what it means to be a professional? How is time control used in relation to home workers and those who collaborate 'virtually' with others?

In terms of studying space, the importance of studying the long run is also important. It is worth keeping in mind that the factory system, concentrating work (or many activities in the value chain) in one location, displaced a more spatially distributed production system of putting out work to cottagers. The current development of internationally distributed production systems raises questions for me about the limits of this trend. To what extent can 'networked' systems be reconciled with managerial interest in the value of organisational commitment as they seek to differentiate their organisations on the basis of service? In this respect, one aspect of the discourse of management which seems to be worth studying is the fashion for creating 'customer experience' functions in service-based operations that stress the need for building close and longer-term relations with customers based on a stable workforce with the appropriate skills and values. Another issue is the full coordination costs of spatial distribution in the form of virtual teams or offshoring. How, indeed, do workers collaborate 'virtually' in different types of work where close coordination and tacit skills are at a premium? How do we understand the discourse of virtual working, with its competing strands of liberation from the traditional workplace and, on the other hand, the 'soft' controls of ever-present technology?

From the foregoing it will be apparent that, in my view, if we are to continue to study work fruitfully, we have to aim explicitly to integrate the themes of time, space and discourse. This is an ambitious demand and is likely to be done best by careful empirical studies over time of particular groups with due consideration of their context, and with a clear recognition that work can be conceptualised in multiple ways. Such research is likely to be based on studies that operate simultaneously at different levels of analysis including the sectoral and macro-organisational down to the micro-task level. It is invariably challenging methodologically because it requires combining ways of understanding the nature of change from an 'objective' perspective with more interpretive frameworks that seek to understand how workers experience the reality of changes to work – indeed what work is. I would see such research asking about the continuities in work and working relations, being mindful of the argument that research may over-focus on the novel and what has changed while disregarding what has not. Studies of work that have an international basis must be particularly valuable, because what the notion of a global economy actually means in the context of work needs to be articulated further. The themes of time, space and discourse powerfully bring home the sheer diffuseness of the concept of work and how workers make sense of it, be it at home, or at the sales conference or as part of a virtual team. The themes of this book provide a good starting point for us to build some general propositions about work and how it is changing: that should be the aim of future research.

References

Ancona, D.G., Okhuysen, G.A. & Perlow, L.A. 2001, 'Taking time to integrate temporal research', *Academy of Management Review* 26(4): 512–30.

Barley, S. & Kunda, G. 2001, 'Bringing work back in', *Organization Science* 12(1): 76–95.

Barney, J. 1991, 'Firm resources and sustained competitive advantage', *Journal of Management* 17(1): 99–120.

Beck, U. 2000, *The Brave New World of Work*, Cambridge, Polity Press.

Bluedorn, A.C. 2002, *The Human Organization of Time: Temporal Realities and Experience*, Stanford University Press.

Bosch, G. 2004, 'Towards a new standard employment relationship in Western Europe', *British Journal of Industrial Relations* 42(4): 617–36.

Castells, M. 1996, *The Rise of the Network Society*, Oxford: Blackwell.

Covaleski, M.A., Dirsmith, M.W., Heian, J.B. & Sajay, S. 1998, 'The calculated and the avowed: techniques of discipline and struggles over identity in the big six public accounting firms', *Administrative Science Quarterly* 43(2): 293–327.

Dickens, L. 2004, 'Problems of fit: changing employment and labour regulation', *British Journal of Industrial Relations* 42(4): 595–616.

Donaldson, L. 1995, *American Anti-Management Theories of Organization*, Cambridge University Press.

Grant, D., Keenoy, T. & Oswick, C. 2001 'Organisational discourse: key contributions and challenges', *International Studies of Management and Organization* 31(3): 5–24.

Greenwood, R. & Hinings, C.R. 1996, 'Understanding radical organizational change: bringing together the old and new institutionalism', *Academy of Management Review* 21(4): 1022–54.

Herzenberg, S., Alic, J. & Wial, H. 1998, *New Rules for a New Economy: Employment and Opportunity in Post-Industrial America*, Ithaca, NY: ILR Press.

Kallinikos, J. 2003, 'Work, human agency and organizational forms: an anatomy of fragmentation', *Organization Studies* 24(4): 595–618.

Nolan, P., & Wood, S. 2003, 'Mapping the future of work', *British Journal of Industrial Relations* 41(2): 165–74.

OECD 2005, *Economic Policy Reforms*, Paris: OECD.

Peiperl, M., Arthur, M., Goffee, R. & Morris, T. 2000, *Career Frontiers: New Conceptions of Working Lives*, Oxford: Oxford University Press.

Sahlin-Andersson, K. & Engwall, L. 2002, *The Expansion of Management Knowledge*, Stanford, Calif.: Stanford Business Books.

Schor, J.B. 1992, *The Overworked American: The Unexpected Decline of Leisure*, New York: Basic Books.

Scott, W.R. 2001, *Institutions and Organizations*, London: Sage.

Taylor, R. 2002, *Britain's World of Work: Myths and Realities*, Swindon: Economic and Social Research Council.

Wood, S. 2000, 'The *BJIR* and industrial relations in the new millennium', *British Journal of Industrial Relations* 38(1): 1–5.

Yakura, E.K. 2001, 'Billables: the valorization of time in consulting', *American Behavioral Scientist* 44(7): 1076–95.

INDEX